Generative AI for Transformational Management

Jeganathan Gomathi Sankar
BSSS Institute of Advanced Studies, India

Arokiaraj David
Al Tareeqah Management Studies, Swiss Business School, UAE

A volume in the Advances in Logistics, Operations, and Management Science (ALOMS) Book Series

IGI Global
Publishing Tomorrow's Research Today

Published in the United States of America by
IGI Global
Business Science Reference (an imprint of IGI Global)
701 E. Chocolate Avenue
Hershey PA, USA 17033
Tel: 717-533-8845
Fax: 717-533-8661
E-mail: cust@igi-global.com
Web site: http://www.igi-global.com

Library of Congress Cataloging-in-Publication Data

CIP DATA PENDING

ISBN13: 9798369355787
Isbn13Softcover: 9798369355794
EISBN13: 9798369355800

British Cataloguing in Publication Data
A Cataloguing in Publication record for this book is available from the British Library.

Table of Contents

Detailed Table of Contents

A universal technology appears that sparks creativity to the point where several sectors undergo complete revolution. The Generative AI is one of these uncommon general-purpose technologies and is poised to bring about exponential transformation and is now consistently supported by research. It has the power to change the competitive landscape and propel businesses towards explosive growth. Businesses will either leap ahead of this technological transformation or fall behind as they race to comprehend its ramifications. In Generative AI and business transformation, potential for strategic and useful business applications are identified by analyzing the platforms, big language models, and technology of generative AI. This chapter focuses on Generative AI role in influencing business strategy.

AI is quickly growing, and its use in commercial decision-making will influence the corporate environment. AI is redefining strategic business decision-making, and the chapter provides a complete view of how AI is changing the corporate world. This chapter examines how AI has disrupted previous decision paradigms and increased organizational agility in business strategy. A thorough literature review analyzes academic and business sources to reveal AI's broad corporate function. Systematic literature reviews are performed to evaluate source credibility and synthesize findings. The chapter also examines AI's corporate challenges and prospects. The chapter's main results demonstrate that AI is a strategic asset that transforms commercial decision-making. AI in company strategy might boost performance and promote sustainability. In conclusion, AI is essential to corporate growth, offering new creative and efficient opportunities. Additionally, a balanced approach to AI integration might emphasize the need of integrating AI with organizations' fundamental values and strategic goals.

This chapter reviews the current state of generative artificial intelligence (AI) and human resource management (HRM). It discusses the current application of Generative AI in the core functional areas of HRM, identifies the main challenges posed by Generative AI, emphasizes the increasing role and influence of Generative AI applications in the workplace, and suggests future research directions. Current applications of Generative AI in HRM include automation, personalization, decision support, and bias reduction in HR processes. However, the urgent challenges related to transparency, bias mitigation, ethical use, and data privacy must be addressed for responsible deployment. This chapter highlights the opportunities for integrating Generative AI in HRM to improve HR processes while ensuring ethical and fair implementation. The future research directions for Generative AI and HRM focus on reducing bias in AI models, developing ethical frameworks, enhancing data privacy, and exploring AI's impact on organizational culture and employee engagement.

The primary goal of the chapter was to examine how, in the Ethiopian environment, an employee's work attitude and AI-based reinforcement learning function as mediators between their psychological intrinsic reward system and the perception of organisational support they receive from their employer. Based on their contribution to the GDP of the economy, the textile industries operating in Ethiopia's industrial parks were chosen as the study area. A quantitative research technique and explanatory research design were employed. A multi-phase sampling method was suggested. To assess discriminant and convergent validity, exploratory confirmatory analysis was carried out using AMOS software. It was discovered that the relationship between an employee's psychological intrinsic reward system and the organization's perceived organisational support was extremely poor in the absence of AI-based re-enforcement

corporate companies and investors to transform their mode of traditional investment planning to technology-oriented investment planning.

Fintech players have always adopted the latest technology that evolve in the market to stay ahead in this competitive industry. In that adoption curve, we are now standing in the place where we are going to witness the adoption of the Generative AI as the next technological phenomenon that will shape the future of Fintech industry. In this chapter, the authors explore the following areas to getter a deeper insight into how Generative AI tends to play in Fintech industry: 1) Generative AI technologies involved in Fintech, 2) application of Generative AI in Fintech, 3) benefits of adopting Generative AI in Fintech, 4) case studies where Generative AI is adopted, 5) challenges and risks in adopting Generative AI, 6) mitigation strategies for the above said challenges and risks, and 7) future trends and developments.

The proliferation of digital transactions in the financial sector when it comes to the 4th Industrial Revolution (41R) has allowed companies to use artificial intelligence. Worryingly, it appears that scant is known about artificial intelligence in the FinTech discourse especially when it comes to African economies. As such, this chapter aims to fill this gap by focusing on the role of artificial intelligence in FinTech. With the utilization of a comprehensive literature review methodology, it was observed that artificial intelligence is of utmost importance as it can augment accuracy, efficiency, fraud detection, effectiveness, human capabilities, and customer experiences; mitigate economic crimes; and accelerate regulatory compliance. Despite these benefits of artificial intelligence in FinTech, it brought to the fore some insurmountable challenges in the financial sector like ethical concerns, human rights issues, social engineering, and fraudulent data generation. The results of the current study are associated with theoretical and practical implications.

In recent times, artificial intelligence (AI) has become an essential component in marketing, leading to the generation of large amounts of data and information, as well as advancements in management software and algorithms. The goal of artificial intelligence is to intelligently imitate human behavior. Artificial intelligence is a rapidly expanding technology, industry, and field of study. AI not only enhances existing marketing strategies, but also introduces innovative ways to deliver value to customers. AI also plays an important role in helping marketers manage marketing projects, support them, create content, and perform other tasks. Research shows that a lack of understanding of AI's capabilities and failed implementation efforts can create additional obstacles for organizations, including investment risks, ethical dilemmas, data issues, recruitment challenges, and negative environmental impacts. Despite being designed to reduce the workload of employees, human intervention is necessary in roles such as management, supervision, and innovation.

Maritime transport is crucial for global trade, transporting over 90% of global goods by volume and facing challenges such as environmental impacts and security threats. Public policy is the key to addressing these issues through regulations that enhance safety, security, and sustainability. Integrating this sector with generative AI can significantly improve predictive maintenance, route optimisation, and accident prevention. AI technologies can process vast amounts of data for real-time decision-making, which is vital for the efficiency and safety of maritime operations. AI can lead to autonomous ships, optimise logistics, and reduce human error. However, integrating AI poses technical barriers such as cybersecurity, significant initial costs, and social hurdles such as job displacement fears. Effective public policy must evolve to address these challenges and promote AI integration while considering ethical and legal implications.

This chapter aims to explore the potential of generative (AI) in improving aspects of tourism experiences. Areas focused on include personalized recommendation systems, content generation for marketing purposes, virtual tour guides, and adaptive travel planning within the tourism industry. It focuses on customization approaches, incorporation of AR and VR technologies, and creation of real-time decision support systems. Moreover, its objective is to understand the ethical utilization of AI in the tourism industry, concerns regarding data privacy, and the incorporation of AI into current tourism infrastructure. It helps to delineate forthcoming research paths and

Preface

Welcome to *Generative AI for Transformational Management*. In this transformative exploration, we navigate the frontiers of artificial intelligence (AI) to unveil its profound impact on the landscape of modern management. This book serves as a beacon, guiding readers through the intersection of cutting-edge generative AI and visionary leadership, offering insights into how these technologies can redefine traditional management paradigms.

As we stand at the nexus of technological innovation and strategic leadership, the potential of generative AI becomes a catalyst for organizational transformation. Through this narrative, we embark on a quest to understand how AI, with its generative capabilities, can empower leaders to make proactive decisions, foster innovation, and navigate the complexities of the digital age. Our journey unfolds with a keen exploration of the symbiotic relationship between generative AI and transformational management. We delve into real-world applications, case studies, and thought-provoking discussions that showcase the transformative potential of AI in reshaping the fabric of contemporary leadership.

This book is not just a guide; it is an invitation to envision and embrace a future where the synergy between generative AI and transformative management propels organizations to unparalleled heights. Together, let us unravel the possibilities, confront challenges, and chart a course for a future where AI becomes an indispensable ally in the pursuit of visionary and transformational leadership. Welcome to a captivating odyssey through the realms of *Generative AI for Transformational Management*.

The objectives of *Generative AI for Transformational Management* are multifaceted, aiming to provide a comprehensive understanding of the intersection between artificial intelligence (AI) and transformative leadership. The book endeavors to bridge the gap between generative AI and leadership by providing a comprehensive synthesis of these two domains. It seeks to offer a holistic understanding of how AI, particularly generative AI, can be integrated into leadership practices to drive transformative outcomes.

Through real-world case studies and practical applications, the book aims to go beyond theoretical discussions. It strives to demonstrate how organizations have successfully implemented generative AI, showcasing tangible examples of transformative practices. With a focus on ethical considerations, the book addresses the responsibility that comes with deploying AI. It explores ethical frameworks and considerations, providing insights into how leaders can navigate the ethical dimensions of AI-driven decision-making.

The intention is to create an engaging and interactive learning experience for readers. Through discussions, reflections, and practical exercises, the book encourages active participation, ensuring that readers not only understand the concepts but also apply them in practical scenarios. Anticipating future trends and innovations, the book aims to provide forward-looking perspectives on the evolving landscape of AI. By doing so, it adds a predictive dimension to current research, helping readers stay abreast of emerging developments.

By providing a comprehensive overview of generative AI's impact on transformational management, the book aims to build a knowledge base that consolidates current research while laying the groundwork for future investigations in this dynamic field. The target audience of this book will be composed of academics, post-graduate students, and researchers working in the field of AI. Moreover, the book will provide insights and support for those academics involved in research supervision.

We hope that this book serves as a valuable resource and inspiration for those who seek to understand and harness the power of generative AI in the realm of transformational management.

ORGANIZATION OF THE BOOK

Chapter 1: Generative AI and Business Strategy

In "Generative AI and Business Strategy," Dina Darwish explores the transformative potential of generative AI as a universal technology capable of revolutionizing multiple sectors. This chapter delves into how generative AI can alter the competitive landscape, driving businesses towards exponential growth. By analyzing platforms, large language models, and generative AI technology, Darwish identifies strategic and practical business applications. The focus is on understanding the role of generative AI in shaping business strategies, highlighting the imperative for businesses to embrace this technological transformation or risk falling behind.

Chapter 2: Artificial Intelligence in Decision-Making: Reinventing Business Strategies

Geetha Manoharan, Sunitha Ashtikkar, and M. Nivedha present a comprehensive view of how AI is redefining strategic business decision-making. This chapter examines AI's disruption of traditional decision paradigms and its enhancement of organizational agility. Through a thorough literature review, the authors synthesize academic and business sources to reveal AI's broad corporate function, addressing both the challenges and opportunities AI presents. The findings underscore AI as a strategic asset that transforms commercial decision-making, boosts performance, and promotes sustainability, emphasizing the integration of AI with core organizational values and strategic goals.

Chapter 3: Exploring the Application of Generative AI in Human Resource Management

Peace Kumah, Ivonne Nketia, and Kwame Asante-Offei review the current state of generative AI in human resource management (HRM). This chapter discusses the application of generative AI in automating, personalizing, and supporting HR processes, while addressing challenges related to transparency, bias mitigation, ethical use, and data privacy. The authors highlight the opportunities for generative AI to improve HR processes and suggest future research directions focused on reducing bias, developing ethical frameworks, enhancing data privacy, and exploring AI's impact on organizational culture and employee engagement.

Chapter 4: Mediated by AI-Based Generative Reinforcement Learning and Work Attitude, Is Intrinsic Reward Transforming Employee's Perceived Organizational Support?

Shashi Kant and Metasebia Adula investigate how AI-based reinforcement learning and employee work attitude mediate the relationship between psychological intrinsic rewards and perceived organizational support in the Ethiopian textile industry. Using quantitative research methods and exploratory confirmatory analysis with AMOS software, the authors find that without these mediators, the relationship is weak. This chapter highlights the critical role of AI and employee attitudes in enhancing organizational support perceptions, providing valuable insights into the mechanisms driving employee motivation and support.

Chapter 5: AI Learning and Work Attitude Mediation Between Reward and Organizational Support in Ethiopia

Continuing their exploration, Shashi Kant and Metasebia Adula analyze the mediator role of AI-based reinforcement learning and employee work attitude between psychological intrinsic rewards and perceived organizational support in Ethiopia's textile industry. Utilizing an explanatory research design and multistage sampling, they demonstrate that AI and work attitudes significantly mediate this relationship. This chapter reinforces the importance of integrating AI in reinforcing learning and shaping positive employee attitudes to strengthen organizational support.

Chapter 6: Using AI-Driven Decision-Making Tools in Corporate Investment Planning

Joel Jebadurai Devapitchai, Krishnapriya S. V., Karuppiah S. P., William Robert P., and Saranya S. explore the critical role of AI in financial sectors, particularly in investment planning. This chapter covers applications of AI techniques such as machine learning, natural language processing, deep learning, and robo-advisors in various investment functions. Through case studies and success stories, the authors illustrate how AI-driven decision-making tools enhance quantitative trading, risk management, portfolio optimization, and more. This chapter serves as a valuable resource for transforming traditional investment planning into technology-oriented approaches.

Chapter 7: Financial Frontiers: How Generative AI is Shaping the Fintech Industry

Gopinath Rajenthran explores the adoption of generative AI in the fintech industry, detailing its transformative impact. This chapter provides insights into generative AI technologies, their applications, benefits, challenges, and mitigation strategies. Through case studies, Rajenthran showcases how generative AI is being adopted in fintech and anticipates future trends and developments. This comprehensive examination highlights generative AI's potential to reshape the fintech landscape, driving innovation and competitive advantage.

Chapter 8: Benefits and Challenges of Artificial Intelligence in FinTech

Mufaro Dzingirai and Peterson Ozili address the role of AI in fintech, especially in the context of African economies. Through a comprehensive literature review, they highlight AI's benefits, including enhanced accuracy, efficiency, fraud detection, and regulatory compliance. However, the chapter also discusses significant challenges such as ethical concerns, human rights issues, and fraudulent data generation. The authors provide theoretical and practical implications, emphasizing AI's transformative potential while acknowledging the hurdles that must be overcome for successful implementation.

Chapter 9: AI in Marketing

Serap Türkyilmaz examines the essential role of AI in marketing, focusing on how it generates data, advances management software, and enhances marketing strategies. This chapter explores AI's capability to imitate human behavior and introduces innovative ways to deliver customer value. Despite its benefits, the chapter also discusses the challenges of AI implementation, including investment risks, ethical dilemmas, and data issues. Türkyilmaz emphasizes the need for human intervention in management, supervision, and innovation, highlighting the balance between AI and human roles in marketing.

Chapter 10: Generative AI for Customized Public Policy in Maritime Transport

Rupesh Kumar and Chhote Lal Yadav discuss the crucial role of Maritime transport for global trade, transporting over 90% of global goods by volume and facing challenges such as environmental impacts and security threats. Public policy is the key to addressing these issues through regulations that enhance safety, security, and sustainability. Integrating this sector with generative AI can significantly improve predictive maintenance, route optimization, and accident prevention. AI technologies can process vast amounts of data for real-time decision-making, which is vital for the efficiency and safety of maritime operations. AI can lead to autonomous ships, optimize logistics, and reduce human error. However, integrating AI poses technical barriers such as cybersecurity, significant initial costs, and social hurdles such as job displacement fears. Effective public policy must evolve to address these challenges and promote AI integration while considering ethical and legal implications.

Chapter 11: Revolutionizing Tourism: The Power of Generative AI

Reena George explores the potential of generative (AI) in improving aspects of tourism experiences. Areas focused on include personalized recommendation systems, content generation for marketing purposes, virtual tour guides, and adaptive travel planning within the tourism industry. It focuses on customization approaches, incorporation of AR and VR technologies, and creation of real-time decision support systems. Moreover, its objective is to understand the ethical utilization of AI in the tourism industry, concerns regarding data privacy, and the incorporation of AI into current tourism infrastructure. It helps to delineate forthcoming research paths and emerging patterns, highlighting the possible influence of AI on the tourism sector and its future. Furthermore, it seeks to elucidate the socio-economic impacts of using AI in the tourist industry, examining its capacity to transform employment patterns, visitor characteristics, and methods for developing destinations. Finally, promotes interdisciplinary discussion in influencing the future of tourism.

Chapter 12: The Improvements in Significance of AI in Experiential and Medical Tourism

Ranjit Barua and Sudipto Datta review how AI has transformed experiential and medical tourism by enhancing specific experiences and healthcare services. AI-powered virtual assistants and recommendation systems personalize tourism experiences, while AI in medical tourism enables precise diagnoses and customized treatments. This chapter discusses AI's role in risk assessment and preventive safety measures, improving overall satisfaction and peace of mind for patients and tourists. The authors highlight ongoing innovations and future developments, showcasing AI's critical impact on these industries.

CONCLUSION

As we conclude this preface to *Generative AI for Transformational Management*, we invite you to embark on an enlightening journey through the multifaceted world of generative AI and its profound implications for modern leadership and organizational strategy. The chapters within this book collectively underscore a pivotal truth: generative AI is not merely a technological advancement but a transformative force that holds the potential to redefine the essence of management and leadership.

Each chapter provides a deep dive into different aspects of AI's integration into various business functions, from strategic decision-making and human resource management to corporate investment planning and marketing. The insights offered by our distinguished contributors illuminate the pathways through which AI can be harnessed to foster innovation, enhance efficiency, and drive sustainable growth. Moreover, the ethical considerations and challenges discussed serve as a vital reminder of the responsibility that accompanies the deployment of such powerful technologies.

Our goal in curating this volume was to create a comprehensive resource that bridges the gap between theoretical frameworks and practical applications, providing readers with both the knowledge and tools necessary to navigate the evolving landscape of AI-driven management. We hope that this book will inspire you to envision new possibilities, confront existing challenges, and embrace the transformative potential of generative AI in your own professional endeavors.

As you delve into the subsequent chapters, we encourage you to engage with the material critically and reflectively. The journey through *Generative AI for Transformational Management* is designed to be interactive and thought-provoking, fostering a deeper understanding of how AI can be a catalyst for transformational leadership and organizational excellence.

Thank you for joining us on this captivating odyssey. We look forward to the innovative and visionary contributions that each reader will bring to the ever-evolving discourse on generative AI and transformational management.

Jeganathan Gomathi Sankar
BSSS Institute of Advanced Studies, India

Arokiaraj David
Al Tareeqah Management Studies, Swiss Business School, UAE

Acknowledgment

We would like to extend our heartfelt gratitude to everyone who contributed to the successful completion of this edited volume.

First and foremost, we express our deep appreciation to the contributing authors. Your scholarly insights and dedication to producing high-quality chapters have significantly enriched this work. Your commitment is the foundation of this book's success.

We are also deeply thankful to our reviewers. Your constructive feedback and careful attention to detail have greatly enhanced the quality of the content presented here.

A special note of thanks goes to our publisher, IGI Global, for their unwavering support throughout the publication process. We extend our sincere appreciation to Nina Eddinger, Assistant Development Editor for IGI Global, whose expertise and guidance have been invaluable.

We are grateful to our families and friends for their patience, understanding, and unwavering support throughout this journey. Your encouragement has been a source of strength and inspiration.

Finally, we wish to acknowledge our readers. We hope that the knowledge and insights contained within these pages will inspire and inform your work in the field of Generative AI.

Thank you all for your contributions and support.

Chapter 1
Generative AI and Business Strategy

Dina Darwish
Ahram Canadian University, Egypt

ABSTRACT

A universal technology appears that sparks creativity to the point where several sectors undergo complete revolution. The Generative AI is one of these uncommon general-purpose technologies and is poised to bring about exponential transformation and is now consistently supported by research. It has the power to change the competitive landscape and propel businesses towards explosive growth. Businesses will either leap ahead of this technological transformation or fall behind as they race to comprehend its ramifications. In Generative AI and business transformation, potential for strategic and useful business applications are identified by analyzing the platforms, big language models, and technology of generative AI. This chapter focuses on Generative AI role in influencing business strategy.

INTRODUCTION

All eyes are suddenly focused on generative AI, yet several companies have successfully implemented AI approaches across numerous business divisions and procedures for a long time. Though only 10% of organizations now experimenting with AI are mature AI organizations. Gartner research indicates that would-be GenAI adopters can learn a great deal from them. Similar to how the internet and earlier innovations like electricity changed society and the economy, generative AI has the potential to do the same. For your company, the question is how AI will advance corporate goals and produce better outcomes. When used effectively, GenAI will become a differentiator and competitive advantage, expanding AI's overall capacity

DOI: 10.4018/979-8-3693-5578-7.ch001

to automate boring and repetitive work and produce novel concepts, ideas, and inventions through predictive analytics. When used effectively, GenAI will strengthen AI's ability to automate monotonous and repetitive work and produce novel insights, concepts, and inventions using machine learning (ML), predictive analytics, and other AI techniques. By generating novel and disruptive opportunities to advance corporate objectives like these, generative AI has the potential to dramatically affect shareholder value through:

Boost income. AI will speed up the process by which businesses develop new products. As they create new medications, less toxic home cleaners, unique tastes and fragrances, new alloys, and quicker and more accurate medical diagnoses, the pharmaceutical, healthcare, and manufacturing sectors (CPG, food and beverage, chemicals, and materials science) will be the first to use AI.
Increase the level of interaction with your customers. Generative AI can increase customer engagement by upending established value chains and business models and empowering companies to produce and deliver content directly to consumers, cutting out conventional middlemen like publishers and distributors.
Cut expenses while raising output. GenAI capabilities, whether through software code generation, chatbot performance optimization, or enhancing the efforts of human workers (e.g., summarizing, simplifying, and classifying content), can streamline procedures and accelerate results. Additionally, GenAI can utilize data that was previously unused and wasted.
This chapter focuses on several topics related to generative AI, like; Generative AI and business strategies, tools and techniques of generative AI in business strategies, benefitting from generative AI, how to gauge AI effectiveness, AI use cases, Challenges, trends and case studies related to generative AI in business strategies, ethical frameworks about using generative AI, and finally future perspectives about generative AI.

BACKGROUND

In recent decades, there have been significant developments in science and technology, resulting in advantages across all areas and specialties. Currently, we find ourselves in a period characterized by groundbreaking advancements, mostly propelled by notable progress in digital technology, including Artificial Intelligence (AI). As a result, analysts expect that AI will have a greater influence on the economy in the future, and there will be a growing interest in its various uses (Melehy, 2023). This suggests that the world is currently seeing an unparalleled revolution in the realm of artificial intelligence, a discipline that strives to enhance its service to humanity (Jutel et al., 2023). Furthermore, the progress in Generative Artificial Intelligence (GAI) has significantly broadened the methods used for automating job tasks related to generating textual material. GAI, specifically utilizing Large Language Models (LLMs), emphasizes the independent generation of innovative content. These LLMs, which are regarded as essential algorithms, signify a significant advancement in the area (Hadi et al., 2023). Following the introduction of a complimentary trial of the ChatGPT-3.5 model by OpenAI in 2022, LLMs experienced a surge in popularity (Mhlanga, 2023). OpenAI is leading the way in the revolution of Artificial Intelligence. The ChatGPT bot has generated considerable excitement in the technology community. Impressively, ChatGPT garnered more than 100 million monthly active users in a mere two and a half months, solidifying its position as the fastest-growing web service ever recorded (Hadi, and Najm, 2023). This remarkable achievement has prompted technology firms to expedite the development of upgrades and novel AI-driven products, such as Bard and Claude, in order to keep pace with this swift technological change (Borji, and Mohammadian, 2023). Feuerriegel et al. (Feuerriegel et al., 2023) define the term "generative" in the field of AI as the ability of an AI system to independently produce new material without any human intervention.

The material, which might be in the form of text, image, audio, or video, conforms to particular standards or rules (Banh and Strobel, 2023). The objective of breakthroughs in Artificial Intelligence is to attain a degree of creativity and inventiveness that exceeds the ability of humans. The objective of ChatGPT is clearly demonstrated by the utilization of its innovative capabilities to streamline and enhance the experience of engaging with technology (Lund and Wang, 2023). However, generative AI is not merely a new technological tool. It is a powerful force that not only changes the way we live and work but also opens up new possibilities in the professional environment (Nah et al., 2023). Specifically, GAI is utilized in diverse fields such as healthcare, education, art, and environment to facilitate and expedite the process of content generation (Morris, 2023). Mao et al. (Mao et al., 2023) state that GAI (Generalized Artificial Intelligence) customizes learning experiences and generates creative educational resources. In addition, Mao et al. (Mao et al., 2023) assert that this technique enables the development of novel and inventive teaching materials derived from educational data. Generative AI in the field of medicine aids in disease diagnosis and healthcare provision (Zhang, and Boulos, 2023). In addition, GAI enables firms to develop impactful marketing materials and promotes innovation in the arts and culture industries (Epstein et al., 2023).

Consequently, GAI surpasses traditional applications and becomes a crucial catalyst for change in multiple sectors. The groundbreaking advancements in Artificial Intelligence, spanning across all industries and disciplines, are seen as a profound revolution that not only significantly affects individuals' daily lives but also has far-reaching implications for organizations (Cardon et al., 2023). This progress highlights the significance of employing sophisticated programs and technology to improve and maintain organizational performance. The pursuit of enhanced efficiency has become a global objective across several industries, including private enterprises, public organizations, and government bodies. As a result, corporate executives are currently contemplating the incorporation of this technology into their business activities. Within this framework, the deliberate utilization of General Artificial Intelligence (GAI) in corporate environments is being acknowledged as a promising remedy to augment job efficiency. Furthermore, the technological advancements in General Artificial Intelligence (GAI) offer a distinct method for organizations to tackle productivity issues inside their organizational structures (Govori, and Sejdija, 2023). Consequently, firms of various magnitudes are actively contemplating the use of AI technology in order to obtain a competitive advantage (Gonçalves et al., 2022). The implementation of GAI has the capacity to significantly enhance productivity by eliminating errors, improving decision-making, and simplifying complex tasks (Wamba-Taguimdje et al., 2020).

MAIN FOCUS OF THE CHAPTER

Generative AI and Business Strategies

The implementation of generative AI is revolutionizing multiple industries by optimizing corporate operations and improving the quality of decision-making. The publications (Turlakova, 2022; Turlakova, 2023) provide guidelines on how AI tools, specifically generative ones, can be used to assist decision-making processes and control the behavior of economic agents in companies. Additionally, these works outline the strategies for achieving economic advantages through the application of AI. The study (Parikh, 2023) examines the various uses of generative AI in software product management, including idea creation and automatic code generation. Additionally, the paper discusses the ethical considerations associated with these applications. Another notable study (Chuma, and de Oliveira, 2023) showcases the application of ChatGPT in the process of gathering research and generating ideas, highlighting its tangible advantages in corporate contexts. The study (Bi, 2023) examines the incorporation of generative artificial intelligence (AI) in corporate management, with a focus on its creative and logical capacities. The writers in (Jospin and Raja, 2023) explore the role of AI in automating chores and improving strategic decision-making. These studies collectively emphasize the significant influence of generative AI on enhancing efficiency, decreasing expenses, and facilitating strategic business choices. Generative AI demonstrates substantial potential across several commercial sectors, augmenting marketing, trade, and healthcare operations. The paper (Oliinyk, 2023) examines the advantages of generative AI in hyper-personalization and customer experience, emphasizing the automated creation of content and enhancement of client engagement. The author explores multiple uses of generative AI, as discussed in research (Taulli, 2023), highlighting its potential to bring about significant changes for businesses. The study (Kuzlu, et al., 2023) investigates the influence of generative AI on medical imaging, drug development, and patient care, while also tackling difficulties related to data privacy and ethical considerations. This research together illustrates the various applications and advantages of generative AI, ranging from improving marketing strategies to transforming healthcare.

In summary, these studies showcase the capabilities of generative AI, but they lack the essential actionable advice for enterprises. In order to close this divide, businesses require well-defined plans for execution, experimental initiatives to assess efficacy, allocation of resources for education and competency enhancement, creation of ethical principles and adherence procedures, utilization of practical examples from actual scenarios, and comprehensive evaluations of costs and benefits. These stages offer a systematic method for implementing generative AI technology and guaranteeing their seamless integration into company operations. The objective of this paper is to analyze the significant capacity of Generative Artificial Intelligence (GenAI) to bring about profound changes in the business realm. This will be achieved by presenting concrete examples of its practical use in different operational areas. The objective is to offer a thorough comprehension of how organizations can utilize advanced GenAI models to improve productivity, stimulate innovation, and establish competitive advantages. The article aims to provide organizations with practical ideas and real-world examples to help them integrate GenAI into their processes. This integration will enable businesses to adapt and succeed in the Fourth Industrial Revolution. Figure 1 illustrates Generative AI location in the ecosystem.

Figure 1. Generative AI's location in the ecosystem

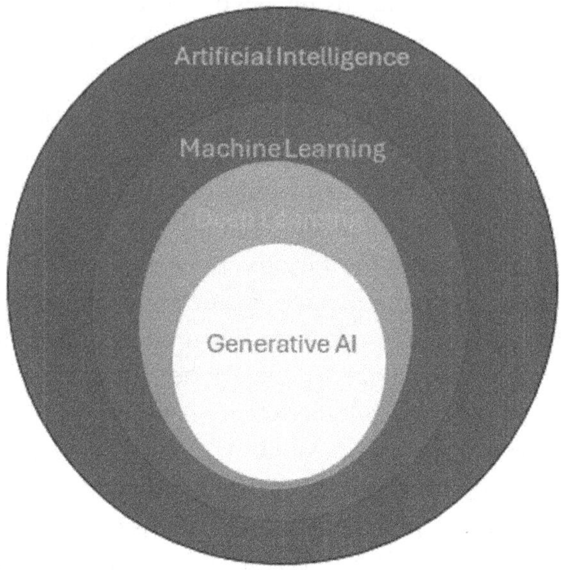

Tools and Techniques of Generative AI in Business Strategies

GenAI, or Generative Artificial Intelligence, has become a powerful and game-changing presence in the commercial realm, providing cutting-edge solutions in different areas of operation. GenAI utilizes sophisticated machine learning models to produce content, automate tasks, and provide opportunities for improved efficiency and creativity. This section examines the pragmatic uses of GenAI in the business sector, emphasizing its wide-ranging skills and presenting concrete examples to demonstrate how firms can leverage this technology to gain a competitive edge.

Generative AI functions exist across several application layers. These layers consist of text, code, picture, speech, video, 3D, and other specialized domains, each providing distinct advantages to enterprises. GenAI has the ability to greatly improve marketing and customer engagement in the field of text generation.

For example, it has the ability to generate captivating and customized marketing materials, enabling firms to efficiently connect with their intended audience. A concrete illustration of this concept is a retail corporation employing GenAI to generate tailored product descriptions and advertising material for every consumer category, hence enhancing online sales and customer contentment. Automated production of sales emails can optimize outreach efforts and improve contact with new clients. This is exemplified by a B2B firm that uses GenAI to create personalized follow-up emails after first client meetings, resulting in higher lead conversion rates. In addition, chatbots and email responders powered by artificial intelligence may effectively manage consumer inquiries, delivering prompt and precise assistance. For instance, an e-commerce platform that employs AI chatbots to handle customer care inquiries might decrease response time and operational expenses. Moreover, GenAI aids in the automation of documentation chores, including the creation of reports and the recording of meeting notes. This benefits consulting businesses by guaranteeing precise and thorough records that can be referred to in the future.

GenAI is a tool that can speed up software development in the field of code generation. It achieves this by automatically producing and documenting code, hence lessening the workload for developers. A software development company can utilize artificial intelligence (AI) to automate monotonous coding processes, enabling engineers to concentrate on more intricate problem-solving endeavors. Moreover, GenAI has the capability to transform natural language queries into SQL instructions, hence simplifying the process of manipulating and retrieving data. For example, a financial services company that utilizes GenAI to empower non-technical employees to create intricate data queries improves the accessibility of data and facilitates decision-making. Furthermore, GenAI has the capability to streamline the process of developing online apps, hence enhancing accessibility and efficiency. This is seen in the way startups are able to rapidly create and launch web applications to expedite the product development cycle.

GenAI has the ability to create and modify images for a wide range of uses, including media, advertising, consumer products, and social media. An advertising agency may utilize artificial intelligence (AI) to generate aesthetically pleasing advertisement materials and social media content, hence enhancing the effectiveness of their marketing campaigns. Furthermore, GenAI may aid designers by producing inventive concepts and preliminary designs, which is advantageous for fashion firms utilizing AI to develop cutting-edge design ideas for new collections, augmenting creativity and minimizing creation cycles. GenAI, a technology in the domain of speech synthesis, has the capability to generate lifelike voiceovers for movies and virtual assistants, hence improving user engagement. One instance is an e-learning platform that utilizes AI-generated voiceovers for educational videos, offering superior audio material and decreasing production expenses. GenAI has the capability to automate the whole video production process, including editing and the creation of completely new video material. GenAI can be employed by a media corporation to automate video editing activities, resulting in accelerated content development and decreased labor expenses. GenAI is capable of generating 3D models and scenarios for several industries including gaming, architecture, and product design.

For example, an architectural firm can utilize GenAI to create lifelike 3D visualizations of building plans, thereby improving client presentations and project planning. GenAI has various specific applications, such as developing lifelike game environments and characters in the gaming industry, automating repetitive business processes using robotic process automation (RPA), producing music compositions and sound effects in the music industry, and aiding scientific research by generating molecular models and simulations. For instance, a game production studio may utilize GenAI to produce intricate game environments and character designs, thereby boosting the overall gameplay experience. By utilizing AI-driven Robotic Process Automation (RPA), a financial institution can automate data entry and reconciliation operations, resulting in a reduction of errors and operational costs. A content creator utilizing GenAI to generate creative background music for videos guarantees the production of distinctive and unencumbered audio tracks. Furthermore, the utilization of artificial intelligence by a pharmaceutical corporation to simulate molecular interactions has the potential to expedite the processes of drug discovery and development.

Generative AI serves as more than a mere content creation tool; it acts as a potent catalyst for driving innovation and enhancing efficiency in company operations. This article will explore real-life instances and case studies, offering practical suggestions on how firms can utilize the power of generative AI to maintain a competitive edge.

Prior to using any technology, such as generative AI, firms must perform comprehensive study and validation to ascertain its feasibility, applicability, and any ramifications. This procedure encompasses multiple pivotal phases, each specifically devised to minimize risks and maximize results.

In the initial phase, known as firm Concept Validation, a prototype is developed to embody the fundamental concept of the firm. The main objectives at this phase are to obtain prompt input from end-users, facilitate internal analysis, and verify the viability of the company concept. By doing this, firms may determine whether the proposed technology is in line with their strategic objectives and fulfils user requirements.

After validating the concept, the subsequent stage involves identifying the technical solution. This stage necessitates the identification of the most advantageous solution for the current situation or the comparison of other possibilities. The goals in this context encompass the identification of the most optimal solution, the removal of technical obstacles, and the comprehension of any technical constraints. This stage is vital as it guarantees that the selected technology is not only technically robust but also the most efficient choice available.

Once a technical solution is determined, the Proof of Technology stage commences. During this stage, businesses assess the practicality and viability of the selected solution. The objectives are to demonstrate the technological viability, mitigate any technical ambiguity, and verify compatibility with current systems. Verifying the functionality of the technology in real-world situations and ensuring its smooth integration with present operations is crucial.

The Clear Project Plan, which is the final stage, entails the execution of a crucial business module with an actual team in order to establish a sense of financial assurance. This phase is centered around fine-tuning timeframes, making more precise cost predictions, and determining the required resources. Through the establishment of a well-defined project plan, organizations can effectively handle expectations, allocate resources optimally, and guarantee a more seamless implementation process.

Companies can methodically and effectively validate and deploy new technologies by following these stages: business concept validation, technical solution identification, proof of technology, and development of a clear project plan. This methodical approach reduces potential hazards, maximizes the efficient use of resources, and increases the probability of successfully integrating technology.

In order to successfully use generative AI technologies, enterprises should adopt a systematic strategy that includes the stages of ideation, solution design and task adaptation, and implementation and integration, as seen in the accompanying graph (Figure 2). Below are pragmatic suggestions for each phase:

To begin brainstorming, it is crucial to identify and assess generative AI application cases. Companies should initiate the analysis of their business processes to identify specific areas where generative AI might provide significant benefits. This entails actively involving stakeholders in order to comprehend areas of dissatisfaction and potential areas for enhancement. For example, a corporation may recognize customer support, content development, or predictive maintenance as promising domains for the application of artificial intelligence. Organizing seminars and brainstorming sessions can facilitate the creation of an extensive inventory of use cases, which should subsequently be ranked according to their practicality and potential influence.

After identifying prospective use cases, the following phase involves designing solutions and adapting tasks accordingly. This entails selecting suitable foundation models or pre-training customized models designed to meet unique company requirements. Timely engineering is essential at this point, as it aids in fine-tuning the AI's answers and enhancing its performance in practical applications. Refining the models by including data particular to the topic improves their precision and pertinence. Furthermore, the integration of input from human specialists is crucial for ongoing enhancement. It is advisable for businesses to create feedback mechanisms that incorporate human perspectives to improve the accuracy and quality of AI outputs. Periodic assessment of the models' performance guarantees that they adhere to the intended criteria and goals.

The last stage involves the implementation and integration of the AI solutions into the current business processes. This entails optimizing the models to be deployed, guaranteeing their efficient performance in the production setting. Companies should prioritize the use of model optimization techniques, such as quantization and pruning, to improve performance and minimize resource usage. Developing applications utilizing large language models (LLMs) necessitates meticulous strategizing and cooperation between AI specialists and business units.

Figure 2. Stages to successfully using generative AI technologies

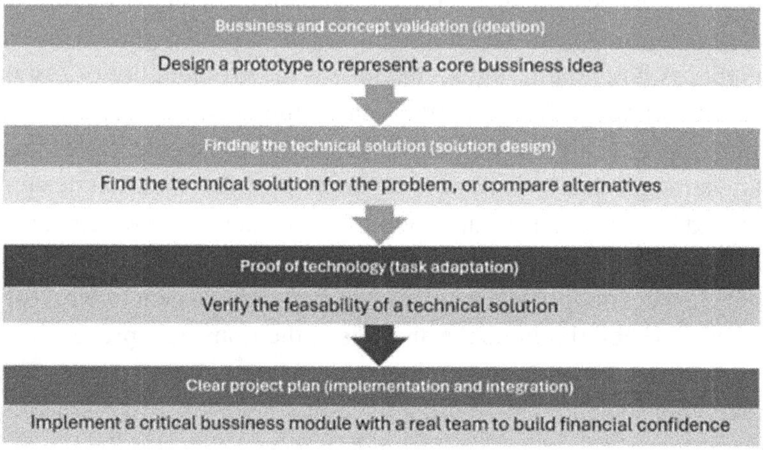

Benefitting from Generative AI

Instead of paying attention to the buzz surrounding generative artificial intelligence, business executives should focus on what they want to accomplish for their organizations, given the early maturity level of this technology. A method that is measured would concentrate on the goals, safeguard and use data in a responsible manner, and guarantee output that is trustworthy and reliable.

Take the Initiative With Your Ambitions

Be disciplined in your examination of whether or not generative artificial intelligence is indeed the appropriate solution for the purpose or problem at hand. Rather than allowing the technology to dictate what you do with it, you should examine it. It is important to begin with a business case that has been well articulated. For the purpose of analyzing the possible rewards, risks, and magnitude of investment, as well as winning the commitment of stakeholders, it is vital to clearly record the business challenge and the desired outcomes. The business case provides the development teams with the information they need to fully define the technical requirements, comprehend the data that is required, and build a solution that is in sync with the resources that your organization possesses.

Protect the Data

Although there is a growing body of evidence suggesting that generative artificial intelligence has the potential to produce remarkable results with the content it is trained on, it is still too soon to leave it entirely on its own in enterprise applications. It is essential to have humans involved in the process of data protection in order to prevent the inappropriate use of sensitive or biassed input data and to keep an eye out for distorted outputs. One of the most important concerns should be the protection of sensitive personal information, such as that of employees or customers, as well as intellectual property and intellectual capital. It is possible that public large language models may only provide minimal safety for sensitive or confidential information, despite the fact that cloud providers and other vendors are working to improve safeguards in this domain.

Make Sure the Output Is Dependable

It is possible to verify that the content that is generated does not contain any aspects that are discriminatory or erroneous, which could potentially cause harm, through the use of confirmation transformers and continuing testing. Because of this transparency, the capacity to explain makes the process easier to understand, and it also helps to create confidence in the final product. There will be an assumption that any endeavor involving generative artificial intelligence will justify its expense, unless the purpose is to do pure research. It is prudent for organizations to take measures to prevent themselves from investing more resources into a project than they extract from it.

Maintain Your Concentration

In spite of the fact that it is possible to establish proof-of-concept prototypes with a modest budget at the outset, it is possible that implementing a production solution would not scale well over time. Smaller, more specialized models that are suited to specific business cases may produce better results and demand a smaller financial commitment for continuing upkeep.

Make Sure You Are on Alert

One of the elements that should be included in a responsible AI framework is privacy and security.

You should begin with solid data. In particular, if the general data maturity of the organization is inadequate, costs might easily inflate out of control. When it comes to generative artificial intelligence business plan development, making investments in foundational data governance, quality, and observation techniques as a prelude will optimize the performance, security, and return on investment of any potential endeavor.

Choose a Way to Gauge AI's Effectiveness

According to a new Gartner poll of a large number of firms using AI, those with the most extensive, in-depth, and tenured expertise with the technology do not gauge success based on the scope of the project, the number of jobs finished, or the final product. Rather, they prioritize business measurements over financial ones, and adhere to use case-specific ad hoc measures and attribution models. Benchmarking occurs both internally and outside. There is a need to determine metrics in advance and evaluate AI use cases' effectiveness promptly and reliably. Among the business measures are those centered on:

Business expansion, such as the possibility for cross-selling, price rises, demand forecasting, and the monetization of additional assets.
Customer success metrics, such as share of wallet, customer happiness, and retention metrics
Cost-effectiveness, such as less inventory, lower production costs, higher worker productivity, and asset optimization.

According to independent data from Gartner, companies that include the AI team in developing success metrics have a higher likelihood of using AI strategically than companies that do not. The AI team should solicit input from data management teams, domain experts, business analysts, risk management leaders, data scientists, and IT developers and leaders when choosing metrics.

USE CASES, CHALLENGES, TRENDS, AND CASE STUDIES

Artificial Intelligence Use Cases in Business

Artificial intelligence (AI) is applied in two main areas: customer support and smart warehouses. Although Sysco has already implemented standard AI and machine learning techniques, the company is currently exploring various applications of generative AI. Presently, its endeavors are bolstering two main domains:

Sysco manages a sales and support system that includes a wide range of products, with a total of around 2 million Stock Keeping Units (SKUs). Among these SKUs, approximately 200,000 are particularly sought after by clients. The company has been utilizing conventional artificial intelligence (AI) and analytics to provide product suggestions. However, generative AI has the ability to integrate unorganized data, such as photos or social media data, in order to gather further information. This will enhance our ability to curate the shopping cart for our customers, fostering greater creativity. By transforming conventional AI into more generative AI, we are observing the emergence of larger shopping carts and increased profit margins.

Sysco's goal is to facilitate a more intelligent and proactive call center. This involves utilizing generative AI to do sentiment analysis, which entails analyzing customer data to gain insights into their emotional state. These insights are then used to develop more impactful scripts for support agents to utilize during customer support conversations.

The organization is utilizing generative AI on the sales side to automate call planning and provide suggestions for next-best actions to team members. Generative AI can assist with menu curation by creating and distributing strategically selected visuals that motivate customers to purchase more products. It can also be used for client segmentation, enabling sales professionals to more effectively tailor their offerings. It is an excellent method to enhance the efficiency of teams and deliver the appropriate product to delight the customer.

The efficiency of any warehouse operation, particularly in the food business, relies heavily on data and algorithms for the movement and tracking of products. Similarly, Sysco is employing artificial intelligence (AI) and generative AI to effectively handle inventory, enhance warehouse operations, and streamline customer deliveries. An instance of this is intelligent substitutes, which refers to the utilization of artificial intelligence to propose alternative products in situations where an item is unavailable or delivery is affected by a weather occurrence. Smart routing use onboard telematics to enhance the management of the company's fleet of trucks. It utilizes data on weather conditions, traffic, and onboard temperature zones to optimize routing in a more flexible manner. Generative AI can also facilitate efficient product selection in the warehouse and loading of trucks.

The novel aspect here is the data that exists outside of a conventional structured database, which can be used to create a more predictive and prescriptive approach. This enables to increase the number of pieces picked per pallet or load trucks more quickly. In the end, the goal is to efficiently manage a warehouse using intelligent methods.

Optimal Strategies for Implementation

There are the following suggestions for companies seeking to enhance their utilization of generative AI.

Incorporate generative AI within a wider technology plan. At Sysco, AI and generative AI are part of a larger automation agenda. Robotic process automation, bots, or classical AI can effectively address the majority of business situations. If those technologies are unable to solve the problem, it is advisable to contemplate constructing something utilizing generative AI capabilities.

Take into consideration the option of purchasing as opposed to constructing. Sysco chooses to acquire AI capabilities, such as robotic process automation bots and tools, rather than developing its own massive language models. This decision is based on Peck's preference for incorporating these skills into the company's existing tool set.

Comprehend the responsibilities and abilities of individuals. Sysco perceives generative AI as a means to increase productivity for humans, rather than as a substitute for employees. Peck stated that instead of establishing a dedicated AI team, Sysco focuses on training and educating its staff in new abilities and ensuring they have access to the necessary technologies.

CIOs have the ability to assume a position of leadership. The majority of CIOs or chief information and digital officers possess strong business acumen and actively contribute to the advancement of transformation and enhancement of business processes. Generative AI presents a new chance for them to elevate their position and exert a significant impact.

Main Challenges Regarding Generative AI

Data privacy is the primary concern regarding generative artificial intelligence. There is a potential for artificial intelligence training models to incorporate customer or employee information that is protected by personal data privacy laws and regulations in a number of nations. Inappropriate use of personally identifiable information or sensitive personal information may result in severe penalties, legal action, and damage to one's reputation.

Data ownership and attribution are important. It may be possible to obtain data for training purposes; however, it is not always apparent whether or not the data in question is protected by copyright or who has the authorization to allow its usage as input for generative artificial intelligence.

Intellectual property rights. In the world of business, intellectual property and intellectual capital are extremely important assets. It is possible that the use of these in data training models or prompts could inadvertently expose confidential information to audiences from outside the organization.

The ability to explain things and transparency. Understanding how an artificial intelligence model operates and how it arrives at its conclusions is what we mean when we talk about transparency. Because generative artificial intelligence makes use of intricate deep learning models and neural networks to recognize patterns and structures within existing data in order to generate new content, it can be challenging to explain how and why a particular output was derived through the use of this technology.

Bias in the data. Source data that contains unintended prejudice or outdated beliefs about protected groups indicates that generative AI would reflect similar biases in the output. This is because the data would involve protected groups. Decision-making is influenced by biassed production, which also has an effect on the reputation of the company.

There are hallucinations. The use of generative artificial intelligence has been observed to provide definite responses that are not supported by the training data, as well as to generate responses when it does not have a response to offer. These mistakes, which are frequently referred to as "hallucinations," cast doubt on the dependability of the output produced by generative robots.

Misinformation is being spread. The application of generative artificial intelligence by malicious actors allows for the publication of false narratives that are intended to manipulate or deceive audiences. Additionally, sophisticated tools have the ability to make hyper-realistic "deepfake" photos, videos, and sounds.

The regulation of AI. As time goes on, an increasing number of legislative and governing organizations are considering the possibility of imposing regulatory constraints on artificial intelligence. The European Union has reached a consensus that would place limitations on the applications of artificial intelligence that are considered to be the most dangerous. Guidelines that are focused on numerous aspects of artificial intelligence policy, including safety, have been put into place in the United States, while federal agencies have been directed to develop regulations.

Long-term viability. Large language models and generative artificial intelligence both demand a significant amount of processing power and energy consumption, which contributes to the generation of carbon dioxide.

Trends Related to Generative AI and Businesses Strategies

When incorporating generative AI, the experimental phase might be compared to sowing seeds in rich soil. This section explores the significance of experimentation in revealing the immense capabilities of generative AI and the intricacies of scaling these experiments to achieve significant business outcomes.

Experimentation is the process in which breakthrough AI applications are developed and refined. It involves the exploration of the realm of possibilities through the process of testing, learning, and iterating. Companies must establish a conducive climate that fosters risk-taking and creativity, enabling a trial-and-error methodology. For example, a technology corporation may engage in the exploration of artificial intelligence to develop innovative features for its products. They may then utilize client input to enhance and perfect their offers.

The process of experimentation is filled with difficulties. A significant challenge is the siloed approach, which restricts AI projects to individual departments instead of being integrated throughout the entire organization. In addition, there is the difficulty of succumbing to short-term thinking, when the emphasis is placed on immediate outcomes rather than the production of long-term value. To overcome these problems, it is necessary to change one's perspective. This involves shifting from focusing on individual projects to adopting a comprehensive approach that encompasses the entire organization. Additionally, the focus should move from seeking immediate benefits to setting long-term strategic objectives.

After successful AI trials have been identified, the next step is to implement them on a larger scale throughout the organization. This entails more than simply integrating technology; it necessitates aligning AI activities with corporate goals, modifying organizational structures, and ensuring that the workforce is prepared for the transition. For instance, a manufacturing corporation may expand an AI pilot project in predictive maintenance from a solitary production line to the entire factory network, resulting in a substantial decrease in downtime and maintenance expenses. The significance of leadership in the process of expanding and implementing artificial intelligence (AI) technology.

Effective leadership is essential during the process of scaling. Leaders must actively promote and support AI efforts, allocate the required resources, and foster a culture that is open to and embraces change. It is necessary to establish a connection between experts in artificial intelligence and leaders in business, ensuring that efforts involving artificial intelligence are in line with the broader company plan and that their value is effectively communicated throughout the organization.

Experimentation and scaling are crucial phases in the process of integrating generative AI. Effective experimentation is crucial for scaling, since it converts individual AI projects into catalysts for enterprise-wide innovation and expansion.

Case Studies Related to Generative AI and Business Strategies

Examinations of Effective Integration Examples

Multiple case studies serve as clear examples of successful integration. A financial services organization employed generative AI to transform its customer service by utilizing AI to produce tailored financial guidance for clients, hence improving customer contentment and operational effectiveness. Another instance involves a healthcare provider that incorporated artificial intelligence into its diagnostic services, resulting in expedited and more precise diagnoses, thereby enhancing patient care.

The Benefits of Utilizing Generative AI-Driven Storytelling in Marketing

Utilizing generative AI-driven storytelling provides numerous benefits in the field of marketing. Generative AI-driven storytelling allows for the development of customized or personalized narratives for clients and certain target segments. These customized stories improve client involvement and strongly connect with individual tastes. In addition, AI models have the capability to generate content on a large scale, hence lowering the time and effort needed to create marketing materials of high quality. Generative AI-driven storytelling allows marketers to explore various storytelling techniques, enhance content, and rapidly evolve based on real-time performance data and feedback. Additionally, it allows for the development of interactive storylines and behaviors that can be tailored to user input or contextual signals, resulting in an enhanced user experience.

An integral aspect of marketing involves delivering appropriate material, in the appropriate tone, timing, and via the appropriate channel. Generative AI-driven storytelling can be utilized by digital marketers to provide a significant consumer experience to the intended audience. These technologies enhance marketing operations and content development by generating original and innovative content. For example, generative AI systems such as Adobe Firefly enhance human creativity and imagination in marketing analytics by incorporating a layer of creative intelligence. Generative AI enhances and reinforces the creativity of digital marketers by generating helpful recommendations for upcoming content, condensing intricate subjects, and presenting stimulating concepts.

Examples of specific instances or situations: Effective Strategies Focused on Human Interaction in Artificial Intelligence Systems

Many organizations have effectively deployed AI strategies that prioritize human needs and preferences. A healthcare provider implemented artificial intelligence (AI) to aid in patient diagnosis, while also giving comprehensive training to medical professionals to effectively collaborate with the new technology. Another instance involves a technological company that integrated artificial intelligence (AI) into its process of developing products, all the while conducting workshops to foster innovation among its staff and inspire them to think imaginatively about how AI may improve their work.

Ensuring that individuals are the central focus of AI strategy is essential for effectively incorporating generative AI into company processes. It entails comprehending and resolving workforce anxieties, promoting a culture of AI education and cooperation, and adhering to ethical AI principles.

ETHICAL FRAMEWORKS AND FUTURE PERSPECTIVES

Ethical Frameworks Integration With Existing Systems

The use of generative AI-driven storytelling raises ethical problems around the production and distribution of manipulative and deceptive narratives. The World Economic Forum has emphasized the significance of tackling the ethical challenges and considerations associated with generative AI. Specifically, they have underlined the need to tackle the collecting and transmission of misleading or inaccurate information through AI. These issues have forced developers such as ChatGPT and OpenAI to mitigate the possibility of producing detrimental or inaccurate results. These firms have implemented bias detection and evaluation systems that periodically assess their AI systems for biases using methods including disparate impact analysis, fairness measures, and statistical tests. Bias mitigation has been observed in research and studies such as the Gender Shades study, which assessed facial recognition systems from prominent corporations and detected elevated error rates for females and individuals with darker skin tones (Roseneil, 2011). In addition, human input is crucial in guaranteeing the integrity and dependability of AI-generated material. Marketers frequently neglect to guarantee the transparency and ethical use of AI-generated materials, therefore leading to infrequent disclosure of its source and nature.

Generative AI poses risks in terms of copyright infringement, the creation of deep-fakes, and other forms of malicious exploitation that specifically target persons, organizations, and government entities. This difficulty has resulted in the presence of biases in training datasets in order to prevent prejudice and stereotypes. In order to overcome these difficulties, marketers can achieve a harmonious equilibrium between ethical deliberation and narrative construction prior to implementing generative AI in marketing. When incorporating generative AI systems, organizations should give priority to fairness, openness, accountability, and privacy. Google has implemented ethical guidelines and review processes to enable ongoing monitoring and accountability for AI systems. In addition, several companies have pursued algorithmic transparency and interpretability by utilizing algorithms that are both interpretable and transparent. By practicing transparency, these companies are able to detect and reduce biases in their decision-making processes. LIME, also known as Local Interpretable Model-agnostic Explanations, is an algorithm designed to offer explanations for individual forecasts.

FUTURE PERSPECTIVES

While the potential of generative AI is thrilling, it is essential to proceed with care. It is necessary to construct fairness criteria in order to guarantee that the narratives generated by AI are inclusive and free from discrimination. Ongoing research is crucial for identifying and correcting biases in generative models. It is crucial to maintain a balance between technology and creativity. Although AI has the ability to produce information, the unique qualities of human touch, intuition, and emotional understanding are still incomparable. Organizations contemplating the implementation of generative AI-driven storytelling should prioritize investing in data diversity and quality. This investment has been proven to be beneficial in producing AI models that are more varied, complete, and reflective of the intended audience. This technique can be improved by implementing appropriate infrastructure that enables smooth integration and meets the computational needs of the current systems. Important factors to consider include high-performance computing infrastructure such as cloud services and GPUs, which are essential for efficient inference procedures and training. Cloud computing programs have been developed using emerging technologies and systems to assist with data management. These programs utilize advanced algorithms that are capable of detecting dangers by leveraging self-learned skills in machine learning. IBM Research has been actively engaged in addressing bias in AI systems and has created the AI Fairness 360 toolbox. These technologies offer users measurements and algorithms that identify and reduce biases in machine learning models. OpenAI, the entity responsible for ChatGPT, has underscored the significance of collaboration and knowledge exchange in tackling AI biases. This company collaborates with the AI research community to tackle ethical challenges.

Delegation-based architectures are capable of assigning resource-intensive tasks to high-performance devices and servers, such as the Server-based Certificate Validation Protocol (SCVP). This technique facilitates the implementation of security protocols such as end-to-end IP security protocols. Security concerns can be enhanced by the utilization of hardware-based techniques that incorporate supplementary hardware security modules such as the Trusted Platform Module (TPM). This technique results in a security paradigm that ensures robust authentication and encryption due to its provision of security-related functions.

Moreover, the implementation of generative AI necessitates a scalable infrastructure capable of meeting the increasing demand for generative AI models. In addition, organizations should give priority to ethical considerations by implementing ethical norms and frameworks that ensure responsible use of generative AI-driven storytelling. Data management and security systems must possess the capability to effectively manage and safeguard substantial amounts of training data while guaranteeing the privacy and security of the data.

REFERENCES

Banh, L., & Strobel, G. (2023). Generative artificial intelligence. *Electronic Markets*, 33(1), 63. 10.1007/s12525-023-00680-1

Bi, Q. (2023). Analysis of the Application of Generative AI in Business Management. *Advances in Economics and Management Research*, 6(1), 36–36. 10.56028/aemr.6.1.36.2023

Borji, A. (2023). Mohammadian, M. Battle of the Wordsmiths: Comparing ChatGPT, GPT-4, Claude, and Bard. Available online: https://papers.ssrn.com/sol3/papers.cfm?abstract_id=4476855

Cardon, P., Getchell, K., Carradini, S., Fleischmann, A. C., & Stapp, J. (2023). Generative AI in the Workplace: Employee Perspectives of ChatGPT Benefits and Organizational Policies. Available online: https://osf.io/preprints/socarxiv/b3ezy10.31235/osf.io/b3ezy

Chuma, E. L., & de Oliveira, G. G. (2023). Generative AI for business decision-making: A case of ChatGPT. *Management Science and Business Decisions*, 3(1), 5–11. 10.52812/msbd.63

Feuerriegel, S., Hartmann, J., Janiesch, C., & Zschech, P. (2023). Generative AI. *Business & Information Systems Engineering*, 66(1), 111–126. 10.1007/s12599-023-00834-7

Gonçalves, R., Dias, Á., Costa, R., Pereira, L., Bento, T., & Rosa, Á. (2022). Gaining competitive advantage through artificial intelligence adoption. *International Journal of Electronic Business*, 1(1), 386–406. 10.1504/IJEB.2022.10044363

Govori, A., & Sejdija, Q. (2023). Future prospects and challenges of integrating artificial intelligence within the business practices of small and medium enterprises. *J. Gov. Regul.*, 12(2), 176–183. 10.22495/jgrv12i2art16

Hadi, M., & Najm, M. (2023). Introduction to ChatGPT: A new revolution of artificial intelligence with machine learning algorithms and cybersecurity. *Sci. Arch.*, 4, 276–285. 10.47587/SA.2023.4406

Hadi, M. U., Al-Tashi, Q., Qureshi, R., Shah, A., Muneer, A., Irfan, M., Zafar, A., Shaikh, M., Akhtar, N., Wu, J., ... (2023). Large Language Models: A Comprehensive Survey of Its Applications, Challenges, Limitations, and Future Prospects. Available online: https://www.techrxiv.org/users/618307/articles/682263-large-language-models-a-comprehensive-survey-of-its-applications-challenges-limitations-and-future-prospects

Jospin Jeya, J., & Raja Ratna, S. (2023). *G*. Generative AI Boosts Business Productivity.

Lund, B., & Wang, T. (2023). Chatting about ChatGPT: How may AI and GPT impact academia and libraries? *Library Hi Tech News*, 40(3), 26–29. 10.1108/LHTN-01-2023-0009

Mao, J., Chen, B., & Liu, J. (2023). Generative Artificial Intelligence in Education and Its Implications for Assessment. *TechTrends*, 68(1), 58–66. 10.1007/s11528-023-00911-4

Melehy, A. K. (2023). The Impact of AI on the Economy: A Comprehensive Analysis. Available online: https://www.researchgate. net/publication/370400293_The_Impact_of_AI_on_the_Economy_A_Comprehensive_Analysis

Mhlanga, D. (2023). The Value of Open AI and Chat GPT for the Current Learning Environments and The Potential Future Uses. SSRN *Electron. J.* 10.2139/ssrn.4439267

Nah, F., Zheng, R., Cai, J., Siau, K., & Chen, L. (2023). Generative AI and ChatGPT: Applications, challenges, and AI-human collaboration. J. Inf. Technol. Case Appl. Res., 25, 277–304.

Oliinyk, I. M. (2023). Prospects for implementing generative artificial intelligence in marketing and trade, Naukovij vìsnik L′otnoï akademìï, vol., p. 110-115.

Parikh, N. A. (2023). Empowering business transformation: The positive impact and ethical considerations of generative AI in software product management – a systematic literature review, Transformational Interventions for Business. *Technology and Health Care*, 269–293.

Roseneil S. (2011). Criticality, not paranoia: A generative register for feminist social research. NORA-Nordic Journal of Feminist and Gender Research, 19(2), 124-31.

Taulli, T. (2023). Generative AI: How ChatGPT and other AI tools will revolutionize business, Berkeley, CA: Apress.

Turlakova, S., & Bohdan, B. (2023). Artificial Intelligence Tools for Managing the Behavior of Economic Agents at Micro Level. *Neuro-Fuzzy Modeling Techniques in Economics*, 12(12), 3–30. 10.33111/nfmte.2023.003

Turlakova S.S. (2022). Conceptual provisions for managing the behavior of economic agents in the digital space using artificial intelligence tools. Economics and entrepreneurship, 49, 40-54.

Wamba-Taguimdje, S., Fosso Wamba, S., Jean Robert, K. K., & Tchatchouang, C. E. (2020). Influence of Artificial Intelligence (AI) on Firm Performance: The Business Value of AI-based Transformation Projects. *Business Process Management Journal*, 26(7), 26. 10.1108/BPMJ-10-2019-0411

Zhang, P., & Kamel Boulos, M. (2023). Generative AI in Medicine and Healthcare: Promises, Opportunities and Challenges. Future Internet, 15, 286.

KEY TERMS AND DEFINITIONS

Robotic Process automation (RPA): is a form of business process automation technology that uses software robots to automate tasks performed by humans.

Graphics Processing Unit (GPU): is a specialized electronic circuit initially designed to accelerate computer graphics and image processing (either on a video card or embedded on motherboards).

Large language models (LLMs): is a computational model notable for its ability to achieve general-purpose language generation and other natural language processing tasks such as classification.

Stock Keeping Units (SKUs): is a scannable code to help vendors track inventory, SKUs often appear as bar codes or QR codes along with alphanumeric digits, and SKUs are also used for units of repair time, services, and warranties.

Chief Information Officer (CIOs): is responsible for developing and implementing an organization's entire IT strategy, managing budgets and overseeing all IT staff.

Trusted Platform Module (TPM): TPM technology is designed to provide hardware-based, security-related functions. A TPM chip is a secure crypto-processor that is designed to carry out cryptographic operations.

Server-based Certificate Validation Protocol (SCVP): is an Internet protocol for determining the path between an X.509 digital certificate and a trusted root (Delegated Path Discovery) and the validation of that path (Delegated Path Validation) according to a particular validation policy.

Chapter 2
Artificial Intelligence in Decision-Making:
Reinventing Business Strategies

Geetha Manoharan
https://orcid.org/0000-0002-8644-8871
SR University, India

Sunitha Purushottam Ashtikkar
SR University, India

M. Nivedha
Robert Gordon University, UK

ABSTRACT

AI is quickly growing, and its use in commercial decision-making will influence the corporate environment. AI is redefining strategic business decision-making, and the chapter provides a complete view of how AI is changing the corporate world. This chapter examines how AI has disrupted previous decision paradigms and increased organizational agility in business strategy. A thorough literature review analyzes academic and business sources to reveal AI's broad corporate function. Systematic literature reviews are performed to evaluate source credibility and synthesize findings. The chapter also examines AI's corporate challenges and prospects. The chapter's main results demonstrate that AI is a strategic asset that transforms commercial decision-making. AI in company strategy might boost performance and promote sustainability. In conclusion, AI is essential to corporate growth, offering new creative and efficient opportunities. Additionally, a balanced approach to AI integration might emphasize the need of integrating AI with organizations' fundamental values and strategic goals.

DOI: 10.4018/979-8-3693-5578-7.ch002

INTRODUCTION

Evolution of Artificial Intelligence in Strategic Business Decisions

Integrating AI into crucial business decisions changes corporate strategy, models, and agility. AI and machine learning are becoming vital in digital transformation, according to Kitsios and Kamariotou (2021). Their rigorous literature review illustrates AI's economic value creation through corporate strategy integration. This convergence makes tactical and strategic AI tool use more difficult and requires more knowledge and ability (Kitsios & Kamariotou, 2021).

AI is gaining importance in business decision-making as strategic management processes evolve (Stipić, 2021; Shameem, A., et al., 2023). The study found that AI-based strategic planning tool can increase corporate success and profitability. Effective AI integration in strategic planning is crucial for organizations to handle complex business situations and make quality decisions for successful outcomes (Stipić, 2021).

Akmaeva et al. (2020) say digitization, including AI, shapes corporate strategy and new business models. Due to pandemic-accelerated socio-economic and political dynamics, their research suggests rethinking corporate management. They promote business AI adoption and the shift from hierarchical to agile, technology-driven paradigms. New company models and strategies for the fast-changing business landscape demand this change (Akmaeva et al., 2020).

AI in strategic business choices is vital to corporations. It might create significant value, rethink strategic planning, and create new firm models. In a digitalized environment, organizations use AI to improve decision-making, corporate performance, and sustainable commercial growth.

Mapping Artificial Intelligence in Corporate Strategy

AI has constantly changed company strategy. Over the past decade, AI has evolved from a novel technology to a strategic business decision-making tool, changing how firms tackle digital challenges and opportunities.

In their extensive analyses, Kitsios and Kamariotou (2021), Mekala, S., et al. (2023), and Lourens, M., et al. (2023) emphasize machine learning developments and their application into business strategy. Their research reveals that AI can tackle complex commercial challenges, but application is difficult. Strategically using AI for commercial value development is difficult without expertise. After a thorough literature review, they provide a theoretical model that links AI technology to organizational strategy, knowledge management, decision-making, and service innovation.

Mithas, Murugesan, and Seetharaman (2020) address AI-era organizational strategy. They highlight how organisations should integrate AI into their digital and IT strategies. Their findings suggest that AI changes a firm's resource and qualification infrastructure but does not fully drive its strategic decisions. It takes an internal reorganization to implement this new architecture in business process strategies. The authors propose that corporations must form governance organizations to define AI doctrine due to the nature of AI-automated decisions.

Delbufalo, Di Bernardo, and Risso (2022) examine human-machine intelligence in digital competitive business. They recommend balancing human and artificial intelligence in decision-making. Their analysis emphasises the need for organisations to adapt their models and responsibilities to intelligent technology. This flexibility is essential for competitiveness and sustainable strategies and programs.

AI improves decision-making, innovates, and creates new value propositions in corporate strategy. AI's position in corporate strategy has evolved to improve machine learning and redefine human and machine intelligence, reflecting a shift toward more flexible, data-driven, and technologically advanced company practices. AI will certainly change the strategic environment, creating new opportunities and challenges for enterprises worldwide.

Artificial Intelligence: Disruption of Conventional Decision Models

AI has changed business decision-making paradigms, changing how strategies are created and implemented. This disruption alters firms' cognitive and strategic processes, not just technology.

El-Namaki (2016) investigates the shift from human-centric to AI-driven company strategy. AI's ability to identify new patterns in big datasets has changed product and market strategy. Several case studies from different industries highlight how AI is influencing company strategies. The study provides a business AI conceptual framework that positions AI as a tool and strategic component.

AI-aided decision-making cognition is studied by Tejeda et al. (2022). They study human AI dependence in cooperative decision-making. Inferring human concealed dependence ways on AI support via a cognitive model shows how AI affects human decision-making. While AI aid is becoming pervasive in decision-making applications, human-AI partnership dynamics must be recognized and managed, the study revealed. Companies need this knowledge to employ AI without damaging human judgment and intuition.

Computer vision-based decision support systems are explored by Meske and Bunde (2020) for trust and transparency in human-AI interaction. Their research highlights the AI 'black box' dilemma, where algorithm complexity undermines confidence. They demonstrate how "Explainable Artificial Intelligence" (XAI) can improve AI system trust by making decision-making more transparent. For ethical and business decision-making, the study emphasizes AI explainability.

AI disrupts business decision models by changing strategic formulation, cognitive processes, and trust and transparency (Singh, C. R., & Manoharan, G., 2024). AI has changed corporate strategy, challenged established paradigms, and required a new approach that mixes human and artificial intelligence. AI will undoubtedly deepen its impact on decision-making processes, creating opportunities and difficulties for digital organizations.

Embracing Business Agility Through Artificial Intelligence

Business success nowadays needs agility. AI drives agility, affecting how organisations make decisions and respond to quickly changing settings like library management (Kumari, S., et al., 2023).

Rajagopal et al. (2022) and Rajchandar, K., et al. (2024) study how AI systems affect business outcomes and organizational decision-making. Their study shows that AI-driven digital frameworks improve decision-making, policy innovation, and decision execution. They explain how AI technologies make company cultures more dynamic and adaptable by analyzing diverse industries. The research shows that AI improves decision-making speed and accuracy, boosting company agility.

Pérez-Campuzano et al. (2021) examine how AI might aid airline strategic decision-making, particularly during COVID-19. They show how AI systems, particularly Machine Learning (ML) approaches, can help make strategic decisions during crises by analyzing markets and estimating costs. The report suggests adopting AI technologies in strategic functions to improve organizations' agility in resource management and competitive analysis.

Strategic agility emphasises decision-making over speed, according to Prange (2020). The study defines corporate agility as flexibility, transformational skills, and response speed. AI helps organizations make quick, educated decisions in chaotic circumstances, keeping them competitive. AI-powered strategic agility requires a deeper awareness of market dynamics and the ability to modify tactics fast, according to study.

AI is crucial to corporate agility. AI's improved analytical powers and faster, more accurate decision-making are changing how firms adapt to environmental changes. AI will increasingly promote nimble corporate methods, opening new options for strategic innovation and competitive advantage.

Conceptual Framework of Artificial Intelligence in Business Context

Strong conceptual frameworks are needed to maximize corporate AI potential. These frameworks help explain how AI can be used in business and decision-making.

Najdawi (2020) proposes an AI ready framework to help enterprises adopt AI. This paradigm is based on Information Systems theories like TOE and Diffusion of Innovation. Najdawi's work emphasizes local circumstances, as shown in the UAE, and focuses on socio-technical aspects of AI application. The framework emphasizes integrating AI activities with organizational skills and environmental elements for successful AI strategy execution.

The Solberg et al. (2022) paradigm ties AI trust to organizational decision-making, explaining AI in business. Their methodology adapts Mayer, Davis, and Schoorman's organizational trust model to AI decision aids. This paradigm emphasises trust, perceived risk, and AI use in organisations. It redefines key ideas and introduces concept like perceived AI decision help control. Businesses benefit from this paradigm because it organizes human-AI decision-making.

Eisenstadt, Althoff, and Langenhan (2020) examine how AI frameworks might help creative and complicated tasks in early architectural design conceptualization. The MetisCBR framework shows how explainable AI and generative adversarial nets can improve AI systems' design skills. This example shows how AI frameworks can be used in corporate contexts beyond data-driven decision-making.

Business AI conceptual frameworks are essential for maximising AI technology's potential. These frameworks organize AI understanding and implementation to align commercial processes with corporate goals and environmental conditions. These frameworks will help firms use AI for strategic advantage and innovation as AI evolves.

PURPOSE OF REVIEW AND GOALS

The goal of this research is to objectively explore the integration and influence of AI in strategic corporate decision-making and its revolutionary role in modern business processes. The goals are:

- To examine how AI is changing strategic decision-making in diverse industries.
- To evaluate how AI improves corporate competitiveness and efficiency.
- To detect AI implementation obstacles and dangers in corporate plans.
- To examine the ethical and social effects of commercial AI deployment.

- Predict AI trends in company strategy and management.

Key Research Queries

In studying AI integration in strategic business decision-making, several major research questions arise. We want to understand how AI is changing business decision-making models from conventional to AI-driven. This involves assessing how AI affects strategic decisions and commercial operations.

Quantifying AI's impact on corporate performance and competitiveness is essential (Durai, S., et al., 2024). This question measures how AI improves corporate efficiency, accuracy, and innovation.

The problems and obstacles firms experience when adopting AI into their plans are also important. Technical, organizational, and change resistance issues are included.

AI's ethical and social impacts on business cannot be ignored. This involves considering the morality and social consequences of AI in business.

Finally, corporate planning AI applications must be foreseen. This study predicts corporate AI trends, breakthroughs, and the shifting landscape, preparing organizations for the next technology wave.

Exploring Uncharted Territories in AI and Business Strategy

Uncharted AI-business strategy integration offers chances and problems. AI is changing corporate approaches and success models.

Esqueda and Melo (2020) innovate AI and game localization and translation. Their research implies that AI-driven solutions could help companies access global consumers across cultures and languages. This microcosm shows how AI may be used across corporate sectors to transcend previous limits, emphasizing its importance in global company plans.

Chuang et al. (2020) examined Creative Design Ltd., a startup that attempted new enterprises. Their case study shows how AI and business techniques can develop in new fields. AI transforms entrepreneurship and business success by helping organizations adapt and survive in fast-changing settings.

Shaheen, Arshad, and Iqbal (2020) argue AI and ML are changing transportation business models. The researchers found that AI helps decision-making, especially in processing and interpreting massive data sets for intelligent transportation systems. AI can streamline company operations and boost efficiency, according to a research.

New AI and business strategy frontiers show dynamic technology-business interaction. AI is establishing new business models, promoting sector innovation and competitiveness. Business possibilities and challenges in these new frontiers require strategic planning and flexibility in the AI age.

Boundaries and Focus of the Analysis

AI's limit and emphasis are evaluated to comprehend its role in strategic corporate decision-making. Company strategy, decision-making, competitive advantage, and operational efficiency are affected by AI.

The research investigates how AI is being integrated into different business models and sectors, stressing its revolutionary potential and challenges. AI impacts data-driven decision-making, consumer interaction, and market analysis.

The review considers commercial AI's ethical and social impacts. This needs careful consideration of privacy, data security, and AI's employment disruption potential.

Finally, the analysis shows how AI will affect company strategy and innovation by examining present patterns and projections. Businesses must be proactive in an AI-driven future.

RESEARCH METHODOLOGY

Business Literature Exploration: AI Blueprint

Organizational literature reviews assure comprehensive coverage and depth of AI in corporate strategy research. Like AI-business research literature selection, Gina and Budree (2020) emphasize business intelligence tool selection essentials. This categorizes studies by AI's involvement in business strategy, focusing on technical and non-technical factors that effect AI integration into company processes.

This context benefits from systematic reviews, say Yin and Fernandez (2020). Their algorithm uses established criteria to select relevant, high-quality documents from reliable resources. The method combines AI research from technological applications to corporate planning.

AI-Business Study Selection Criteria

AI business research projects are chosen utilizing many factors. The Stojanović et al. (2016) strategy for discovering business process improvement methodologies can also be used to choose AI-business literature. The approach suggests assessing AI's relevance to company strategy, the studies' methodological rigor, and their business implications.

Júnior et al. (2020) emphasize the importance of a thorough literature review for understanding enterprise architecture in healthcare systems. Their careful selection and evaluation disagreement assessment resemble AI-business research. This fair and comprehensive review of AI's role in business includes methodology, tools, best practices, and selection criteria.

Our AI-business literature exploration and study selection procedures are robust. This ensures AI's technical and strategic functions in business strategy are understood.

Dissecting AI Business Research Themes

Artificial intelligence business research thematic analysis examines key literature subjects. Vergara-Villegas et al. (2021) demonstrated this strategy in their AI for Industry 4.0 thematic issue. Thematic analysis helps label and understand AI applications in industry, from IoT infrastructures to decision-making. Identifying AI's multiple effects on company plans and operations requires this method.

The Thematic Analysis Grid by Anderson, Lees, and Avery (2015) simplifies academic literature theme synthesis. Organized literature reviews help researchers find field consensus and differences. This grid helps AI business researchers map knowledge and find gaps and patterns.

AI Business Insights Synthesis Method

An AI business insights synthesis mechanism must weave facts into a tale. Kreines and Kreines (2019) suggest synthesizing business research with AI technologies for objective scientific text analysis. AI maps the scientific scene and finds important topics and trends. This method is beneficial for synthesizing AI business research because the literature is vast and the themes diverse.

Corporate strategy and operations synthesis involves collecting, evaluating, and interpreting data. This requires extensive AI technology and commercial application understanding. Corporate strategies should be based on actionable findings in an AI-driven market.

FINDINGS

AI-Integrated Business Management Strategies

AI in corporate management changes decision-making and operations. Recent academic research feeds this AI-integrated corporate management strategies area.

Ling, Lin, and Yang (2017) suggest using AI to assess firm risk and profit. They predict business performance rating using random projection, data envelopment analysis, and AI. AI can enhance business decision-making, especially in dynamic environments where traditional models may fail (Lin, Lin, & Yang, 2017).

Amine Belhadi et al. (2022) build reliable supply chains with AI. Their comprehensive multi-criteria decision-making strategy builds supply-chain resilience using AI algorithms. This study shows how AI improves supply chain management, a critical company function. Fuzzy logic, machine learning, and agent-based systems demonstrate how AI may address complex business challenges (Belhadi, Kamble, Wamba, & Queiroz, 2022).

Vagin et al. (2022) and Tripathi, M. A., et al. (2023) study AI and Big Data in business management environmental decision-making. Their research shows these tools optimize economic-environmental decisions.

This study shows how AI can be used for sustainable business practices, a growing corporate strategy (Vagin, Klimenko, Telegina, & Aleksashina, 2022).

AI is used in risk assessment, supply chain resilience, and sustainable decision-making in business management. These studies show how AI may improve corporate decision-making, enabling strategic planning and operational efficiency.

Role of AI in Business Skill Enhancement

AI has transformed worker development, merging business and technology skills. Here's how AI is transforming corporate skill development.

Digital leadership is essential, according to Bai-Ngern and Tubtiang (2020). They say tech-savvy CEOs are needed to integrate AI into company operations and foster creativity and collaboration. Leadership training must emphasize AI literacy and its promise and limitations. The research advises educating AI-based strategic thinking for competitive advantage.

ElZomor et al. (2020) examine how AI and robotics may impact design, engineering, and construction. According to their analysis, new technologies change job skills and increase economic growth, empowering diverse workforces. This study reveals that AI-driven educational tools improve learning and workplace diversity.

Smolarek and Scrivener (2021) and Deviprasad, S., et al. (2023) describe Up-Skill Houston, a business-driven education reform initiative Their research shows how AI and digital technologies link workforce capabilities to industrial needs. The program stresses a labor market-relevant education, notably in AI- and automation-heavy businesses. AI provides real-time labor market data to advise and change educational curricula, according to the study.

Business skills are strengthened by AI beyond technical skills. AI-augmented workplaces value emotional intelligence, critical thinking, and adaptability. AI analytics can discover skill gaps and adjust instruction. This holistic skill development equips workers for AI's complex interpersonal, ethical, and technical challenges.

Technical and soft skills developed by AI increase commercial ability. These studies show how AI may revolutionize workforce development, emphasizing the necessity for new training and education in the digital age (Razak, A., et al., 2023). Skill upgrading will help companies stay competitive and build a robust, adaptive workforce as they adopt AI.

AI Impacts Corporate Performance Metrics

AI has transformed performance measurements and analysis in corporate business and financial management. This section examines how AI transforms business performance indicators using recent scholarly research.

Rasheed, Ishaq, and Rehman (2021) fully examined AI's involvement in Pakistani financial and corporate company management. Their analysis shows that AI has transformed financial management and corporate enterprise. According to studies, 80% of senior corporate leaders believe AI enhances productivity and opens new markets. Based on AI adoption, the report divides firms into four maturity clusters: Pioneers, Investigators, Experimenters, and Passives. This classification clarifies how different firms use AI to improve performance. Pioneer organizations that completely comprehend and apply AI have improved performance indicators, according to the data.

Lin and Chang (2021) examine corporate governance and dynamic business performance in semiconductors. Their research shows that AI can alter business governance and performance. The paper suggests using AI for automatic warning systems in corporate governance to identify and mitigate risks and improve performance indicators. This technique shows how AI may improve corporate governance transparency and accountability, improving performance.

Jiang et al. (2021) provide an HPC AI system benchmarking method for commercial and research computing. Valid FLOPS, a novel metric, stresses throughput and target quality in the study. This comprehensive AI system efficiency statistic is crucial to AI's impact on corporate performance. The research emphasizes benchmarking AI systems to appropriately assess their impact on corporate performance measures.

Performance measurements are being assessed and interpreted differently due to AI in corporate business and financial management. The research covered here show how AI is increasing company performance, from efficiency and business potential to corporate governance and benchmarking. AI's impact on corporate performance indicators will undoubtedly expand, giving firms new insights and chances to optimize operations and strategy.

Facilitating Inclusive Business Practices With AI

AI has improved operational efficiency and enabled inclusive and socially responsible business models. Recent scholarly research examines how AI is promoting inclusive corporate practices.

CSR and inclusive business in Peruvian business are explained in detail by Negro (2019). AI improves these notions, especially in underdeveloped economies, according to the study. Negro believes AI can identify and address social and economic inequalities, supporting inclusive business practises. AI can identify priorities and construct poverty reduction and sustainable development strategies from massive data sets.

AI boosts CSR's competitive edge and corporate performance, say Mai and Nguyen (2021). AI-driven CSR activities, notably ethical, legal, and benevolent ones, improve corporate advantage, according to their Vietnamese study. AI can scan and analyze massive data sets to help companies make CSR investment decisions, boosting their success and reputation.

Arenas-Torres, Bustamante-Ubilla, and Campos-Troncoso study Chilean firm ethics and CSR in 2021. Research shows AI standardizing social responsibility methods. AI helps companies incorporate CSR into their operations, boosting diversity, environment, and community.

Corporate social responsibility and inclusive business practices benefit from AI. These studies show AI's ability to identify social and economic inequalities, improve CSR decision-making, standardize social responsibility, and align business operations with global sustainability goals (Kumar, C. S., et al., 2024). As AI advances, it will promote inclusive and responsible business models, giving enterprises new ways to benefit society.

AI Tools for Business Challenges

AI is essential for solving corporate problems in the fast-changing commercial and technological world. AI integration demands deep knowledge of ethics, company culture, sustainability, and technology. Attard-Frost, De los Ríos, and Walters (2023) suggest that AI ethical guidelines should consider political and economic impacts beyond algorithmic decision-making in corporate activities. This mindset is needed to employ AI ethically in business.

Frost, Jeske, and Ottersböck (2020) highlight AI leadership and company culture for digital transformation. They argue AI and hybrid business models require new management and culture. Management and staff skills are developed together with technical change. The report shows that many companies underestimate the importance of these skills for digital success.

AI in business also need sustainability. Business culture impacts sustainable AI adoption, according to Isensee, Griese, and Teuteberg (2021). They suggest normative Sustainable Artificial Intelligence (SAI) informed by sustainability-focused corporate culture. The study reveals how company culture might affect SAI handling, proving that corporate culture affects AI sustainability.

Integrating AI into corporate processes presents challenges and opportunities. AI deployment ethics are crucial. As AI systems become more complex and influential in decision-making, businesses must ensure they are fair, accountable, transparent, and sustainable. AI ethics must consider economic and political factors as well as technology.

Another problem is changing corporate culture to integrate AI. Executives and employees must adapt to AI-driven business models. Companies must educate employees to use AI effectively. A culture of continuous learning and innovation supports workplace technology adoption.

Sustainable business practices are growing, and AI brings benefits and problems. To fulfill sustainability goals, AI may optimize resource use, eliminate waste, and improve efficiency. AI systems can use too much computer power, harming the environment. Therefore, companies must balance AI use with sustainability, environmental, and social goals.

AI business challenges require a holistic approach that considers ethics, culture, and sustainability. Businesses must create comprehensive AI policies that address these challenges to deploy AI sustainably. Business procedures, culture, and ethics must adapt with technology. AI can help businesses grow in the digital age by solving difficulties.

ANALYSIS AND DISCUSSIONS

Decoding AI's Impact on Business Choices

Modern corporate strategy uses AI to make decisions, transforming management and operations. This strategic transformation affects firm decision-making, not just technology.

Rajagopal et al. (2022) emphasize AI's transformation of company culture. AI-driven digital frameworks improve corporate decision-making, they argue. AI systems use data analytics and machine learning to gain previously unattainable insights to improve decision-making. This transformation provides a more purposeful and intelligent approach to decision-making that can handle complex scenarios with agility and precision, not just automation.

AI-era managerial decision-making is examined by Tabesh (2022) and Ashiq et al. (2023). The study reveals how AI and machine learning are improving decision-making through analysis and intuition. Advanced AI algorithms help managers assess company issues. Tabesh stresses that AI can enhance decision-making but should not replace it.

Ethical AI business activities are examined by Attard-Frost et al. (2023). Their work promotes ethical corporate AI adoption. The study showed that AI can improve decision-making, but data privacy, algorithmic bias, and transparency must be addressed. Ethics are essential to employing AI properly and sustainably in business.

Besides operational efficiency, AI affects strategic planning and organizational development. AI helped corporations analyze enormous amounts of data, discover trends, and predict market moves for more strategic decision-making. Success in today's fast-paced corporate environment requires quick market adaptation.

AI's decision-making role isn't limited to big companies. SMEs profit from AI integration. AI technologies give SMEs insights and efficiency formerly reserved for larger enterprises with more resources. Technology democratization helps small enterprises compete with big ones.

AI in commercial decision-making alters strategy and operations. This boosts productivity, analysis, and strategy. An ethical balance between human intuition and machine-driven analytics is needed for this transition. AI will influence company strategy and choices, creating new opportunities and challenges for businesses across sectors.

Business AI: A Sector-Wide Comparison

AI has changed corporate operations and competition in several industries. Recently conducted research compares AI's impact across sectors.

Dobre et al. (2020) link AI's history to the Dotcom era, demonstrating its durability and growth potential despite early worries. In contrast to Dotcom, AI is well embedded into key global economic sectors, suggesting a more sustainable growth trajectory. Schumpeterian creative destruction in AI occurs when larger firms purchase breakthrough startups, changing the competitive landscape.

In 2017, Papadimitriou et al. examined high-tech companies and knowledge-intensive services. Their research reveals that information intensiveness encourages innovation in these fields. In AI, knowledge development and leveraging are key competitive advantages.

Global robotics, a crucial AI market, is examined by Makedon et al. (2021). AI and robotics are transforming production and consumption, ushering in a new technological order. The study shows how robotics market expansion affects global innovation. This investigation shows how AI-driven robotics are transforming markets and economic roles.

AI impacts strategic pricing decisions across industries, according to Indrani et al. (2020). These studies illustrate that product, market, and business environment characteristics affect pricing strategies across sectors. AI can optimize pricing decisions, a crucial economic strategy, according to this study.

Businesses integrate AI differently depending on the sector and AI applications. From resilience and development potential in the AI industry to knowledge intensiveness in high-tech and service industries, revolutionary robot influence, and strategic pricing decision-making, AI's role is complex and sector-dependent. AI organizations need these insights to solve their specific problems and possibilities.

Unique Business AI Implementation Challenges

AI integration into corporate initiatives both challenges and opportunity. Ruokonen and Ritala (2023) say an AI-first approach requires a strong understanding of the firm's position and capabilities. In deploying AI for strategic advantage, digital tycoons, niche carvers, and asset augmenters face diverse challenges. Tech titans and digital tycoons must innovate to succeed. Niche carvers must find new methods to use AI in niche markets, while asset augmenters must add AI to assets to boost value.

Moving this argument to education, Owoc, Sawicka, and Weichbroth (2019) and Manoharan, G., et al. (2023) underline the shifting nature of business AI use. They emphasize that AI technology adoption requires knowledge of the technology and sector-specific challenges and opportunities. AI's strengths in learning and operational efficiency must be acknowledged and implementation challenges like data protection and bias perpetuated addressed.

Fenwick, Vermeulen, and Corrales (2018) address corporate AI environmental and regulatory challenges. They believe AI navigation requires changing regulatory and innovation contexts. Dynamic regulation, including regulatory sandboxes, allows experimentation and adaption in fast-changing areas. Innovation ecosystems allow large firms to partner with AI-focused startups, which boosts technology and business. AI's disruptive potential makes Fintech ecosystems vital.

So, handling disruptive AI technology strategically involves many ways. Businesses need AI capabilities and an ecosystem to integrate them into processes and business models. Balance technological innovation, regulatory compliance, and ecosystem collaboration.

Business AI implementation is cultural and technological. Businesses must embrace change, encourage creativity, and adapt to rapid AI technology breakthroughs. To maximise AI's potential and transform it into a strategic asset that supports long-term growth and sustainability, businesses must undergo this cultural shift.

As AI-using sectors vary, so do business AI implementation issues. Strategic alignment, sector-specific issues, regulatory compliance, and ecosystem growth are difficult for businesses. AI must be integrated into company strategy addressing its technological, cultural, regulatory, and collaborative aspects.

Vision for AI in Business Decision Processes

Businesses adjust strategy and operations when AI is used to make decisions. Rajagopal et al. (2022) study why AI-driven frameworks change business culture. Their research suggests AI helps corporate decision-making. AI improves procedure and results by making judgments more precisely. AI analytics automate judgments and improve strategic choices in this shift.

To elaborate, Ilieva et al. (2021) study business intelligence AI and ML. Their next-generation analytics uses AI for predictive modeling and data-driven insights. Strategies like AI integration into BI platforms assist organizations predict market trends, customer behavior, and operational inefficiencies. AI's e-commerce predictive powers improve forecasting, consumer segmentation, marketing, and customer experiences.

A review by Simões et al. (2022) and R. Kiran, G. R., et al. (2024) examines future AI and digital transformation trends. AI's versatility in digital transformation is shown by its impact on healthcare, education, and tourism.

This comprehensive examination emphasizes AI's role in future corporate strategies and operations. Businesses may better plan for future challenges and opportunities by employing AI for value aggregation.

AI integration into commercial decision-making is difficult. The right balance between human and AI-driven decision-making is crucial. Rajagopal et al. (2022) propose a new comparative analysis paradigm. They propose combining human and AI-based decision-making to improve organizational judgment efficiency. Participative management, where internal stakeholders oversee AI-business choices, is stressed in this concept.

AI decision-making ethics are another issue. Businesses must ensure ethical and responsible usage of AI technologies as they become more advanced. Considerations include data privacy, AI algorithm bias, and the social consequences of AI-driven judgments. Businesses must carefully handle these issues to maximize AI's impact on decision-making and employee well-being (Alex Rajesh G., & Florence Sheeba J., 2022).

AI in corporate decision processes will present significant potential and difficulties (Manoharan, G., et al., 2024). Business strategy and operations will increasingly depend on AI as it evolves. Businesses that successfully integrate AI into their decision-making processes may adapt to changing market dynamics, predict future trends, and make better strategic decisions. AI's ethical and practical challenges must be considered during integration. AI may be used for innovation, efficiency, and growth, not just automation.

CONCLUSION

A comprehensive literature review supported this study on AI in strategic business decision-making. AI's emergence, evolution, and impact on corporate practices were the main focus. An exhaustive analysis of academic and corporate sources explained AI's business role.

Business AI is difficult, as shown by a detailed literature study. It established a strong framework for examining sources and integrating findings to comprehend AI's role in organizational strategy and decision-making. This strategy allows a thorough dive into AI's disruption of traditional decision models, business agility, and skill augmentation.

A study reveals that AI is a strategic advantage that impacts company decisions. AI-powered business management solutions improve performance and encourage inclusivity. The report also stressed the necessity for AI-ready corporate cultures and sustainable company futures due to AI's unique challenges and opportunities.

In conclusion, AI drives company strategy with unparalleled creativity and efficiency. AI integration into corporate practises is complex and requires strategic alignment with core values and aims. This research suggests adopting AI as a technology that drives holistic growth and sustainability. AI will change commercial decision-making and organizational dynamics.

REFERENCES

Abdulwahid, A. H., Pattnaik, M., Palav, M. R., Babu, S. T., Manoharan, G., & Selvi, G. P. (2023, April). Library Management System Using Artificial Intelligence. In *2023 Eighth International Conference on Science Technology Engineering and Mathematics (ICONSTEM)* (pp. 1-7). IEEE.

Akmaeva, R., Arykbaev, R., Epifanova, N., & Glinchevskiy, E. 2020. Influence of digitalization upon formation of corporate strategy and new business models of modern organizations. In SHS Web of Conferences (Vol. 89, p. 03003). *EDP Sciences*. DOI: 10.1051/shsconf/20208903003

Alex Rajesh G., & Florence Sheeba J. (2022). A Study on Exploring Perceptions of Emotional Intelligence among Educators. *IJFANS International Journal of Food and Nutritional Sciences*, ISSN PRINT 2319-1775 Online 2320-7876.

Anderson, D., Lees, B., & Avery, B. 2015, June. Reviewing the literature using the Thematic Analysis Grid. In European Conference on Research Methodology for Business and Management Studies. Valetta, Malta: *Academic Conferences and Publishing International* (pp. 455-457).

Arenas-Torres, F., Bustamante-Ubilla, M., & Campos-Troncoso, R. (2021). The incidence of social responsibility in the adoption of business practices. *Sustainability (Basel)*, 13(5), 2794. 10.3390/su13052794

Ashiq, V. M., Fredrik, E. T., Kumar, N. K., Torres-Cruz, F., Colque, J. P. B., & Manoharan, G. (2023, September). A Deep Learning Approaches for Natural Language Processing and Sentiment Analysis in Social Media. In 2023 6th International Conference on Contemporary Computing and Informatics (IC3I) (Vol. 6, pp. 1746-1750). IEEE.

Attard-Frost, B., De los Ríos, A., & Walters, D. R. (2023). The ethics of AI business practices: A review of 47 AI ethics guidelines. *AI and Ethics*, 3(2), 389–406. 10.1007/s43681-022-00156-6

Bai-Ngern, K., & Tubtiang, A. 2020. Leadership in the Digital Era. In 2020 *5th International STEM Education Conference* (iSTEM-Ed) (pp. 127-130). IEEE. DOI: 10.1109/iSTEM-Ed50324.2020.9332712

Belhadi, A., Kamble, S., Fosso Wamba, S., & Queiroz, M. M. (2022). Building supply-chain resilience: An artificial intelligence-based technique and decision-making framework. *International Journal of Production Research*, 60(14), 4487–4507. 10.1080/00207543.2021.1950935

Chuang, Y. H., Kang, T. C., Chang, W. C., & Chen, P. J. (2020). Creative Design Ltd.: The path to youth entrepreneurship. *Emerald Emerging Markets Case Studies*, 10(2), 1–17. 10.1108/EEMCS-07-2019-0182

Ćormarković, T., Dražeta, L. and Njeguš, A., 2022. The levels of artificial intelligence application in human resource systems. *The European Journal of Applied Economics*, 19(2). DOI: .10.5937/EJAE19-39535

Delbufalo, E., Di Bernardo, M., & Risso, M. (2022). Human-Machine Interaction and AI for Competitive Business in the Digital Era. *Symphonya*, (2), 134–143. 10.4468/2022.2.12delbufalo.dibernardo.risso

Deviprasad, S., Madhumithaa, N., Vikas, I. W., Yadav, A., & Manoharan, G. (2023). The Machine Learning-Based Task Automation Framework for Human Resource Management in MNC Companies. *Engineering Proceedings*, 59(1), 63.

Dobre, R., Bulin, D., Iorgulescu, M.C. & Oehler-Sincai, I.M. (2020). Artificial Intelligence Sector: The Next Technology Bubble? A Comparative Analysis with Dotcom Based on Stock Market Data. *Romanian Economic Journal*, (76).

Durai, S., Manoharan, G., & Ashtikar, S. P. (2024). *Harnessing Artificial Intelligence: Pioneering Sustainable Solutions for a Greener Future. Social and Ethical Implications of AI in Finance for Sustainability*. IGI Global. 10.4018/979-8-3693-2881-1.ch003

Durai, S., Manoharan, G., Priya, T. S., Jayanthi, R., Razak, A., & Ashtikar, S. P. (2024). It is quantifying the Impacts of Artificial Intelligence Implementations in Marketing. In *Smart and Sustainable Interactive Marketing* (pp. 120–144). IGI Global. 10.4018/979-8-3693-1339-8.ch008

Eisenstadt, V., Althoff, K. D., & Langenhan, C. (2020). Student Graduation Projects in the Context of Framework for AI-Based Support of Early Conceptual Phases in Architecture. *In LWDA* (pp. 174-179).

El-Namaki, M.S.S. (2016). How Companies are Applying AI to the Business Strategy Formulation. DOI: */JOURNAL.SIJBPG05080I*10.19085

ElZomor, M., Pradhananga, P., Santi, G., & Vassigh, S. (2020, June). Preparing the future workforce of architecture, engineering, and construction for robotic automation processes. *2020 ASEE Virtual Annual Conference ContentAccess*. 10.18260/1-2--35082

Esqueda, M. D., & Melo, B. C. (2020). The uncharted territory in Uncharted 3: Expectancy vs. Professional norms in translated games. *Belas Infiéis*, 9(4), 173–199. 10.26512/belasinfieis.v9.n4.2020.26449

Fenwick, M., Vermeulen, E. P., & Corrales, M. (2018). Business and regulatory responses to artificial intelligence: Dynamic regulation, innovation ecosystems and the strategic management of disruptive technology. In Robotics, AI and the Future of Law (pp. 81–103). Springer Singapore., 1007/978-981-13-2874-9_4. 10.1007/978-981-13-2874-9_4

Frost, M., Jeske, T., & Ottersböck, N. (2020). Leadership and corporate culture as key factors for thriving digital change. In Advances in Human Factors and Systems Interaction: Proceedings of the AHFE 2020 Virtual Conference on Human Factors and Systems Interaction, July 16-20, 2020, USA (pp. 55-61). *Springer International Publishing*. 10.1007/978-3-030-51369-6_8

Gina, B., & Budree, A. (2020). A review of literature on critical factors that drive the selection of business intelligence tools. *In 2020 International Conference on Artificial Intelligence, Big Data, Computing and Data Communication Systems (icABCD)* (pp. 1-7). IEEE. 10.1109/icABCD49160.2020.9183852

Ilieva, R., Ivanova, M., Peycheva, T., & Nikolov, Y. (2021). Modelling in support of decision making in business intelligence. In *Integration Challenges for Analytics, Business Intelligence, and Data Mining* (pp. 115–144). IGI Global. 10.4018/978-1-7998-5781-5.ch006

Indrani, M.W., Naidoo, M. & Wickremasinghe, G. (2020). Comparative analysis of pricing decisions made by listed companies representing different industry sectors: evidence from Sri Lanka. DOI: */IJABF.V6I1.53*.4038

Isensee, C., Griese, K. M., & Teuteberg, F. (2021). Sustainable artificial intelligence: A corporate culture perspective. In Sustainability Management Forum| Nachhaltigkeits Management Forum(Vol. 29, No. 3-4, pp. 217-230). Berlin/Heidelberg: *Springer Berlin Heidelberg*. 10.1007/s00550-021-00524-6

Jiang, Z., Gao, W., Tang, F., Wang, L., Xiong, X., Luo, C., Lan, C., Li, H., & Zhan, J. (2021). Hpc ai500 v2. 0: The methodology, tools, and metrics for benchmarking hpc ai systems. In *IEEE International Conference on Cluster Computing* (CLUSTER) (pp. 47-58). IEEE. 10.1109/Cluster48925.2021.00022

Júnior, S. H. D. L., Silva, F. Í. C., Albuquerque, G. S. G., de Medeiros, F. P. A., & Lira, H. B. (2020). Enterprise Architecture in Healthcare Systems: A systematic literature review. *arXiv preprint arXiv:2007.06767*. 10.17632/44bygxg8w3.1

Kiran, R. G. R., Manoharan, G., Durai, S., Ashtikar, S. P., & Kunchala. (2024). Higher Education in India and the Influence of Online Certification Programs. Evaluating Global Accreditation Standards for Higher Education. IGI Global.

Kitsios, F., & Kamariotou, M. (2021). Artificial intelligence and business strategy towards digital transformation: A research agenda. *Sustainability (Basel)*, 13(4), 2025. 10.3390/su13042025

Kreines, M. G., & Kreines, E. M. (2019). Artificial Intelligence Tools for Business Applications: Objective Map of Science and Analysis of Texts. *In 2019 IEEE 21st Conference on Business Informatics (CBI)* (Vol. 1, pp. 445-451). IEEE. 10.1109/CBI.2019.00058

Kumar, C. S., Vani, D. D., Damodar, K., Manoharan, G., & Veerapaga, N. (2024). Climate Change Mitigation Through AI Solutions. In Gastronomic Sustainability Solutions for Community and Tourism Resilience (pp. 37-59). IGI Global. 10.4018/979-8-3693-4135-3.ch003

Lin, C.-C. & Chang, S.-F. (2021). Using AI to Improve Corporate Governance. 10.1051/e3sconf/202124503063

Lin, W.-K., Lin, S.-J., & Yang, T.-N. (2017). Integrated Business Prestige and Artificial Intelligence for Corporate Decision Making in Dynamic Environments. 10.1080/01969722.2017.1284533

Lourens, M., Sharma, S., Pulugu, R., Gehlot, A., Manoharan, G., & Kapila, D. (2023, May). Machine learning-based predictive analytics and big data in the automotive sector. In 2023 3rd International Conference on Advance Computing and Innovative Technologies in Engineering (ICACITE) (pp. 1043-1048). IEEE. 10.1109/ICACITE57410.2023.10182665

Mai, K. N., & Nguyen, A. K. T. (2021). The Impact of Corporate Social Responsibility Performance on Competitive Advantage and Business Success: A Case of Vietnamese Enterprises. *International Journal of Asian Business and Information Management*, 12(3), 1–15. 10.4018/IJABIM.294095

Makedon, V., Mykhailenko, O., & Vazov, R. (2021). Dominants and Features of Growth of the World Market of Robotics. *European Journal of Management Issues*, 29(3), 133–141. 10.15421/192113

Manoharan, G., Ashtikar, S. P., & Nivedha, M. (2024). Integrating Artificial Intelligence in Library Management: An Emerging Trend. AI-Assisted Library Reconstruction, 144-157.

Manoharan, G., Ashtikar, S. P., & Nivedha, M. (2024). Harnessing the Power of Artificial Intelligence in Reinventing the Manufacturing Sector. In Using Real-Time Data and AI for Thrust Manufacturing (pp. 113-137). IGI Global. 10.4018/979-8-3693-2615-2.ch007

Manoharan, G., Durai, S., Ashtikar, S. P., & Kumari, N. (2024). Artificial Intelligence in Marketing Applications. In Artificial Intelligence for Business (pp. 40-70). Productivity Press.

Manoharan, G., Durai, S., Rajesh, G. A., & Ashtikar, S. P. (2023). A Study on the Application of Natural Language Processing Used in Business Analytics for Better Management Decisions: A Literature Review. Artificial Intelligence and Knowledge Processing, 249-261.

Manoharan, G., Durai, S., Rajesh, G. A., & Ashtikar, S. P. (2024). A Study on the Application of Expert Systems as a Support System for Business Decisions: A Literature Review. Artificial Intelligence and Knowledge Processing, 279-289.

Manoharan, G., Jalaja, V., Sathe, M. A., Lourens, M., & Suresh, K. (2023, December). Machine Learning and Data Privacy in Human Resource Management. In 2023 4th International Conference on Computation, Automation and Knowledge Management (ICCAKM) (pp. 1-6). IEEE. 10.1109/ICCAKM58659.2023.10449576

Manoharan, G., Rao, C. G., Ashtikar, S. P., Kumar, S., & Nivedha, M. (2024). Voyage Virtuoso: Artificial Intelligence in Transforming Tourism. In Utilizing Smart Technology and AI in Hybrid Tourism and Hospitality (pp. 79-97). IGI Global.

Manoharan, G., Razak, A., Rajchandar, K., Nithya, G., Durai, S., & Ashtikar, S. P. (2024). Digital Learning for Professional Development in Varied Fields of Service Sectors: Embracing Technological Advancements. In Embracing Technological Advancements for Lifelong Learning (pp. 111-137). IGI Global.

Manoharan, G., Razak, A., Rao, B. S., Singh, R., Ashtikar, S. P., & Nivedha, M. (2024). Navigating the Crescendo of Challenges in Harnessing Artificial Intelligence for Disaster Management. In Predicting Natural Disasters With AI and Machine Learning (pp. 64-94). IGI Global. 10.4018/979-8-3693-2280-2.ch003

Manoharan, G., Razak, A., Rao, C. G., Ashtikar, S. P., & Nivedha, M. (2024). Artificial Intelligence at the Helm: Steering the Modern Business Landscape Toward Progress. In The Ethical Frontier of AI and Data Analysis (pp. 72-99). IGI Global.

Mekala, S., Bhuvana, M., Gupta, D. B., Bhatt, V., Kunekar, P., & Manoharan, G. (2023, September). Natural Language Processing and Deep Learning Techniques to Improve Sentiment Analysis in Social Media Texts. In 2023 6th International Conference on Contemporary Computing and Informatics (IC3I) (Vol. 6, pp. 1751-1755). IEEE. 10.1109/IC3I59117.2023.10397735

Meske, C., & Bunde, E. (2020). Transparency and trust in human-AI-interaction: The role of model-agnostic explanations in computer vision-based decision support. In Artificial Intelligence in HCI: First International Conference, AI-HCI 2020, Held as Part of the 22nd HCI International Conference, HCII 2020, Copenhagen, Denmark, July 19–24, 2020, Proceedings 22(pp. 54-69). Springer International Publishing. 10.1007/978-3-030-50334-5_4

Mithas, S., Murugesan, S., & Seetharaman, P. (2020). What is your artificial intelligence strategy? *IT Professional*, 22(2), 4–9. 10.1109/MITP.2019.2957620

Najdawi, A. (2020). Assessing AI readiness across organizations: the case of UAE. In 2020 11th International Conference on Computing, Communication and Networking Technologies (ICCCNT) (pp. 1-5). IEEE. DOI: 10.1109/ICCCNT49239.2020.9225386

Negro, A. R., & Mesia, R. (2019). Organization and Society: Understanding Corporate Social Responsibility and The Inclusive Business in The Peruvian Business Environment. *Journal of Applied Business & Economics*, 21(5). Advance online publication. 10.33423/jabe.v21i5.2275

Nguyen, M. Q., Nguyen, T. K. C., & Pham, H. G. (2022). Sustainable Development under the Impacts of the Fourth Industrial Revolution and the Role of Corporate Culture Renovation. *VNU Journal of Science: Policy and Management Studies*, 38(3). Advance online publication. 10.25073/2588-1116/vnupam.4412

Owoc, M. L., Sawicka, A., & Weichbroth, P. (2019). Artificial intelligence technologies in education: benefits, challenges and strategies of implementation. In *IFIP International Workshop on Artificial Intelligence for Knowledge Management* (pp. 37-58). Cham: Springer International Publishing. DOI: 1007/978-3-030-85001-2_4

Papadimitriou, L., Mpartzeliotis, K., Nikas, S., & Vessala, M. (2017). A Comparative Analysis of Knowledge-Based Firms in High-Tech Sectors and Knowledge Intensive Business Services. In Strategic Innovative Marketing: 4th IC-SIM, Mykonos, Greece 2015(pp. 419-424). Springer International Publishing. DOI: 10.1007/978-3-319-33865-1_52

Paulauskaite-Taraseviciene, A., Lagzdinyte-Budnike, I., Gaiziuniene, L., Sukacke, V., & Daniuseviciute-Brazaite, L. (2022). Assessing education for sustainable development in engineering study programs: A case of AI ecosystem creation. *Sustainability (Basel)*, 14(3), 1702. 10.3390/su14031702

Pérez-Campuzano, D., Ortega, P. M., Andrada, L. R., & López-Lázaro, A. (2021). Artificial Intelligence potential within airlines: A review on how AI can enhance strategic decision-making in times of COVID-19. *Journal of Airline and Airport Management*, 11(2), 53–72. 10.3926/jairm.189

Perucica, N., & Andjelkovic, K. (2022). Is the future of AI sustainable? A case study of the European Union. Transforming Government: People. *Process and Policy*, 16(3), 347–358. 1108/tg-06-2021-0106

Prange, C. I. (2020). Strategic agility–decision-making beyond speed. In Academy of Management Proceedings (Vol. 2020, No. 1, p. 12499). Academy of Management. 10.5465/AMBPP.2020.12499abstract

Rajagopal, N. K., Qureshi, N. I., Durga, S., Ramirez Asis, E. H., Huerta Soto, R. M., Gupta, S. K., & Deepak, S. (2022). Future of business culture: An artificial intelligence-driven digital framework for organization decision-making process. *Complexity*, 2022(1), 1–14. 10.1155/2022/7796507

Rajchandar, K., Kothandaraman, D., Manoharan, G., & Kabanda, G. (n.d.). Robotics and its Navigation Techniques: The Present and Future Revelations. Handbook of Artificial Intelligence and Wearables, 189-204.

Rajchandar, K., Manoharan, G., & Ashtikar, S. P. (2024, February). Robustness in Natural Language Processing: Addressing Challenges in Text-based AI Systems. In 2024 11th International Conference on Computing for Sustainable Global Development (INDIACom) (pp. 1435-1439). IEEE.

Raji, B. S. (2022). Exploring how artificial intelligence (AI) can support start-ups to manage crisis situations for future sustainable business in the agri-food industry. In *Future Role of Sustainable Innovative Technologies in Crisis Management* (pp. 192–213). IGI Global. 10.4018/978-1-7998-9815-3.ch014

Raji, B. S. (n.d.). Exploring How Artificial Intelligence (AI) Can Support Start-Ups to Manage Crisis Situations for Future Sustainable Business in the Agri-Food Industry. DOI: 4018/978-1-7998-9815-3.ch014

Rasheed, R., & Ishaq, M.N. & ur Rehman, H. (2021). Artificial Intelligence in Corporate Business and Financial Management: A Performance Analysis from Pakistan. Review of Education. *Administration & Law*, 4(4), 847–860.

Razak, A., Nayak, M. P., Manoharan, G., Durai, S., Rajesh, G. A., Rao, C. B., & Ashtikar, S. P. (2023). Reigniting the power of artificial intelligence in education sector for the educators and students competence. In *Artificial Intelligence and Machine Learning in Smart City Planning* (pp. 103–116). Elsevier. 10.1016/B978-0-323-99503-0.00009-0

Ruokonen, M., & Ritala, P. (2023). How to succeed with an AI-first strategy? *The Journal of Business Strategy*. Advance online publication. 10.1108/JBS-08-2023-0178

Samarasinghe, K., & Medis, A. (2020, March 26). Artificial Intelligence Based Strategic Human Resource Management (AISHRM) For Industry 4.0. *Global Journal of Management and Business Research*, 7–13. Advance online publication. 10.34257/GJMBRGVOl20IS2PG7

Shaheen, M., Arshad, M., & Iqbal, O. (2020). Role and Key Applications of Artificial Intelligence & Machine Learning in Transportation. *European Journal of Technology*, 4(1), 47–59. 10.47672/ejt.632

Shameem, A., Ramachandran, K. K., Sharma, A., Singh, R., Selvaraj, F. J., & Manoharan, G. (2023, May). The rising importance of AI in boosting the efficiency of online advertising in developing countries. In 2023 3rd International Conference on Advance Computing and Innovative Technologies in Engineering (ICACITE) (pp. 1762-1766). IEEE. 10.1109/ICACITE57410.2023.10182754

Simões, R. V., Parreiras, M. V. C., Da Silva, A. C. C., Barbosa, C. E., de Lima, Y. O., & de Souza, J. M. (2022). Artificial intelligence and digital transformation: analyzing future trends. In *2022 IEEE International Conference on Systems, Man, and Cybernetics (SMC)*(pp. 1462-1467). IEEE. 10.1109/SMC53654.2022.9945429

Singh, C. R., & Manoharan, G. (2024). Strengthening Resilience: AI and Machine Learning in Emergency Decision-Making for Natural Disasters. In Internet of Things and AI for Natural Disaster Management and Prediction (pp. 249-278). IGI Global.

Smolarek, B. B., & Scrivener, L. (2021). Examining business-driven education reform by new policy actors: A discursive analysis of UpSkill Houston. *Journal of Education Policy*, 36(3), 349–366. 10.1080/02680939.2019.1686539

Solberg, E., Kaarstad, M., Eitrheim, M. H. R., Bisio, R., Reegård, K., & Bloch, M. (2022). A conceptual model of trust, perceived risk, and reliance on AI decision aids. *Group & Organization Management*, 47(2), 187–222. 10.1177/10596011221081238

Stipić, V. V. (2021). Interaction of strategic management processes and achieved corporate profitability: Evidence from Croatia. In BH Ekonomski forum(No. 13, pp. 133-149). Ekonomski fakultet-Univerzitet u Zenici.

Stojanović, D., Slović, D., Tomašević, I., & Simeunović, B. (2016). Model for selection of business process improvement methodologies. In *19th International Toulon-Verona Conference on Excellence in Services* (Vol. 5, pp. 453-467). Huelva.

Svistunov, V. M., Kuzina, G. P., & Lobachev, V. V. (2021). Inevitability of company's corporate culture transformation under conditions of new management technologies. In Engineering Economics: Decisions and Solutions from Eurasian Perspective (pp. 613-623). Springer International Publishing. 10.1007/978-3-030-53277-2_73

Tabesh, P. (2022). Who's making the decisions? How managers can harness artificial intelligence and remain in charge. Journal of Business Strategy, 43(6), pp.373-380. *The Journal of Business Strategy*, 2021. Advance online publication. 10.1108/JBS-05-2021-0090

Tariq, M. U., Poulin, M., & Abonamah, A. A. (2021). Achieving operational excellence through artificial intelligence: Driving forces and barriers. *Frontiers in Psychology*, 12, 686624. 10.3389/fpsyg.2021.68662434305744

Tejeda, H., Kumar, A., Smyth, P., & Steyvers, M. (2022). AI-assisted decision-making: A cognitive modeling approach to infer latent reliance strategies. *Computational Brain & Behavior*, 5(4), 491–508. 10.1007/s42113-022-00157-y

Tripathi, M. A., Tripathi, R., Effendy, F., Manoharan, G., Paul, M. J., & Aarif, M. (2023, January). An In-Depth Analysis of the Role That ML and Big Data Play in Driving Digital Marketing's Paradigm Shift. In *2023 International Conference on Computer Communication and Informatics (ICCCI)* (pp. 1-6). IEEE. 10.1109/ICCCI56745.2023.10128357

Vagin, S. G., Klimenko, V. A., Telegina, Z. A., & Aleksashina, T. V. (2022). Improving environmental decision-making in environmental business-management using big data and AI. *Frontiers in Environmental Science*, 10, 951306. 10.3389/fenvs.2022.951306

Vergara Villegas, O. O., Nandayapa, M., Sossa Azuela, J. H., Cossio Franco, E. G., & Rubin Linares, G. T. (2021). Introduction to the Thematic Issue on Artificial Intelligence for Industry 4.0. *Computación y Sistemas*, 25(4), 681–682. 10.13053/cys-25-4-4057

Yin, J., & Fernandez, V. (2020). A systematic review on business analytics. *Journal of Industrial Engineering and Management*, 13(2), 283–295. 10.3926/jiem.3030

Chapter 3
Exploring the Application of Generative AI in Human Resource Management

Peace Kumah
Knutsford University College, Ghana

Ivonne Kuma Nketia
https://orcid.org/0009-0003-8320-2475
University of Ghana, Ghana

Winfred Yaokumah
https://orcid.org/0000-0001-7756-1832
University of Ghana, Ghana

Kwame Okwabi Asante-Offei
https://orcid.org/0000-0002-0944-5503
Accra Technical University, Ghana

ABSTRACT

This chapter reviews the current state of generative artificial intelligence (AI) and human resource management (HRM). It discusses the current application of Generative AI in the core functional areas of HRM, identifies the main challenges posed by Generative AI, emphasizes the increasing role and influence of Generative AI applications in the workplace, and suggests future research directions. Current applications of Generative AI in HRM include automation, personalization, decision support, and bias reduction in HR processes. However, the urgent challenges related to transparency, bias mitigation, ethical use, and data privacy must be addressed

DOI: 10.4018/979-8-3693-5578-7.ch003

for responsible deployment. This chapter highlights the opportunities for integrating Generative AI in HRM to improve HR processes while ensuring ethical and fair implementation. The future research directions for Generative AI and HRM focus on reducing bias in AI models, developing ethical frameworks, enhancing data privacy, and exploring AI's impact on organizational culture and employee engagement.

INTRODUCTION

Human Resource Management (HRM) involves strategically managing an organization's most important asset - its people. HRM aligns the organization's human capital with its strategic objectives, fosters employee engagement and development, and creates a positive work culture that supports organizational success (Al-Dmour, 2020). The key components of HRM include recruitment and selection, training and development, performance management, compensation and benefits, employee relations, diversity and inclusion, employee engagement, health and safety, succession planning, and workforce planning (Kaur, 2021). Recruitment and selection entails attracting and hiring the right talent for the organization through job postings, interviews, and assessments (Qamar et al., 2021). Training and development involve providing employees with the necessary skills and knowledge to perform their jobs effectively and grow within the organization (Bandari, 2019).

Another HRM function is performance management, which consists of evaluating and managing employee performance through feedback, goal setting, and performance appraisals (Brindha & Rhytheema, 2023). Compensation and benefits are also essential functions of HRM, as they involve designing and administering competitive salary and benefits packages to attract and retain top talent (Malik et al., 2022). Employee relations are also crucial, including handling grievances and conflicts and ensuring a positive work environment (Yahia et al., 2021). HR planning is another critical function of HRM, as it involves forecasting future workforce needs and developing strategies to meet organizational goals (Malik et al., 2022). Legal compliance is also an essential aspect of HRM, ensuring that the organization complies with labour laws and regulations related to employment practices (Babelova et al., 2023).

Performing these functions effectively and efficiently in today's dynamic business environment is challenging (Bhattacharyya et al., 2020). These challenges may include finding and retaining top talent, ensuring high employee engagement and motivation levels, providing relevant training and development opportunities to enhance employees' skills and capabilities, and effectively evaluating and managing employee performance. However, Generative AI has great potential in HRM to handle some complex tasks (Akpamah & Matkó, 2021). It can enhance HRM practices, processes, and activities in various ways (Akpamah & Matkó, 2021). The implications of generative AI for HR leaders include improved decision-making, automation of tasks, personalized employee experiences, strategic planning, compliance, and enhanced employee engagement, ultimately contributing to a more efficient and effective HR function. Thus, Generative AI holds significant potential to revolutionize various aspects of HRM practices (Johnson, Coggburn, & Valcik, 2022).

The use of Generative AI in HRM offers both benefits and challenges. Automating repetitive tasks can improve efficiency, but over-reliance on AI-generated content may reduce the human touch in HR interactions (Tacheva & Ramasubramanian, 2023). Generative AI also enables personalization and customization, but ensuring the accuracy and relevance of AI-generated content to meet diverse employee needs can be challenging. Additionally, Generative AI provides decision support by offering data-driven insights but concerns about transparency and accountability of AI-generated decisions may arise (Shin, Koerber, & Lim, 2024). While Generative AI has the potential to reduce bias in HR processes, unintentional biases in AI models or training data can lead to discriminatory outcomes (Peng & Zhao, 2024). Generative AI enhances data privacy and security, but safeguarding employee privacy and confidential data remains crucial (Johnson, Coggburn, & Valcik, 2022). Overall, a balanced approach is needed to leverage the benefits of Generative AI while addressing the challenges to ensure ethical, fair, and practical implementation in the workplace.

The purpose of this chapter is to (a) review the current state of the field of Generative AI and HRM, (b) discuss the current and potential application of Generative AI in the core functional areas of HRM, (c) identify the main challenges posed by Generative AI, and (d) concludes by identifying future research directions in HRM and practice that emphasize the increasing role and influence of Generative AI applications in the workplace. By addressing these objectives, the chapter contributes to advancing the understanding of how Generative AI can be leveraged to improve HR processes and employee experiences while emphasizing the importance of ethical and fair implementation. Additionally, the chapter sheds light on the opportunities and challenges associated with integrating Generative AI in HRM, highlighting the need for responsible deployment and ethical considerations in using AI technologies in the workplace.

BACKGROUND

Human Resource Information System

Before the advent of computers and technology, human resources professionals would separate, and file employee data received as a paper application during the recruiting process. Subsequently, these records were kept in different directories. This was ineffective and tedious. As a result, a human resource information system (HRIS) was developed. HRIS is a system that supports companies with payroll, handling administrative duties, and evaluating, preserving, and collecting data on their human resources (Randle et al., 2017). It allows organizations to monitor employees' personal information (Bali, 2019). Usually, a database is used for this, or even more commonly, several linked databases. HRIS enables HR representatives to take ownership and accountability for the system (Bali, 2019).

The functionalities of HRIS are diverse and encompass various aspects of human resource management. HRIS helps in payroll management by accurately determining employee pay and efficiently handling employee promotions and salaries (Ali Quaosar & Rahman, 2021). It can be categorized into transactional, traditional, and organizational development functions, including staff planning, hiring, training, and compensation management (Randle et al., 2017). HRIS also fosters paper-free HR management by disseminating policies and automating HR processes (Zahari et al., 2018). Moreover, HRIS is crucial in entering and analyzing data on skills inventories, job openings, and performance evaluations, enabling informed decision-making and retaining important organizational data (Zahari et al., 2018). Ultimately, HRIS can lead to reduced administrative expenses, increased productivity, faster decision-making, and improved employee services.

Several studies have focused on designing and implementing HRIS. For example, Siregar and Dachyar (2018) identified five crucial HRIS performance criteria, including data presentation, speed and accuracy, accessibility, timely delivery of information, and satisfaction of HR demands. Novianti and Qadri (2020) developed a web-based HRIS to manage human resources, which enabled remote attendance tracking for employees working from home. Baswardono et al. (2019) assessed an HRIS to address issues with payroll, work evaluation, staff management, and attendance in small and medium-sized businesses in Indonesia. Chakraborty and Khan (2019) examined a corporate hospital in India to understand how HRIS contributes to providing high-quality medical treatment. Al-Dmour (2020) analyzed the connection between employee performance in Jordan's five-star hotels and the use of HRIS, finding that it significantly improved worker performance and engagement. Weeramanthrie et al. (2017) developed an HRIS to bridge the knowledge gap between management's understanding of employee behavior and the actual conduct of the organization's employees. Lastly, Suffian and Zahari (2017) examined the effects of the Malaysian government's human resources management information systems (HRMIS) on workers' productivity and happiness, finding that the use of HRMIS, user attributes, and organizational support positively impacted the satisfaction of employees.

The implementation of HRIS systems is not without significant challenges. The high costs associated with purchasing and maintaining the hardware and software and the need for user training have deterred many organizations, particularly smaller firms with limited resources (Sharma, 2022). The security of HRIS is another concern, as any breach in data safeguarding can lead to unauthorized disclosure or manipulation of sensitive information, potentially resulting in legal or financial repercussions for the company (Babelova et al., 2023). Moreover, poorly designed user interfaces can create a negative user experience, discouraging employees from using HRIS (Sakthi et al., 2023).

Generative AI and HRM

Generative AI is a new area of artificial intelligence utilized to produce original writing, audio, and image material (Okolo, 2023). Unlike conventional artificial learning tools focusing on classification and prediction, generative AI tools can produce novel content. Some Generative AI tools use a large language model (LLM). LLMs' objective is to independently discover patterns and connections in the data without being specifically instructed on what they should search for. To achieve this, LLMs use several methods. After assimilating these patterns, the model can produce fresh instances that closely resemble the training set (Hacker et al., 2023).

Artificial Intelligence (AI) has revolutionized various aspects of HRM. Generative AI is applied in multiple HR activities such as talent search, training, performance analysis, career development, and staff turnover (Yahia et al., 2021). AI-driven technologies have revolutionized HRM, particularly in recruitment and selection processes (Qamar et al., 2021). The implementation of AI in HRM involves a range of techniques such as expert systems (Malik et al., 2022), fuzzy logic (Qamar et al., 2021), artificial neural networks, data mining, genetic algorithms (Zhang et al., 2021), and machine learning (Hamilton & Davison, 2022;). These techniques are employed in different HR functions, including HR planning, compensation (Malik et al., 2022), labor management, decision-making (Kimseng et al., 2020), staff selection, workforce planning, performance evaluation, and turnover prediction (Hamilton & Davison, 2022). Thus, the integration of AI in HRM represents a paradigm shift, blending traditional methods with cutting-edge technology and providing invaluable support to HR managers in decision-making processes, thereby enhancing overall HR activities.

Furthermore, Generative AI plays a crucial role in employee engagement and retention methods (Agarwal, 2022) through sentiment analysis of feedback and personalized career progression recommendations (Neelam et al., 2023). Natural Language Processing (NLP) has also gained significance in HRM, with NLP-powered chatbots and sentiment analysis contributing to effective communication and understanding of employee sentiments. Generative AI and machine learning have significantly enhanced HR processes, from talent evaluation and workforce planning to candidate assessment and engagement (Ali et al., 2022; Jagwani et al., 2023).

APPLICATION OF GENERATIVE AI IN HRM

Human Resource Management practices encompass organizations' strategies, policies, and activities for effectively managing their workforce. These practices are designed to attract, develop, motivate, and retain employees to achieve organizational goals. Standard HRM practices include recruitment and selection, training and development, performance management, compensation and benefits, employee relations, diversity and inclusion, employee engagement, health and safety programs, succession planning, and workforce planning (Kimseng et al., 2020; Malik et al., 2022). They are essential for shaping organizational culture, improving employee performance, and driving overall business success. This section describes the key HRM processes and discusses how Generative AI is helping to support these processes. Figure 1 summarizes HRM practices, methods, and activities.

Figure 1. HRM practices, processes, and activities

Recruitment and Selection

Recruitment and selection processes are essential for organizations to attract, assess, and hire qualified candidates (Singh & Sahoo, 2023). Critical steps in recruitment and selection processes include identifying job requirements (Choudhary, 2022), sourcing candidates through various methods, screening resumes, conducting interviews, assessing candidates, performing reference and background checks, making job offers, facilitating onboarding, and seeking feedback for continuous improvement (Rathore, 2023). These processes help organizations attract top talent, make informed hiring decisions, and effectively integrate new employees into the company culture. Generative AI is increasingly prevalent in recruitment and selection processes, offering various benefits. It is used for resume screening, where algorithms analyze resumes to identify relevant skills and experiences, and for initial screening through AI-powered chatbots (Madanchian, Taherdoost, & Mohamed, 2023). Additionally, Generative AI is utilized for candidate matching based on job requirements, interview assistance, predictive analytics, and personalized candidate experiences. Leveraging generative AI in recruitment and selection processes allows organizations to streamline talent acquisition, improve efficiency, enhance candidate experience, and make data-driven decisions to identify the best-fit candidates for their roles (Mannuru et al., 2023). Some specific ways in which Generative AI is used in recruitment and selection include:

- Resume Screening: AI algorithms analyze resumes to identify relevant skills and experiences, helping recruiters efficiently shortlist candidates (Li, Lassiter, Oh, & Lee, 2021).
- Chatbots for Initial Screening: AI-powered chatbots engage with candidates in real-time, asking questions to assess their qualifications and suitability for the role.
- Candidate Matching: AI algorithms match candidate profiles with job requirements based on keywords, skills, and experience.
- Interview Assistance: AI tools like ChatGPT assist recruiters in generating interview questions, evaluating candidate responses, and providing feedback (Rana, 2018).
- Predictive Analytics: AI analyzes historical data to predict the likelihood of a candidate's success in a particular role (Bandari, 2019).
- Personalized Candidate Experience: AI tailors communication, provides feedback, and offers job recommendations based on individual preferences, enhancing candidate engagement.

Performance Management

Performance Management involves various activities and processes to improve employee performance and achieve organizational objectives. Critical components of performance management include setting clear and specific performance goals, providing ongoing feedback, conducting regular performance appraisals, creating development plans, recognizing and rewarding high performers, addressing performance issues, and planning for future leadership needs (Nicastro, 2020). By implementing these activities and processes, organizations can enhance employee performance, drive productivity, and achieve strategic objectives (Kaur & Gandolfi, 2023). Generative AI is increasingly used in performance management to improve employee evaluation and development. It is utilized in various ways, such as generating personalized feedback based on performance data, predicting future performance trends, setting goals, recommending learning opportunities, automating performance reviews, and identifying high-potential employees. Organizations can use generative AI to streamline performance evaluation processes, provide personalized feedback, predict performance trends, and support employee development, ultimately contributing to overall organizational success. Some specific ways Generative AI is used in performance management include:

- Feedback Generation: Generative AI tools can generate personalized feedback for employees based on performance data, evaluations, and goals to help them understand their strengths and areas for improvement (Mogaji et al., 2021).
- Performance Prediction: Generative AI algorithms analyze historical performance data to predict future trends, helping managers identify potential performance issues and take proactive measures (Kaur, 2021).
- Goal Setting and Alignment: Generative AI can help set SMART goals for employees and align them with organizational objectives based on individual performance data and career aspirations.
- Skill Development: AI-powered platforms recommend personalized learning opportunities to employees based on their performance gaps and career goals (Mhlanga, 2021).
- Performance Reviews Automation: Generative AI automates the performance review process, saving time for managers and ensuring a more objective evaluation of employee performance.
- Identifying High-Potential Employees: AI algorithms identify employees within an organization based on their performance data, skills, and career trajectory, aiding in talent management and succession planning.

Compensation and Benefits

Compensation and Benefits are essential aspects of Human Resource Management that aim to attract, retain, and motivate employees. Key activities and processes related to Compensation and Benefits include job analysis, conducting salary surveys, designing salary structures, implementing performance-based pay, managing employee benefits programs, conducting compensation reviews, transparent communication of compensation and benefits, job evaluation, compensation planning, and benefits enrolment (Pataranutaporn et al., 2021). Effectively managing these activities and processes enables organizations to attract and retain top talent, motivate employees, and gain a competitive advantage in the labor market.

Generative AI is increasingly used in compensation and benefits management to streamline processes, enhance decision-making, and personalize employee offerings. It is utilized in salary benchmarking (analyzing market data, industry trends, and internal factors to benchmark salaries for different roles, ensuring competitive compensation packages), personalized compensation packages (assessing individual employee data, performance metrics, and preferences to recommend personalized compensation packages, including bonuses and incentives tailored to each employee), and benefits optimization (analyzing employee demographics, preferences, and usage patterns to optimize benefits offerings, recommending packages that align with employees' needs and promote well-being) (Kaur & Gandolfi, 2023).

Other ways Generative AI supports Compensation and Benefits processes include cost analysis and budgeting (analyzing historical compensation data, market trends, and budget constraints to optimize compensation and benefits spending and ensure cost-effectiveness), predictive analytics for retention (predicting employee turnover risks based on factors such as compensation satisfaction, benefits utilization, and performance data, helping to address retention issues proactively) (Lengnick-Hall et al., 2018), and compliance monitoring (monitoring compensation and benefits practices to ensure compliance with legal regulations, industry standards, and internal policies, flagging any discrepancies for timely resolution). Employing Generative AI in compensation and benefits management helps organizations optimize their reward strategies, personalize offerings, ensure cost-effectiveness, and enhance employee satisfaction, ultimately attracting and retaining top talent and maintaining competitive compensation practices.

Employee Relations

Employee Relations activities and processes are designed to cultivate positive relationships between employees and the organization. These activities include establishing open communication channels, encouraging feedback, resolving conflicts, promoting employee engagement, nurturing a positive workplace culture, supporting employee wellness, providing performance management support, developing and communicating policies, and recognizing employee contributions (Kaur & Gandolfi, 2023). By focusing on these activities, organizations can create a positive work environment, boost employee morale, and build strong relationships that contribute to overall organizational success. In the modern era, the role of AI in employee relations is becoming increasingly significant. Generative AI is now used to enhance communication, engagement, and overall employee experience. It is employed in various ways, such as through chatbots for employee support, feedback analysis, conflict resolution, employee engagement analysis, performance coaching, and cultural alignment assessment (Fallucchi et al., 2020). These AI-driven solutions are revolutionizing how organizations improve communication, address conflicts proactively, boost employee engagement, and foster a positive work environment.

They empower HR professionals and managers to understand employee needs better, promote collaboration, and strengthen organizational relationships.

AI algorithms can analyze employee feedback from surveys, performance evaluations, and other sources to identify trends, sentiments, and areas of concern within the organization (Houde et al., 2020). This analysis helps HR professionals and managers understand employee perceptions and take targeted actions to improve employee relations. However, the real power of AI lies in its ability to identify and address conflicts proactively. Generative AI tools can assist in identifying potential conflicts or issues within teams based on communication patterns, performance data, and other indicators. This proactive approach to conflict resolution is a game-changer, as it allows HR professionals and managers to intervene before issues escalate, promoting a positive work environment. AI-powered platforms can analyze employee engagement data, such as activity participation, feedback responses, and communication patterns, to assess overall engagement levels (Bongard, 2019). This analysis helps in designing targeted engagement initiatives to boost morale and productivity. Generative AI can provide employees with personalized coaching and development recommendations based on performance data, career goals, and feedback (Qadir, 2022). AI coaching systems can support employee growth by guiding skill development, goal setting, and career advancement. AI algorithms can analyze employee behavior, interactions, and feedback to assess organizational cultural alignment. This analysis helps identify cultural strengths, areas for improvement, and ways to promote a cohesive and inclusive work culture.

Diversity and Inclusion

Diversity and Inclusion initiatives are crucial for fostering a workplace that embraces and respects employee differences. Key activities and processes related to D&I include diversity training to raise awareness about unconscious bias and cultural competence, diversity recruitment strategies, the establishment of Employee Resource Groups (ERGs) to promote diversity and inclusion, inclusive leadership development, tracking and reporting of diversity metrics, reviewing and updating HR policies to support diversity, the establishment of diversity councils, cross-cultural communication training, and celebrating diversity through events and workshops (Soto, 2020). Implementing these activities and processes can help create a more inclusive and equitable workplace where all employees feel valued, respected, and empowered to contribute their best. Generative AI is increasingly used in diversity and inclusion initiatives to promote equity, reduce bias, and foster a more inclusive work environment. It is utilized in various ways, including bias detection and mitigation, diverse candidate sourcing, inclusive language analysis, diversity training and development, inclusive decision-making, and employee resource group support.

Generative AI helps organizations identify and address biases, promote diversity in recruitment and decision-making, foster inclusive communication, and support employee development, ultimately creating a more diverse, equitable, and inclusive workplace culture.

AI algorithms can analyze recruitment, performance, and promotion data to identify biases in decision-making processes (Kaur & Gandolfi, 2023). Generative AI tools can be crucial in detecting and mitigating biases related to gender, race, age, and other factors, thereby ensuring fair and inclusive practices (Dwivedi et al., 2021). Furthermore, AI-powered platforms can assist in sourcing diverse candidates by analyzing job descriptions, candidate profiles, and recruitment channels. These tools can also recommend strategies to attract a more diverse pool of candidates and promote inclusivity in the hiring process. Additionally, AI algorithms can analyze communication patterns, job postings, and employee interactions to identify and suggest the use of inclusive language. Generative AI tools can help organizations create a more welcoming environment by promoting gender-neutral, culturally sensitive, and inclusive language.

In diversity training, generative AI can provide personalized learning experiences for employees, offering interactive modules, simulations, and feedback to enhance their understanding of diversity and inclusion concepts. Moreover, AI algorithms can assess inclusivity by analyzing team dynamics, collaboration patterns, and decision-making processes. Generative AI tools can provide valuable insights to leaders and managers on promoting diverse perspectives, equitable participation, and inclusive decision-making practices. Lastly, AI-powered platforms can support employee resource groups by providing resources, facilitating communication, organizing events, helping employee resource groups promote diversity and inclusion initiatives, and supporting underrepresented employee groups.

Training and Development

Training and development activities and processes are crucial aspects of Human Resource Management that aim to improve employees' knowledge, skills, and abilities. These initiatives help employees to grow professionally, adapt to changing job requirements, and contribute effectively to organizational success. Some common activities and processes include training programs, onboarding for new employees, skill development, career development, performance management training, professional development, cross-training, leadership development, e-learning, and feedback and coaching. Investing in these activities and processes can lead to enhanced employee performance, increased job satisfaction, and a culture of continuous learning and growth within the organization.

Generative AI is increasingly being used in training and development to offer personalized learning experiences, assess and address skill gaps effectively, and enhance employee engagement and retention (Kaur & Gandolfi, 2023). It is utilized in various ways, including personalized learning paths, adaptive learning modules, skill assessment and gap analysis, interactive training content, feedback and coaching, and language learning support (Jalil et al., 2023). These AI-driven solutions help organizations optimize their training programs, improve learning outcomes, and support continuous skill development in a dynamic work environment. AI-powered platforms can analyze employee skills, learning preferences, and performance data to recommend personalized learning paths. AI algorithms can suggest relevant courses, resources, and activities tailored to individual learning needs and goals. Additionally, AI algorithms can adapt training modules based on personal progress, feedback, and performance and dynamically adjust learning materials' difficulty level, content, and pace. AI can also assess employee skills, identify skill gaps, generate interactive and engaging training content, and provide real-time feedback and coaching during training sessions (Surameery & Shakor, 2023). Furthermore, AI-powered language learning platforms can assist employees in improving their language skills through interactive exercises, pronunciation feedback, and conversational practice tailored to individual proficiency levels.

Health and Safety

Health and Safety involves implementing practices and policies to ensure the well-being and safety of employees in the workplace. This includes compliance with regulations, risk assessment and management, safety training, provision of safety equipment and facilities, health promotion programs, workplace ergonomics, incident reporting and investigation, emergency preparedness, health and safety committees, and continuous improvement. Prioritizing Health and Safety in HRM helps create a safe and healthy work environment, reduce workplace injuries and illnesses, and demonstrate a commitment to employee well-being.

Generative AI is increasingly used in health and safety initiatives to enhance workplace safety, improve health outcomes, and mitigate risks. It is utilized in predictive analytics for safety, health monitoring and surveillance, safety training simulations, risk assessment and management, emergency response optimization, and occupational health and wellness programs. By leveraging generative AI, organizations can enhance workplace safety, prevent accidents, and improve health outcomes (Pataranutaporn et al., 2021). These AI-driven solutions help prioritize employee well-being, comply with safety regulations, and foster a safe and healthy work environment for all employees. AI algorithms can analyze historical data, incident reports, and environmental factors to predict potential safety hazards in the workplace. Generative AI tools can effectively identify patterns, trends, and risk factors to prevent accidents and ensure a safer work environment. Furthermore, AI-powered systems can monitor employee health data, including vital signs, movement patterns, and environmental exposures, to detect early signs of health issues or fatigue. By providing real-time alerts and recommendations, generative AI tools can promote employee well-being and prevent health-related incidents (Mohajan, 2019).

In addition, generative AI can create realistic simulations and scenarios for safety training programs. AI algorithms can generate interactive training modules that simulate hazardous situations, emergency responses, and safety protocols to prepare employees for potential risks in a controlled environment. Moreover, AI algorithms can assess workplace risks by analyzing data on equipment maintenance, operational procedures, and employee behavior. Generative AI tools can help organizations identify high-risk areas, prioritize safety measures, and develop risk mitigation strategies to prevent accidents and injuries. AI-powered systems can further optimize emergency response procedures by analyzing incident severity, response times, and resource allocation data. Generative AI tools can provide real-time recommendations for efficient emergency response coordination, communication, and decision-making to minimize the impact of emergencies. Furthermore, generative AI can support occupational health and wellness programs by analyzing employee health data, conducting risk assessments, and recommending preventive measures. AI algorithms can assist in designing tailored wellness initiatives, ergonomic improvements, and mental health support services to promote employee well-being and productivity.

Succession Planning

Succession planning training activities and processes are essential for identifying and developing future leaders within an organization. These activities include identifying key positions, conducting talent assessments, creating individual development plans, implementing leadership development programs, providing mentoring and coaching, offering job rotations, conducting succession planning workshops, managing performance, assigning cross-functional projects, and providing ongoing feedback and evaluation. By implementing these activities, organizations can build a pipeline of talented leaders, ensure continuity in leadership roles, and drive long-term organizational success. Generative AI is increasingly used in succession planning to identify high-potential employees, assess leadership capabilities, and develop talent pipelines for future leadership roles (Arun, 2020). It is used for talent identification and assessment, skills mapping and development, succession readiness assessments, leadership development programs, succession planning scenarios, and data-driven decision-making.

AI algorithms have the capability to analyze employee performance data, skills assessments, and behavioral traits to identify high-potential individuals within the organization (Tambe, Cappelli, & Yakubovich, 2019). Generative AI tools can evaluate leadership competencies, growth potential, and readiness for leadership roles to establish a talent pool for succession planning. AI-powered platforms can map employee skills, competencies, and career aspirations to potential future roles within the organization. Additionally, AI algorithms can recommend personalized development plans, training opportunities, and mentorship programs to prepare employees for succession into critical positions. Furthermore, AI algorithms can conduct readiness assessments for potential successors by evaluating their preparedness for specific leadership roles. By analyzing performance data, feedback from peers and supervisors, and psychometric assessments, generative AI tools can determine candidates' readiness for succession.

Generative AI can also facilitate the design and delivery of leadership development programs tailored to the needs of potential successors. Moreover, AI-powered platforms can generate personalized learning experiences, coaching sessions, and feedback mechanisms to enhance the leadership capabilities of identified high-potential employees. AI algorithms can simulate succession planning scenarios based on various factors such as retirement, promotions, and unexpected departures. Generative AI tools can assist organizations in modeling different succession scenarios, assessing the impact of leadership changes, and developing contingency plans to ensure a smooth transition of critical roles. Finally, AI-powered systems can provide data-driven insights and recommendations for succession planning decisions by analyzing workforce data, performance metrics, and talent analytics to support informed decision-making in identifying, developing, and promoting future leaders within the organization. By leveraging generative AI in succession planning, organizations can proactively identify and develop future leaders, build a robust talent pipeline, and ensure continuity in leadership roles.

Workforce Planning

Workforce planning ensures that an organization's workforce aligns with its strategic goals. This involves analyzing current workforce capabilities, forecasting future needs, and developing strategies to ensure the right talent is in place. Some key activities include aligning with strategic goals, analyzing the current workforce, forecasting future needs, assessing talent availability, identifying skills gaps, succession planning, talent acquisition strategies, training and development programs, workforce flexibility, performance management, and monitoring and evaluation.

Organizations can effectively manage talent needs, improve workforce performance, and drive sustainable business growth by implementing these activities.

Generative AI is increasingly used in workforce planning to optimize management, predict future talent needs, and align organizational goals with human resource strategies. It is utilized in demand forecasting to analyze historical data and market trends to predict fluctuations in staffing requirements and identify skill gaps. AI-powered platforms map employee skills to organizational goals, conduct gap analyses, and recommend training opportunities. Additionally, AI algorithms optimize resource utilization, recommend staffing levels and task assignments, and integrate succession planning with workforce planning strategies. AI-powered systems also analyze diversity metrics, inclusion initiatives, and bias detection to promote diversity and inclusion in workforce planning. Furthermore, AI algorithms can simulate workforce planning scenarios based on different variables and help organizations model various workforce scenarios, assess the impact of strategic decisions, and develop contingency plans for workforce resilience. Leveraging generative AI in workforce planning helps organizations optimize talent management strategies, align workforce capabilities with business objectives, and enhance workforce agility and adaptability, enabling them to make data-driven decisions and create a flexible and responsive workforce.

Employee Engagement

Employee engagement activities and processes are essential for creating a positive work environment and enhancing organizational performance. These activities include establishing effective communication channels, implementing feedback mechanisms, recognizing and rewarding employees, providing professional development opportunities, offering work-life balance initiatives, and implementing employee well-being programs. Additionally, team building activities, career pathing, empowerment, diversity and inclusion initiatives, and performance management and feedback are crucial for fostering a positive work culture and improving employee morale and retention. Generative AI is increasingly used in employee engagement to enhance communication, personalize interactions, and foster a positive work environment. It is utilized in various ways, including personalized communication through chatbots and virtual assistants, analyzing feedback and surveys to gauge engagement levels, automating recognition and rewards programs, recommending customized learning and development opportunities, monitoring employee well-being, and conducting sentiment analysis.

AI-powered tools such as chatbots and virtual assistants provide personalized communication and support to employees by offering information on company policies, benefits, and resources, as well as personalized recommendations. These tools can also analyze employee feedback and survey responses to assess engagement levels, generate insights, and recommend actions to enhance satisfaction and well-being. Additionally, AI can automate recognition and rewards programs, recommend personalized rewards, and facilitate peer-to-peer recognition to boost morale and motivation. AI-powered systems can also recommend personalized learning and development opportunities based on skills, career goals, and performance evaluations. They can monitor employee well-being, stress levels, and work-life balance, and offer support and resources to help manage stress and maintain overall well-being. Lastly, AI-powered platforms conduct sentiment analysis on employee surveys, social media posts, and communication channels to gauge sentiment and engagement, identify areas of concern, measure satisfaction, and recommend interventions to enhance engagement and retention.

GENERATIVE AI TOOLS USED IN HRM

With its diverse branches encompassing recruitment, employee onboarding, training, performance analysis, support, and offboarding, HRM has been greatly bolstered by the efficiency of Generative AI tools. This section describes the functionalities and applications of these tools, empowering HR professionals with the knowledge to leverage them effectively in their work. There are several Generative AI tools available. Some common ones include ChatGPT, Google Bard, ChatGPT, DALL-E, Midjorney, and Synthesia (Okolo, 2023).

ChatGPT

OpenAI released ChatGPT, a Generative AI tool, to the public on November 30, 2022. ChatGPT uses OpenAI's GPT-3.5 language model technology, which has produced responses that resemble those of a human after being trained on a vast amount of text data (Torre, 2024). ChatGPT utilizes the Transformer Neural Network Architecture. This architecture improves efficiency by selectively focusing on various parts while handling lengthy and complicated input sequences (Al-Amin et al., 2024). ChatGPT can retrieve pertinent corresponding data from users' past discussions to offer a more tailored answer. Consequently, ChatGPT can have more profound and more intelligible interactions with users to provide insightful information. (Naik et al., 2023). It utilizes a chat interface and incorporates the history of its conversation with a user to provide interactive and fine-tuned text responses (Lozie et al., 2024).

ChatGPT functionalities are applied to HRM in the following ways:

- Generative ChatGPT is transforming the HR recruitment procedure. Applications, profiles, and Curriculum Vita data can be employed to train ChatGPT. ChatGPT quickly assesses resumes, carries out preliminary screenings, and goes a step further to mimic conventional employment interviews by utilizing natural language processing (Rane, 2023). In addition, ChatGPT directs supervisors and hiring managers to narrow their search to the most eligible prospects to enhance the compatibility between the hired applicant and the respective vacancy position (Ooi et al., 2023).
- ChatGPT supports employee growth and skill development. It facilitates customized learning experiences and adapts information to suit individual needs. This promotes training and development activities (Rane, 2023).
- ChatGPT offers a forum for employees to ask questions and receive prompt responses, which helps enhance relations between HR departments and employees (Korzynski et al., 2023). HR can also use ChatGPT to answer frequently asked questions (Naik et al., 2023), saving time and creating efficiency for other more critical HR tasks. Also, ChatGPT makes real-time communication possible, improving organizational Responsiveness (Naik et al., 2023). Creating a feeling of community raises staff happiness and performance.
- ChatGPT enhances data analysis (Yang, Wang, & Lyu, 2023). It can analyze key performance indicators like sales numbers, project delivery costs, and consumer experience ratings. Additionally, it can consider information from other sources, such as project schedules, client reviews, and personnel activity logs. This all-encompassing method allows ChatGPT to deliver a highly objective and thorough employee productivity evaluation (Rathnayake & Gunawardana, 2023).

Google Bard

Another Generative AI tool used in HRM is the Google Bard AI. It was released on February 7, 2023. Like ChatGPT, Bard also uses the Transformer Neural Network Architecture, making it indispensable for interpreting and creating languages (Al-Amin et al., 2024). Bard is comparatively less prejudiced than ChatGPT (Singh et al. (2023). It uses natural language processing to respond in real time. According to Google, Bard can assist with innovative initiatives, clarify complex subjects, and gather data from various online sources. (Aydin, 2023). Bard functionalities are applied to HRM in the following ways:

- Google Bard enhances predictive hiring by evaluating employment-related data and determining the core competencies needed for a position. Moreover, depending on employee conduct and previous encounters, it can determine if a staff member is attempting to resign from their position.

- It precisely determines future employment requirements by rigorously analyzing historical recruiting data trends and patterns. For organizations, this ability is significant because it enables prior anticipation of their hiring needs (Rathnayake & Gunawardana, 2023).
- It can facilitate collaborative learning by matching an experienced coworker with a staff member's question. It also answers in real-time the planned questions that workers ask throughout skill development sessions (Ooi et al., 2023). Thus, Bard supports employee growth and development.
- It facilitates strategic HR planning. This can address internal HR analytical data to give insight into employee turnover, inactivity, and a variety of HR data, as well as external proof by referencing systematic evaluations of the effects of policy and other initiatives aimed at enhancing personnel management (Budhwar et al., 2023)

DALL-E

DALL-E (Denoising Autoencoder for Learned Language Embeddings) is a Generative AI tool developed by the OpenAI company (Nistler & Tomas, 2023). It was initially launched in 2021, and then an advanced version, DALL-E2, was launched in April 2022 (Bendel, 2023). It generates detailed, high-quality photos using a cutting-edge deep-learning algorithm (Zhou & Nabus, 2023). It can produce imaginative and fantastical visuals beyond what is generally thought possible for image synthesis tools (Fezari et al., 2023). DALL-E functionalities are applied to HRM in several ways:

- DALL-E, with its unique ability to visually convey safety regulations, safe work procedures, or hazard warning signs, is a valuable tool for HRM (Lozie et al., 2024). The highly realistic images it produces can make a lasting impression on staff, effectively explaining safety protocols, impacts, and mitigation factors.
- DALL-E has excellent image content production capabilities. Thus, HRM can utilize it during employee workshops for training. These images can enhance training sessions, producing high-level images and illustrations of various job scenarios (Fezari et al., 2023).
- During recruitment and onboarding, HRM can use DALL-E for virtual tours of company facilities.
- DALL-E plays a crucial role in employee support through surveys and data analysis. Its AI-generated visuals provide adaptability and versatility, sup-

porting feedback analysis, surveys, and performance data analysis. Similarly, Midjorney can be used in HRM to provide images that explain the company's key strategies, enhancing the understanding of vital information and performance indicators for the company.

Midjorney

Midjorney is a Generative AI tool for generating graphics. It was released in February 2022. Midjorney aims to identify the connections between text and images by training a machine-learning model on a vast collection of visuals with accompanying text descriptions (Adetayo, 2024). Generative AI enables the production of an image that corresponds with a description input by the user in the chat window (Nistler & Tomas, 2023). Midjorney functionalities are applied to HRM in the following ways:

- Midjorney can generate HRM recruitment and onboarding tasks such as logo creation, image production for recruitment fliers and notices, and animations. For smaller companies, this can save costs and ensure efficient use of time and other resources.
- During recruitment, Midjorney plays a crucial role in providing a visual perspective on job roles (Larsen, 2023). It can generate accurate images in the job description that highly depict the job requirements and candidate qualifications, giving candidates a clearer understanding of the role and equipping them with a visual mindset.
- HRM can use Midjorney to provide images that explain the company's key strategies. Images that explain vital information and performance indicators for the company can be described using Midjorney's high-level image generation.
- Midjorney can generate images during training sessions that enhance explaining concepts to employees. Visualizing core concepts can improve employee performance on the job.

Synthesia

Synthesia is a Generative AI tool that produces text-to-video content featuring lifelike computer actors (avatars) (Cacicio & Riggs, 2023). Synthesia can produce expert videos with a variety of avatars. It generates voice in 120 distinct languages (Gozalo-Brizuela & Garrido-Merchán, 2023). Synthesia can create realistic virtual simulations, significantly enhancing more cost-effective, innovative, and accessible training methods (Leiker, 2023). Its functionalities are applied to HRM in several ways:

- Synthesia-generated videos can enhance employee training and development programs by providing crisp educational content on job requirements through automated resource generation. With the assistance of Synthesia, employees can be upskilled to ensure they are up to date with new methods. Also, re-skilling employees when work requirements change can be enhanced with instructional videos generated by Synthesia. This reduces the cost of conventional training programs and time constraints.
- During onboarding, virtual tours can be performed, and recruits can use Synthesia-generated simulations. This saves HR time performing tasks requiring significant attention (Joseph, 2023).
- Synthesia AI can be employed to create safety videos, policy, and code of conduct videos and transform HR-related articles into HR-related videos, creating practicality and more transparent communication between HR and employees. Thus, communication is automated through Synthesia

CHALLENGES AND RECOMMENDATIONS FOR USING GENERATIVE AI IN HRM

Despite the benefits of using Generative AI to support HRM functions, Generative AI is faced with ethical, social, and economic challenges. These challenges may include bias and discrimination, privacy and data security, transparency and accountability, job displacement and workforce changes, employee trust and engagement, ethical use of employee data, and algorithmic fairness (Shin, Koerber, & Lim, 2024).

Generative AI algorithms utilized in HRM processes, such as recruitment and performance evaluation, have the potential to perpetuate biases present in the training data, resulting in discriminatory outcomes against groups (Peng & Zhao, 2024). These AI systems often handle employees' sensitive personal data, raising concerns about data privacy, security breaches, and potential misuse of information. The opacity of Generative AI decision-making in HRM can make it challenging to comprehend how specific outcomes are achieved, raising questions about accountability and the ability to contest or appeal AI-generated decisions. Automating specific HR tasks through Generative AI may lead to the displacement of human workers, necessitating organizations to address the impact on their workforce and potentially retrain employees for new roles. Using Generative AI in HRM processes may influence employee trust in the fairness and impartiality of decisions, potentially affecting engagement and morale within the organization.

Generative AI in educational settings presents challenges as students may rely on it for writing assignments without critical engagement, potentially affecting the assessment of their work and requiring a re-evaluation of teaching methods. However, the implementation and maintenance of Generative AI systems can be costly, creating accessibility issues for smaller organizations and individuals, thus widening the gap between those who can afford it and those who cannot, leading to increased inequality. The rapid advancement of Generative AI also raises concerns about the need for regulations to ensure responsible development and deployment, as legal frameworks may struggle to keep pace with AI's evolving capabilities, resulting in potential gaps in oversight and accountability (Patel, 2023). Organizations must ensure that AI systems in HRM adhere to ethical standards in collecting, storing, and using employee data while respecting individual rights and maintaining confidentiality. Furthermore, it's essential to design Generative AI algorithms used in HRM to promote fairness and equity, especially in areas like recruitment, promotion, and performance evaluation, to prevent discrimination and bias.

Implementing and maintaining Generative AI systems can be costly, making them inaccessible to smaller organizations or individuals. This can create a divide between those who can afford it and those who cannot, leading to further inequality. The rapid advancement of Generative AI raises concerns about the need for regulations to ensure responsible development and deployment. Legal frameworks may struggle to keep pace with AI's evolving capabilities, leading to potential gaps in oversight and accountability (Patel, 2023). Organizations must ensure that AI systems in HRM adhere to ethical standards in collecting, storing, and using employee data, respecting individual rights and maintaining confidentiality, and ensuring that Generative AI algorithms used in HRM are designed to promote fairness and equity, particularly in areas like recruitment, promotion, and performance evaluation, to prevent discrimination and bias.

To effectively address ethical, social, and economic concerns, organizations must establish robust governance frameworks to tackle ethical issues related to bias, discrimination, privacy, transparency, and accountability in implementing AI in HRM. To foster employee trust and engagement, it is crucial to prioritize transparency, data privacy, and security in AI deployment. Continuous communication with employees is essential to ensure ethical AI deployment in HRM practices. While leveraging Generative AI in HRM can offer benefits like efficiency and personalization, organizations must also consider the importance of maintaining a human touch in HR interactions and ensuring the accuracy and relevance of AI-generated content. Addressing concerns about transparency and accountability of AI-generated decisions is vital to upholding trust in HR processes. Mitigating unintentional biases in AI models and training data is necessary to prevent discriminatory outcomes in HR practices. Organizations should also prioritize safeguarding employee privacy and confidential data when using Generative AI for HR-related content generation and decision support. It's crucial to continuously monitor and improve AI models in HRM to ensure ongoing accuracy, relevance, and alignment with organizational goals.

FUTURE RESEARCH DIRECTIONS

Future research in Generative AI in Human Resource Management (HRM) should focus on:

- Reducing bias in AI models used in HR processes to ensure fair recruitment and performance evaluation outcomes.
- Research into developing ethical frameworks for responsible AI deployment in HRM, data privacy and security, transparency in AI processes, and employee acceptance of AI in HRM.
- Research that explores using AI to enhance performance evaluation and personalized training materials and study AI's impact on organizational culture, employee engagement, and the balance between automation and human involvement in HRM interactions.
- Mechanisms for continuously monitoring and improving AI models in HRM are essential for ensuring ongoing accuracy, relevance, and alignment with organizational goals.

These future research directions aim to address challenges, promote ethical and responsible use of AI technologies, and advance the understanding of Generative AI in HRM practices.

CONCLUSION

This chapter emphasizes the significant potential of Generative AI to revolutionize HRM practices by automating tasks, providing personalized experiences, supporting decision-making processes, and reducing bias in HR processes. While Generative AI offers benefits such as efficiency, personalization, and decision support, challenges related to transparency, bias mitigation, ethical use, and data privacy must be addressed for responsible deployment in HRM. The paper underscores the importance of a balanced approach to leveraging Generative AI in HRM, considering both the benefits and challenges associated with AI technologies. By highlighting the opportunities and challenges of integrating Generative AI in HRM, the chapter aims to improve HR processes, enhance employee experiences, and drive organizational performance while ensuring ethical and fair implementation of AI technologies in the workplace.

REFERENCES

Adetayo, A. J. (2024). Reimagining learning through AI art: The promise of DALL-E and MidJourney for education and libraries. *Library Hi Tech News*. Advance online publication. 10.1108/LHTN-01-2024-0005

Agarwal, A. (2022). AI adoption by human resource management: A study of its antecedents and impact on HR system effectiveness. *Foresight*, 67–81.

Akpamah, P., & Matkó, A. (2021). Information Technology deployment in Human Resource Management: A case study in deprived regions. *International Review of Applied Sciences and Engineering*, 13(1), 1–10. 10.1556/1848.2021.00278

Al-Amin, M., Shazed Ali, M., Salam, A., Khan, A., Ali, A., Ullah, A., Alam, N., & Chowdhury, S. K. (2024). History of generative Artificial Intelligence (AI) chatbots: past, present, and future development.

Al-Dmour, R. H. (2020). The influence of HRIS usage on employee performance and mediating effects of employee engagement in five-star hotels in Jordan. *International Journal of Information Systems in the Service Sector*, 12(3), 1–18. 10.4018/IJISSS.2020070101

Ali, I., Mughal, N., Khan, Z. H., Ahmed, J., & Mujtaba, G. (2022). Resume Classification System using Natural Language Processing and Machine Learning Techniques. *Mehran University Research Journal of Engineering and Technology*, 41(1), 65–79. 10.22581/muet1982.2201.07

Ali Quaosar, G. M. A., & Rahman, M. (2021). Human Resource Information Systems (HRIS) of Developing Countries in 21st Century: Review and Prospects. *Journal of Human Resource and Sustainability Studies*, 09(03), 470–483. 10.4236/jhrss.2021.93030

Arun, C. (2020). AI and the Global South: Designing for other worlds. In The Oxford Handbook of Ethics of AI. Oxford Academic. 588–606. https://papers.ssrn. com/sol3/papers.cfm?abstract_id=3403010

Aydin, Ö. (2023). Google Bard Generated Literature Review: Metaverse. *Journal of AI, 1*(7). doi:https://bard.google.com

Babelova, Z. G., Vranakova, N., & Starecek, A. (2023). *The Integration of HR Information Systems Utilization in Industrial Enterprises*. Mm Science Journal.

Bali, S. A. (2019). An analytical study of human resource information system applications in modern human resources management. *Int. J. Sustainable Agricultural Management and Informatics, 5*(4).

Bandari, V. (2019). Exploring the transformational potential of emerging technologies in human resource analytics: a comparative study of IoT, AI, and cloud computing applications. *Journal of Humanities and Applied Science Research*, 15-27.

Baswardono, W., Cahyana, R., Rahayu, S., & Nashrulloh, M. R. (2019). Design of human resource information system for micro, small, and medium enterprises. *Journal of Physics: Conference Series*, 1402(6), 066056. Advance online publication. 10.1088/1742-6596/1402/6/066056

Bendel, O. (2023). Image synthesis from an ethical perspective. *AI & Society*. Advance online publication. 10.1007/s00146-023-01780-4

Bhattacharyya, D. S., Shafique, S., Akhter, S., Rahman, A., Islam, M. Z., Rahman, N., & Anwar, I. (2020). Challenges and facilitators of implementing an information communication and technology (ICT)-based human resources management tool in the government health sector in Bangladesh: Protocol for an exploratory qualitative research study. *BMJ Open*, 10.33318122

Brindha, S., & Rhytheema, D. (2023). Predictive HR Analytics: Pioneering Innovation in the Workplace. *European Chemical Bulletin*, 820–835.

Budhwar, P., Chowdhury, S., Wood, G., Aguinis, H., Bamber, G. J., Beltran, J. R., Boselie, P., Lee Cooke, F., Decker, S., DeNisi, A., Dey, P. K., Guest, D., Knoblich, A. J., Malik, A., Paauwe, J., Papagiannidis, S., Patel, C., Pereira, V., Ren, S., . . . Varma, A. (2023). Human resource management in the age of generative artificial intelligence: Perspectives and research directions on ChatGPT. *In Human Resource Management Journal, 33*(3), 606–659.

Cacicio, S., & Riggs, R. (2023). Bridging Resource Gaps in Adult Education: The Role of Generative AI. *Adult Literacy Education: The International Journal of Literacy, Language, and Numeracy*, 5(3), 80–86. 10.35847/SCacicio.RRiggs.5.3.80

Chakraborty, M., & Khan, A. M. K. (2019). A case study on the importance of Human Resource Information System in the Healthcare sector of a corporate Hospital in India. IEEE 2019 International Conference on Digitization (ICD). 10.1109/ICD47981.2019.9105864

Choudhary, S. (2022). AI in Organizations a Helping hand of HR. ResearchGate.

Falletta, S. (2014). In search of HR intelligence: Evidence-based HR analytics practices in high performing companies. *People and Strategy*, 36(4), 28.

Fezari, M., Al-Dahoud, A., & Al-Dahoud, A. (2023). Augmenting Reality: The Power of Generative AI. https://www.spaceo.ai/wp-content/uploads/2023/02/OpenAI-GPT-3-Architecture.jpg

Gozalo-Brizuela, R., & Garrido-Merchán, E. C. (2023). A survey of Generative AI Applications. doi:http://arxiv.org/abs/2306.02781

Hacker, P., Engel, A., & Mauer, M. (2023). Regulating ChatGPT and other Large Generative AI Models. *ACM International Conference Proceeding Series*, 1112–1123. 10.1145/3593013.3594067

Hamilton, R., & Davison, H. (2022). Legal and Ethical Challenges for HR in Machine Learning. *Employee Responsibilities and Rights Journal*, 34(1), 19–39. Advance online publication. 10.1007/s10672-021-09377-z

Jagwani, V., Meghani, S., Pai, K., & Dhage, S. (2023). Resume Evaluation through Latent Dirichlet Allocation and Natural Language Processing for Effective Candidate Selection. doi:arXiv:2307.15752v1.

Johnson, J. A., Coggburn, J. D., & Valcik, N. A. (2022). Artificial Intelligence and Public Human Resource Management: Questions for Research and Practice. *Public Personnel Management*, 51(4), 539–560. 10.1177/00910260221126498

Joseph, J. (2023). Conceptual Framework of Open and Distance Learning (ODL) for Studio-Based Architectural Design Courses Assessing the Potential of Laboratory Instructional Tool through Synthesia AI: A Case Study on Student Learning Outcome.

Kaur, M. (2021). Adoption of Artificial Intelligence in Human Resource Management: A Conceptual Model. *Indian Journal of Industrial Relations*, 57, 331.

Kaur, M., & Gandolfi, F. (2023). Research on Artificial Intelligence in Human Resource Management: Trends and Prospects. *Global Journal of Management and Business Research*, 23(1).

Kimseng, T., Javed, A., Jeenanunta, C., & Kohda, Y. (2020). Applications of Fuzzy Logic to Reconfigure Human Resource Management Practices for Promoting Product Innovation in Formal and Non-Formal R&D Firms. *Journal of Open Innovation*, 6(2), 38. Advance online publication. 10.3390/joitmc6020038

Korzynski, P., Mazurek, G., Altmann, A., Ejdys, J., Kazlauskaite, R., Paliszkiewicz, J., Wach, K., & Ziemba, E. (2023). Generative artificial intelligence as a new context for management theories: Analysis of ChatGPT. *Central European Management Journal*, 31(1), 3–13. 10.1108/CEMJ-02-2023-0091

Larsen, G. (2023). Boutique Staffing Firm Internship: How AI is Changing the Staffing Boutique Staffing Firm Internship: How AI is Changing the Staffing Industry. Retrieved from https://scholarworks.uark.edu/finnuht/113

Li, L., Lassiter, T., Oh, J., & Lee, M. K. (2021). Algorithmic Hiring in Practice: Recruiter and HR Professional's Perspectives on AI Use in Hiring. Proceedings of the 2021 AAAI/ACM Conference on AI, Ethics, and Society. Association for Computing Machinery, 166–176. Retrieved from 10.1145/3461702.3462531

Lozie, D. R., Omasa, R., Hesami, S., Zaman, S., Kajbaf, M., & Malik, A. R. (2024). Examining the impact of generative artificial intelligence on work dynamics. *Human Resources Management and Services*, 6(2), 3420. Advance online publication. 10.18282/hrms.v6i2.3420

Madanchian, M., Taherdoost, H., & Mohamed, N. (2023). AI-Based Human Resource Management Tools and Techniques; A Systematic Literature Review. *Procedia Computer Science*, 229, 367–377. 10.1016/j.procs.2023.12.039

Malik, A., Thevisuthan, P., & Sliva, T. (2022). Artificial Intelligence, Employee Engagement, Experience, and HRM. In Malik, A. (Ed.), *Strategic Human Resource Management and Employment Relations* (pp. 171–184). Springer. 10.1007/978-3-030-90955-0_16

Mannuru, N. R., Shahriar, S., Teel, Z. A., Wang, T., Lund, B. D., Tijani, S., Pohboon, C. O., Agbaji, D., Alhassan, J., Galley, J., Kousari, R., Ogbadu-Oladapo, L., Saurav, S. K., Srivastava, A., Tummuru, S. P., Uppala, S., & Vaidya, P. (2023). Artificial intelligence in developing countries: The impact of generative artificial intelligence (AI) technologies for development. *Information Development*, 1–19. 10.1177/02666669231200628

Mogaji, E., Balakrishnan, J., Nwoba, A. C., & Nguyen, N. P. (2021). Emerging-market consumers' interactions with banking chatbots. *Telematics and Informatics*, 65, 101711. 10.1016/j.tele.2021.101711

Mohajan, H. K. (2019). The first industrial revolution: Creation of a new global human era. *Journal of Social Sciences and Humanities*, 5(4), 377–387.

Naik, I., Naik, D., & Naik, N. (2023). Chat Generative Pre-Trained Transformer (ChatGPT): Comprehending its Operational Structure, AI Techniques, Working, Features and Limitations. 3rd IEEE International Conference on ICT in Business Industry and Government, ICTBIG 2023. 10.1109/ICTBIG59752.2023.10456201

Neelam, K., Rahul, P. S., & Brijesh, S. a. (2023). Artificial intelligence and HRM: identifying future research Agenda using systematic literature review and bibliometric analysis. *Management Review Quarterly*, 455-493.

Nicastro, D. (2020). 7 Ways Artificial Intelligence Is Reinventing Human Resources. Retrieved from https://www.cmswire.com/digital-workplace/7-ways-artificial-intelligence-is-reinventing-human-resources/

Nistler, J., & Tomas, P. (2023). Graphical use of AI. Retrieved from https://www.vtei.cz/2023/04/

Novianti, W., & Qadri, F. (2020). Design of Information System Human Resource Management. *IOP Conference Series. Materials Science and Engineering*, 879(1), 012126. Advance online publication. 10.1088/1757-899X/879/1/012126

Okolo, C. T. (2023). The Promise and Perils of Generative AI: Case Studies in an African Context. *ACM International Conference Proceeding Series*, 266–270. Retrieved from 10.1145/3628096.3629066

Ooi, K. B., Tan, G. W. H., Al-Emran, M., Al-Sharafi, M. A., Capatina, A., Chakraborty, A., Dwivedi, Y. K., Huang, T. L., Kar, A. K., Lee, V. H., Loh, X. M., Micu, A., Mikalef, P., Mogaji, E., Pandey, N., Raman, R., Rana, N. P., Sarker, P., Sharma, A., & Wong, L. W. (2023). The Potential of Generative Artificial Intelligence Across Disciplines: Perspectives and Future Directions. *Journal of Computer Information Systems*, 1–32. Advance online publication. 10.1080/08874417.2023.2261010

Pataranutaporn, P., Danry, V., Leong, J., Punpongsanon, P., Novy, D., Maes, P., & Sra, M. (2021). AI-generated characters for supporting personalized learning and well-being. *Nature Machine Intelligence*, 3(12), 1013–1022. 10.1038/s42256-021-00417-9

Peng, L., & Zhao, B. (2024). Navigating the Ethical Landscape Behind ChatGPT. *Big Data & Society*, 1-5(1). Advance online publication. 10.1177/20539517241237488

Qamar, Y., Agrawal, R., Samad, T., & Jabbour, C. (2021). When technology meets people: The interplay of artificial intelligence and human resource management. *Journal of Enterprise Information Management*, 34(5), 1339–1370. Advance online publication. 10.1108/JEIM-11-2020-0436

Rana, T. (2018). The Future of HR in the Presence of AI: A Conceptual Study. SSRN *Electronic Journal*. 10.2139/ssrn.3335670

Randle, O. A., Coleman, A., & Kekwaletswe, R. (2017). *Towards a Motivational based Model for Effective Use of Human Resource Information System in South African Universities*. IEEE. 10.23919/i-Society.2017.8354672

Rane, N. (2023). Role and Challenges of ChatGPT and Similar Generative Artificial Intelligence in Human Resource Management. SSRN *Electronic Journal*. 10.2139/ssrn.4603230

Rathnayake, C., & Gunawardana, A. (2023). *The Role of Generative AI in Enhancing Human Resource Management Recruitment*. Training, and Performance Evaluation Perspectives. In International Journal of Social Analytics.

Rathore, S. (2023). The Impact of AI on Recruitment and Selection Processes: Analysing the role of AI in automating and enhancing. *International Journal for Global Academic & Scientific Research*, 78-93.

Sakthi, S., Nathan, K., & Karthi, D. R. (2023). Future of Electronic Human Resource Management in the IT Sector. Retrieved from http://eelet.org.uk

Sharma, A. (2022). HRIS-Challenges, Obstacles and Implementation. *Parichay Maharaja Surajmal Institute Journal of Applied Research*, 5(1), 49–53.

Shin, D., Koerber, A., & Lim, J. S. (2024). Impact of misinformation from generative AI on user information processing: How people understand misinformation from generative AI. *New Media & Society*, 1–31. 10.1177/14614448241234040

Singh, A., & Sahoo, D. (2023). Revolutionizing Recruitment: Harnessing the Power of Technology. *IRE Journals*, 6(12), 1343–1355.

Siregar, E., & Dachyar, M. (2018). Determining Criteria of Human Resource Information System that Affect Human Resource Performance in Companies Using DEMATEL-Based ANP Method. https://doi.org/10.1051/matecconf/2018248030

Suffian, A., & Zahari, M. (2017). User Satisfaction on Human Resource Management Information System (HRMIS): A Case Study at Terengganu Police Contingent, Malaysia. Journal of Biological and Environmental Sciences. Retrieved from https://www.researchgate.net/publication/322758387

Tacheva, Z., & Ramasubramanian, S. (2023). *Challenging AI Empire: Toward a Decolonial and Queer Framework of Data Resurgence*. Advance. 10.31124/advance.22012724.v1

Tambe, P., Cappelli, P., & Yakubovich, V. (2019). Artificial intelligence in human resources management: Challenges and a path forward. *California Management Review*, 61(4), 15–42. 10.1177/0008125619867910

Torre, G. (2024). Save Time With ChatGPT. *Talent Development*, 78(5), 18–19.

Weeramanthrie, T. T., Thilakumara, C. N., Wijesiri, K. N. A. C., Fernando, N. I., Thelijjagoda, S., & Gamage, A. (2017). ARROW: A Web-Based Employee Turnover Analysis Tool for Effective Human Resource Management in Large-Scale Organizations.

Yahia, N. B., Jihen, H., & Colomo-Palacios, R. (2021). From Big Data to Deep Data to Support People Analytics for Employee Attrition Prediction. *IEEE Access : Practical Innovations, Open Solutions*, 99, 1. 10.1109/ACCESS.2021.3074559

Yang, X., Wang, Q., & Lyu, J. (2023). Assessing ChatGPT's Educational Capabilities and Application Potential. *ECNU Review of Education*, 1-15.

Zahari, A. S. M., Harun, M. A., Hamzah, S. F. M., & Salleh, S. M. (2018). The influence of Human Resource Management Information System (HRMIS) Application towards Employees Efficiency and Satisfaction. *Journal of Physics: Conference Series*, 1019(1), 012077. Advance online publication. 10.1088/1742-6596/1019/1/012077

Zhang, Y., Xu, S., Zhang, L., & Yang, M. (2021). Big data and human resource management research: An integrative review and new directions for future research. *Journal of Business Research*, 133, 34–50. 10.1016/j.jbusres.2021.04.019

Zhou, K.-Q., & Nabus, H. (2023). The Ethical Implications of DALL-E: Opportunities and Challenges. *Mesopotamian Journal of Computer Science*, 17–23.

KEY TERMS AND DEFINITIONS

Artificial Intelligence (AI): A simulation of human intelligence processes by machines, especially computer systems, which can adapt and learn from experience, making them capable of performing tasks that typically require human intelligence.

ChatGPT: A conversational AI model that is a deep learning model capable of generating human-like text based on the input it receives. It is designed to engage in natural and coherent conversations with users, providing responses that are contextually relevant and linguistically accurate.

Employee Relations: The management of the relationship between an organization and its employees, focusing on creating a positive work environment, fostering effective communication, resolving conflicts, and promoting mutual understanding and cooperation between management and staff.

Generative Artificial Intelligence: Artificial Intelligence systems that can create new content, such as images, text, or music, based on patterns and examples from existing data.

Human Resource Management: A strategic approach to managing people. It encompasses the processes, practices, and policies related to recruiting, hiring, training, developing, compensating, and retaining employees to achieve organizational goals effectively and efficiently.

Performance Management: A systematic process that involves setting clear expectations, monitoring progress, providing feedback, and evaluating individual and organizational performance to achieve strategic goals.

Recruitment and Selection: Processes that involve attracting, identifying, and hiring the most qualified candidates for job positions within an organization.

Succession Planning: A strategic process that involves identifying and developing internal talent to fill key leadership positions within an organization in the event of planned or unplanned vacancies.

Training and Development: A process of enhancing employees' skills, knowledge, abilities, and competencies to improve their performance, productivity, and effectiveness in their current roles or prepare them for future responsibilities within the organization.

Workforce Planning: A strategic process that involves analyzing and forecasting an organization's current and future workforce needs to ensure that it has the right talent in the right place at the right time to achieve its business objectives.

Chapter 4
Mediated by AI-Based Generative Re-Enforcement Learning and Work Attitude:
Are Intrinsic Rewards Transforming Employee Perceived Organizational Support?

Shashi Kant
https://orcid.org/0000-0003-4722-5736
Bule Hora University, Ethiopia

Metasebia Adula
https://orcid.org/0000-0001-5732-2850
Bule Hora University, Ethiopia

ABSTRACT

The primary goal of the chapter was to examine how, in the Ethiopian environment, an employee's work attitude and AI-based reinforcement learning function as mediators between their psychological intrinsic reward system and the perception of organisational support they receive from their employer. Based on their contribution to the GDP of the economy, the textile industries operating in Ethiopia's industrial parks were chosen as the study area. A quantitative research technique and explanatory research design were employed. A multi-phase sampling method was suggested. To assess discriminant and convergent validity, exploratory confirmatory analysis was carried out using AMOS software. It was discovered that the

DOI: 10.4018/979-8-3693-5578-7.ch004

relationship between an employee's psychological intrinsic reward system and the organization's perceived organisational support was extremely poor in the absence of AI-based re-enforcement learning and the employee's work attitude as a mediator. Thus, the work attitude of employees and artificial intelligence (AI) function as a complete mediator.

INTRODUCTION

A sort of machine learning technology called Generative re-enforcement learning (GRL) teaches an agent how to behave in a way that maximizes a reward (Emmanuel & Nwuzor, 2021). By making mistakes and getting feedback—that is, incentives or penalties—for its activities, the agent learns by doing and then modifying its behavior to get the intended result. When there is a clear objective but an unclear method to get there, Generative re-enforcement learning (GRL) works well (Kassa & Tsigu, 2022).

Generative re-enforcement learning (GRL) and generative AI are connected in that they both belong to the larger category of machine learning (Verma et al., 2022). While generative AI is concentrated on producing new data that mimics the training data, Generative re-enforcement learning (GRL) is a technique for teaching agents to do actions. For instance, the two can be used to train a generative model to generate desired outputs using Generative re-enforcement learning (GRL) (Emmanuel & Nwuzor, 2021).

Generally speaking, psychological intrinsic reward systems have an impact on Generative re-enforcement learning (GRL) (AI) and employee work attitudes. They also have an impact on how supportive an organization is seen by employees (Peponi et al., 2022; Mbebeb & Tanyi, 2019). Employee emotional committed behavior is the result of the psychological intrinsic reward system, which also enhances employee attitude, Generative re-enforcement learning (GRL) (AI), and commitment (Kant et al., 2023; Verma et al., 2022). According to Pathan et al. (2018), psychological intrinsic reward systems have a substantial role in Generative re-enforcement learning (GRL) (AI) and an organization's capacity to recruit, retain, and inspire high-potential employees, as well as in achieving better levels of perceived organizational support.

The impact of the extrinsic psychological intrinsic reward system on employee commitment changes based on the degree of artificial intelligence (AI) reinforcement (Danilwan & Dirhamsyah, 2022). It appears to differ greatly depending on the person and industry (Kassa & Tsigu, 2022). Generative re-enforcement learning (GRL) (AI) is a psychological process that is systematically delivered through both internal and extrinsic reward systems (Adula et al., 2022; Seeck et al., 2017). It benefits both the employer and the employee in tandem (Naser, 2021).

Research has shown that organization support is not well implemented in African nations, particularly in Ethiopia. As a result, employees find it difficult to form a strong bond with their employers (Elita & Sinthia, 2021). Thus, despite improved application of human resource methods, work attitude is unable to grow in Ethiopian companies (Kassa & Tsigu, 2022). When scientists looked for the cause of it, they discovered the fundamental truth. The issue was that intrinsic reward and effort were incompatible. They are unable to develop a psychological bond with the organization as a result. The rate of discontent, estrangement, and employee turnover is rising daily, which results in a decline in organizational growth and a lack of interest in psychological organizational learning (Seeck et al., 2017). In order to enhance psychological organizational learning, it ought to be integrated with psychological intrinsic reward (Adula et. a., 2023).

Physically delivering psychologically meaningful incentives is typically challenging (Shaw, 2021). However, implementing new technology enables workers to become more productive, negotiate greater pay, and obtain better jobs (Naser, 2021). It was established that learning results from reward. According to Edward Thorndike's S-R theory, stimulus results in resources that genuinely function (Mbebeb & Tanyi, 2019). Employees' cognitive Generative re-enforcement learning (GRL) will therefore be enhanced if psychological intrinsic rewards are given to them (Kassa & Tsigu, 2022). Additionally, research showed that artificial intelligence (AI) is the primary factor employed by innovation-based enterprises to advance cognitive Generative re-enforcement learning (GRL) to its highest potential (Emmanuel & Nwuzor, 2021).

Thus, the current study examined how employees' perceptions of organizational support in the textile companies operating in Ethiopian industrial parks were influenced by their work attitudes and the use of AI-based Generative re-enforcement learning (GRL). The textile enterprises operating inside Ethiopia's industrial park were chosen due to their technological foundation and substantial contribution to the GDP of the region under investigation.

LITERATURE REVIEW

Combining generative AI with reinforcement learning methods, generative reinforcement learning (GRL) seeks to develop AI systems that can produce new information while also picking up skills via trial and error. The AI model in a generative reinforcement learning setup consists of two primary parts (Kassa & Tsigu, 2022):

1. *Generative Model:* This is the system component in charge of creating new material, such text, photos, and other types of data. Variational Auto-encoders (VAEs) and Generative Adversarial Networks (GANs) are two examples of generative AI approaches that are used to train this component.
2. *Reinforcement Learning Agent:* It is the system component that uses interactions with its surroundings to learn how to carry out a certain activity or accomplish a goal. Based on how well it performs, the agent is rewarded or penalized, and it modifies its behavior to maximize rewards.

Integrating the model's generating powers with the reinforcement learning agent's goal-oriented learning and decision-making processes is the fundamental principle underpinning GRL. The reinforcement learning agent may assess and choose the most promising new candidate solutions or actions that the generative model generates, giving the generative model feedback to enhance its output (Adula et al., 2022; Seeck et al., 2017). In fields where there is a wide range of potential answers and the work is creative or open-ended, this method can be especially helpful (Naser, 2021).

The system can more efficiently explore this region and find innovative, high-performing solutions by fusing generative capabilities with reinforcement learning. Creative tasks like creating music, art, or stories; designing intricate systems like molecules, materials, or architectures; solving open-ended optimization problems; and enabling autonomous agents to adapt and pick up new skills in dynamic environments are a few potential uses for generative reinforcement learning (Mbebeb & Tanyi, 2019). In general, generative reinforcement learning is a fascinating field of study that seeks to develop AI systems that can learn from and get better through interaction with their surroundings, in addition to being able to produce new ideas.

A mix of computer vision, sensor data analytics, and machine learning algorithms would probably be used in the particular Generative AI systems being evaluated for usage in Ethiopian garment manufacturers. The AI systems would continually watch and record worker activity across the production floor using cameras, motion sensors, and other devices. This data would be analyzed by computer vision algorithms to measure parameters such as worker attendance, production speed, quality of output, and safety compliance (Kassa & Tsigu, 2022).

According to Ramachandran et al. (2022) and Adula & Kant (2022), the Generative AI system would assess each employee's productivity and contributions using machine learning models based on the performance data gathered. The algorithms would include qualitative aspects like problem-solving, cooperation, and protocol adherence in addition to quantitative measures. After that, the Generative AI would decide on suitable incentives for the top-performing employees, such as bonuses, promotions, or other awards. The system would employ pre-established formulae and thresholds to clearly determine the award amounts and eligibility.

The goal is to replace human subjectivity and biases in compensation choices with an objective, data-driven procedure. Fairness would be encouraged as employees would be able to observe how their work is evaluated and prizes are given out. Of course, there are legitimate worries about privacy invasions, possible algorithmic biases, and an excessive dependence on Generative AI systems (Kant et al., 2023). To make sure the Generative AI is making impartial and equitable choices, it would be necessary to have strong testing, monitoring, and appeals procedures. It will also be crucial to give employees a say in how the Generative AI systems are implemented and to be transparent about how the systems function. To resolve any problems that may come up, constant communication among factory management, employees, and Generative AI specialists will be necessary (Verma et al., 2022).

These Generative AI-powered performance tracking and incentives systems have the potential to make Ethiopian garment factories more equal and inspiring places to work, provided the proper safety measures are put in place and the labor is given the support it needs.

THEORETICAL CONTRIBUTION

A framework based on two factor theory, resource-based view, social exchange theory, and a review of the literature on employees' perceived organizational support, AI-based Generative re-enforcement learning (GRL), psychological intrinsic reward, and work attitude are used to theoretically investigate the strategic question, "Is psychological intrinsic reward augment the employees' perceived organizational support when mediated by work attitude and AI based Generative re-enforcement learning (GRL) in Ethiopia?" In this theoretical paradigm, employees' perceptions of their organizations' support are the dependent variable, while psychological intrinsic pleasure is the independent variable. Furthermore, the association among employees' perceptions of organizational support and psychological intrinsic reward was mediated by work attitude and AI-based Generative re-enforcement learning (GRL).

The significance of intrinsic psychological benefits, such job satisfaction and personal development, in inspiring people is underscored by Herzberg's Two-Factor Theory. According to Penrose's Resource-Based View, businesses may get a competitive edge by making use of their special internal resources, such as organizational support and psychological intrinsic incentives (Danilwan & Dirhamsyah, 2022). Wernerfelt's RBV emphasizes how outside variables, including industry rivalry, influence how well an organization performs. According to Ramachandran et al. (2022) and Adula & Kant (2022), Barney's Resource-Based View (RBV) emphasizes the importance of an organization's internal resources, especially its VRIO (valuable, rare, inimitable, and organized) resources, as major sources of long-term competitive advantage.

According to Homans' Social interchange Theory, the interchange of benefits and costs among people and organizations shapes social behavior, including the attitudes of employees towards their jobs. All things considered, these theories offer insightful information on the variables affecting worker motivation, organizational effectiveness, and competitive advantage (Adula et al., 2022; Seeck et al., 2017). Organizations may create strategies that enhance employee engagement, productivity, and overall performance by comprehending and implementing these theories (Kassa & Tsigu, 2022).

Empirical Literature Review

1. Organizational Perceived organizational support and Psychological intrinsic reward System

According to Verma et al. (2022) there is a favorable association among the psychological intrinsic reward system of employees and the perceived organizational support inside the company. A psychological intrinsic reward system influences people's behavior and well-being and is correlated with how effectively the organization is seen to support them, both of which can result in positive organizational outcomes and support (Panch et al., 2018). Increased job satisfaction leads to improved individual and team performance in organizations that prioritize employees' psychological intrinsic reward systems (Ramachandran et al., 2022; Adula & Kant, 2022). Nonetheless, other researchers came to the conclusion that there is an association between the apparent administrative care and the employee's psychological intrinsic reward system (Naser, 2021). Thus, the researcher employed SEM analysis to test the theory and determine whether or not it has a substantial link in order to verify this inconclusive idea. The information gap of inconclusive idea is filled by this study.

H1: Employee Perceptions of Organizational Support and Their Psychological Intrinsic Reward System Are Substantially Correlated

2. Employee's Work Attitude and Psychological intrinsic reward System

By providing "bonuses, profit sharing, wage incentive, extra allowances," and other financial and psychological incentives, many organizations improve the work attitudes of their employees (Shaw, 2021). According to Pathan et al. (2018), intrinsic rewards cultivate a positive attitude in employees and foster a long-term connection. According to Wakjira and Kant (2022), industries provide financial incentives with inherent psychological value in order to improve workers' work attitudes and perceptions of industry support from peers. Researchers claim that there is a favorable and substantial correlation among the psychological intrinsic reward system in the industrial sector and employees' work attitudes (Seeck et al., 2017). Research indicates that an worker's assertiveness is strictly connected to their expectations, which are based on the idea that their industry would value their work and provide perceived organizational support through a variety of financial, psychological, and intrinsic incentive systems (Emmanuel & Nwuzor, 2021).

Employees stay engaged, devoted, and consider the business to be their home and do not consider switching to another industry if it meets their expectations (Hao et al., 2022). It therefore leads to driving aspects that are essential for the industry's reputability and sustained growth—high levels of employee dedication, engagement, and belonging (Naser, 2021). The researcher used SEM analysis to test the theory to determine whether or not it has a substantial association, as some scholars had concluded that there is no substantial association among an worker's work attitude and their psychological intrinsic reward system (Mbebeb & Tanyi, 2019). The information vacuum created by ambiguous ideas is filled by this study.

H2: There Is a Substantial Positive Association Among Psychological Intrinsic Reward System and Worker's Work Attitude

3. Organizational perceived organizational support and Employee work attitude

The impact of an employee's assertiveness on objective accomplishment and working efficacy, that in turn affects firm performance and productivity, has been well documented in the literature (Widarko & Anwarodin, 2022; Adula et al., 2022; Al-Awar et. a., 2022). Employee earnestness to assistance the association attain its objectives is therefore shown in their work attitude (Dhir & Chakraborty, 2021). Many studies have examined a variety of work attitude factors and how they affect emotional, continuous, and normative commitment in addition to employee participation and organizational citizenship among textile industry employees (Panch et al., 2018).

As well as referring to the department of an employee's work attitude and the organization's perceived organizational support, it also denotes connection to the organization's perceived organizational support (Verma et al., 2022). According to the Component Model of Organizational Work Attitude, employees' demand for commitment, participation, and organizational citizenship behaviors drives their desire to identify with their workplace and industry (Kassa & Tsigu, 2022). An employee with a work attitude is one who sticks with the firm by showing up for work on a regular basis, working a full day (or longer), safeguarding the company's objectives, and so on (Ismael et al., 2022; Seeck et al., 2017). In summary, several research studies have been carried out across diverse industries and nations concerning employees' work attitudes and their impact on perceived organizational support.

Numerous scholars have conducted studies in the setting of the Horn of Africa, looking at the association among workers' work attitudes and perceived organizational support in the textile sector (Naser, 2021). In order to examine perceived organizational support of textile industries and operators, the studies included a number of constructs to be examined in the Ethiopian textile industry in the Horn of Africa. These constructs included motivation, financial perceived organizational support, and employee satisfaction (Junça Silva & Coelho, 2022).

Research revealed that, in the Ethiopian setting, perceptions of organizational support for textiles were greatly impacted by HRM practices (Dhir & Chakraborty, 2021). The study by Neudert et al. (2020) examined the association among HRM practices, work attitude, and perceived organizational support for textiles and discovered a positive correlation among these indicated components. A negative correlation was discovered when the association among an employee's work attitude and their perception of the organization's support was examined (Emmanuel & Nwuzor, 2021). The association among an employee's work attitude and the organization's perceived support of the Ethiopian textile industry in Southern Africa has not been studied by the researcher.

H3: The Work Attitude of Employees and the Perceived Support From the Organization Are Substantially Correlated

4. Employee Work Attitude's Mediating Role

In the manufacturing and service sectors, psychological intrinsic incentive systems are powerful and effective methods for changing employees' behavior and are crucial for both parties' task achievement (Danilwan & Dirhamsyah, 2022). According to academics, the psychological intrinsic reward system is in line with organizational objectives; as a result, these factors inspire workers, and task accompaniment results in job satisfaction (Naser, 2021).

The psychological intrinsic incentive system of an organization has a substantial impact on employee actions since it provides perceived organizational support for their performance (Dhir & Chakraborty, 2021). A strong psychological intrinsic incentive system gives a business a competitive edge by keeping seasoned workers on board (Mbebeb & Tanyi, 2019).discovered that a psychological intrinsic reward system is a valuable instrument for raising employee motivation and behavior to deliver quality work and encourage improved performance at work (Shaw, 2021). Researchers have examined how the psychological intrinsic reward system influences employee motivation and behavioral change in the industrial, textile, and food industries (Stergiou, 2022).

H4: Employee Work's Attitude Plays a Mediation Among Psychological Intrinsic Reward System and Perceived Administrative Support

4. Generative re-enforcement learning (GRL) (AI) and Employee Psychological intrinsic reward System

Generative re-enforcement learning (GRL) is not dependent on the explicit correction of suboptimal actions or the display of labeled input/output pairs, as supervised learning is (Danilwan & Dirhamsyah, 2022). Rather, the focus is on striking a balance among venturing into frontiers and making use of the knowledge that is currently available (Kassa & Tsigu, 2022). In order to maximize the "reward function" or any additional user-provided restoration signal that builds from the immediate rewards, the agent uses generated learning through reinforcement (GRL) to build a perfect or almost optimal strategy. Comparable structures seem to exist in animal cognition (Dhir & Chakraborty, 2021). For instance, neurological brains interpret signals such as hunger and pain as negative stimuli and signals like as euphoria and food intake to be advantageous benefits (Shaw, 2021).

Neudert et al. (2020) state that studies in the field of machine learning called generative re-enforcement learning (GRL) (RL) have shown how intelligent agents should behave in a particular setting to maximize the concept of accumulated reward. Together with supervised learning and unsupervised learning, generative reinforcement learning (GRL) is one of the three primary machine learning paradigms (Verma et al., 2022).

Developers provide a way to penalize undesirable behavior and reward favorable behavior in dynamic re-enforcement learning (GRL) (Mbebeb & Tanyi, 2019). Danilwan and Dirhamsyah (2022) claim that this tactic gives advantageous qualities to desired behaviors in an effort to motivate the agent to participate in them and opposing opinions to undesirable behaviors in an effort to stop them.

H5: Generative Re-Enforcement Learning (GRL) and the Employee Psychological Intrinsic Reward System Are Closely Related (AI)

5. Employee Perceived organizational support and Generative re-enforcement learning (GRL)

    Generative re-enforcement learning (GRL) is a technique in machine learning training that rewards good actions and penalizes undesired ones (Stergiou, 2022).A Generative re-enforcement learning (GRL) agent is an organism that is being educated to see and understand its surroundings, behave appropriately, and learn from its mistakes (Elita & Sinthia, 2021). Overall, the results demonstrate that incentives have no negative impact on intrinsic motivation (Al-Awar et al., 2022). Research on interaction effects shows that verbal praise boosts intrinsic motivation (Adula et al., 2022). People are negatively impacted when they obtain expected material rewards for completing a job alone (Adula et al., 2022).

    AI-based solutions enable businesses to increase employee engagement for both on-site and remote workers in a variety of ways (Naser, 2021). These methods include providing 24/7 assistance, real-time performance monitoring, learning and development, and dispute resolution (Mbebeb & Tanyi, 2019). By utilizing AI's ability to analyze massive amounts of data and provide insightful learning, organizations may improve their decision-making in a number of areas, such as strategy, marketing, and operations (Kassa & Tsigu, 2022). AI helps organizations be highly successful in motivating their workers and promoting employee engagement by exposing individuals to a variety of success levers, such as efficacy in decision making and learning, collaboration, experimentation, and information sharing (Verma et al., 2022).

H6: There Is a Substantial Effect of Generative Re-Enforcement Learning (GRL) on Employee Perceived Organizational Support

6. Mediating Role of Generative re-enforcement learning (GRL)

The textile business must recognize that effective psychological intrinsic incentives are necessary for managing Generative re-enforcement learning (GRL) (AI) and handling employee behavior. (Al-Awar et. all., 2022). Thus, in order to obtain Generative re-enforcement learning (GRL) (AI) and organizational perceived organizational support, the textile sector must implement an efficient psychological intrinsic incentives system (Stergiou, 2022). Generative re-enforcement learning (GRL) (AI) has the most potential to influence employee behavior in the workplace. good Generative re-enforcement learning (GRL) (PRL) fosters good behavior and commitment in the workplace by instilling in the worker a sense of attachment to their work and surroundings (Neudert et al., 2020).

Promotion, Generative re-enforcement learning (GRL) (AI), attractive and high-paying jobs, and employee satisfaction all contributed to employee engagement and motivation, which in turn affected the industry's perception of organizational support (Kassa & Tsigu, 2022). Conversely, research on the impact of Generative re-enforcement learning (GRL) (AI) on organizations revealed that it was not substantial (Shaw, 2021). However, AI was shown to be crucial in providing exceptional organizational assistance as recognized by the organizations. In exchange for their efforts to improve and create their high-quality product, employees are motivated by Generative re-enforcement learning (GRL) (AI), which helps management increase employee satisfaction (Dhir & Chakraborty, 2021). The goal of the current study is to investigate how Generative re-enforcement learning (GRL) (AI) mediates the association among the perceived organizational support in the textile sector in Horn Africa, Ethiopia, and the psychological intrinsic reward system of employees (Mbebeb & Tanyi, 2019). Employee commitment, connection, and participation are enhanced by positive Generative re-enforcement learning (GRL) (AI), and this is substantial for the industry since it affects how organizations are considered to assist one another (Verma et al., 2022). Generative re-enforcement learning (GRL) (AI) and perceived organizational support have been directly linked in a number of nations, including Pakistan, Vietnam, Ghana, Malaysia, New Zealand, and Turkey (Neudert et al., 2020). Conversely, a small number of studies showed a negligible correlation among AI-enhanced Generative re-enforcement learning (GRL) and felt organizational support inside an organization. Therefore, the researcher employed SEM analysis to evaluate the theory and validate this ambiguous concept.

H7: *Generative re-enforcement learning (GRL) (AI) plays a mediating role among the psychological intrinsic reward system of employees and their perception of organizational support.*

Figure 1. Schematic representation of the interaction among AI-based generative re-enforcement learning (GRL), work attitude, and intrinsic reward transformation (Reviewed literature, 2023)

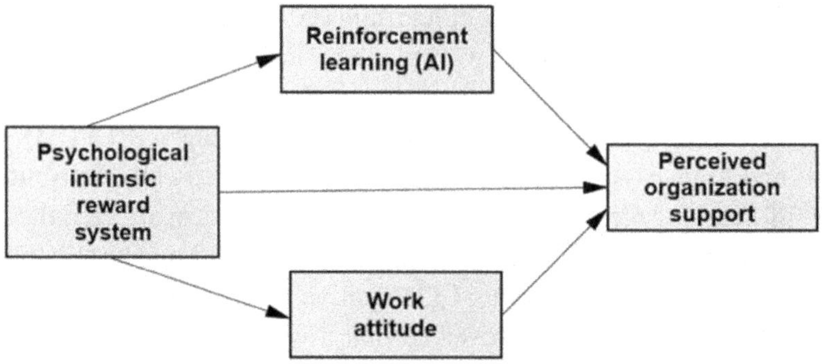

RESEARCH METHODOLOGY

In order to get understanding of the stated research topic, researchers used a mix of ontology and epistemology techniques in the form of pragmatism, applying the pragmatic paradigm. The logic of pragmatic inquiry is based on the application of induction (sequence identification), deduction (the theory and assumption verification), and abduction (identifying and relying on the best explanation among a range of alternatives for comprehending) (Verma et al., 2022). In this study, a method of quantitative investigation was adopted because the study's objectives can only be addressed by using an exploratory investigation approach.

TARGET POPULATION AND SAMPLING TECHNIQUE

The primary focus of this study was Ethiopia's public textile and fabric industry. According to Mbebeb and Tanyi (2019), Ethiopia has ten public industrial parks. There are ten (twenty-eight) distinct owners who produce textiles and fabric inside Ethiopia's ten public textile and cloth enterprises. Researchers only choose factories with at than three years of operational experience in order to obtain enough data. Accordingly, the study's sample frame consisted of 24 (twenty-four) industries that employ 398762 people in the textile and fabric sector (Kassa & Tsigu, 2022).

Managers from the textile and apparel industries, the director of human resources, team leaders, and employers were chosen at random from each organization. After being written in English, the questionnaire was translated into Amharic, the regional language of Ethiopia, and Afan Oromo.

SAMPLE SIZE

The Dillman sampling formula (2000) was utilized by the researchers to minimize coverage error in the research survey and to calculate the study's representative sample. The multi-stage sample technique was employed in the study's sampling methodology. In order to choose government textile industries based on the GTP-II plan, which aims to elevate Ethiopia to lower middle income status by 2025, researchers initially employed purposive sampling. Stratified sampling, which separates the population into homogenous subpopulations from a heterogeneous sample, was employed in the second step. Due to the varied nature of the sector, researchers must use stratified sampling to guarantee that every attribute in the sample was accurately represented. Following that, the responders were chosen via the application of methodical using sampling intervals.

$$[(X)\ (q)\ (1\text{-}q)] = x[(X\text{-}1)] \,/\, (Z/Y)2 + (q)\ [(1\text{-}q)]$$

$$= (39876 \pm 0.5)\ (1\text{-}0.5)][(39876\text{-}1)]\ (1\text{-}0.5) + (0.5)\ (1\text{-}0.05/1.96)2]{=}383$$

39876 people work in the textile and clothing sector throughout the three industrial parks. A sample size of 383 people was chosen, or around 0.75% of the whole population. Since a sample size of at least 381 is usually advised for populations this size, this sample size is thought to be sufficient for carrying out substantial statistical analysis. A stratified random sampling technique was used to choose the sample, guaranteeing that it is representative of the population with regard to key attributes like geography and industry. This technique improves the accuracy of the results and lessens bias.

DISCUSSION

Assortment adequacy is measured by the KMO, and a factor analysis cannot be approved if it is less than 0.5. When correlation tendencies are reasonably compact, as indicated by a value close to 1, factor analysis can provide identifiable and reliable factors. Table 1 displays the KMO value.

Table 1. Data adequacy test

Kaiser Meyer Olkin: Measure of data Adequacy		**.854**
Sphericity Test: Bartlett's	Chi- Square (Approx.)	1603.425
	Df	31
	Sig.	.000

Source: AMOS Output (2024)

The outcomes of the data sufficiency test show that the data are appropriate for factor analysis. The KMO value, or Kaiser-Meyer-Olkin sample adequacy metric, is 0.854, which is considered to be very good. This implies that factor assessment would be a very suitable application of the information. The significant results of the Bartlett's test of sphericity ($p < 0.05$) suggest that the data are not spherically distributed. This suggests that each of the variables have a connection with one another, which is necessary for factor analysis. Overall, the results of the examination for data sufficiency indicate that the data are appropriate for factor analysis. Considering the significant degree of shared heterogeneity among the variables and the good connection that exists between the data, factor analysis is probably going to be able to find any underlying factors.

CONSTRUCT VERIFICATION

A form of statistics for confirming the arrangement of factors of a collection of observable variables is verifying factor analysis (Tufa et al., 2023). Investigators may additionally evaluate hypotheses using CFA that are based on the relationships between the underlying structure's visible parameters. Using CFA, a researcher can investigate the assumption that there is a relationship among the variables that appear and the implicit assumptions that underlie them.

Figure 2. Confirmatory factor analysis (AMOS Output, 2024)

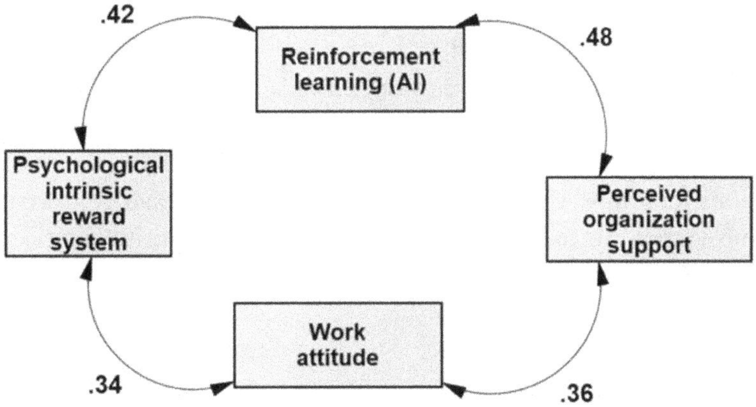

The initial approximation in Figure 2 illustrates the relationship between worker disposition and perceived support from the organization. The predicted covariance of 0.36 shows a discovery on an approximately distributed normally random variable with a standard deviation of 0.029. If the 0.05 significant amount assumption in the section "distribution presumptions for Amos model" were true, then any of the essential ratio in excess of 1.96 in magnitude would be considered substantial. The projection of the standard error (S.E.) of the coefficient of variation, 0.029 Critical Ratio, which is significantly higher than 1.96 at the threshold of 0.05, indicates that there existed autocorrelation among the variables in question.

Table 2. Validity convergent

			Estimate	S.E.	C.R.	P
EOPS	**<-->**	**EW**	**.24**	**.019**	**7.197**	***
ERW	<-->	EW	.26	.029	6.903	***
ERW	<-->	EOPS	.20	.018	7.398	***
ERW	<-->	RL	.19	.019	8.004	***
EOPS	<-->	RL	.26	.028	7.372	***

Source: AMOS Output (2024)

The initial approximation displayed in Table 2 is the connection between ERW and EOPS. The observation is on an approximately normally dispersed random variable with substantial covariance at its center, having a standard variance of 0.036 and a projected covariance of 0.275. Any crucial ratio more than 1.96 would be deemed major if the Amos model's section dispersion assumptions are adhered to, which sets an important threshold of 0.05. The critical ratio, or the calculation of the standard error, or S.E., of the covariance, is higher than 1.96 at the threshold of 0.05, suggesting a significant divergence from zero in the original similarity among the variables being studied.

The correlation among employee work attitude and EOPS is the first estimate to be shown. With a standard deviation of 0.026, the estimated covariance of 0.0190 indicates that, assuming the significance level of 0.05 in the section "Distribution Assumptions for Amos Model," any critical ratio greater than 1.96 would be considered substantial. Since the covariance estimate's (S.E.) critical ratio of 0.026 is more than 1.96.

DISCRIMINANT VALIDITY

Proof for discriminatory accuracy is the finding that assessments of characteristics that, on paper, are supposed to be considerably associated with one another are really not found to be considerably correlated with one another. As seen by the association data in Table 3, discriminant accuracy coefficients should, in theory, be significantly less than convergent legitimacy coefficients.

Table 3. Discriminant validity

Eigen Initial values		**Sums Extraction of Loading Squared**		
Sum	**(%) Deviations**	**Sum**	**(%) Deviations**	**Sum cumulative (%)**
3.791	46.98	4.03	51.09	46.98
1.012	12.54	0.99	14.07	59.05
Average Variance Explained			0.5905	
Square root (Ave)			**0.779**	
Variables	**RW**	**WA**	**RL**	**EOPS**
RW	1			
WA	.29	1		
RL	.39	.43	1	
EOPS	.38	.29	.37	1

Source: AMOS Output (2024)

When compared to the comparable correlation of all other variables, the Average Variance Explained (AVE) square root was determined to be more than 0.779. As can be observed, the correlation among RW, WA, RL, and EOPS was less than that of AVE (0.779). Consequently, discriminating validity is attained since the AVE's square root is greater than the sum of all correlation values.

Figure 3. Equation model (AMOS Output, 2024)

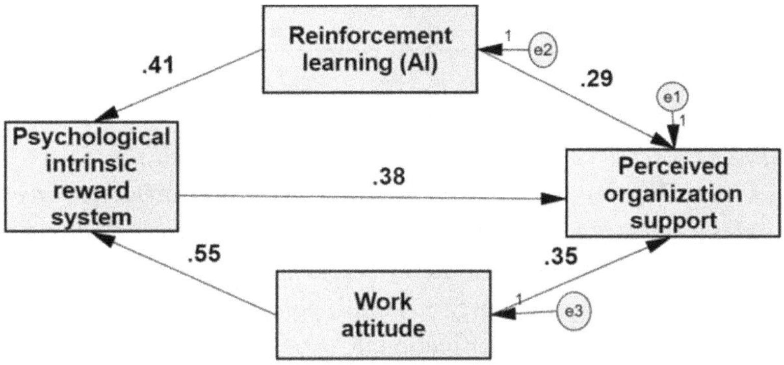

Table 4. Indices of model fit

P	Chi Sq* Degree of freedom	Fitness- Good Index	C-F-I	T-L-I	R-M-S-E-A
0.39	2.98	0.96	0.94	0.95	.008

Source: AMOS Output (2024)

Based on Table 4 and Figure 3 data, a satisfactory model fit is indicated by a Chi square divided by degree of freedom value of 2.98, which is a minimum or not over 2. The goodness fit index is 0.9753 larger than 0.95, the index of comparative fit is 0.936 above 0.95, the root mean square error of estimate is 0.025 less than 0.05, and the root mean of residual.017 is less than 0.05. The complete fit model is so good. Since the parameter that is relevant in this instance is the GFI for the standard model, GFI has drawn the greatest attention. The recommended model's Goodness of Fit Index (GFI) is 0.973, which is greater than 0.95.

INVESTIGATION FOR MEDIATION

ERW affects EOPS by 0.487. EW acts as a mediator among ERW and EOPS. Using the mediation theory and predictors with job-related attitudes towards the researcher's work, researchers employed the Barron and Kenny (1987) model. The mediation idea was expanded upon. Using the SPSSvs.26 process macros, researchers were able to first investigate the association among work attitude mediation and predictors displayed under Table 5.

Table 5. Mediation analysis

	ERW	EW	EOPS
EW	.699	---	.049
RL	.559	.199	----
EOPS	.491	.229	----

Source: AMOS Output (2024)

There was a 0.70 overall impact. There is a 0.48 indirect influence on employees' work attitudes. Following Baron and Kenny (1987), an investigation was conducted to determine if the employee work attitude mediates the link among the psychological intrinsic reward system and the organization's perceived organizational support of the textile industry. Following verification that our survey satisfied all requirements set out by investigators. The results of the two experiments indicated that the work attitude of the employees and their perception of the organization's support for the textile industry are mediated by the employees' psychological intrinsic reward system.

The connection among an employee's psychological intrinsic reward system and the organization's perceived organizational support of the textile industry was found to be directly mediated by the employee's work attitude, as indicated by the results, which also showed an effect of the employee's psychological intrinsic reward system on affects as a mediating variable, 0.70 for employee work attitude (p less than 1%) and a overall effect mediated by employee work attitude of 0.70 (p less than 1%). However, since $p > 0.001$, p was determined to be 0.51, and RL behavior was shown to be a mediator among RW and EW rather than RW and EOPS. As seen in Figure 4, this circumstance is regarded as parallel mediation.

Figure 4. Serial mediation (AMOS Output, 2024)

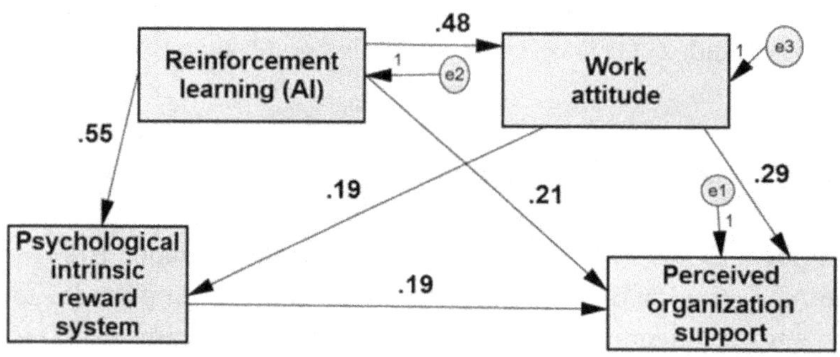

A mediation impact of the employee's work attitude at a significance level of 0.05 is 0.70 on the employee's psychological intrinsic reward system and organizational perceived organizational support, according to the results of the Structure

Equation Modelling (SEM), as illustrated by Figure 4. The cumulative direct effect was determined to be 0.48, or the total effect. Additionally, the association among the employee's perceived organizational support for the textile sector and their psychological intrinsic reward system is represented by the subsidiary influence of 0.69 at precision of 0.05, which also reflects the employee's work attitude. The overall impact is 0.69. Behavior of dependent variable or the dependent variable's behavior as described by the Table 5 presence mediator predictor of Mediation Analysis as shown in figure 4.

CONCLUSION

The main objective of the study was to ascertain the role that a staff member's job mindset played as a mediator between their emotional intrinsic incentive system and their impression of the company's support. Based on the analysis of data using AMOS software, it was demonstrated that, in the event that an employee's work attitude did not function as a mediator, the association between the psychological inherent reward system and the sense of supportive environment of the organization is very fragile in the form of a standardized govern influence; instead, it is quite potent in the form of an uniform total impact when worker attitude is present as an intermediary factor.

A bootstrapping test was used to assess the mediation's significance in statistics. The findings of both studies showed that staff work attitude acts as a mediator in the relationship among cognitive fundamental incentive system and perceived support from organizations for the clothing industry. It was discovered that the workers' work attitudes entirely mitigate this connection. Therefore, it can be concluded that the link under investigation is entirely mediated by the worker's employment attitude, which acts as a mediator between the person's behavioral intrinsic motivation and the perception of institutional backing inside the company.

DISCUSSION

This is a more thorough explanation of the potential applications of artificial intelligence (AI) in rewarding workers in Ethiopian garment manufacturers, along with some background information and possible issues. Artificial intelligence (AI) technologies have the potential to autonomously monitor and assess worker productivity, output quality, and other critical variables in Ethiopian garment manufacturers. Based on each employee's performance, these systems might then utilize algorithms to determine what incentives and prizes are acceptable for them. The

AI would quantify each worker's contribution objectively by analyzing data from cameras, sensors, and other sources.

The objective would be to establish a more equitable and open procedure for employee compensation by utilizing AI to manage a rewards program. In order to calculate incentives, the AI may consider a wide range of parameters, which would assist to minimize human biases or partiality. Employees may be eligible for bonuses, promotions, or other rewards purely on the basis of their individual performance and merits. Although it draws on previous automation and computerization initiatives in the industry, the application of AI in textile manufacturing is a relatively recent development. Early worries included the possibility of employment losses as robots and artificial intelligence replace some manual labor. Concerns have also been raised concerning the possibility that AI systems would treat and reward employees in an unfair or prejudiced manner.

Proponents counter that by offering transparent, impartial measures for assessment and reward, AI may actually empower workers. When implemented carefully, the AI-driven incentives system may encourage the improvement of skills, boost employee satisfaction, and keep the manufacturers competitive. Ensuring that the incentives are allocated equally would need rigorous testing and monitoring of the AI systems. The final result of AI in Ethiopian garment manufacturers will rely on how the technology is developed and implemented. AI-powered incentives programs have the ability to improve equity and inspire employees in the workplace with the correct safety measures and worker involvement. However, issues with worker privacy, algorithmic bias, and job security must be handled carefully.

LIMITATIONS AND FUTURE DIRECTIONS

The complicated nature of the suggested model, which includes several mediating and interacting factors, may be one of its main weaknesses. Given that work attitude, intrinsic reward, AI-based generative reinforcement learning (GRL), and perceived organizational support are all likely impacted by a variety of contextual and individual variables, it may be difficult to establish definitive causal links among these dimensions. Furthermore, these characteristics may not be easily measured or operationalized. Sophisticated evaluation instruments and procedures may be necessary to accurately capture the subtleties of work attitude, intrinsic pleasure, and perceived organizational support. If these measurement issues are not resolved, the study's findings may lose their validity and reliability.

The results' potential for generalization might be another flaw. The corporate setting, culture, and execution of the GRL system may have a substantial impact on how well GRL changes employee attitudes. If these contextual considerations are not taken into consideration, the study's relevance to a wider range of organizational contexts may be limited. Notwithstanding these possible drawbacks, the suggested study may substantially advance our knowledge of generative AI and its uses in organizational behavior. If the study is effective in illustrating how GRL might affect employee attitudes and perceptions, it may pave the way for the future integration of cutting-edge AI technology with established frameworks from organizational psychology.

Results like these may have a big impact on employee motivation, engagement, and perceived support—all of which are vital for a successful business. Further methodological insights into the planning and execution of GRL-based interventions in organizational contexts may be provided by the study, which might influence future investigations and real-world implementations. Generally, if the research design and methodology are sound and sufficiently address the complex issues inherent in the proposed model, the investigation's potential benefits to the knowledge about generative AI and its potential uses in the organizational context are encouraging, even though it is challenging to evaluate the chapter's specific weaknesses without access to the full research.

REFERENCES

Adula, M., & Kant, S. (2022). Interpretative Phenomenological Perceptional Study of Women Entrepreneurs Facing Challenges in Entrepreneurial Activity in the Horn of Africa. *Journal of Entrepreneurship, Management, and Innovation*, 4(2), 321–335.

Adula, M., Kant, S., & Birbirsa, Z. A. (2022). Systematic Literature Review on Human Resource Management Effect on Organization Perceived organizational support. *Annals of Human Resource Management Research*, 2(2), 131–146.

Adula, M., Kant, S., & Birbirsa, Z. A. (2023). Qualitative Analysis with MAXQDA Approach: HRM Practices effect on Organization Perceived organizational support with Mediation of Employee Work Attitude in Textile Industries of Ethiopia. *Advanced Qualitative Research*, 1(1), 1–14.

Al-Awar, M. S., Al-Habeet, A., & Gafer, A., Al-Amery, B., Edrees, W. H., & Al-Asbahi, A. (2022). Job satisfaction at clinical laboratories in Sana'a hospitals, Yemen, using the application of Herzberg's two-factor theory of motivation. *Al- Razi University. Journal for Medical Sciences*, 6(1).

Danilwan, Y., & Dirhamsyah, I. P. (2022). The Impact of The Psychological intrinsic reward on The Organizational Perceived organizational support: Does Ethical Climate Matter? *Journal of Positive School Psychology*, 6(3), 1–16.

Dhir, S., & Chakraborty, T. (2021). Does the perceived efficiency of the HR department matter in influencing satisfaction and employee perceived organizational support? *International Journal of Productivity and Perceived organizational support Management*, (ahead-of-print).

Elita, Y., & Sinthia, R. (2021). Knowledge Sharing Behavior Reviewed From a Social Exchange Perspective. *International Conference on Educational Sciences and Teacher Profession (ICETeP 2020)* (pp. 509-512). Atlantis Press.

Emmanuel, N., & Nwuzor, J. (2021). Employee and Organizational Perceived organizational support: Employees Perception of Intrinsic and Extrinsic Psychological intrinsic rewards System. *Applied Journal of Economics. Management and Social Sciences*, 2(1), 26–32.

Hao, J., Zhang, G., Liu, W., Zou, H., & Wang, Y. (2022). Autotune control algorithm based on relay feedback and adaptive neural network for attitude tracking of nonlinear AUG system. *Ocean Engineering*, 250, 111051.

Ismael, F., Hussein, B., Ibrahim, M. S., & Akoye, S. (2022). The mediation role of organization citizenship behavior among employee motivation and productivity: Analysis of Pharmaceutical Industries in KRG. *International Journal of Humanities and Education Development*, 4(1), 10–22.

Junça Silva, A., & Coelho, N. (2022). The moderating role of organizational culture on the association among workers' attitudes towards telework and happiness. *Kybernetes*.

Kant, S., Belay, B., & Dabaso, A. (2023). Coffee Logistics Operation Knowledge Effect on Cooperative Associations Functionalism in Ethiopia with Mediation of Cybernetics and Local People Knowledge Base. *Journal of Production, Operations Management and Economics, 3*(1), 21-33.

Kassa, A. G., & Tsigu, G. T. (2022). Corporate entrepreneurship, employee engagement and innovation: A resource-based view and a social exchange theory perspective. *The International Journal of Organizational Analysis*, 30(6), 1694–1711.

Mbebeb, F. E., & Tanyi, F. B. B. (2019). Alternative Options In Building Workers' incentives: Effects On Job Satisfaction And Perceived Organizational Support In Local Context. *Global Journal of Human Resource Management*, 7(2), 38–53.

Naser, M. Z. (2021). An engineer's guide to eXplainable Artificial Intelligence and Interpretable Machine Learning: Navigating causality, forced goodness, and the false perception of inference. *Automation in Construction*, 129, 103821.

Neudert, L. M., Knuutila, A., & Howard, P. N. (2020). *Global attitudes towards AI, machine learning & automated decision making*. Working paper 2020.10, Oxford Commission on AI & Good Governance.

Panch, T., Szolovits, P., & Atun, R. (2018). Artificial intelligence, machine learning and health systems. *Journal of Global Health*, 8(2).

Peponi, A., Morgado, P., & Kumble, P. (2022). Life cycle thinking and machine learning for urban metabolism assessment and prediction. *Sustainable Cities and Society*, 80, 103754.

Ramachandran, K. K., Mary, A. A. S., Hawladar, S., Asokk, D., Bhaskar, B., & Pitroda, J. R. (2022). Machine learning and role of artificial intelligence in optimizing work perceived organizational support and employee behavior. *Materials Today: Proceedings*, 51, 2327–2331.

Rudra Kumar, M., & Gunjan, V. K. (2022, May). Machine Learning Based Solutions for Human Resource Systems Management. In *ICCCE 2021: Proceedings of the 4th International Conference on Communications and Cyber Physical Engineering* (pp. 1239-1249). Singapore: Springer Nature Singapore.

Seeck, H., & Diehl, M. R. (2017). A literature review on HRM and innovation–taking stock and future directions. *International Journal of Human Resource Management*, 28(6), 913–944.

Shaw, J. D. (2021). The resource-based view and its use in strategic human resource management research: The elegant and inglorious. *Journal of Management*, 47(7), 1787–1795.

Stergiou, D. P. (2022). *Social Exchange Theory. Encyclopedia of Tourism Management and Marketing*. Edward Elgar Publishing.

Tufa, G., Kant, S., & Dinber, G. N. (2023). Meta- Analysis: Qualitative Review of Human Resource Management Studies. *Advanced Qualitative Research*, 1(1), 42–62.

Verma, A., Lamsal, K., & Verma, P. (2022). An investigation of skill requirements in artificial intelligence and machine learning job advertisements. *Industry and Higher Education*, 36(1), 63–73.

Wakjira, G. G., & Kant, S. (2022). Significance of Market Orientation on Business Perceived organizational support With Mediating Role of Employee And Customer Satisfaction In Ethiopia Banks. *Partners Universal International Research Journal*, 1(4), 118–125.

Widarko, A., & Anwarodin, M. K. (2022). Work Motivation and Organizational Culture on Work Perceived organizational support: Organizational Citizenship Behavior (OCB) as Mediating Variable. *Golden Ratio of Human Resource Management*, 2(2), 123–138.

Xia, H., Wang, Y., Jasimuddin, S., Zhang, J. Z., & Thomas, A. (2022). A big-data-driven matching model based on deep Generative re-enforcement learning (GRL) for cotton blending. *International Journal of Production Research*, 1–19.

KEY TERMS AND DEFINITIONS

AI-Based Solutions: Technological approaches that meet a range of goals or issues by utilizing machine learning capabilities.

Artificial Intelligence (AI): The subject of research concentrated on building robots or systems that are capable of learning, solving problems, making decisions, and perceiving—tasks that normally require intellect from humans.

Cognitive: Having to do with or pertaining to perception, recall, evaluation, and logic as cognitive processes.

Generative AI: Artificial intelligence (AI) algorithms that, using their training information and supporting models, can produce new text, picture, or voice material.

Generative Model: A kind of predictive model that goes beyond simple classification or prediction to produce fresh data samples that resemble the set used for training.

Generative Re-Enforcement Learning: Parametric reinforcement learning combined with algorithmic learning to allow agents to learn and produce novel actions or responses.

Innovation: The procedure of bringing in fresh or enhanced goods, services, methods, or concepts that benefit a company or its customer base.

Intrinsic Reward: Self-satisfying or internally generated benefits, including a feeling of development or achievement, as opposed to incentives or rewards from outside sources.

Machine Learning: A branch of machine learning that allows systems—without intentional programming—to train and consequently become better over time.

Organization's Capacity: The potential of a group to use assets and skills together to accomplish objectives in an efficient manner.

Perceived Organizational Support: The conviction among workers that their supervisor appreciates their work and is concerned regarding their welfare.

Work Attitude: Someone's general attitude, sentiments, and convictions regarding their employment or workplace.

Chapter 5
AI Learning and Work Attitude Mediation Between Reward and Organizational Support in Ethiopia

Shashi Kant
https://orcid.org/0000-0003-4722-5736
Bule Hora University, Ethiopia

Metasebia Adula
https://orcid.org/0000-0001-5732-2850
Bule Hora University, Ethiopia

ABSTRACT

The chapter's main focus was to analyze the mediator role of employee work attitude and AI-based re-enforcement learning in between employee psychological intrinsic reward system and organization perceived organizational support in context of Ethiopia. Study area was selected as textile industries working in industrial park of Ethiopia on the basis of their contribution to the GDP of the economy. Explanatory research design and quantitative research approach were used. A multistage sampling technique was implied. With AMOS software, exploratory confirmatory analysis was conducted to measure discriminate and convergent validity. It was found that in absence of AI-based re-enforcement learning and employee work attitude as a mediator relation between employee psychological intrinsic reward system and organization perceived organizational support was very weak. Therefore, employee work attitude and reinforcement learning (AI) behave like full mediators between

DOI: 10.4018/979-8-3693-5578-7.ch005

psychological intrinsic reward and organization perceived organizational.

INTRODUCTION

Psychological intrinsic reward systems have a major effect on reinforcement learning (AI) and organization's ability to acquire, retain and motivate high potential employee's and ultimately getting the higher levels of perceived organizational support (Panch et. al., 2018). Extrinsic psychological intrinsic reward system effected the employee commitment and its extent varies according to the level of reinforcement learning (AI) (Danilwan & Dirhamsyah, 2022). It seems vary widely with the individual and industry (Kassa & Tsigu, 2022). Both intrinsic and extrinsic reward system psychologically provides a systematic way to deliver positive consequences in form of reinforcement learning (AI) (Adula et. al., 2022; Seeck et. al., 2017). It gives mutual benefit for both employer and employee's (Naser, 2021). In generally psychological intrinsic reward systems influences the both employee's work attitude and reinforcement learning (AI); and both influenced the organizational perceived organizational support (Peponi et. al., 2022; Mbebeb & Tanyi, 2019).

Employee psychological intrinsic reward system improves employee attitude, reinforcement learning (AI), commitment and all it leads to employee affective committed behavior (Kant et. al., 2023; Verma et al., 2022). If employees enjoy their work because of presence of reinforcement learning (AI), they feel more confident in their abilities to succeed in the tasks assigned, and appreciate the role they are assigned, they are far more likely to have a positive attitude in the Poor employee attitudes and address attitude problems such as negativity and laziness (Al-Awar et. a., 2022).

Studies manifested that, in the context of African countries, especially in Ethiopia organization support is very weakly practiced therefore employees not able to attach with the organization (Elita & Sinthia, 2021). Therefore work attitude not able to develop in Ethiopia industries in spite of better implementation of human resource practices (Kassa & Tsigu, 2022). When researchers were find the reason behind that they found the ground level reality. The problem was intrinsic reward was not compatible with efforts. Therefore they are not able to attach psychologically with the organization. Dissatisfaction, alienation and turnover rate is increasing day by day; that leads to decreasing organization growth and disinterest in psychological organizational learning (Seeck et. al., 2017). If psychological organizational learning needs to improve, it should be assimilated with psychological intrinsic reward (Adula et. a., 2023).

Most of times; it will be difficult to provide psychological intrinsic rewards in the physical terms (Shaw, 2021). But adoption of new technology helps work to increase their efficiency and helps to bargain their efforts and to get better work (Naser, 2021). It was founded that reward leads to learning. Stimulus leads to resource truly works as founded by S-R theory of Edward Thorndike (Mbebeb & Tanyi, 2019). Therefore psychological intrinsic rewards if provided to employees their cognitive reinforcement learning will be augmented (Kassa & Tsigu, 2022). Also studies depicted that; to take cognitive reinforcement learning to its maximum level Artificial learning (AI) is the major determinant used by the innovation based industries (Emmanuel & Nwuzor, 2021). Therefore present study investigated the role of work attitude and AI based reinforcement learning augmented the effect of psychological intrinsic reward towards employees perceived organizational support in textile industries working in industrial park of Ethiopia. Textile industries working in industrial park of Ethiopia were selected because they are based on technology and largest contributors to GDP in the study area.

By creating a solid theoretical basis through meta-analysis, the chapter stressed the significance of incorporating pertinent theoretical frameworks and models offered in the next section, "theoretical contribution." It examined and analysed the theories that have been proposed that are relevant to the study of AI learning and work attitudes in Ethiopia, including theories of motivation, organisational behaviour, and human resource management. The chapter created a strong theoretical framework by outlining the study's theoretical foundations and how they relate to the research questions and hypotheses.

The literature on AI learning, work attitude mediation, incentive systems, and organizational support in Ethiopia was critically examined in this chapter. It pointed out shortcomings, contradictions, and gaps in the state of the art and study findings. Contextual elements specific to Ethiopia that might affect the connections between AI learning, work attitudes, incentive structures, and organizational support were analyzed. These gaps and restrictions have the effect of identifying areas in need of more study and advancement in the subject.

The chapter included suggestions for more study in order to make a more significant contribution to the body of current scholarship. These suggestions, which attempt to fill in the gaps and overcome the limits found, are predicated on a critical review of the literature. Some recommendations may be to look at how Ethiopian culture affects AI learning and work attitudes, or to look into the long-term effects of AI learning on staff engagement and motivation. Other ideas would be to look into the efficacy of certain reward programmers and organizational support systems. The chapter also included research tools or methodologies, such mixed-methods studies and longitudinal study designs that can offer a more thorough grasp of the subject.

Thus, the chapter strengthens its theoretical foundation and adds more significantly to the body of knowledge on AI learning and work attitude mediation between reward and organizational support in Ethiopia by improving organizational clarity, theoretical integration, critical analysis, and recommendations for future research.

THEORETICAL CONTRIBUTION

Strategic question "Is psychological intrinsic reward augment the employees perceived organizational support when mediated by work attitude and AI based re-enforcement learning in Ethiopia" is theoretically investigated using a framework built on Two factor Theory; Resource based view, Social Exchange theory and a study of the literature on employees perceived organizational support; AI based re-enforcement learning; psychological intrinsic reward, and work attitude. Psychological intrinsic reward is the independent variable in this theoretical framework, and employees perceived organizational support is the dependent variable. Additionally, while work attitude and AI based re-enforcement learning mediated the association among Psychological intrinsic reward and employee's perceived organizational support. In table 1, Meta analysis of theories is presented. The growth of investigate scheme based on the proxies in present investigation is discussed in the Table 1.

Table 1. Meta Analysis of Theory

	Theory	Based Studies	Contribution of theory	Variable extracted
1	Two factor Theory (Herzberg 1959)	Emmanuel & Nwuzor, 2021; Al-Awar et. a., 2022; Kassa & Tsigu, 2022	Intrinsic psychological intrinsic reward comes from the work attitude.	Psychological intrinsic reward system
2	Resource based view (Penrose, 1959)	Verma et al., 2022; Panch et. al., 2018	Psychological intrinsic rewarding system is improving performance.	Psychological intrinsic reward; organizational support
3	RBV (Wernerfelt, 1984)	Naser, 2021; Kassa & Tsigu, 2022	Focus on external environment.	psychological intrinsic reward system
4	RBV (Barney, 1991)	Mbebeb & Tanyi, 2019; Shaw, 2021	VRIO is an Internal resource.	Psychological intrinsic reward; work attitude
5	Social Exchange theory (Homans, 1958)	Naser, 2021, Al-Awar et. a., 2022	Social behavior as exchange	Employee's work attitude

Source: Researchers Meta-Analysis (2023)

Historical development of Concept of Psychological intrinsic reward System was presented in Table 2 in form of Meta analysis of Psychological intrinsic reward System.

Table 2. Meta analysis of Concept of Psychological intrinsic reward System

	Author(s)	Definition
1	Smyth (1968)	Employees who act in the preferred organizational manner will get psychological intrinsic reward in form of recognition.
2	Bishop (1987)	Explained that pay relates to productivity and psychological intrinsic reward system relate to size of the firm. Psychological intrinsic rewards.
3	Bowen & Radhakrishna (1991)	Employee psychological intrinsic reward system can be designed by include job enlargement, job enrichment, in employee.
4	Ajila (1997)	Extrinsic cost and or receive external psychological intrinsic rewards for job.
5	Bartol (1999)	Compensation for their employees, behavior oriented or outcome-oriented
6	White & Drucker (2000)	Psychological intrinsic reward systems are comprised psychological intrinsic rewards.
7	Jacobsen & Thorsvik (2002)	Employees will be penalized or no psychological intrinsic reward was distributed.

Source: Researchers Meta-Analysis (2023)

EMPIRICAL LITERATURE REVIEW

Psychological Intrinsic Reward System and Organizational Perceived Organizational Support

Psychological intrinsic reward system is linked to the perceived organizational support of the organization and has an influence on their behavior and well-being, which can lead to good organizational results and good perceived organizational support (Panch et. al., 2018). Organizations that emphasize employee's psychological intrinsic reward systems increase job satisfaction, which translates into better individual and team results (Ramachandran et. al., 2022; Adula & Kant, 2022). Researchers in previous studies have argued that there is a positive relationship between employee psychological intrinsic reward system and organizational perceived organizational support (Verma et al., 2022). Howeever, some scholars was concluded that employee psychological intrinsic reward system and organization perceived organizational support have insignificant relationship (Naser, 2021). So, in order to check this inconclusive idea, the researcher used SEM analysis test the theory either this theory have significant relationship or not. This study fills the knowledge gap of inconclusive idea.

The association between perceived organizational support and psychological intrinsic rewards has been the subject of several researches in the larger body of literature (Kant et al., 2023; Verma et al., 2022; Naser, 2021, Al-Awar et al., 2022). The majority of these investigations point to a favorable correlation between the two constructs. Workers are more likely to feel supported by their company if they believe that it values and rewards their intrinsic motivations. Consequently, better performance, greater levels of commitment, and work satisfaction may result from this sense of organizational support.

The social exchange theory is one theoretical framework that aids in the explanation of this interaction. This idea holds that mutual duties and trust form the basis of a reciprocal connection between employees and their organization (Naser, 2021, Al-Awar et. a., 2022). Employees believe their company is meeting their own needs and promoting their self-actualization when they receive psychological intrinsic incentives. Because people feel their organisation cares about their growth and well-being, this view enhances their sense of organizational support.

H1: There Is a Significant Relationship Between Employee's Psychological Intrinsic Reward System and Organization Perceived Organizational Support

Table 3. Effect Size of Work Attitude Studies

	Study name	Partial Correl ation	CI Lo wer	CI Up per	Weight %
	Emmanuel & Nwuzor, 2021	0.36	0.1	0.5	6.8
	Gheitani et.al., 2018	0.78	0.6	0.9	9.5
	Anwar; 2021	0.64	0.2	1.0	2.0
	Pang & Lu, 2018	0.68	0.6	0.7	20.5
	Hoque et al., 2018	0.65	0.5	0.7	19.6
	Hee & Jing, 2018	0.65	0.5	0.7	20.4
	Al-Ali et al., 2019	0.69	0.6	0.7	20.9

Source: Meta Essential Output (2023)

Figure 1. Forest Plot

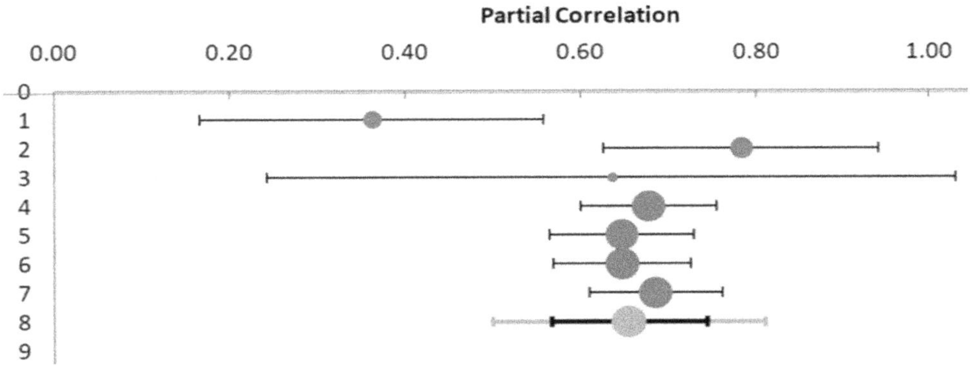

Source: Meta Essential Output (2023)

In Figure 1; *combined* effect of most recent seven used studies founded as 0.67, which indicated a moderate to a strong effect size with a Z-value of 18.21 that founded as significant at one tailed p-value less than 0.05 as shown in Table 3:

Table 4. Heterogeneity

Q	**12.09**
P_Q	0.060
I^2	50.35%
T^2	0.00
T	0.05
Trim and Fill	**On**
Estimator for missing studies	Linear
Search from mean	Left
Number of imputed studies	0

Source: Meta Essential Output (2023)

Drawn forest plot in Figure 1; depicted that apart from one study other 6 studies concentrated on the upper part of the funnel; it depicted heterogeneity in Table 4 used studies. Also I^2 (50.35%) manifested a large value. Therefore no publication bias founded in used seven studies.

Psychological Intrinsic Reward System and Employee's Work Attitude

Financial and non-financial incentives stimulate employee's work attitude and have continuous relationship (Panch et. al., 2018). Industries offer finical psychological intrinsic rewards to enhance employee's work attitude and increase industry perceived organizational support (Wakjira & Kant, 2022). Many organizations enhance employee's work attitude by financial psychological intrinsic reward system of industry through "bonus; profit sharing; wage incentive; extra allowances" (Shaw, 2021). According to researcher arguments psychological intrinsic reward system of the manufacturing industry has a positive and significant relationship with employee's work attitude (Seeck et. al., 2017). Scholar suggested that employee's attitude is more relay with employee's expectation that means expect from their industry to appreciate their job perceived organizational support though difference financial psychological intrinsic reward system (Emmanuel & Nwuzor, 2021). If industry meet employee's expectations, they remain committed, involved and fill industry as their home to their work and do not think about moving to other industry (Hao el. Al., 2022).

Therefore, it results in pushing factors of highly commitment, engagement and belongingness of employee's necessary for sustainable growth, reputability of the industry (Naser, 2021). However, some scholars was conclude employee psychological intrinsic reward system and employee's work attitude have insignificant relationship (Mbebeb & Tanyi, 2019); so in order to check this inconclusive idea the researcher used SEM analysis test the theory either this theories have significant relationship or not. This study fills the knowledge gap of inconclusive idea.

The total job happiness of employees is substantially influenced by psychological intrinsic incentives. People are more likely to report greater levels of job satisfaction when they believe their employment to be intrinsically fulfilling, pleasurable, and consistent with their beliefs (Emmanuel & Nwuzor, 2021). Sense of autonomy, mastery, and purpose that is fostered by intrinsic incentives increases workers' motivation and engagement at work. People are more likely to be self-driven, passionate, and committed to their work when they are genuinely motivated (Shaw, 2021).

Workers that experience psychological intrinsic pleasures in their jobs tend to become more devoted and committed to the company. They relate to the organization's objectives, principles, and mission on a deeper level (Dhir & Chakraborty, 2021).

H2: There Is a Significant Positive Relationship Between Psychological Intrinsic Reward System and Employee's Work Attitude

Employee Work Attitude and Organizational Perceived Organizational Support

Literature has extensively described employee work attitude results in achievement of goals and effectiveness in operations which influence organizational success and productivity (Widarko & Anwarodin, 2022; Adula et. al., 2022). There is a direct connection between employee's work attitude like commitment, involvement and organizational citizenship behavior brings employee satisfaction (Al-Awar et. a., 2022). Accordingly, employee work attitude represents employee sincerity to assist the company to accomplish its goals (Dhir & Chakraborty, 2021). Lot of studies studied a set of employee's work attitude determinants and their impact on affective, continuance and normative commitment as well as employee involvement and organizational citizen ship of textile industries employee (Panch et. al., 2018).

Belonging to employee's work attitude and organization perceived organizational support referred to department of it, further it refers as attachment towards organizational perceived organizational support (Verma et al., 2022). Component Model of Organizational work attitude claims that employees desire to attach themselves with their workplace and industry as a need for commitment, involvement and organizational citizenship behaviors (Kassa & Tsigu, 2022). Employee work attitude is one who stays with organization through attends work regularly, puts in a full day (and maybe more), protects company assets, goals, and so on (Ismael et. al., 2022; Seeck et. al., 2017). In a nutshell, there are various studies that have been conducted in different industries and countries on employee's work attitude and its effect on organizational perceived organizational support and findings found to be inconclusive as described in the earlier portion of the current study.

In the horn of Africa context, studies of various researchers including examined the relation of employee's work attitude and organizational perceived organizational support in the textile industry (Naser, 2021). The studies included various constructs to be examined in the textile industry of the Ethiopia in the horn of Africa region which considered motivation, financial perceived organizational support and employee's satisfaction for examining perceived organizational support of textile industries and operators (Junça Silva & Coelho, 2022).

Studies stated that human resource management practices significantly influenced perceived organizational support of textile in the Ethiopian context (Dhir & Chakraborty, 2021). The examination of association between human resource management practices, work attitude, and perceived organizational support of textile was investigated and found a positive relation between these stated constructs in the study by (Shaw, 2021). The examination of association between employee's work attitude and perceived organizational support of organization was investigated and found a negative relation (Emmanuel & Nwuzor, 2021). The researcher has not come across any study that examines the relationship between employee's work attitude and organization perceived organizational support of Ethiopian textile industry in the Southern Africa region.

H3: There Is a Significant Positive Relationship Between Employee's Work Attitude and Organizational Perceived Organizational Support

Mediating Role of Employee's Work Attitude in Between Employee Psychological Intrinsic Reward System and Organizational Perceived Organizational Support

Employee decisions in the workplace are strongly influenced by the organization's psychological intrinsic reward system in exchange for their job perceived organizational support (Dhir & Chakraborty, 2021). An effective psychological intrinsic reward system helps an organization gain a competitive advantage by retaining experienced employees (Mbebeb & Tanyi, 2019).; found psychological intrinsic reward system is an important tool in improving employee's motivation and behavior to provide quality and to support employees for performing better at the workplace (Shaw, 2021). The psychological intrinsic reward system has been study in manufacturing industry, textile industry and food manufacturing industry make employees motivate and bring behavioral change (Stergiou, 2022).

In manufacturing and, service sector psychological intrinsic reward system as a strong and positive behavior change tools of employee's and important mechanism of job accomplishment of both (Danilwan & Dirhamsyah, 2022). Scholars have argued that the psychological intrinsic reward system is consistent with organizational goals therefore, these things create employee motivation and task accompaniment leads to job satisfaction (Naser, 2021).

H4: Mediating Role of Employee's Work Attitude Positive and Statistically Significant Relationship Between Employee Psychological intrinsic Reward System and Organizational Perceived Organizational Support

Employee Psychological Intrinsic Reward System and Reinforcement Learning (AI)

The field of machine learning known as reinforcement learning (RL) studies showed how intelligent agents should behave in a given environment to maximise the concept of cumulative reward (Neudert et. al., 2020). Along with supervised learning and unsupervised learning, reinforcement learning is one of the three fundamental machine learning paradigms (Verma et al., 2022).

In contrast to supervised learning, reinforcement learning does not need the presentation of labelled input/output pairings or the explicit correction of suboptimal actions (Danilwan & Dirhamsyah, 2022). Instead, the emphasis is on striking a balance between utilisation of existing knowledge and exploration of unexplored terrain (Kassa & Tsigu, 2022). In order to maximise the "reward function" or other user-provided reinforcement signal that builds up from the immediate rewards, the agent uses reinforcement learning to develop an optimal or nearly optimal policy. Similar processes seem to take place in animal psychology (Dhir & Chakraborty, 2021). Biological brains, for instance, are designed to perceive signals like pain and hunger as negative reinforcements and pleasure and food intake as positive reinforcements (Shaw, 2021).

Animals can learn to adopt behaviours that maximise these rewards in certain situations (Elita & Sinthia, 2021). This shows that animals are able to learn through reinforcement. Reinforcement learning, a subfield of artificial intelligence (AI) that enables agents to learn from their own actions and feedback, relies heavily on a reward function (Al-Awar et. a., 2022). A reward function affects the agent's behaviour and learning by defining the objective and providing feedback. The agent in reinforcement learning is rewarded for making decisions that result in successful states (Stergiou, 2022). Rewards can be given straight away, such as obtaining a point for each positive action, or they can be given later, such as receiving a point at the conclusion of the episode if the objective was accomplished (Elita & Sinthia, 2021).

Developers provide a way of rewarding desired behaviours and penalising undesirable behaviours in reinforcement learning (Mbebeb & Tanyi, 2019). This approach gives desired behaviours positive values in order to motivate the agent to engage in them, while undesirable behaviours are given negative values in order to deter them (Danilwan & Dirhamsyah, 2022).

H5: There Is a Significant Positive Relationship Between Employee Psychological Intrinsic Reward System and Reinforcement Learning (AI)

Reinforcement Learning (AI) and Employee Perceived Organizational Support

Organisations may now boost employee engagement for both onsite and remote workers in a number of ways thanks to AI based systems (Naser, 2021), including by offering round-the-clock support, real-time performance monitoring, learning and development, and conflict resolution (Mbebeb & Tanyi, 2019). Organisations may make better decisions in a variety of areas, including as strategy, marketing, and operations, by taking advantage of AI's capacity to process enormous volumes of data and produce insightful learning (Kassa & Tsigu, 2022). By introducing people to numerous levers of success like efficacy in decision making and learning, collaboration, experimentation, and information sharing, AI assists organisations in being very successful in inspiring their employees and encouraging employee engagement (Verma et al., 2022).

By adapting products and systems to the unique requirements and preferences of each user, AI-driven personalization and adaptation can increase productivity (Dhir & Chakraborty, 2021). One such is AI-powered adaptive learning systems, which can assess a worker's prior knowledge and preferred learning methods to develop specialised training courses (Neudert et. al., 2020). Logically, when the reward when employed by the agent for its learning in its environment, it maximizes their perception towards the support provided by the organization (Shaw, 2021).

A machine learning training method called reinforcement learning rewards desired behaviours and penalises undesirable ones (Stergiou, 2022).The creature being trained, known as a reinforcement learning agent, is often capable of perceiving and interpreting its environment, acting accordingly, and learning through mistakes (Elita & Sinthia, 2021). Overall, the findings show that rewards do not lessen intrinsic motivation (Al-Awar et. a., 2022). Verbal praise increases intrinsic motivation, according to research that looks at interaction effects (Adula et. al., 2022). When people receive anticipated tangible incentives merely for performing a task, this has a negative impact alone (Adula et. al., 2022).

H6: There Is a Significant Positive Relationship Between Reinforcement Learning (AI) and Employee Perceived Organizational Support

Mediating Role of Reinforcement Learning (AI) in Between Employee Psychological intrinsic Reward System and Employee Perceived Organizational Support

Attractive and high-salaried, promotion and reinforcement learning (AI) were satisfied and create employee's engagement and motivation that show influence on industry perceived organizational support (Kassa & Tsigu, 2022). On the contrary, the studies conducted to examining influence of reinforcement learning (AI) on organizational found insignificant (Shaw, 2021), but reinforcement learning (AI) found to be important in delivering outstanding on organizational perceived organizational support. Reinforcement learning (AI) motivates employee's in return of their efforts to enrich and develop their quality product and management in return gain employee's satisfaction (Dhir & Chakraborty, 2021).

Management of reinforcement learning (AI) in textile industry and handle employee's behavior in not an easy task for organization, so industry must acknowledge effective psychological intrinsic rewards (Al-Awar et. a., 2022). Therefore, textile industry must initiate effective psychological intrinsic rewards system to gain their reinforcement learning (AI) and organizational perceived organizational support (Stergiou, 2022). At the work environment, reinforcement learning (AI) can have the greatest impact on employee behavior. The positive reinforcement learning (AI) of the employee at work creates in the employee's mind the commitment, attachment to his job and working environment, more attachment to his job and creates positive behavior (Neudert et. al., 2020).

The current study intends to examine the mediating role of reinforcement learning (AI) between employees psychological intrinsic reward system and industry perceived organizational support in textile in horn Africa, Ethiopia (Mbebeb & Tanyi, 2019). Positive reinforcement learning (AI) brings employee commitment, attachment and involvement this important to the industry, as they influence organizational perceived organizational support (Verma et al., 2022). The direct link has been explored between reinforcement learning (AI) and organizational perceived organizational support in various countries including Pakistan, Vietnam, Ghana, Malaysia, and New Zealand Turkey (Neudert et. al., 2020). On the contrary, few study depicted insignificant relation between reinforcement learning (AI) and organizational perceived organizational support. So, in order to check this inconclusive idea, the researcher used SEM analysis to test the theory and to fills the knowledge gap of inconclusive idea.

H7: Mediating Role of Reinforcement Learning (AI) in Between Employee Psychological Intrinsic Reward System and Organizational Perceived Organizational Support

The growth of investigate Conceptual testing Framework in present investigation is discussed in the Figure 2.

Figure 2. Conceptual Framework

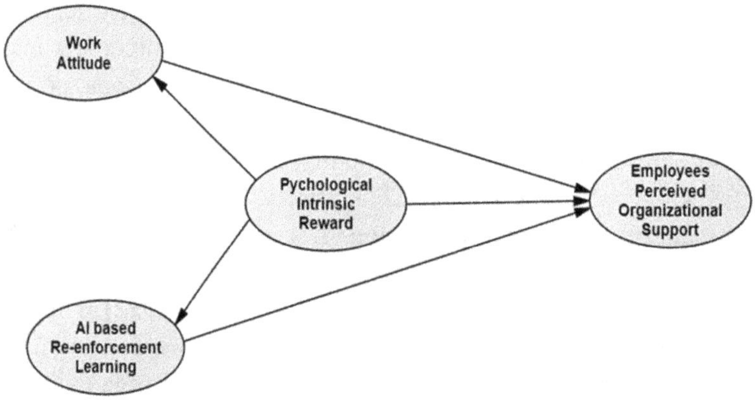

Source: Researchers own study model, 2023

RESEARCH PHILOSOPHY AND METHODOLOGY

Researchers applied the pragmatic paradigm in present research by use combination of ontology and epistemology approaches in form of pragmatism to gain insight into the stated research problem. The logic of pragmatic inquiry includes the use of induction (discovery of patterns), deduction (testing of theories and hypotheses), and abduction (uncovering and relying on the best of a set of explanations for understanding (Verma et al., 2022). Study employed quantitative research design. Since the research questions of this study requires the exploratory research approach.

TARGET POPULATION AND SAMPLING TECHNIQUE

This study was focused on public textiles and cloth industries available in Ethiopia. The ten public industrial parks in Ethiopia are namely; Hawasa Industrial Park, Mekelle Industrial Park, Knobloch Industrial Park, Adama Industrial Park, DBL Industrial Park in Mekelle, Debar Birahan Industrial Park, Jimma Industrial Park and Bahir Dar Industrial Park (Mbebeb & Tanyi, 2019).

In Ethiopia there are 10 public textile and cloth industries but inside these industries there are 28 (twenty-eight) different owner who manufacture textile and cloth. To get sufficient data researchers only selects those factories that have more than three years working experience. Thus, the sampling frame of the study was 24 (twenty-four) textile and cloth industry in 24 (twenty-four) industries with 46903 employees (Kassa & Tsigu, 2022).

Textile and cloth industry managers, Director of human resource manager, team leader and employers were selected randomly from each company. Once the questionnaire was prepared in English, it was translated into Ethiopia regional language Amharic and Afan Oromo.

SAMPLE SIZE DETERMINATION

The researchers employed Dillman sampling formula (2000) in order to determine the representative sample of the study and also used to minimize coverage error in the research survey. The sampling technique of the study was used the multi-stage sampling technique. At the first researchers used the purposive sampling to select government textile industries on the base of GTP-II plan to make Ethiopia a lower middle income country by 2025. At the second stage, stratified sampling was used that divides the population into homogeneous sub populations from a heterogeneous sample. The characteristics of the industry are heterogeneous so that researchers rely on stratified sampling to ensure that all characteristics in the sample was represented correctly. After that, the respondents were selected by the use of systematic sampling that involves selecting items from the list of employees using sampling intervals. This means that every "nth" data sample is selected from a large data set is the respondent.

$$n = [(N)\ (p)\ (1\text{-}p)] / [(N\text{-}1)]\ (B/C)^2 + (p)\ (1\text{-}p)]$$

$$n = (46903)\ (0.5)\ (1\text{-}0.5)] / [(46903\text{-}1)]\ (0.05/1.96)^2 + (0.5)\ (1\text{-}\ 0.5)] = 381$$

Thus, proportionate stratified method, the sample size of each stratum is proportionate to the population size of the stratum of textile and cloth industry illustrated on table 6 Sample Size.

Table 5. Sample Size

N O	Textile and cloth industry	Number of employees	Proportion n	Sample size
1	Hawass industry park	25,026	203	203
2	Adama industry park	3,598	29	29
3	Bole Lemi Industry park	16,111	131	131
	Total	**46903**	**363**	**363**

Source: AMOS Output, 2023

DATA ANALYSIS

Test for Reliability

The KMO measures the sampling adequacy which should be greater than 0.5 for a satisfactory factor analysis to accept and a value close to 1 indicates that patterns of correlations are relatively compact and so factor analysis yield distinct and reliable factors the measurement of KMO illustrated in Table 6.

Table 6. Bartlett's and KMO Test

Kaiser Meyer Olkin: Measure of data Adequacy		**.784**
Sphericity Test: Bartlett's	Chi- Square (Approx.)	1591.763
	Df	28
	Sig.	.000

Source: AMOS Output, 2023

The KMO measures the sampling adequacy which should be greater than 0.5 for a satisfactory factor analysis to accept and a value close to 1 indicates that patterns of correlations are relatively compact and so factor analysis yield distinct and reliable factors. For employee psychological intrinsic rewards have two factors recognition and motivation.

Convergent Validity

The degree to which different measures of a construct that theoretically should be connected are really related is known as convergent validity.

Table 7. Convergent validity

	Factor Loading	comu = (Load F^2)	1- LF^2
Psychological intrinsic reward	0.52	0.27	0.72
Work Attitude	0.58	0.34	0.65
Reinforcement Learning	0.51	0.26	0.73
Perceived organizational support	0.62	0.39	0.60
Total	2.24		2.72
a = sum of LF + (1-LF^2)			4.96
b= sum of LF			2.25
CR = (b/a)			**0.46**

Source: AMOS Output, 2023

Convergent validity result manifested that the items in given measure converged therefore they represented the underlying construct and convergent validity was established. The mean of the squared loadings of each indicator connected to a build was used to calculate the Average variance explained (AVE). When sum of LF (loading factors) was divided by LF + (1-LF^2); convergent validity was founded as 0.46. In terms of statistics, convergent validity is proven when the Average Variance Extracted (AVE) value is near to 0.50.

CONFIRMATORY FACTOR ANALYSIS

Confirmatory factor analysis is a statistical technique used to verify the factor structure of a set of observed variables (Tufa et. al., 2023). CFA also allows researchers to test hypotheses based on the relationships between observed variables underlying structure. CFA allows the researcher to test the hypothesis that a relationship between observed variables and their underlying latent constructs exists.

Figure 3 Confirmatory Factor Analysis

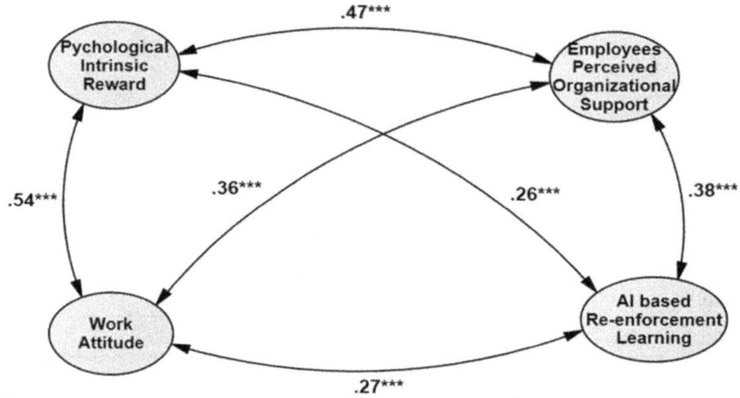

Source: AMOS Output, 2023

The first estimate displayed in figure 3 is the covariance employee perceived organization support and employee work attitude. The covariance is estimated to be 0.36 shows an observation on an approximately normally distributed random variable centered around the population covariance with a standard deviation of .029, that is, if the assumption in the section "distribution assumptions for Amos model the significant level of 0.05, any critical ration that exceeds 1.96 in magnitude would be significant. Estimate of standard error (S.E) of the covariance, .029 Critical Ratio is more than 1.96 at 0.05 significance level therefore covariance between variables existed.

Table 8. Convergent validity

			Estimate	S.E.	C.R.	P
EOPS	**<-->**	**EW**	**.23**	**.02**	**8.0**	***
ERW	<-->	EW	.27	.03	7.6	***
ERW	<-->	EOPS	.19	.02	7.4	***
ERW	<-->	RL	.22	.02	7.8	***
EOPS	<-->	RL	.25	.03	7.4	***

Source: AMOS Output, 2023

The first estimate displayed is the covariance ERW and EOPS. The covariance is estimated to be .275 shows an observation on an approximately normally distributed random variable centered around the population covariance with a standard deviation of .036, that is, if the assumption in the section distribution assumptions for Amos model the significant level of 0.05, any critical ration that exceeds 1.96 in magnitude would be significant. Estimate of standard error (S.E) of the covariance, .036 Critical Ration is more than 1.96 at 0.05 significance level their fore covariance between variables is significantly difference from zero.

The first estimate displayed is the covariance EOPS and employee work attitude. The covariance is estimated to be .0190 shows an observation on an approximately normally distributed random variable centered around the population covariance with a standard deviation of .026, that is, if the assumption in the section "distribution assumptions for Amos model the significant level of 0.05, any critical ration that exceeds 1.96 in magnitude would be significant. Estimate of standard error (S.E) of the covariance, .026 Critical Rations is more than 1.96 at 0.05 significance level therefore covariance between variables was significantly difference from zero.

DISCRIMINANT VALIDITY

Discriminant validity is demonstrated by evidence that measures of constructs that theoretically should not be highly related to each other are, in fact, not found to be highly correlated to each other. Practically speaking, discriminant validity coefficients should be noticeably smaller in magnitude than convergent validity coefficients the result shown under table correlation table 9.

Table 9. Total Variance Explained

Initial Eigen values		**Extraction Sums of Squared Loadings**		
Total	**% Variance**	**Total**	**% Variance**	**Cum %**
3.8	47.8	3.8	47.8	47.8
1.0	13.7	1.0	13.7	61.5
AVE			.615	
Ave square root			**0.784**	
Variables	**RW**	**WA**	**RL**	**EOPS**
RW	1			
WA	.33	1		
RL	.41	.45	1	
EOPS	.41	.32	.41	1

**. Correlation is significant at the 0.01 level (2- tailed).
Source: AMOS Output, 2023

Average Variance Explained (AVE) square root was founded was 0.784; which when compared to the corresponding correlation of other all variables; it found to be more than that. As we seen AVE (0.784) was more than correlation between RW,

WA, RL and EOPS. Therefore discriminate validity achieved because square root of AVE is more than other all correlation values.

Model Fit Indices

Figure 4. Educational Model

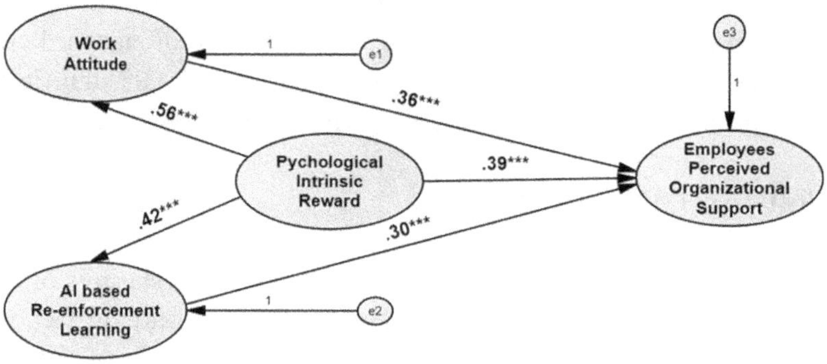

Source: AMOS Output, 2023

Table 10. Model Fit indices

P	CMIN/DF	GFI	CFI	TLI	RMSEA
0.4	3.08	0.97	0.93	0.96	.025

Source: AMOS Output, 2023

From the above table 10 and figure 4 result shows that CMIN/DF value is 3.080 which is at least or not more than 2 which indicates good model fit, root mean ofresidual.017 is less than 0.05, goodness fit indices 0.9753 greater than 0.95, comparative fit index 0.936 greater than 0.95 and root mean square error of approximation 0.025 less than 0.05. Therefore, the overall fit model is good. The value of interest here is the GFI for the default model, so main focus was on GFI. GFI is 0.973 that is more than 0.95 indicated that Goodness of Fit Index for the proposed Model.

Mediation Analysis

EOPS affected by ERW by 0.487. EW mediates in between ERW and EOPS. Researchers used the Barron and Kenny (1987) model by using the mediation theory, predictors with attitudes of work toward researcher's work. The theory of mediation was further developed. To examine the relationship between predictors and work attitude mediation, researchers first used the SPSSvs.26 process macros.

After demonstrating the confirmatory results of the Hayes process, the researchers further analyzed the mediation of work attitudes in employee psychological intrinsic reward systems and employee's work attitude Model Fit indices result shown under table (11).

Table 11. Mediation Analysis & Total Effect

	ERW	EW	EOPS
EW	.704	.000	.051
RL	.562	.203	.000
EOPS	.487	.233	.000

Source: AMOS Output, 2023

The Total effect was 0.70. Indirect effect on employee work attitude is 0.48. In order to assess whether the relationship between employee psychological intrinsic reward system and organization perceived organizational support of textile industry is mediated by employee work attitude were undertaken following Baron and Kenny (1987) After ensuring that our survey met all the requisites established by these authors, the macro Process 3.0 from SPSS (version 26.0) developed by Hayes was used. Both tests showed that both employee work attitude and mediate the relationship between employee psychological intrinsic reward system and organization perceived organizational support of textile industry.

The results indicated an effect of employee psychological intrinsic reward system on affects as a mediating variable, 0.70 for employee work attitude ($p>0.001$), with a total effect (direct + indirect effects) mediated by employee work attitude of 0.70 ($p > 0.001$), suggesting that employee work attitude directly mediated the relationship between employee's psychological intrinsic reward system and organization perceived organizational support of textile industry. But as $p > 0.001$, p founded as 0.51 and RL behavior was founded as mediator not between RW and EOPS but between RW and EW. This situation considered as parallel mediation as shown by figure 5.

Figure 5. Parallel Mediation

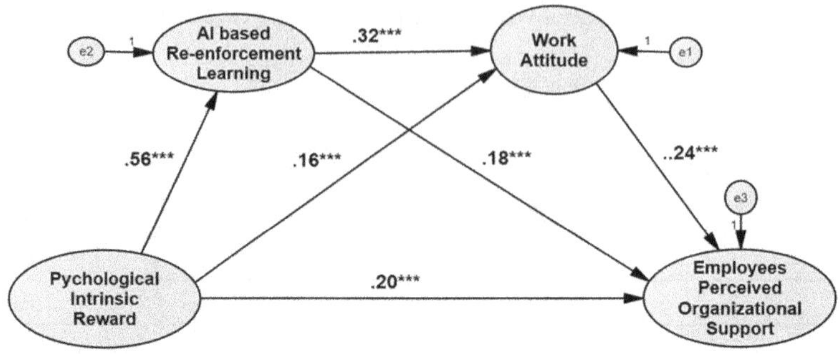

Source: AMOS Output, 2023

The SEM (Structure Equation Modeling) as shown by figure 5 manifested work attitude results have a mediation effect of the employee work attitude at a significance level of 0.05 is 0.70onemployee's psychological intrinsic reward system and organizational perceived organizational support. The overall effect was found 0.48, which represents the accumulation of the direct effect. And the indirect effect of 0.70 at the significance level of 0.05 represents the employee's work attitude, and the relationship between the employee's psychological intrinsic reward system and the perceived organizational support of the textile industry. The combined effect of all found predictors on textile industry perceived organizational support is 0.70. The dependent variable or behavior of the dependent variable explained by the presence mediator predictor the Table 11 show the result of Mediation Analysis & total effect in addition Figure 3 Path analysis study result.

DISCUSSION

In the Ethiopian context, the chapter "AI Learning and Work Attitude Mediation between Reward and Organizational Support in Ethiopia" examines the connections between reward systems, organizational support, work attitudes, and AI learning. A critical and analytical evaluation is necessary to determine if the data in this chapter effectively depicts the concerns, difficulties, and patterns associated with the book's suggested topic. The link between AI learning, work attitudes, incentive systems, and organizational support in Ethiopia was brought into sharper perspective in this chapter. It recognized and tackled the main concerns and challenges surrounding the effects of AI learning on workers' attitudes towards their jobs when incentive structures and organizational support are in place.

The chapter contributes to the body of literature by emphasizing how crucial it is to comprehend this connection within Ethiopia's particular setting. All things considered, the theme's concerns, difficulties, and trends are well communicated. The chapter included a more thorough assessment of the unique possibilities and difficulties in the Ethiopian setting that result from the deployment of AI learning in Ethiopia in order to better improve the clarity of the issues, problems, and trends. This entails taking organizational procedures, cultural aspects, and any implementation hurdles into account. will provide a thorough analysis of the most recent advancements and trends in AI learning, as well as information on work attitudes, incentive schemes, and organizational support.

This chapter shows a thorough grasp of the body of current knowledge and helps to place the study within the broader area. By examining the theoretical background, current research, and possible connections between AI learning, work attitudes, incentive systems, and organizational support, the chapter showed a respectably high degree of analysis. It is clear those pertinent theories and models have been used, enabling a theoretical integration that advances the goals of the research. Deeper critical examination and review of the literature are still possible, nevertheless.

The chapter conducted a more thorough critical examination of the body of literature, including a discussion of the advantages and disadvantages of earlier research, in order to support the analytical judgment. This would serve as a basis for future study by assisting in the identification of gaps and inconsistencies in the present body of knowledge.

CONCLUSION

Study main focus was on to access the role of employee work attitude as a mediator in between employee psychological intrinsic reward system and organization perceived organizational support. On the base of data analysis with help of AMOS software it was found that in absence of employee work attitude as a mediator relation between psychological intrinsic reward system and organization perceived organizational support is very weak in the form of standardized direct effect. But because of the presence of employee work attitude as a mediator relation between psychological intrinsic reward system and organization perceived organizational support is very strong in the form of standardized total effect. In order to test the statistical significance of mediation, bootstrapping test was run (10,000 runs). Both tests showed that both employee work attitude mediate the relationship between psychological intrinsic reward system and organization perceived organizational support of textile industry. It showed that employee work attitude fully mediates this relation. So, it is concluded that employee work attitude as a mediator between employee psychological intrinsic reward system and organization perceived organizational support fully mediate the relation in the study area.

Data Availability Statement

The data supporting reliability of the findings were embedded in the research analysis.

Conflict of Interest

In this piece of research, the authors declare no conflicts of interest.

Funding

The author wishes to state that there was no funding support for this study.

Data Availability

Data or information for this study will be made available upon request from the corresponding author.

Declarations

Competing interests: The authors declare no competing interests.

REFERENCES

Adula, M., & Kant, S. (2022). Interpretative Phenomenological Perceptional Study of Women Entrepreneurs Facing Challenges in Entrepreneurial Activity in the Horn of Africa. *Journal of Entrepreneurship, Management, and Innovation*, 4(2), 321–335.

Adula, M., Kant, S., & Birbirsa, Z. A. (2022). Systematic Literature Review on Human Resource Management Effect on Organization Perceived organizational support. *Annals of Human Resource Management Research*, 2(2), 131–146.

Adula, M., Kant, S., & Birbirsa, Z. A. (2023). Qualitative Analysis with MAXQDA Approach: HRM Practices effect on Organization Perceived organizational support with Mediation of Employee Work Attitude in Textile Industries of Ethiopia. *Advanced Qualitative Research*, 1(1), 1–14.

Al-Awar, M. S., Al-Habeet, A., & Gafer, A., Al- Amery, B., Edrees, W. H., & Al-Asbahi, A. (2022). Job satisfaction at clinical laboratories in Sana'a hospitals, Yemen, using the application of Herzberg's two-factor theory of motivation. *Al- Razi University. Journal for Medical Sciences*, 6(1).

Danilwan, Y., & Dirhamsyah, I. P. (2022). The Impact of The Psychological intrinsic reward on The Organizational Perceived organizational support: Does Ethical Climate Matter? *Journal of Positive School Psychology*, 6(3), 1–16.

Dhir, S., & Chakraborty, T. (2021). Does the perceived efficiency of the HR department matter in influencing satisfaction and employee perceived organizational support? *International Journal of Productivity and Perceived organizational support Management*, (ahead-of-print).

Elita, Y., & Sinthia, R. (2021). Knowledge Sharing Behavior Reviewed From a Social Exchange Perspective. *International Conference on Educational Sciences and Teacher Profession (ICETeP 2020)* (pp. 509-512). Atlantis Press.

Emmanuel, N., & Nwuzor, J. (2021). Employee and Organisational Perceived organizational support: Employees Perception of Intrinsic and Extrinsic Psychological intrinsic rewards System. *Applied Journal of Economics. Management and Social Sciences*, 2(1), 26–32.

Hao, J., Zhang, G., Liu, W., Zou, H., & Wang, Y. (2022). Autotune control algorithm based on relay feedback and adaptive neural network for attitude tracking of nonlinear AUG system. *Ocean Engineering*, 250, 111051.

Ismael, F., Hussein, B., Ibrahim, M. S., & Akoye, S. (2022). The mediation role of organization citizenship behaviour between employee motivation and productivity: Analysis of Pharmaceutical Industries in KRG. *International Journal of Humanities and Education Development*, 4(1), 10–22.

Junça Silva, A., & Coelho, N. (2022). The moderating role of organizational culture on the relationship between workers' attitudes towards telework and happiness. *Kybernetes*.

Kant, S., Belay, B., & Dabaso, A. (2023). Coffee Logistics Operation Knowledge Effect on Cooperative Associations Functionalism in Ethiopia with Mediation of Cybernetics and Local People Knowledge Base. *Journal of Production, Operations Management and Economics, 3*(1), 21-33.

Kassa, A. G., & Tsigu, G. T. (2022). Corporate entrepreneurship, employee engagement and innovation: A resource-based view and a social exchange theory perspective. *The International Journal of Organizational Analysis*, 30(6), 1694–1711.

Mbebeb, F. E., & Tanyi, F. B. B. (2019). Alternative Options In Building Workers' incentives: Effects On Job Satisfaction And Perceived Organizational Support In Local Context. *Global Journal of Human Resource Management*, 7(2), 38–53.

Naser, M. Z. (2021). An engineer's guide to eXplainable Artificial Intelligence and Interpretable Machine Learning: Navigating causality, forced goodness, and the false perception of inference. *Automation in Construction*, 129, 103821.

Neudert, L. M., Knuutila, A., & Howard, P. N. (2020). *Global attitudes towards AI, machine learning & automated decision making*. Working paper 2020.10, Oxford Commission on AI & Good Governance.

Panch, T., Szolovits, P., & Atun, R. (2018). Artificial intelligence, machine learning and health systems. *Journal of Global Health*, 8(2).

Peponi, A., Morgado, P., & Kumble, P. (2022). Life cycle thinking and machine learning for urban metabolism assessment and prediction. *Sustainable Cities and Society*, 80, 103754.

Ramachandran, K. K., Mary, A. A. S., Hawladar, S., Asokk, D., Bhaskar, B., & Pitroda, J. R. (2022). Machine learning and role of artificial intelligence in optimizing work perceived organizational support and employee behavior. *Materials Today: Proceedings*, 51, 2327–2331.

Rudra Kumar, M., & Gunjan, V. K. (2022, May). Machine Learning Based Solutions for Human Resource Systems Management. In *ICCCE 2021: Proceedings of the 4th International Conference on Communications and Cyber Physical Engineering* (pp. 1239-1249). Singapore: Springer Nature Singapore.

Seeck, H., & Diehl, M. R. (2017). A literature review on HRM and innovation–taking stock and future directions. *International Journal of Human Resource Management*, 28(6), 913–944.

Shaw, J. D. (2021). The resource-based view and its use in strategic human resource management research: The elegant and inglorious. *Journal of Management*, 47(7), 1787–1795.

Stergiou, D. P. (2022). *Social Exchange Theory. Encyclopedia of Tourism Management and Marketing*. Edward Elgar Publishing.

Tufa, G., Kant, S., & Dinber, G. N. (2023). Meta- Analysis: Qualitative Review of Human Resource Management Studies. *Advanced Qualitative Research*, 1(1), 42–62.

Verma, A., Lamsal, K., & Verma, P. (2022). An investigation of skill requirements in artificial intelligence and machine learning job advertisements. *Industry and Higher Education*, 36(1), 63–73.

Wakjira, G. G., & Kant, S. (2022). Significance of Market Orientation on Business Perceived organizational support With Mediating Role of Employee And Customer Satisfaction In Ethiopia Banks. *Partners Universal International Research Journal*, 1(4), 118–125.

Widarko, A., & Anwarodin, M. K. (2022). Work Motivation and Organizational Culture on Work Perceived organizational support: Organizational Citizenship Behavior (OCB) as Mediating Variable. *Golden Ratio of Human Resource Management*, 2(2), 123–138.

Xia, H., Wang, Y., Jasimuddin, S., Zhang, J. Z., & Thomas, A. (2022). A big-data-driven matching model based on deep reinforcement learning for cotton blending. *International Journal of Production Research*, 1–19.

Chapter 6
Using AI-Driven Decision-Making Tools in Corporate Investment Planning

Joel Jebadurai Devapitchai
https://orcid.org/0000-0002-6947-8497
St. Joseph's College of Engineering, India

Krishnapriya S. V.
St. Joseph's College of Engineering, India

Karuppiah S. P.
St. Joseph's College of Engineering, India

William Robert P.
https://orcid.org/0009-0000-5568-9210
Saveetha School of Management, Saveetha Institute of Medical and Technical Sciences, Chennai, India

S. Saranya
NPR College of Engineering and Technology, Dindigul, India

ABSTRACT

Artificial intelligence plays a crucial role in financial sectors, especially in investment planning. It enhanced or replaced traditional investment planning by applying AI techniques such as machine learning, natural language processing, deep learning, and robo-advisors. This chapter presented the applications of AI-enabled decision-making tools in various functional areas of corporate investment planning such as

DOI: 10.4018/979-8-3693-5578-7.ch006

quantitative trading algorithms, risk management systems, portfolio optimization tools, algorithmic trading, forecasting and prediction of securities market, automated portfolio building, data analysis, asset management, and personalized investment advice. Also, this chapter presented the case studies, success stories, and benefits of AI applications in corporate investment planning. This chapter will be very useful for corporate companies and investors to transform their mode of traditional investment planning to technology-oriented investment planning.

INTRODUCTION

In today's fast-paced business environment, where speed and precision are vital for sustained growth and staying ahead of the competition, investment planning plays a pivotal role in strategic decision-making. Effectively allocating resources, seizing new opportunities, and mitigating risks are essential tasks for businesses across all industries. Traditional investment planning methods typically rely on market research, expert opinions, and historical data analysis. However, with the rapid proliferation of data and the increasing complexity of financial markets, these traditional approaches struggle to provide timely and accurate insights (Ren 2021). In traditional investment planning, identifying investment opportunities and assessing risks involves meticulous analysis of financial statements, market trends, industry dynamics, and macroeconomic indicators. While these methods have yielded some success, they are inherently constrained by human biases, information disparities, and the sluggish processing of vast datasets.

The term "Artificial Intelligence" was coined in the early days of computing when automated computations could only execute a limited number of arithmetic operations in a single program run. There was optimism that AI would eventually match and even surpass human intelligence in terms of processing speed as electronic computing became more accessible in the late 1940s. However, despite several promising advancements, unforeseen challenges and limitations abruptly tempered these lofty expectations (Lu 2019). The emergence of Artificial Intelligence (AI) technologies has revolutionized the investment planning landscape, empowering human decision-making with advanced computational capabilities. In particular, machine learning algorithms have showcased remarkable proficiency in unravelling complex datasets and uncovering latent patterns. By leveraging historical data, machine learning models can identify correlations, trends, and anomalies that traditional methods may overlook. Moreover, their iterative nature enables continuous refinement and adaptation to evolving market dynamics. The capacity of Artificial Intelligence (AI) to unveil concealed patterns and correlations within financial data, beyond the scope of human analysts, stands as a primary driver for its adoption in investment planning. AI systems harness machine learning algorithms to scrutinize historical market trends, macroeconomic indicators, corporate financial statements, and unconventional data sources, thereby uncovering predictive signals and anomalies (Miziołek 2021). Subsequently, these insights can inform investment strategies and guide portfolio allocation decisions.

There are five sections to this chapter. The goals and methodology are covered in the first section. The second section explores AI strategies used in corporate investment planning. The application of AI approaches to various functional areas of corporate financial planning is examined in the third section. The benefits and challenges of AI are discussed in the fourth section. The fifth and final section includes case studies, success stories, predictions for the future, and closing thoughts about artificial intelligence's place in corporate investment planning.

This chapter is framed with the following objectives. They are.

1. The first objective of this study is to understand AI tools used in corporate investment planning such as Machine Learning, Natural Language Processing, Deep Learning, and Robo-Advisors.
2. The second objective covered the AI applications in various functional areas of corporate investment planning such as Quantitative Trading Algorithms, Risk Management Systems, Portfolio Optimization Tools, Algorithmic Trading, Forecasting and Prediction of Securities Market, Automated Portfolio Building, Data Analysis, Asset Management and Personalized Investment Advice.
3. Benefits, challenges, case studies, and success stories of AI in corporate investment planning are presented in the third objective.

METHODOLOGY

This chapter is purely based on the secondary data. It is collected from various sources such as books, websites, journals, and so on. The collected data represented the AI tools used in corporate investment planning such as Machine Learning (ML), Natural Language Processing (NLP), Deep Learning, and Robo-Advisors. In addition, AI tools application areas such as Quantitative Trading Algorithms, Risk Management Systems, Portfolio Optimization Tools, Algorithmic Trading, Forecasting and Prediction of Securities Market, Automated Portfolio Building, Data Analysis, Asset Management, and Personalized Investment Advice also collected and presented in this book chapter.

ARTIFICIAL INTELLIGENCE DECISION-MAKING TOOLS IN CORPORATE INVESTMENT PLANNING

Machine Learning

At the core of AI-driven investment planning tools lie Machine Learning (ML) algorithms. These algorithms are adept at analyzing vast repositories of historical financial data, uncovering trends, correlations, and anomalies that may elude human analysts. Supervised learning techniques like regression analysis and decision trees are commonly employed for tasks such as optimizing portfolio allocation, identifying investment opportunities, and forecasting stock prices (Prasad & Seetharaman 2021). Additionally, unsupervised learning algorithms, including clustering and dimensionality reduction, play a crucial role in identifying related market segments and unveiling latent structures within financial datasets.

Fintech Studios is an analytics and intelligent search engine tailored for financial experts, providing access to a vast array of business and financial resources (https://www.fintechstudios.com). Leveraging artificial intelligence and machine learning technologies, the platform swiftly sifts through millions of sources in 49 languages, including blogs, news, research, and big data analytics. This comprehensive solution caters to a diverse range of financial professionals, from brokers and consultants to individuals in hedge funds and private equity firms, enabling them to access essential information tailored to their needs efficiently.

U.S. Bank has integrated Artificial Intelligence (AI) into its operations to automate customer account management and loan application processing tasks. This automation allows professionals to focus on strategic initiatives. Furthermore, U.S. Bank leverages machine learning and AI to enhance the banking experience for customers by tailoring services to their needs (www.usbank.com). This approach enables the bank to introduce new products and offer more efficient financial solutions based on individual applications.

Natural Language Processing (NLP)

The term "Natural Language Processing" (NLP) refers to a class of computing techniques that are used to process or produce speech and text. These techniques include natural language understanding, which deduces meaning from spoken or written text; voice recognition, which translates spoken language into text; speech generation, which produces text into speech; and natural language generation, which creates natural language data from other data sources. Natural language financial forecasting is a hot topic in finance. It takes sentiment analysis from social media and financial news and uses it to feed algorithms that forecast the movement of financial data. Because information about stocks and foreign exchange rates is readily available, Natural Language Processing (NLP) can be used in these markets.

Unstructured data sources such as news articles, social media feeds, analyst reports, and earnings call transcripts necessitate the utilization of Natural Language Processing (NLP) techniques for processing and analysis. Within the realm of NLP, sentiment analysis plays a crucial role in evaluating investor and market sentiment, shedding light on the potential impact of news stories, public opinion, and corporate statements on stock prices and market movements (Chen 2023). Through the extraction of valuable information from textual data, both quantitative and qualitative, NLP systems empower investors to make data-driven decisions.

The objective of the NLP is to determine whether to buy, sell, or hold assets. While portfolio managers traditionally handle these responsibilities directly or with the assistance of an AI decision engine, NLP and Natural Language Generation (NLG) can aid in crafting the narrative behind AI-supported decisions. NLP/G processes input and decision data amalgamative to generate an impartial report elucidating the decision-making process, including potential counteracting factors. Proprietary technologies subject data to a series of stress tests to elucidate the drivers behind an AI decision engine, including investment engines. Portfolio managers can leverage this narrative for evaluating and endorsing trades, or for reporting to regulators, clients, or other portfolio managers regarding the rationale behind each trade. This data enables portfolio managers to update and manage AI decision algorithms effectively (Konstantinidis 2023). By utilizing technology to offer an unbiased explanation of the reasoning behind each trade, companies can demonstrate to clients and regulators their understanding and control over trading algorithms. NLP/G functions as a decision support technology during this stage, while the AI component autonomously makes the investment decisions.

Financial markets are profoundly influenced by news sentiment. NLP-based sentiment analysis of news articles and social media posts can significantly impact stock market predictions (Rehman et.al. 2024). By assessing the sentiment associated with financial news, investors and traders can make more informed decisions.

Deep Learning Models

Deep learning, a subset of machine learning, utilizes multi-layered neural networks to discern intricate patterns and relationships within data. Within investment planning, an increasing array of deep learning models is employed for tasks such as sentiment analysis, time series forecasting, and anomaly detection. Examples of these models include Convolutional Neural Networks (CNNs) and Recurrent Neural Networks (RNNs), which excel in processing sequential data and extracting high-level features from raw data, making them well-suited for analyzing financial time series data and identifying patterns in market trends (Hung et.al. 2024).

In the realm of finance, both structured and unstructured data, such as text and documents, are prevalent. Deep learning is beneficial for financial institutions by transforming unstructured data into machine-readable and structured formats. For example, banks can utilize Deep Learning to extract financial data from annual reports posted on regulatory platforms, thereby enabling the classification and prediction of information from structured data sources (Hassani 2020). Highly structured data, like stock market information, can be leveraged to automate trading operations.

Robo-Advisors

Robo-advisors are computer programs designed to offer personalized investment advice to individual investors. These programs have recently garnered significant attention due to their ability to lower entry barriers for retail investors. Their main function is to create algorithms, known as recommender systems, that generate optimal portfolios tailored to investors' risk preferences. Moreover, robo-advisors can incorporate various AI applications into portfolio management, trading, and risk management. By leveraging AI's success in these areas, robo-advisors can deliver portfolios with superior out-of-sample performance, automatically rebalance portfolios, manage risks, and minimize transaction costs. Because robo-advisors are more affordable than human advisors and offer a simplified interface, they make investing more beneficial and accessible for retail investors.

Robo-advisors are AI-driven platforms designed to provide investors with automated portfolio management and investment guidance. These systems analyze investors' risk tolerance, financial preferences, and investment objectives using algorithms to offer personalized investment portfolio recommendations. Utilizing Machine Learning (ML) algorithms, Natural Language Processing (NLP) techniques, and optimization algorithms, Robo-advisors aim to minimize risk and maximize returns within predefined parameters.

Many investors prefer making routine purchases and allocating additional funds to their portfolios regularly. Automatic investment plans are commonplace, allowing investors to authorize automated purchases (Phoon & Koh 2018). Whether the Robo-advisor autonomously distributes funds or merely facilitates their transfer to clients for confirmation, automated purchases must be permitted.

Schwab Intelligent Portfolios is a notable Robo-advisor offering features such as automated portfolio rebalancing, a diverse selection of Exchange-Traded Funds (ETFs), and personalized portfolio management.

Societe Generale Bank, a leader in financial services, has integrated RPA into its workflow to handle time-consuming and tiresome tasks. They may offer superior customer care and change the company model with the aid of RPA bots (Huang et.al., 2024).

AI Application Areas in Corporate Investment Planning

Quantitative Trading Algorithms

Utilizing artificial intelligence (AI) methodologies, quantitative trading algorithms—commonly known as algorithmic trading or automated trading—execute trades based on predetermined rules, algorithms, and quantitative models. These algorithms aim to detect trading opportunities and execute orders with minimal human intervention by analyzing real-time market data, including price fluctuations, trading volumes, and order book dynamics (Dakalbab 2024). To adapt to changing market conditions and enhance trading performance, quantitative trading algorithms often incorporate machine learning models. These strategies encompass trend-following, mean-reversion, arbitrage, and statistical arbitrage.

Large Institutional Investors typically employ algorithms to execute substantial trades. These firms seek to conceal their trades by distributing them across multiple exchanges or brokers to prevent their transactions from impacting market prices (Cohen 2022). Algorithmic pattern recognition is employed to identify these significant trades, allowing for the construction of models to recognize trends in large trades within a company. While this approach can aid in identifying stocks to purchase before significant trades affect prices, it necessitates robust High-Frequency Trading (HFT) systems.

Several High-Frequency Trading (HFT) companies have prospered by utilizing ultra-fast algorithms, such as Virtu Financial and Citadel Securities. These businesses profit by making a lot of trades quickly and taking advantage of little pricing differences. The success of HFT serves as an example of how algorithmic execution speed and accuracy can result in profitability. The U.S. saw a flash crash on May 6, 2010, during which the Dow Jones Industrial Average fell by about 1,000 points in a matter of minutes (Dong et.al. 2024). An element of the sudden and sharp collapse in the market was ascribed to algorithmic trading. Algorithms used in high-frequency trading increased the volatility and set off a chain reaction of sell orders. This episode highlights the possible dangers of algorithmic trading, which calls for constant observation and circuit breakers to stop such disturbances.

Risk Management Systems

With AI-driven risk management systems, corporate investors can detect, assess, and mitigate a range of risks linked to their investment portfolios. Employing ML algorithms, these systems analyze historical data to pinpoint trends signaling potential hazards like operational, credit, liquidity, and market risks (Schuett 2023). By continuously measuring and monitoring these risks in real-time, these systems enable investors to make informed decisions, protecting their portfolios and maximizing risk-adjusted returns.

In today's business landscape, traditional approaches to risk identification encounter numerous challenges. These methods often struggle to adapt to the dynamic and evolving nature of risks as they rely heavily on past data and preset criteria. Additionally, traditional techniques face difficulties in processing the vast volume of real-time data, hindering their ability to swiftly detect new risks (Naim 2022). Their manual nature, lack of predictive capabilities, and inability to address contemporary issues such as cyber threats, rapidly evolving regulations, and operational hazards further limit their effectiveness.

Artificial intelligence (AI) revolutionizes the field of risk identification by employing machine learning and predictive analytics. Unlike previous methodologies, AI operates in real-time, enabling organizations to assess vast and dynamic datasets promptly. Through predictive analytics, AI systems can recognize patterns, trends, and anomalies, facilitating a proactive approach to risk detection. Furthermore, machine learning models enhance the system's capability to identify and comprehend new threats, including those that have not been previously identified, through continuous learning and adaptation.

ZestFinance exemplifies the application of AI and machine learning in risk management. Founded by a former chief information officer of Google, ZestFinance collaborated with Baidu, China's leading search engine, in 2016 to enhance Baidu's loan offerings (Maurya et.al. 2024). Baidu's interest in providing small loans to retail customers who shopped on their marketplace prompted this collaboration.

Lending in the Chinese market poses unique challenges due to the limited credit ratings or profiles of the population, with less than 20% having such records (Jebadurai et.al. 2024). In the absence of traditional credit history, lending to individuals with minimal or no credit profiles carries inherent risks. ZestFinance leverages its access to Baidu's extensive member database, which includes data on search and purchase behaviors, to assist Baidu in assessing loan applicants' creditworthiness (Hidayat et.al. 2024).

With access to thousands of data points for each customer, ZestFinance enables quick decisions on loan approvals. During the reported testing of its technology in 2017, Baidu experienced a significant 150% increase in small-item lending within just two months, showcasing the effectiveness of ZestFinance's approach.

Portfolio Optimization Tools

Artificial Intelligence (AI) methodologies are designed to construct and adjust investment portfolios with specific objectives in mind, such as maximizing returns, reducing risk, or achieving a designated asset allocation. Employing optimization techniques such as multi-objective optimization, modern portfolio theory, and mean-variance optimization, these tools determine the optimal asset allocation strategy that minimizes risk and maximizes returns while accounting for investors' constraints and preferences (Gunjan & Bhattacharyya 2023). AI-powered portfolio optimization tools can efficiently construct robust portfolios tailored to investors' requirements, considering factors such as transaction costs, liquidity constraints, and market impact.

AI excels in processing vast financial databases, providing investors with rapid, data-driven insights. By eliminating emotional biases, it enables rational decision-making based on historical performance and current market conditions. Additionally, AI continuously monitors portfolios in real-time, swiftly responding to market fluctuations to optimize profits and mitigate risks. A key advantage of AI is its ability to enhance diversification techniques by uncovering previously unrecognized asset correlations and facilitating the construction of resilient, well-diversified portfolios capable of weathering market volatility (Ban et.al. 2019). Furthermore, by automating processes, AI-driven portfolio management reduces costs and enhances the accessibility and affordability of investment solutions.

AI serves as a valuable tool for portfolio optimization, aiding investors in identifying a portfolio that aligns with their specific needs regarding time horizon and risk tolerance. Additionally, when combined with modern portfolio theory, AI can assist in constructing a portfolio of stocks situated on the efficient frontier, thereby maximizing returns for a given level of risk.

For example, Capestart offers comprehensive machine learning solutions tailored for the financial sector. These solutions facilitate the optimization of portfolio performance, asset management, risk mitigation, credit score analysis, and loan approval processes, and even enhance customer engagement through intelligent chatbots (Rane et.al. 2024).

Algorithmic Trading

Algorithmic trading, also known as automated trading, black-box trading, or algo-trading, involves executing trades using computer programs that follow predetermined sets of instructions known as algorithms. The aim is to generate profits more swiftly and consistently than a human trader could achieve. These instructions can be based on various factors such as mathematical models, timing, costs, or quantities (Cohen 2022). Algo trading removes the influence of human emotions from trading decisions, thereby enhancing systematic trading and market liquidity, while also offering profit opportunities for traders.

AI significantly influences trading through algorithmic trading, which automates various stages of the trading process. This method has grown in asset management due to three recent developments:

Technological Advances

Enhanced computing power, data science, and telecommunications have transformed financial markets. Computers can now gather and analyze vast data sets and execute trades in milliseconds without human intervention.

Breakthroughs in Quantitative Finance and Machine Learning

These advancements equip computers to perform sophisticated financial analysis more quickly and efficiently than humans.

Market Complexity and Scale

The rapid pace, increasing complexity, and scale of financial markets, along with the emergence of new financial products, make it challenging for humans to track markets and make real-time decisions. Advanced AI techniques, such as Artificial Neural Networks (ANNs), can now operate in near real-time.

Algorithmic trading strategies often rely on technical analysis, which predicts future asset returns using past stock and market data. While fundamental analysis is possible, high-frequency trading typically finds it less effective due to the lower frequency of fundamental data. Evidence suggests technical indicators are more successful than fundamental ones in generating profitable AI-based trading signals, leading to a stronger presence of AI in technical analysis.

Traditional technical analysis primarily uses historical price and trading volume data. Price-based strategies model trends (like momentum or reversal) and cycles to forecast future returns, while volume-based strategies predict future returns based on recent investor trading activity. Modern technical analysis also integrates information from diverse sources, such as fund flows, investor trades, and textual data from news articles or online sources. AI techniques, particularly natural language processing (NLP), are valuable for analyzing these new, unstructured data sources.

An automated trading strategy is implemented to buy 50 shares of a stock when its 50-day moving average crosses above the 200-day moving average. Conversely, when the stock's 50-day moving average falls below the 200-day moving average, shares of the company are sold. Utilizing these two simple commands, computer software continuously monitors the stock price and moving average indicators. Once the predefined conditions are met, the software executes buy and sell orders without the need for manual intervention from the trader (Dakalbab et.al. 2024). This automated process efficiently identifies trade opportunities and eliminates the necessity for traders to manually input orders or monitor real-time charts and prices.

Forecasting and Prediction of Securities Market

AI can predict future price movements across various asset classes like stocks, bonds, and currencies by analyzing historical data and market conditions. Investment firms are increasingly leveraging machine learning models to enhance their forecasting accuracy, identifying patterns and correlations that human analysts might overlook (Chopra & Sharma 2021).

For instance, Two Sigma, a New York-based investment firm, incorporates High-Frequency Trading (HFT) techniques alongside AI and ML technology. This strategy allows them to execute profitable trades faster by analyzing both quantitative and qualitative data from diverse marketplaces.

Rebellion Research offers AI-powered investment strategies to its clients, such as the Global Equity strategy, which utilizes ML algorithms to adapt to the dynamic nature of the market.

Bridgewater Associates an American asset management company, has been utilizing AI for market predictions and improving traders' efficiency for several years (Oyeniyi et.al. 2024). In 2022, the company introduced its new AI-based algorithm, "I Know First," designed to analyze daily market events and generate forecasts for over 7,000 corporate assets.

Automated Portfolio Building

Automated investing refers to the technology-driven approach to investment management, where mathematical models and algorithms are utilized to invest on behalf of customers. This streamlined and cost-effective option is particularly appealing to tech-savvy investors (Haddadian et.al. 2022). However, potential users must understand how the program's features align with their specific financial goals and investment objectives to effectively utilize automated investing.

Robo-advisors like Wealth Front and Betterment automate the traditional process of engaging with a financial advisor to discuss investment goals, timeframes, and risk tolerances. These platforms guide users through a questionnaire to generate a tailored portfolio based on their criteria. Artificial intelligence is often employed alongside the questionnaire and model scoring to identify the optimal combination of individual stocks for the portfolio. Moreover, automated portfolios are designed to automatically rebalance if the allocations deviate significantly from the chosen portfolio's targets.

Investment Data Analysis

AI can analyze data from non-traditional sources such as online traffic, satellite imagery, and consumer purchasing trends, providing insights into the operations of specific businesses or sectors (Gao, 2020). By incorporating alternative data into their investment models, investors can gain a competitive edge and identify investment opportunities that may not be apparent from conventional financial data.

In the next five years from 2024, alternative data is expected to revolutionize the landscape of active investment management, impacting not only hedge fund management but also long-only mutual funds and private equity managers (Swathi & Pahuja 2024). Companies that fail to adapt their investment practices within this timeframe risk losing market share to competitors who effectively leverage alternative data in their trading signals and securities valuation processes.

For example, Eagle Alpha has witnessed significant hedge funds leading the adoption of alternative data. Over time, the organization has expanded its services to encompass approximately 500 datasets across 24 categories. Mutual fund managers and private equity firms are increasingly recognizing the potential of alternative data to generate alpha (Bandyopadhyay 2024). Eagle Alpha anticipates that as the industry evolves, the necessity to incorporate alternative data will grow, with those who resist this trend losing their competitive advantage to firms harnessing these new sources of information.

Asset Management

In 2022, approximately $2.6 billion was invested in the global artificial intelligence market for asset management. Analysts at Grand View Research predict that this market will experience a compound annual growth rate of 24.5% from 2023 to 2030. Investment firms are increasingly recognizing the value of using AI as a tool for asset management, aiding them in meeting market performance targets and attracting new clients (Zhao et.al. 2024).

For instance, Vanguard's CEO has embraced AI as a vital tool for managing investment companies and as a dynamic force in asset management. Speaking at the Investment Company Institute Leadership Summit in Washington, D.C., in May, Buckley noted that CEOs' perceptions of investment firms are evolving due to technology. He emphasized the role of generative AI in automating routine cognitive tasks, highlighting how this revolutionizes traditional processes. Vanguard already utilizes AI technology to operate as a robo-advisor, leveraging its Exchange-Traded Funds (ETFs) to create personalized retirement portfolios for clients.

Personalized Investment Advice

AI programs are increasingly capable of offering personalized investment advice, as exemplified by Magnifi. Utilizing real-time investing advice through ChatGPT and other AI techniques, Magnifi functions as a trading platform akin to an AI-powered version of Robinhood. Available as a smartphone application, Magnifi facilitates stock and fund trading, allowing users to construct investment portfolios.

What sets Magnifi apart is its incorporation of an AI assistant, akin to ChatGPT, which actively monitors users' investment portfolios. This AI assistant provides insights into portfolio performance, diversification level, and associated risk, offering a personalized investment experience.

Benefits of Artificial Intelligence in Corporate Investment Planning

The following are the benefits of Artificial Intelligence in corporate investment planning (Zhao 2022). They are.

Increased Performance
Utilizing AI for investment planning could potentially enable investors to surpass traditional methods in terms of investment performance. AI algorithms may uncover more efficient avenues for generating alpha, thereby enhancing risk-adjusted returns in investment portfolios.
Cost Savings
In contrast to traditional investment management approaches, AI-driven investment planning can yield savings in operational expenses. Over time, significant cost reductions may arise from the automation of repetitive tasks such as trade execution, portfolio rebalancing, and data collection and analysis.
Flexibility and Adaptability

AI systems exhibit flexibility, swiftly adjusting to new data inputs, evolving investment strategies, and fluctuating market conditions. This adaptability empowers investment planners to capitalize on opportunities, mitigate risks, and respond promptly to emerging trends amid changing market dynamics.

Efficiency and Automation

AI streamlines and automates various investment planning processes, such as trade execution, portfolio construction, rebalancing, and data analysis. As a result of this automation, investment professionals can focus on more high-value tasks such as strategic decision-making and nurturing client relationships. This not only enhances efficiency but also reduces the need for manual labor.

CHALLENGES

Dwivedi et.al. 2021 presented the following challenges of Artificial Intelligence in corporate investment planning. They are.

Data Availability and Quality

Accessing high-quality data is crucial for AI-driven investment planning. However, corporate data often suffers from issues such as being incomplete, outdated, or inconsistent, which can undermine the accuracy and reliability of AI models. Ensuring data availability and quality poses a significant challenge, especially for companies dealing with sensitive data or operating in complex environments.

Complexity of Financial Markets

Financial markets are inherently complex, characterized by the dynamic interplay of various elements such as market sentiment, geopolitical events, economic indicators, and regulatory shifts. AI methodologies must navigate this complexity to generate valuable insights for investment planning. In the corporate realm, developing AI models capable of accurately capturing and comprehending these intricacies remains a significant challenge.

Ethical and Regulatory Considerations

Concerns about Data Privacy, Fairness, and Compliance are some of the ethical and regulatory issues that AI-driven investment planning brings up. For example, CCPA and GDPR standards must be followed when using personal data to guide investment decisions. Furthermore, AI algorithms need to be created without biases that can unfairly affect demographic groups or provide unethical results.

AI systems are rapidly being utilized to automate trading, risk assessment, and loan approvals since they can make choices more quickly than people. These automatic judgments, meanwhile, raise the possibility of prejudice, inaccuracy, and even discrimination in some situations.

AI systems' capacity to magnify preexisting prejudice is a major ethical worry. Certain groups may be unjustly favored over others in judgments made by AI systems that have been trained on data sets that contain preexisting biases.

Because AI systems don't comprehend the ethical issues and human context, they might potentially result in unjust or inconsistent outcomes.

The possibility for AI to be utilized maliciously, such as insider trading or money laundering, raises further ethical concerns. Artificial intelligence (AI) has the potential to enable quick and covert manipulation of financial data, which might be used for nefarious purposes.

The matter of privacy comes last. AI-driven systems can gather enormous volumes of personal data about users, which may be utilized for marketing or surveillance objectives. Furthermore, if the information these systems contain is not adequately secured, hackers or other bad actors may be able to access it.

Collaboration between humans and AI

While AI can enhance decision-making processes, it cannot entirely supplant human knowledge and intuition. Integrating AI-driven insights with domain expertise and strategic objectives poses challenges when human decision-makers and AI systems fail to collaborate effectively. Moreover, ensuring the successful implementation of AI recommendations requires human stakeholders to have confidence in and accept them.

Cost and Resource Constraints

Implementing AI-driven investment planning systems requires significant investments in talent, data, and technical infrastructure. Cost and resource limitations may hinder the adoption of advanced AI technology, particularly for smaller businesses. Corporate decision-makers face the critical task of evaluating the potential benefits of AI-driven investment planning about associated expenses

Model interpretability

Deep learning and machine learning are examples of AI systems that often operate as “Black Boxes,” making it difficult to understand the rationale behind their decisions. The lack of clear interpretability in these models can pose significant challenges in investment planning, where accountability and transparency are crucial. If corporate stakeholders cannot grasp the underlying logic behind AI-driven recommendations, they may hesitate to rely on them.

TRADITIONAL VS. AI-BASED CORPORATE INVESTMENT PLANNING

The differences between traditional and AI-based investment planning are discussed below (Addy et.al 2024).

Table 1. Traditional vs. AI-based corporate investment planning

Sl. No	*Traditional corporate investment planning*	*AI-Based corporate investment planning*
1	It is a static one	It is a dynamic one
2	It is answering the question of 'What'	It is answering the question of 'Why' and 'how'
3	It is driven by hypotheses	It is driven by data
4	It is used with conventional techniques	It is used with algorithms and contemporary techniques
5	Lack of prediction about future financial position	Prediction of future financial position easy.
6	High time consuming	Less time consuming

CASE STUDIES AND SUCCESS STORIES

Founded in 1988, Ping An, with a workforce of 1.8 million, stands as the largest insurance firm globally. Dedicated to delivering technology-enabled retail financial services encompassing investing, banking, and insurance, Ping An has developed extensive capabilities in five ecosystems: financial services, healthcare, auto services, real estate services, and smart city services, leveraging ABCDS (Artificial Intelligence, Blockchain, Cloud computing, Big data, and Information security) technology.

Benefiting from a rich repository of superior financial data, Ping An has recognized the potential of big data to meet users' personalized needs and propel commercial growth since establishing its AI team in 2015, comprising fewer than ten members initially. Over four years, the team has expanded to 1,000 members and operates across diverse business domains.

Ping An SMART Flash Claim streamlines vehicle damage recognition through image processing, managing tens of thousands of daily claims. Customers simply capture images of their damaged vehicles and submit claims on-site, with the system swiftly processing claims within seconds, providing precise payment calculations. This automated system integrates several key modules, including picture quality assessment, insured vehicle validation, car part segmentation, damage identification, payment calculation, and fraud detection.

For over a year, the system has been operational at Ping An, efficiently handling over 30,000 claims daily. Not only does it enhance claim processing efficiency and customer satisfaction, but it also mitigates potential fraud worth billions of yuan. This system is now accessible to the insurance industry via the Ping An One Connect platform. Ping An manages over 11 million claims annually, with 98.7% settled within a day and 60% processed through self-service channels.

Ping An developed OlaTop, another application in corporate risk assessment, given China's more than 70 million registered enterprises. Information is sourced from commercial registrations, daily operations, public announcements (including news and social media), and business relationships (such as supply chain, investment, legal, and executive connections). To organize and analyze this dynamic data, Ping An developed OlaTop, an enterprise knowledge graph application. Leveraging advanced AI technologies like knowledge graphs, Natural Language Processing (NLP), and machine learning, OlaTop effectively addresses traditional enterprise operation analysis challenges, offering tailored solutions across risk management, precision marketing, smart investment, and public service domains.

Several AI techniques were developed to power the AI+ Flash Claim platform, including image processing, segmentation, object detection, recognition, and knowledge graph utilization. In the case of OlaTop, millions of legal proceedings are automatically interpreted, and over 40 million lawsuit relationships are integrated into the graph. Deep graph analysis algorithms are applied to support business decisions, such as risk assessment.

Business logics are directly embedded into OlaTop, with different risk events tailored for investments, bonds, and loans, and related signals extracted through sentiment analysis from social and news data. Additionally, different orders of upstream and downstream relationships serve as risk indicators, where the impact of risk events propagates through the graph network and decays based on relationship orders.

A further instance is the Canadian Imperial Bank of Commerce (CIBC), which has instituted an AI Ethics Council to supervise the use of moral AI procedures and created an AI Ethics Code. The council's multidisciplinary membership, which includes representatives from risk management, legal, and compliance, guarantees a thorough approach to handling ethical issues (.

In 2019, the Apple Card came under scrutiny due to accusations of gender discrimination. Reports indicated that the algorithm used to determine credit limits allegedly exhibited bias against women.

For instance, to offer direction and supervision on the moral use of AI, the Dutch bank ING formed an AI Ethics Advisory Council made up of both internal and external experts. This council makes sure that AI systems adhere to the bank's ethical standards and values by reviewing AI initiatives, evaluating possible risks, and considering moral consequences.

AI TRENDS IN CORPORATE INVESTMENT PLANNING

The investment planning landscape in the corporate world is evolving significantly due to several AI trends. Firstly, predictive analytics powered by machine learning algorithms enable businesses to forecast market trends, identify investment opportunities, and optimize portfolio allocations. Secondly, Natural Language Processing (NLP) techniques streamline the analysis of unstructured data like news articles, social media posts, and analyst reports, extracting valuable insights for informed decision-making. Thirdly, the adoption of reinforcement learning algorithms enables firms to dynamically adjust investment strategies in real-time, responding promptly to changing market conditions for better asset allocation and risk management (Raja, et.al 2024). Additionally, the rise of AI-driven robo-advisors offers automated portfolio management and investment advice, catering to both individual and institutional investors. Overall, these AI advancements are revolutionizing investment planning, empowering faster and more data-driven decision-making processes.

CONCLUSION

Incorporating Artificial Intelligence (AI) methods into corporate investment planning represents a significant shift in how businesses approach financial decision-making. Leveraging machine learning, natural language processing, reinforcement learning, and robo-advisors, AI enables enterprises to harness vast datasets, generate actionable insights, optimize portfolio allocations, and effectively mitigate risks. The utilization of AI in investment planning offers numerous benefits, including enhanced efficiency, accuracy, and adaptability to changing market dynamics. By leveraging AI, businesses can drive long-term value creation and gain a competitive advantage through quicker and more informed investment decisions. However, several challenges need to be addressed before AI approaches can be seamlessly integrated into investment planning. These challenges include ensuring data availability and quality, addressing biases and interpretability issues in models, and navigating ethical and legal considerations. Overcoming these obstacles requires collaboration among regulators, data scientists, and business leaders to establish robust governance frameworks and ethical standards. Ultimately, the convergence of AI-driven insights and human expertise will shape the future of business investment planning. By embracing AI technologies and fostering collaboration between humans and machines, businesses can capitalize on new opportunities for growth and innovation in the dynamic financial landscape.

ABBREVIATIONS

AI- Artificial Intelligence
ML- Machine Learning
NLP- Natural Language Processing
CNN- Convolutional Neural Networks
RNN- Recurrent Neural Networks
ETFs- Exchange-Traded Funds
HFT- High-Frequency Trading

REFERENCES

Addy, W. A., Ajayi-Nifise, A. O., Bello, B. G., Tula, S. T., Odeyemi, O., & Falaiye, T. (2024). Transforming financial planning with AI-driven analysis: A review and application insights. *World Journal of Advanced Engineering Technology and Sciences*, 11(1), 240–257. 10.30574/wjaets.2024.11.1.0053

Ban, G. Y., El Karoui, N., & Lim, A. E. (2018). Machine learning and portfolio optimization. *Management Science*, 64(3), 1136–1154. 10.1287/mnsc.2016.2644

Bandyopadhyay, I. (2024). Implementation Of An Artificial Intelligence And Machine Learning Powered Financial Decision-Support System For Stock Market Speculators. *Educational Administration: Theory and Practice*, 30(4), 203–209.

Chen, Y. (2023). Designing an Investment Research System for Asset Management Based on Natural Language Processing (Doctoral dissertation, Massachusetts Institute of Technology).

Chopra, R., & Sharma, G. D. (2021). Application of artificial intelligence in stock market forecasting: A critique, review, and research agenda. *Journal of Risk and Financial Management*, 14(11), 526. 10.3390/jrfm14110526

Cohen, G. (2022). Artificial Intelligence in Trading the Financial Markets. *International Journal of Economics & Business Administration*, 10(1), 101–110. 10.35808/ijeba/751

Cohen, G. (2022). Algorithmic trading and financial forecasting using advanced artificial intelligence methodologies. *Mathematics*, 10(18), 3302. 10.3390/math10183302

Dakalbab, F., Talib, M. A., Nassir, Q., & Ishak, T. (2024). Artificial intelligence techniques in financial trading: A systematic literature review. *Journal of King Saud University. Computer and Information Sciences*, 36(3), 102015. 10.1016/j.jksuci.2024.102015

Dakalbab, F., Talib, M. A., Nassir, Q., & Ishak, T. (2024). Artificial intelligence techniques in financial trading: A systematic literature review. *Journal of King Saud University. Computer and Information Sciences*, 36(3), 102015. 10.1016/j.jksuci.2024.102015

Dong, Z., Xin, Z., Liu, D., & Yu, F. (2024). The impact of artificial intelligence application on company environmental investment in Chinese manufacturing companies. *International Review of Financial Analysis*, 95, 103403. 10.1016/j.irfa.2024.103403

Dwivedi, Y. K., Hughes, L., Ismagilova, E., Aarts, G., Coombs, C., Crick, T., Duan, Y., Dwivedi, R., Edwards, J., Eirug, A., Galanos, V., Ilavarasan, P. V., Janssen, M., Jones, P., Kar, A. K., Kizgin, H., Kronemann, B., Lal, B., Lucini, B., & Williams, M. D. (2021). Artificial Intelligence (AI): Multidisciplinary perspectives on emerging challenges, opportunities, and agenda for research, practice, and policy. *International Journal of Information Management*, 57, 101994. 10.1016/j.ijinfomgt.2019.08.002

Gao, Z. (2020). The application of artificial intelligence in stock investment. *Journal of Physics: Conference Series*, 1453(1), 012069. 10.1088/1742-6596/1453/1/012069

Gunjan, A., & Bhattacharyya, S. (2023). A brief review of portfolio optimization techniques. *Artificial Intelligence Review*, 56(5), 3847–3886. 10.1007/s10462-022-10273-7

Haddadian, H., Baky Haskuee, M., & Zomorodian, G. (2022). A hybrid artificial intelligence approach to portfolio management. *Iranian Journal of Finance*, 6(1), 1–27. 10.30699/ijf.2021.287131.1237

Hassani, H., Huang, X., Silva, E., & Ghodsi, M. (2020). Deep learning and implementations in banking. *Annals of Data Science*, 7(3), 433–446. 10.1007/s40745-020-00300-1

Hidayat, M., Defitri, S. Y., & Hilman, H. (2024). The Impact of Artificial Intelligence (AI) on Financial Management. *Management Studies and Business Journal Productivity*, 1(1), 123–129. 10.62207/s298rx18

Huang, Z., Che, C., Zheng, H., & Li, C. (2024). Research on Generative Artificial Intelligence for Virtual Financial Robo-Advisor. *Academic Journal of Science and Technology*, 10(1), 74–80. 10.54097/30r2kk80

Hung, M. C., Hsia, P. H., Kuang, X. J., & Lin, S. K. (2024). Intelligent portfolio construction via news sentiment analysis. *International Review of Economics & Finance*, 89, 605–617. 10.1016/j.iref.2023.07.103

Jebadurai, D. J., Sheela, M. V., Rajeshkumar, L., Soundarya, M., Meena, R., Manickam, T., . . . Manikandan, M. (2024). AI-Driven Decision-Making and Optimization in Modern Agriculture Sectors. In Using Traditional Design Methods to Enhance AI-Driven Decision Making (pp. 269-288). IGI Global.

Konstantinidis, T., Farres, A. B., Xu, Y. L., Constantinides, T. G., & Mandic, D. P. (2023, June). Financial News Classification Model for NLP-based Bond Portfolio Construction. In 2023 24th International Conference on Digital Signal Processing (DSP) (pp. 1-5). IEEE.

Lu, Y. (2019). Artificial intelligence: A survey on evolution, models, applications and future trends. *Journal of Management Analytics*, 6(1), 1–29. 10.1080/23270012.2019.1570365

Maurya, S., Verma, R., Khilnani, L., Bhakuni, A. S., Kumar, M., & Rakesh, N. (2024, March). Effect of AI on the Financial Sector: Risk Control, Investment Decision-making, and Business Outcome. In 2024 11th International Conference on Reliability, Infocom Technologies and Optimization (Trends and Future Directions) (ICRITO) (pp. 1-7). IEEE.

Miziołek, T. (2021). Employing artificial intelligence in investment management. In *The Digitalization of Financial Markets* (pp. 161–174). Routledge. 10.4324/9781003095354-9

Naim, A. (2022). Role of artificial intelligence in business risk management. American Journal of Business Management. *Economics and Banking*, 1, 55–66.

Oyeniyi, L. D., Ugochukwu, C. E., & Mhlongo, N. Z. (2024). Transforming financial planning with AI-driven analysis: A review and application insights. *Finance & Accounting Research Journal*, 6(4), 626–647. 10.51594/farj.v6i4.1037

Phoon, K. F., & Koh, C. C. F. (2018). Robo-advisors and wealth management. *Journal of Alternative Investments*, 20(3), 79–94. 10.3905/jai.2018.20.3.079

Prasad, A., & Seetharaman, A. (2021). Importance of machine learning in making investment decisions in the stock market. *Vikalpa*, 46(4), 209–222. 10.1177/02560909211059992

Raja, S., Jebadurai, D. J., Ivan, L., Mykola, R. V., Ruslan, K., & Nadiia, P. R. (2024). Impact of Artificial Intelligence in Students' Learning Life. In *AI in Business: Opportunities and Limitations* (Vol. 2, pp. 3–17). Springer Nature Switzerland. 10.1007/978-3-031-49544-1_1

Rane, N., Choudhary, S., & Rane, J. (2024). Artificial Intelligence-driven corporate finance: enhancing efficiency and decision-making through machine learning, natural language processing, and robotic process automation in corporate governance and sustainability. Natural Language Processing, and Robotic Process Automation in Corporate Governance and Sustainability (February 8, 2024).

Rehman, M., Dhiman, D. B., & Cheema, G. S. (2024). Minds and Machines: Impact of Emotional Intelligence on Investment Decisions with Mediating the Role of Artificial Intelligence. International Journal of Engineering, Business and Management, *8*(1), 1-10.

Ren, J. (2021). Research on financial investment decisions based on artificial intelligence algorithms. *IEEE Sensors Journal*, 21(22), 25190–25197. 10.1109/JSEN.2021.3104038

Schuett, J. (2023). Risk management in the Artificial Intelligence Act. *European Journal of Risk Regulation*, 1–19. 10.1017/err.2023.1

Swathi, G., & Pahuja, A. (2024). FinTech Frontiers: Cloud Computing and Artificial Intelligence Applications for Intelligent Finance Investment and Blockchain in the Financial Sector. *International Journal of Intelligent Systems and Applications in Engineering*, 12(4s), 654–659.

Zhao, J. (2022). Artificial intelligence and corporate decisions: Fantasy, reality or destiny. *Cath. UL Rev.*, 71, 663.

Zhao, Z., Chen, Y., Bangash, A. A., Adams, B., & Hassan, A. E. (2024). An Empirical Study of Challenges in Machine Learning Asset Management. arXiv preprint arXiv:2402.15990.

KEY TERMS AND DEFINITIONS

Artificial Intelligence: Artificial intelligence, or AI, is a technology that enables computers and machines to simulate human intelligence and problem-solving capabilities.

Asset Management: Asset management is the practice of buying, selling, and managing investments, commensurate with specific risk tolerances, to increase wealth over time.

Institutional Investors: Organizations that invest, include insurance companies, depository institutions, pension funds, investment companies, mutual funds, and endowment funds.

Investment Planning: Investment planning is the process of identifying financial goals and creating a strategy to achieve them through investments. It involves assessing risk tolerance, and time horizon, and selecting appropriate investment options to grow wealth over time.

Machine Learning: Machine learning (ML) is a branch of artificial intelligence (AI) and computer science that focuses on using data and algorithms to enable AI to imitate the way that humans learn, gradually improving its accuracy.

Natural Language Processing: Natural language processing (NLP) is a subfield of computer science and artificial intelligence (AI) that uses machine learning to enable computers to understand and communicate with human language.

Portfolio Optimization: Portfolio optimization is a quantitative method used in finance to select the best mix of assets for an investment portfolio, aiming to achieve maximum return at a chosen level of risk.

Risk Management: Risk management identifies, assesses, and controls financial, legal, strategic, and security risks to an organization's capital and earnings.

Robo-Advisors: A robo-advisor is a type of automated financial advisor that provides algorithm-driven wealth management services with little to no human intervention.

Securities Market: A financial securities market is a marketplace where individuals and organizations buy and sell various securities such as stocks, bonds, and derivatives.

Chapter 7
Financial Frontiers:
How Generative AI Is Shaping the Fintech Industry

Gopinath Rajenthran
Commonwealth Bank of Australia, Australia

ABSTRACT

Fintech players have always adopted the latest technology that evolve in the market to stay ahead in this competitive industry. In that adoption curve, we are now standing in the place where we are going to witness the adoption of the Generative AI as the next technological phenomenon that will shape the future of Fintech industry. In this chapter, the authors explore the following areas to getter a deeper insight into how Generative AI tends to play in Fintech industry: 1) Generative AI technologies involved in Fintech, 2) application of Generative AI in Fintech, 3) benefits of adopting Generative AI in Fintech, 4) case studies where Generative AI is adopted, 5) challenges and risks in adopting Generative AI, 6) mitigation strategies for the above said challenges and risks, and 7) future trends and developments.

INTRODUCTION

Fintech is the adoption of Information Technology as a tool to facilitate and or enhance accessibility to perform financial transactions through digital channels. Fintech has played a key role in today's modern world transforming the traditional 'Over the counter' Banking to Digital Banking where the customers are no longer required to visit the branch physically for their day-to-day financial transactions. The late 90s and early 2000s saw the adoption of Internet as an evolution that helped digitise the finance sector. The customers required a physical device like laptop or computer and a moderate internet connection to access the finance services using

DOI: 10.4018/979-8-3693-5578-7.ch007

Internet Banking platform. The late 2000s and early 2010s saw the rise of mobile banking where a Mobile Banking Application or popularly a 'Mobile App' took digitisation of the Finance Sector to the next level where a computer or laptop is no longer. The customers can now initiate and complete a digital transaction anywhere anytime at the touch of a button using a mobile device. Fintech products has democratized access of the financial services. Fintech players have always adopted the latest technology that evolve in the market to stay ahead in this competitive industry. In that adoption curve, we are now standing in the place where we are going to witness the adoption of the Generative AI as the next technological phenomenon that will shape the future of Fintech Industry.

TECHNOLOGIES INVOLVED IN GENERATIVE AI

Machine Learning

Machine learning (ML) is a part of Artificial Intelligence (AI). It helps to perform the work by developing algorithms. Machine learning is widely used in fintech industry, health industry, transportation etc. With the help of the statistical models like regression, clustering, mean etc that helps to follow the instructions given by the customer to perform the tasks (Harshvardhan et al., 2020). The application of machine learning in widely used in fintech industry is to be identifying the fraudulent transactions by detecting the fraud in the transaction data and to assess the creditworthiness of the customer based on considering various factor and advising them a proper investment portfolio (Alwahedi et al., 2024). Relevant data related to fintech is collected from various sources, processing into an information, using appropriate model data is being assessed, evaluated and implement in the real-world application. It should be continuously monitored and whenever and wherever need it should be updated. Fraud detection in one the most important application of the machine learning in Fintech. By analyzing the customers historical transactions, it can identify the pattern of fraudulent activity involved in the account and marked it as suspicious transaction. Fintech industry use machine learning to offer the customized products and services and tailored based financial advice for investment which enhances customer loyalty (Harshvardhan et al., 2020).

Deep Learning

Deep learning is a part of machine learning with advance technology like responding to the voice message (speech recognition), object detection, image classification, converting the spoken language to written language, converting written language into spoken language. The queries raised by the customer is passed through various process to offer solutions. Deep learning algorithm identifies the fraud by analysing the fraudulent behaviour. It adopts new fraudulent techniques to offer solutions (Soori et al., 2023).

Natural Language Processing

Natural Language Processing (NLP) is a field of artificial intelligence that focuses on the interaction between computers and human language. By utilizing algorithms and machine learning, NLP enables computers to understand, interpret, and generate human language. Applications of NLP include language translation, sentiment analysis, and chatbots (Chowdhary & Chowdhary, 2020). Key techniques involve parsing, tokenization, and semantic analysis. NLP bridges the gap between human communication and computer understanding, making technology more accessible and intuitive. As the technology advances, it holds the promise of transforming industries by enabling more efficient and natural interactions between humans and machines (Fanni et al., 2023).

Blockchain and AI Integration

AI can analyze the transaction patterns to identify fraud whereas the blockchain will help us to know the honesty of the transactions it also ensures the transparency, security and compliance of the data used. Blockchain and AI integration creates a powerful synergy, enhancing the capabilities of both technologies. Blockchain provides a decentralized, transparent, and secure ledger system, ensuring data integrity and trust (David et al., 2023). AI, on the other hand, leverages this trustworthy data to make intelligent decisions, improve efficiency, and enable automation. The integration enhances data security in AI applications, reducing risks of data tampering. It also facilitates the creation of decentralized AI models, promoting collaborative learning without compromising privacy (Sankar et al., 2022). Together, blockchain and AI drive innovation in various sectors, including finance, healthcare, and supply chain, fostering a more secure and intelligent digital future (Sankar, 2024).

APPLICATION OF GENERATIVE AI IN FINTECH

Enhanced Customer Service

AI interacts with the customers to know their needs and preferences in terms of any additional services needed or solutions to the problems they encounter. It acts as a financial advisor by offering the recommendations and solutions to the problems you faced (Rani et., 2024). For e.g. The frequent problem faced by the customer is lack of transparency or misinformation about their service charges. At the time of offering the services they do not disclose or emphasis on the service charges. If you ask the service charges queries to the AI, it will give you a correct information at a faster rate. Sometimes it will also give you all splits up of the charges which you are paying, and it will suggest you the best payment mode to reduce your cost. It simply understands the customer's common problems and work closely for better solutions. It reduces the customer service human work and supports the customers 24/7 thus enhancing an increase in customer the satisfaction. Chatbots are the most common use of generative AI to enhance customer service. It provides convenience to the customers to clarify their queries at less time with no cost (Khan & Iqbal, 2020).

Bias Free Credit Scoring and Lending

AI is revolutionizing the credit scoring and lending processes by providing more accurate and fair assessments of creditworthiness. Traditional credit scoring models rely heavily on credit history, which can be limiting for individuals with little or no credit history. AI, however, can analyze alternative data sources, such as social media activity, utility bill payments, and even mobile phone usage, to assess an individual's creditworthiness (Jammalamadaka & Itapu, 2023). Machine learning algorithms can identify patterns and correlations within this data, offering a more comprehensive and nuanced understanding of a borrower's financial behaviour. This approach not only improves the accuracy of credit scoring but also expands access to credit for underserved populations, promoting financial inclusion (Hearn, 2023). In the lending process, AI can automate and streamline tasks such as document verification, risk assessment, and loan approval. By reducing manual intervention, AI-driven systems can expedite the lending process, enhance operational efficiency, and reduce the risk of human error (Dessain et al., 2023). When the customer is interested to know their credit scoring, they can seek assistance from the AI. It has an ability to explain the customer about their credit assessment by quickly assessing their transaction history and offer them more accurate assessment of their creditworthiness with greater security, privacy, accountability etc. It will accurately predict the customers repaying capacity by analysing their information and offer suggestions in their financial processes (Hearn, 2023; Jammalamadaka & Itapu, 2023). AI has a capacity to analyse a data from various source at faster speed to analyse the risk assessment of the customer efficiently with less or no mistake, ensure transparency, no bias and compliance which enhance the fraud detection capabilities and improves overall customer experience (Dessain et al., 2023).

More Personalization of Digital Banking

Covid has made customer to adapt to digitalization. Now a days all the customers have convenience of all the services at their fingertips. Many fintech companies offer personalized services to the customer via email, customer support, mobile banking, internet banking, AI can assist the customer with personalised financial advice like investment opportunities, saving plans, manage finance, offer products and services which aligns with their financial goals by analysing their financial history and spending habits (Gigante & Zago, 2023). It offers more personalized services like offer 24/7 support with chatbots, quickly solve the customer issues and queries. Customers can avail their debit card, credit card without visiting the bank. They can access to your financial statement, check your daily transactions by single click in their mobile banking app or in internet banking (Sheth et al., 2022). All the organisation started moving towards green environment and paper-less transactions. Even you can open a saving account online by uploading all the necessary documents. AI-powered systems can analyse vast amounts of data to understand individual customer preferences, behaviours, and financial goals. This enables financial institutions to offer personalized products and services, enhancing customer satisfaction and loyalty (Yalamati, 2023). For example, AI-driven robo-advisors provide personalized investment advice based on an individual's financial goals, risk tolerance, and market conditions. These robo-advisors continuously monitor and adjust investment portfolios, ensuring they align with the client's objectives (Sheth et al., 2022). This level of personalization, previously available only to high-net-worth individuals, is now accessible to a broader audience. AI also powers chatbots and virtual assistants that provide real-time, personalized support to customers. These AI-driven tools can answer queries, provide financial advice, and assist with transactions, offering a seamless and engaging customer experience (Gigante & Zago, 2023; Yalamati, 2023).

Fraud Detection and Prevention

Fraud exists in all walks of life and detecting and preventing fraud plays a pivotal role in all industry. Fraud detection has been a challenge in Fintech industry. When there are frequent fraudulent transactions in their account customer will have negative opinion towards the organisation and It will affect the good will of the organisation. There has been a massive increase in the fraud from the covid 19 pandemic. Financial frauds are like hacking the credit card or debit card details and using it (Alzahrani & Aljabri, 2022; Bao et al., 2022). AI will check the account, detect the fraudulent transactions by analysing the transaction patterns of the customer and credit the amount to their respective account (Bao et al., 2022). For eg a bank must analyse the transaction details of the customer and their spending patterns. The debit card of the customer is used only in India for the purchase of last 10 years. Even a previous transaction was from India suddenly there is a transaction like hotel booking in a different country (USA) it is a fraudulent activity (Mohanty & Mishra, 2023). When there is frequent fraud activities take place in an account then the card has to be temporally blocked. Organisation started using AI to detect and prevent fraud.

Algorithmic Trading

Algorithmic Trading is a big transformation of the fintech industry. All the trading has been transferred from human to technologies. AI is an application procedure or commands used for solving a problem or queries of the customer (Addy et al., 2024). It carried out the instructions in a specific order to answer the queries raised by the users. It will have answer / data to offer solutions. Whenever customer enquire about information it can answer them in fractions of a second, with low cost without the involvement of the human being. Algorithmic trading is reliable because it ensures transparency, accountability, fair practices and follows ethical principles and regulations (Cohen, 2022). Example - AI algorithms is widely used in the stock market to analysis and process a historical data of the stock market behaviour and help the investors to plan their investment accordingly. Machine learning models can process vast amounts of historical and real-time data, identifying patterns and trends that may be indicative of future market movements. These models can adapt to changing market conditions, improving their predictive accuracy over time. High-frequency trading (HFT), a subset of algorithmic trading, relies heavily on AI to execute many trades in fractions of a second, capitalizing on minute price discrepancies (Ferreira et al., 2021; Addy et al., 2024). AI-driven trading systems can also incorporate sentiment analysis, evaluating news articles, social media posts, and other textual data to gauge market sentiment. This information can be used to inform trading strategies, helping traders make more informed decisions (Cohen, 2022).

Democratization of Financial Services

We have various investment opportunities to increase the wealth management. Each opportunities have its own risk. It provides personalized investment advice based on the individual income, needs, goals and risk levels (Tan, 2021).

Robotic Advisors like Chatbots

Robotic advisor plays a pivotal role in fintech by assisting the customer to manager their investment effectively. Robotic advisor will provide automated assistance to the customers. They are available round the clock and support their querier at any time and anywhere in the world (Sabir et al., 2023). It will offer the customized solutions to the users based on the questions asked. It will answer them within a second without wasting the valuable time of the customers and able to answers any questions. It will be like an Interactive session to enhance the knowledge related to your queries. It also ensures the security of the information which you have revealed at the time of your enquiry (Roh et al., 2023).

BENEFITS OF ADOPTING GENERATIVE AI IN FINTECH

Data Driven Decision Making

The financial transactions performed by the end users generate large volume of data. The Fintech industry harness this data to make key decisions. These decisions require manual efforts and the results derived more often only after detailed analysis involving large amount of time and human resources (Yusof & Roslan, 2023). For example, preparing the financial performance report of an organisation involves such tedious manual tasks and are often published only as monthly, quarterly bi-annual or annual report. The Generative AI has the potential to harness this data by using AI algorithms. As AI algorithms evolve, they will grow to be capable of producing such reports real time thus benefiting the top-level management to arrive at key decisions more instantly than relying on periodic reports (Tian & Han, 2021). The AI Algorithms can help customers take an Improvised approach in transactional decision-making scenarios like trading. Before getting involved in a trading event for instance buying shares of a company or creating a long position or short position on a particular share, the participant must arrive at a decision after analysing large volume of data (Awotunde et al., 2021). Often this decision making results in a biased outcome like emotional buying. But with AI taking over this key process, an unbiased decision can be made since it is data driven algorithmic in nature rather than emotional (Yusof & Roslan, 2023).

Automation

AI Algorithms being capable of handling complex decision-making workflows, many repetitive tasks that are often handled by support analysts can now be automated. This adaptability can be a win-win situation for both Fintech Service providers as well as the end users (Huang & Lee, 2022). The service providers can improve the end user experience by reducing the turnaround time for decisions like loan approvals and risk assessments while the customers can get to know the outcome of their applications much sooner rather than waiting for the analysts to come back with their decision in days or weeks and in some cases extending over to several months (Cao et al., 2021). As the AI Algorithms evolve over a period, key business processes can slowly be automated. For instance, customer credit risk assessments, profiling the customers based on the type of transactions they perform, unfolding new offers to the targeted audience to improve customer satisfaction and so on (Jain et al., 2023). AI-Driven chatbots and virtual assistants can handle routine queries thus enhancing the customer experience by not only reducing the turnaround time but also providing response real time (Huang & Lee, 2022).

Fraud Detection Capabilities

With more and more customers on-boarding into digital banking, the volume of transactions is going to increase exponentially over the coming years. So, more the transactions are, so is the fraudulent activities especially where money is involved in the play. The Fintech players are obliged to ensure that their IT infrastructure is immune to cyber-attacks, phishing and all the other possible vulnerabilities (Alzahrani & Aljabri, 2022; Bao et al., 2022). AI Powered fintech solutions can offer faster, secure and seamless transactions. The major fintech players have already started to explore using AI Algorithms to perform predictive analysis, analyse real-time transaction patterns and quickly identify suspicious activities thus preventing unauthorized transactions (Bao et al., 2022).

Tailor Made Financial Solutions

Traditional portfolio management is a financial solution that is often made available only to the high-net-worth individuals due to the financial expertise required for the solution. The AI-Powered artificial advisors can offer customers personalised investment strategies by understanding their risk appetite, financial goals considering the current markets conditions. And this can only be possible by integrating AI Algorithms into the financial services sector that looks after portfolio management (Abrokwah-Larbi, 2023).

Conversational Transactions

A conventional financial transaction would involve the customer logging into his/her account and following the step-by-step procedure like entering the password and navigating to the transaction page to initiate the transaction. Await and verify that the transaction has completed. Log off from the application. Just imagine if this step-by-step procedure is translated into a conversation between the application and the customer. Generative AI can make this possible. Voice activated payments or the 'Conversation Transactions' can become possible with AI powered Financial Technology. With the right security parameters set up, this can help visually challenged customers to use Fintech on their own (Aggarwal & Singh, 2024).

Reduce Illegal Insider Trading

Generative AI can help reducing unethical and illegal activities like insider trading. Major public organisations gather their financial performance information for over a defined period say quarterly or annually and then publish them. Insider Trading is often possible only because of the non-public, material information about a public company's stock being accessible to someone within the organization (Alqurayn et al., 2024). With AI-Empowered financial systems, the material information can be collected, aggregated and documented real time. So, the organisations can generate these this data just before making them public, thus avoiding the room for possibility of insider trading (Esen et al., 2019).

CHALLENGES AND RISKS IN ADOPTING GENERATIVE AI

The fintech industry, characterized by its use of technology to improve financial services, has been rapidly evolving. Generative AI, a subset of artificial intelligence that can generate new content based on existing data, has emerged as a transformative force within this sector. Its applications range from personalized customer interactions to advanced fraud detection and predictive analytics. However, the adoption of generative AI in fintech is fraught with significant challenges and risks. This essay explores these issues in depth, providing a comprehensive overview of the hurdles and potential dangers associated with integrating generative AI into the financial technology landscape (Huang et al., 2024).

Data Quality and Availability

One of the primary challenges in adopting generative AI in fintech is ensuring high data quality and availability. Generative AI models rely heavily on large datasets to learn and make accurate predictions (Sankar, 2024). However, financial data is often dispersed across various systems and formats, leading to inconsistencies and inaccuracies. Poor data quality can result in flawed AI models, which may produce unreliable or biased outputs (Huang et al., 2024). Moreover, access to vast amounts of data is often restricted by privacy laws and data-sharing limitations. Regulations like the General Data Protection Regulation (GDPR) in Europe impose strict controls on how personal data is collected, stored, and used (Sankar, 2024). Fintech companies must navigate these regulations carefully to ensure compliance while still gathering the data necessary for training AI models. Balancing data accessibility with privacy concerns is a significant hurdle that requires robust data governance frameworks (Huang et al., 2024).

Regulatory Compliance

The fintech industry is heavily regulated, and the introduction of generative AI adds another layer of complexity. Financial institutions must ensure that their AI applications comply with a myriad of laws and regulations, including Anti-Money Laundering (AML) and Know Your Customer (KYC) requirements. These regulations are designed to prevent fraud, money laundering, and other illicit activities, but they also pose challenges for AI adoption (Truby et al., 2020). Regulators are often wary of new technologies, and the opacity of AI models can exacerbate these concerns. Traditional financial systems are built on principles of transparency and accountability, but AI models, especially complex ones, can function as "black boxes," making it difficult to understand how decisions are made. This lack of transparency can hinder regulatory approval and lead to legal challenges. Fintech companies must work closely with regulators to ensure that AI models are transparent, explainable, and compliant with existing laws (Lee, 2020).

Integration With Legacy Systems

Many financial institutions operate on legacy systems that are deeply entrenched in their operations. These systems, often built decades ago, may not be compatible with modern AI technologies. Integrating generative AI with these legacy systems is a formidable challenge. It requires significant investment in technology upgrades, data migration, and system interoperability (Cao, 2020). Legacy systems are typically not designed to handle the scale and complexity of AI applications. They may lack the processing power and data storage capabilities needed to support advanced AI models. Furthermore, the integration process can be disruptive, potentially causing downtime and affecting customer service (Ashta & Herrmann, 2021). Fintech companies must carefully plan and execute integration strategies to minimize disruptions and ensure a smooth transition to AI-enabled systems.

Technical Expertise

The successful adoption of generative AI in fintech requires specialized technical expertise. Developing, deploying, and maintaining AI models necessitates skills in machine learning, data science, and software engineering. However, there is a shortage of professionals with these skills, making it challenging for fintech companies to recruit and retain the necessary talent. Additionally, the fast-paced nature of AI research means that knowledge and skills can quickly become outdated (Ooi et al., 2023). Continuous learning and development are essential to keep up with the latest advancements. Fintech companies must invest in training and development programs to ensure their teams remain at the cutting edge of AI technology (Ashta & Herrmann, 2021). Collaborations with academic institutions and AI research organizations can also help bridge the skills gap and foster innovation.

Scalability

Scalability is another critical challenge in adopting generative AI in fintech. Financial institutions handle large volumes of transactions and customer interactions daily. AI solutions must be able to scale effectively to manage this high demand without compromising performance or accuracy. Scaling AI models requires robust infrastructure, including powerful computing resources and efficient data management systems (Ooi et al., 2023; Ashta & Herrmann, 2021). Cloud computing can offer scalable solutions, but it also introduces concerns about data security and privacy. Fintech companies must carefully evaluate their infrastructure needs and choose scalable solutions that align with their business goals and regulatory requirements (Cao, 2020).

Ethical Considerations

Ethical considerations play a significant role in the adoption of generative AI in fintech. AI models can inadvertently perpetuate or even exacerbate biases present in the training data (Cao, 2020). For example, if historical lending data reflects discriminatory practices, an AI model trained on this data may continue to make biased lending decisions. Ensuring fairness and transparency in AI decision-making is paramount. Fintech companies must implement rigorous testing and validation processes to identify and mitigate biases (Ashta & Herrmann, 2021). Developing ethical AI frameworks that prioritize fairness, accountability, and transparency is essential. Additionally, engaging with diverse stakeholders, including customers, regulators, and advocacy groups, can help ensure that AI systems are designed and deployed responsibly.

Security and Privacy Risks

Security and privacy are critical concerns in the fintech industry, and the adoption of generative AI introduces new risks. AI systems can be targets for cyberattacks, potentially exposing sensitive financial data. Protecting AI models and the data they process requires robust security measures, including encryption, access controls, and continuous monitoring (Kar & Kushwaha, 2023). Moreover, AI models themselves can inadvertently leak sensitive information. For instance, generative models trained on customer data might inadvertently generate outputs that reveal personal information. Ensuring data privacy and preventing unintended data leakage is essential (Ashta & Herrmann, 2021). Fintech companies must implement privacy-preserving techniques, such as differential privacy, to protect customer data while still leveraging AI capabilities.

Bias and Fairness

Bias in AI models is a significant risk in the fintech industry. AI systems trained on biased data can make unfair decisions, leading to discrimination against certain customer groups. This can have serious legal and reputational consequences for financial institutions. Addressing bias requires a comprehensive approach that includes diverse and representative training data, rigorous testing for biases, and ongoing monitoring of AI models (Kar & Kushwaha, 2023). Transparent and explainable AI models are also crucial for identifying and mitigating biases. Fintech companies must prioritize fairness and inclusivity in their AI development processes to ensure that all customers are treated equitably (Cao, 2020).

Operational Risk

Operational risk is a critical consideration when adopting generative AI in fintech. AI models can fail or make incorrect predictions, leading to financial losses and reputational damage. For example, an AI system used for credit scoring might incorrectly assess a customer's creditworthiness, resulting in either unjust loan approvals or rejections. Continuous monitoring and validation of AI models are essential to mitigate operational risks (Ashta & Herrmann, 2021). Fintech companies must establish robust risk management frameworks that include regular audits, performance evaluations, and contingency plans for AI system failures. Building resilient AI systems that can adapt to changing conditions and recover quickly from errors is crucial for maintaining operational stability (Shanmuganathan, 2020).

Dependency Risk

The adoption of generative AI can lead to increased dependency on AI systems. Over-reliance on AI can create vulnerabilities if the AI systems fail or if there are disruptions in the technology supply chain. For example, a sudden change in market conditions might render an AI model obsolete, requiring rapid updates and recalibrations (Shanmuganathan, 2020). Fintech companies must maintain a balance between human oversight and AI automation. Ensuring that human experts remain involved in critical decision-making processes can help mitigate dependency risks. Additionally, developing robust AI governance frameworks that include clear roles and responsibilities for AI oversight can enhance resilience and reduce the risk of over-reliance on AI systems (Cao, 2020).

Market Risk

The financial market is highly dynamic, and rapid changes can impact the effectiveness of AI models. For instance, economic downturns, regulatory changes, or shifts in consumer behaviour can render existing AI models less accurate or relevant. Fintech companies must be prepared to adapt their AI systems to changing market conditions (Shanmuganathan, 2020). Regularly updating and retraining AI models is essential to ensure they remain effective in dynamic environments. Continuous learning and adaptive algorithms can help AI systems stay relevant and accurate. Additionally, fintech companies should invest in market research and predictive analytics to anticipate and respond to market changes proactively (Ashta & Herrmann, 2021).

Legal and Compliance Risks

Non-compliance with regulatory requirements poses significant legal and compliance risks for fintech companies adopting generative AI. Regulatory bodies may impose fines, penalties, and other sanctions for non-compliance, leading to financial losses and reputational damage (Ashta & Herrmann, 2021). To mitigate these risks, fintech companies must establish robust compliance frameworks that ensure adherence to all relevant laws and regulations (Cao, 2020). This includes conducting regular compliance audits, engaging with legal experts, and staying informed about regulatory developments. Proactive engagement with regulators and participation in industry forums can also help fintech companies navigate the regulatory landscape and ensure compliance with evolving standards (Ashta & Herrmann, 2021).

MITIGATION STRATEGIES

Addressing the challenges and risks associated with adopting generative AI in fintech requires a multi-faceted approach. The following mitigation strategies can help fintech companies navigate these complexities. Ensuring high data quality, secure storage, and compliance with data privacy regulations is essential. Implementing data governance frameworks and using privacy-preserving techniques can help protect customer data and ensure AI models are trained on accurate and representative data (Cao, 2020). Regularly testing AI models for accuracy, fairness, and robustness is crucial. Fintech companies should implement rigorous validation processes to identify and mitigate biases and ensure AI models perform reliably (Cao et al., 2021). Implementing systems to continuously monitor AI performance and detect anomalies or biases is essential. Real-time monitoring can help identify issues early and prevent potential risks (Cao, 2020; Cao et al., 2021). Developing AI models that provide clear, understandable decision-making processes is crucial for regulatory compliance and customer trust. Transparent and explainable AI systems can help demystify AI decisions and ensure accountability (Cao et al., 2021). Establishing ethical guidelines and practices for AI development and deployment can help ensure that AI systems are designed and used responsibly. Engaging with diverse stakeholders and prioritizing fairness and inclusivity are key components of ethical AI frameworks (Cao, 2020). Proactively engaging with regulators can help fintech companies ensure compliance and influence policy development. Participating in industry forums and collaborating with regulatory bodies can provide (Cao et al., 2021).

CASE STUDIES WHERE GENERATIVE AI IS ADOPTED

AI has significantly transformed the financial technology (fintech) sector by introducing automation, enhancing customer service, and improving decision-making processes. Here are a few notable case studies that highlight the diverse applications of AI in fintech:

Robo-Advisors: Betterment and Wealthfront (Wong, 2021)

Betterment and Wealthfront are prominent examples of robo-advisors using AI to manage investment portfolios. These platforms use algorithms to provide financial advice and manage client investments with minimal human intervention. Betterment Uses AI to optimize tax strategies, recommend asset allocations, and personalize investment plans based on individual goals and risk tolerance. It employs algorithms to perform tax-loss harvesting, which helps minimize tax liabilities. Wealthfront Utilizes AI to provide personalized financial planning. Its Path tool uses AI to analyse financial data and simulate different scenarios to help clients understand their financial health and plan for future goals.

Fraud Detection: PayPal (Mohanty & Mishra, 2023)

PayPal employs machine learning algorithms to detect and prevent fraudulent transactions. By analysing vast amounts of transaction data, PayPal's AI system identifies patterns and anomalies that may indicate fraudulent activity. Real-Time Analysis: PayPal's AI system processes transactions in real-time, allowing it to flag and investigate suspicious activities immediately. This helps reduce financial losses and protect user accounts. Adaptive Learning: The system continuously learns from new data, improving its accuracy and ability to detect emerging fraud tactic.

Credit Scoring: ZestFinance (Hearn, 2023)

ZestFinance leverages AI to revolutionize credit scoring and underwriting. Traditional credit scoring models rely heavily on credit history, which can be limiting for individuals with sparse credit records. Zest Finance's AI model considers a broader range of data points. Alternative Data: The AI system incorporates non-traditional data sources, such as utility payments, social media activity, and other behavioural data, to assess creditworthiness. Fairer Lending: By using AI, ZestFinance aims to provide fairer credit assessments, expanding access to credit for underserved populations.

Personalized Banking: Bank of America's Erica (Gigante & Zago, 2023)

Bank of America introduced Erica, an AI-powered virtual assistant, to enhance customer service and provide personalized banking experiences. Natural Language Processing (NLP): Erica uses NLP to understand and respond to customer queries via text or voice. It can help with tasks such as checking account balances, paying bills, and providing budgeting tips. Proactive Alerts: Erica proactively provides financial insights and alerts customers about potential issues, such as unusual spending patterns or upcoming bills, helping them manage their finances more effectively.

Algorithmic Trading: Renaissance Technologies (Addy eta al., 2024)

Renaissance Technologies is a hedge fund known for its use of AI and quantitative models to execute trades. The firm's Medallion Fund is famous for its high returns, driven by sophisticated AI algorithms. Data-Driven Decisions: The fund uses machine learning to analyse vast amounts of financial data, identify trading opportunities, and execute trades with precision. Risk Management: AI models also help in assessing and mitigating risks by continuously monitoring market conditions and adjusting strategies accordingly.

Chatbots and Customer Support: Lemonade (La Barbera, 2023)

Lemonade, an insurance company, uses AI to streamline its customer service and claims processing. AI Chatbots: Lemonade's AI chatbot, Maya, assists customers with purchasing policies and filing claims. The chatbot provides instant responses, improving customer satisfaction and reducing operational costs. Claims Processing: The AI system processes claim quickly by analysing the details provided by customers, cross-referencing with policy information, and making decisions in real-time.

These case studies demonstrate the transformative impact of AI in fintech, showcasing its potential to improve efficiency, enhance customer experiences, and drive innovation across various financial services.

FUTURE TRENDS AND DEVELOPMENTS

Enhanced Personalization

One of the most significant future trends in AI for fintech is enhanced personalization. As AI technologies advance, they will enable financial institutions to provide highly tailored services to their customers. AI algorithms can analyse vast amounts of data, including transaction histories, social media activity, and even biometric data, to gain deep insights into individual preferences and behaviours (Sheth et al., 2022; Gigante & Zago, 2023).

- **Personalized Financial Planning**: AI-driven financial planning tools will become more sophisticated, offering customized investment advice, retirement planning, and budgeting assistance based on real-time analysis of a user's financial situation and goals.
- **Targeted Marketing**: Financial institutions will leverage AI to create more effective marketing strategies. By analysing customer data, AI can identify the most relevant products and services for everyone, leading to higher conversion rates and customer satisfaction.
- **Dynamic Pricing and Offers**: AI will enable dynamic pricing models and personalized offers. For instance, credit card companies could adjust interest rates and rewards based on a customer's spending patterns and creditworthiness, ensuring more competitive and attractive offerings.

Advanced Fraud Detection and Prevention

As fintech continues to grow, so does the sophistication of financial fraud. AI will play a crucial role in enhancing fraud detection and prevention capabilities. Future AI systems will be able to identify fraudulent activities with greater accuracy and speed, minimizing losses and protecting customers (Alzahrani & Aljabri, 2022; Mohanty & Mishra, 2023).

- **Behavioural Biometrics**: AI will analyse behavioural biometrics, such as typing patterns, mouse movements, and touchscreen interactions, to detect fraudulent activities. These biometric markers are difficult for fraudsters to replicate, providing an additional layer of security.
- **Real-time Monitoring**: AI-powered systems will continuously monitor transactions in real-time, flagging suspicious activities instantly. Machine learning algorithms will evolve to recognize new and emerging fraud patterns, staying ahead of cybercriminals.
- **Enhanced Identity Verification**: AI will improve identity verification processes through advanced techniques like DIP (Digital Image Processing), facial recognition, voice recognition, and even blockchain-based identity solutions. These technologies will make it harder for fraudsters to impersonate legitimate customers.

AI-Driven Customer Support

Customer support is a critical area where AI is set to make significant strides. AI-powered chatbots and virtual assistants will become more prevalent and sophisticated, offering efficient and personalized customer service (Sheth et al., 2022).

- **Natural Language Processing (NLP)**: Advances in NLP will enable chatbots to understand and respond to customer queries more accurately. These chatbots will handle a broader range of customer interactions, from answering basic questions to resolving complex issues.
- **Proactive Support**: AI will enable proactive customer support by anticipating customer needs and addressing potential issues before they arise. For example, if an AI system detects unusual spending patterns, it can notify the customer and help.
- **Multi-Channel Integration**: AI-driven customer support systems will seamlessly integrate across multiple channels, including social media, mobile apps, and websites. This ensures consistent and efficient service delivery, regardless of the platform used by the customer.

Improved Risk Management

Risk management is a critical aspect of financial services, and AI is poised to revolutionize this area. Advanced AI algorithms will enhance risk assessment, monitoring, and mitigation strategies, leading to more robust financial systems (Ashta & Herrmann, 2021).

- **Predictive Analytics**: AI will leverage predictive analytics to forecast market trends, credit risks, and potential financial crises. By analysing historical data and identifying patterns, AI can help financial institutions make informed decisions and mitigate risks.
- **Real-time Risk Monitoring**: AI will enable continuous monitoring of financial risks in real-time. This allows institutions to identify and respond to emerging threats swiftly, minimizing potential losses.
- **Stress Testing**: AI-driven stress testing models will become more sophisticated, simulating various economic scenarios to assess the resilience of financial institutions. This will help regulators and institutions ensure stability in the face of economic uncertainties.

Blockchain and AI Integration

The integration of AI and blockchain technology is set to create new opportunities and efficiencies in the fintech industry. Blockchain's decentralized and transparent nature, combined with AI's analytical capabilities, will transform various financial processes (Odeyemi et al., 2024).

- **Smart Contracts**: AI can enhance smart contracts by automating and optimizing contract execution. For instance, AI algorithms can monitor contract conditions in real-time and trigger actions when specific criteria are met, reducing the need for manual intervention.
- **Fraud Detection and Compliance**: AI and blockchain together can improve fraud detection and compliance. Blockchain's immutable ledger ensures transparency, while AI analyses transaction data to identify suspicious activities and ensure regulatory compliance.
- **Decentralized Finance (DeFi)**: The rise of DeFi platforms, which use blockchain and AI to offer financial services without traditional intermediaries, will continue to grow. AI can enhance DeFi platforms by providing risk assessment, automated trading, and personalized financial advice.

AI in Investment Management

Investment management is another area where AI is set to make significant advancements. AI-driven tools and platforms will offer more precise investment strategies, improving returns and reducing risks for investors (Addy et al., 2024).

- **Robo-Advisors**: AI-powered robo-advisors will become more sophisticated, offering personalized investment portfolios based on individual risk tolerance, financial goals, and market conditions. These robo-advisors will continuously optimize portfolios, ensuring maximum returns.
- **Algorithmic Trading**: AI algorithms will play a more prominent role in algorithmic trading, analysing vast amounts of data to identify profitable trading opportunities. These algorithms will execute trades at high speeds, maximizing gains and minimizing losses.
- **Sentiment Analysis**: AI will leverage sentiment analysis to gauge market sentiment by analysing news articles, social media posts, and other textual data. This information will help investors make informed decisions based on market sentiment and trends.

Enhanced Regulatory Compliance

Regulatory compliance is a significant challenge for financial institutions, and AI can streamline and enhance compliance processes. AI-driven compliance tools will help institutions navigate complex regulatory landscapes and ensure adherence to laws and regulations (Truby et al., 2020).

- **RegTech Solutions**: AI-powered regulatory technology (RegTech) solutions will automate compliance processes, reducing the burden on financial institutions. These solutions will monitor regulatory changes, analyse compliance data, and generate reports, ensuring timely and accurate compliance.
- **Anti-Money Laundering (AML)**: AI will improve AML efforts by identifying suspicious transactions and patterns indicative of money laundering. Machine learning algorithms will continuously learn from new data, enhancing their ability to detect and prevent illicit activities.
- **Know Your Customer (KYC)**: AI will streamline KYC processes by automating identity verification and due diligence. Advanced AI systems will analyse various data sources to verify customer identities quickly and accurately, reducing onboarding times and improving customer experiences.

Quantum Computing and AI

Quantum computing, though still in its early stages, has the potential to revolutionize AI in fintech. Quantum computers can process vast amounts of data at unprecedented speeds, enabling more complex AI models and algorithms (Fernández Pérez et al., 2022).

- **Enhanced Computational Power**: Quantum computing will provide the computational power needed for more sophisticated AI models. This will enable financial institutions to solve complex problems, such as risk modelling and portfolio optimization, more efficiently.
- **Secure Transactions**: Quantum computing will enhance the security of financial transactions through quantum encryption methods. This will protect sensitive financial data from cyber threats and ensure secure communication channels.
- **Optimized Algorithms**: Quantum AI algorithms will optimize various financial processes, from trading strategies to fraud detection. The speed and efficiency of quantum computing will enable real-time decision-making and improve overall financial performance.

Collaboration and Ecosystem Development

The future of AI in fintech will involve greater collaboration between financial institutions, technology providers, regulators, and other stakeholders. Building a robust ecosystem will drive innovation and ensure the responsible adoption of AI (Cao et al., 2021).

- **Partnerships and Alliances**: Financial institutions will form strategic partnerships with AI startups, technology firms, and academic institutions. These collaborations will foster innovation, knowledge sharing, and the development of cutting-edge AI solutions.
- **Industry Standards**: The fintech industry will work towards establishing industry standards and best practices for AI adoption. Standardization will ensure interoperability, transparency, and ethical AI use across the sector.
- **Regulatory Collaboration**: Financial institutions and regulators will collaborate more closely to develop AI-friendly regulatory frameworks. This collaboration will ensure that AI innovations comply with regulations while fostering a supportive environment for AI growth.

CONCLUSION

The integration of artificial intelligence (AI) within the financial technology (Fintech) sector is heralding a significant transformation in the financial industry. This technological advancement is fostering the development of innovative solutions aimed at enhancing operational efficiency, reducing operational costs, and elevating the overall customer experience. AI-driven systems are being utilized across various facets of financial services, including but not limited to fraud detection, credit scoring, personalized financial advice, and regulatory compliance. One of the most prominent applications of AI in Fintech is in the realm of fraud detection and prevention (Ashta & Herrmann, 2021). Traditional methods of identifying fraudulent activities often rely on rule-based systems that can be circumvented by sophisticated fraudsters. In contrast, AI systems leverage machine learning algorithms to analyze vast amounts of transaction data in real-time, identifying patterns and anomalies that may indicate fraudulent behavior. This capability not only improves the accuracy of fraud detection but also significantly reduces the time required to identify and respond to potential threats. Credit scoring is another area where AI is making a substantial impact. Conventional credit scoring models are based on a limited set of financial metrics, which can sometimes result in inaccurate assessments of an individual's creditworthiness. AI-driven credit scoring systems, however, incorporate a broader range of data points, including social media activity, payment history, and other non-traditional data sources (Cao, 2020). This comprehensive approach enables more accurate and inclusive credit assessments, providing opportunities for individuals who may have been overlooked by traditional credit scoring models. Personalized financial advice is becoming increasingly accessible through the use of AI. Financial institutions are leveraging AI algorithms to analyze customer data and provide tailored recommendations that align with individual financial goals and risk appetites. This personalized approach not only enhances customer satisfaction but also fosters greater engagement and loyalty (Ashta & Herrmann, 2021). For example, AI-powered robo-advisors can offer investment advice based on a user's financial situation and goals, providing a level of service that was previously only available through human financial advisors.

Regulatory compliance is another critical area where AI is proving to be invaluable. The financial industry is heavily regulated, and compliance with these regulations can be both time-consuming and costly. AI systems can automate many aspects of the compliance process, such as monitoring transactions for suspicious activity and ensuring adherence to anti-money laundering (AML) regulations. By automating these processes, financial institutions can reduce the risk of non-compliance and the associated penalties while also freeing up resources to focus on other strategic initiatives (Aggarwal & Singh, 2024). Despite the numerous benefits, the adoption of AI in Fintech also presents several challenges. One of the primary concerns is data privacy (Sankar & David, 2024). The use of AI requires access to vast amounts of data, raising concerns about how this data is collected, stored, and used. Ensuring that data privacy regulations are adhered to is crucial to maintaining customer trust and avoiding legal repercussions. Model interpretability is another significant challenge. AI systems, particularly those based on deep learning, can often function as "black boxes," making it difficult to understand how decisions are made. This lack of transparency can be problematic, especially in areas such as credit scoring and fraud detection, where understanding the rationale behind decisions is essential (Ashta & Herrmann, 2021).

Regulatory compliance is further complicated by the rapid pace of technological advancement. As AI systems evolve, regulatory frameworks must also adapt to address new risks and ensure that these systems are used responsibly. This requires ongoing collaboration between financial institutions, regulators, and technology providers. Ethical considerations also play a critical role in the adoption of AI in Fintech. Issues such as bias in AI algorithms, the potential for job displacement, and the ethical use of customer data must be carefully considered and addressed to ensure that the benefits of AI are realized in a fair and equitable manner. Looking ahead, the prospects for AI in Fintech are promising. Advanced personalization, integration with blockchain technology, the development of autonomous financial agents, and the promotion of financial inclusion are just a few areas where AI has the potential to drive significant innovation. As technology continues to evolve, addressing the challenges associated with AI adoption will be crucial to unlocking its full potential and creating a more efficient, inclusive, and innovative financial ecosystem.

REFERENCES

Abrokwah-Larbi, K. (2023). The role of generative artificial intelligence (GAI) in customer personalisation (CP) development in SMEs: A theoretical framework and research propositions. *Industrial Artificial Intelligence*, 1(1), 11. 10.1007/s44244-023-00012-4

Addy, W. A., Ajayi-Nifise, A. O., Bello, B. G., Tula, S. T., Odeyem, O., & Falaiye, T. (2024). Algorithmic Trading and AI: A Review of Strategies and Market Impact. *World Journal of Advanced Engineering Technology and Sciences*, 11(1), 258–267. 10.30574/wjaets.2024.11.1.0054

Aggarwal, N., & Singh, K. B. (2024). Evolution and Adoption of Conversational Artificial Intelligence in the Banking Industry. *Conversational Artificial Intelligence*, 85-93.

Alqurayn, A., Kulendran, N., & Ihalanayake, R. (2024). An event study of potential insider trading in the Saudi stock market. *Cogent Economics & Finance*, 12(1), 2367368. 10.1080/23322039.2024.2367368

Alwahedi, F., Aldhaheri, A., Ferrag, M. A., Battah, A., & Tihanyi, N. (2024). Machine learning techniques for IoT security: Current research and future vision with generative AI and large language models. *Internet of Things and Cyber-Physical Systems*.

Alzahrani, R. A., & Aljabri, M. (2022). AI-based techniques for Ad click fraud detection and prevention: Review and research directions. *Journal of Sensor and Actuator Networks*, 12(1), 4. 10.3390/jsan12010004

Ashta, A., & Herrmann, H. (2021). Artificial intelligence and fintech: An overview of opportunities and risks for banking, investments, and microfinance. *Strategic Change*, 30(3), 211–222. 10.1002/jsc.2404

Awotunde, J. B., Adeniyi, E. A., Ogundokun, R. O., & Ayo, F. E. (2021). Application of big data with fintech in financial services. In *Fintech with artificial intelligence, big data, and blockchain* (pp. 107–132). Springer Singapore. 10.1007/978-981-33-6137-9_3

Bao, Y., Hilary, G., & Ke, B. (2022). Artificial intelligence and fraud detection. *Innovative Technology at the Interface of Finance and Operations*, I, 223–247. 10.1007/978-3-030-75729-8_8

Cao, L. (2022). Ai in finance: Challenges, techniques, and opportunities. *ACM Computing Surveys*, 55(3), 1–38. 10.1145/3502289

Cao, L., Yang, Q., & Yu, P. S. (2021). Data science and AI in FinTech: An overview. *International Journal of Data Science and Analytics*, 12(2), 81–99. 10.1007/s41060-021-00278-w

Chowdhary, K., & Chowdhary, K. R. (2020). Natural language processing. *Fundamentals of artificial intelligence*, 603-649.

Cohen, G. (2022). Algorithmic trading and financial forecasting using advanced artificial intelligence methodologies. *Mathematics*, 10(18), 3302. 10.3390/math10183302

David, A., Ahmed, R. R., Ganesh Kumar, C., & Sankar, J. G. (2020). Consumer purchasing process of organic food product: An empirical analysis. *Journal of Management Systems. Quality - Access to Success*, 21(177), 128–132.

David, A., Chandirasekaran, G., & Sankar, J. G. (2023, November). Blockchain and Artificial Intelligence in Food Industry-Case Analysis of Ripe. Io Firm. In *Proceedings of the 5th International Conference on Information Management & Machine Intelligence* (pp. 1-6).

David, A., Jeganathan, G. S., Sikandar, M. D., & Azam, S. A. (2023, May). Internet Users Top Concerns Ensuring Data Privacy, Security, and Protection. In *Arokiaraj David, Jeganathan Gomathi Sankar & Md Sikandar Azam, —Internet Users Top Concerns Ensuring Data Privacy, Security, and Protection , 10th International Conference on Multidisciplinary Research and Modern Education, ISBN* (No. 978-920, pp. 5-20241).

David, A., Maheswari, M., Sankar, G., Christy, F., Karuppannan, A., & Banumathi, M. (2023). Mental illness of Pregnant Women determined by Covid-19: An Empirical Analysis of Pre-and- Post Delivery. *The Saybold Report Journal*, 18(03), 1706–1721.

Dessain, J., Bentaleb, N., & Vinas, F. (2023, July). Cost of Explainability in AI: An Example with Credit Scoring Models. In *World Conference on Explainable Artificial Intelligence* (pp. 498-516). Cham: Springer Nature Switzerland. 10.1007/978-3-031-44064-9_26

Esen, M. F., Bilgic, E., & Basdas, U. (2019). How to detect illegal corporate insider trading? A data mining approach for detecting suspicious insider transactions. *International Journal of Intelligent Systems in Accounting Finance & Management*, 26(2), 60–70. 10.1002/isaf.1446

Fanni, S. C., Febi, M., Aghakhanyan, G., & Neri, E. (2023). Natural language processing. In *Introduction to Artificial Intelligence* (pp. 87–99). Springer International Publishing. 10.1007/978-3-031-25928-9_5

Fernández Pérez, I., Prieta, F. D. L., Rodríguez-González, S., Corchado, J. M., & Prieto, J. (2022, July). Quantum AI: achievements and challenges in the interplay of quantum computing and artificial intelligence. In *International Symposium on Ambient Intelligence* (pp. 155-166). Cham: Springer International Publishing.

Ferreira, F. G., Gandomi, A. H., & Cardoso, R. T. (2021). Artificial intelligence applied to stock market trading: A review. *IEEE Access : Practical Innovations, Open Solutions*, 9, 30898–30917. 10.1109/ACCESS.2021.3058133

Ganeshkumar, C., David, A., & Sankar, J. G. (2024). Blockchain Technology Acceptance in Agribusiness Industry. In Idrees, S. M., & Nowostawski, M. (Eds.), *Blockchain Transformations. Signals and Communication Technology*. Springer., 10.1007/978-3-031-49593-9_15

Ganeshkumar, C., David, A., Sankar, J. G., & Saginala, M. (2023). Application of Drone Technology in Agriculture: A Predictive Forecasting of Pest and Disease Incidence. In *Applying Drone Technologies and Robotics for Agricultural Sustainability* (pp. 50–81). IGI Global.

Ganeshkumar, C., Sankar, J. G., & David, A. (2023). Adoption of Big Data Analytics: Determinants and Performances Among Food Industries. *International Journal of Business Intelligence Research*, 14(1), 1–17. 10.4018/IJBIR.317419

Ganeshkumar, C., Sankar, J. G., & David, A. (2023). Impact of Artificial Intelligence on Agriculture Value Chain Performance: Agritech Perspective. In *Blockchain, IoT, and AI Technologies for Supply Chain Management* (pp. 71-98). CRC Press.

Gigante, G., & Zago, A. (2023). DARQ technologies in the financial sector: Artificial intelligence applications in personalized banking. *Qualitative Research in Financial Markets*, 15(1), 29–57. 10.1108/QRFM-02-2021-0025

Harshvardhan, G. M., Gourisaria, M. K., Pandey, M., & Rautaray, S. S. (2020). A comprehensive survey and analysis of generative models in machine learning. *Computer Science Review*, 38, 100285. 10.1016/j.cosrev.2020.100285

Hearn, A. (2023). The collateralized personality: Creditability and resistance in the age of automated credit-scoring and lending. *Cultural Studies*, 37(1), 123–148. 10.1080/09502386.2022.2042576

Huang, K., Huang, J., & Catteddu, D. (2024). GenAI Data Security. In *Generative AI Security: Theories and Practices* (pp. 133–162). Springer Nature Switzerland. 10.1007/978-3-031-54252-7_5

Huang, S. Y., & Lee, C. J. (2022). Predicting continuance intention to fintech chatbot. *Computers in Human Behavior*, 129, 107027. 10.1016/j.chb.2021.107027

Huang, Z., Che, C., Zheng, H., & Li, C. (2024). Research on Generative Artificial Intelligence for Virtual Financial Robo-Advisor. *Academic Journal of Science and Technology*, 10(1), 74–80. 10.54097/30r2kk80

Jain, R., Prajapati, D., & Dangi, A. (2023). Transforming the financial sector: A review of recent advancements in FinTech. *Available atSSRN* 4380348.

Jammalamadaka, K. R., & Itapu, S. (2023). Responsible AI in automated credit scoring systems. *AI and Ethics*, 3(2), 485–495. 10.1007/s43681-022-00175-3

Jeganathan, G. S., David, A., & Ilangovan, K. (2022). Determination of Hospitality Services Quality and Customer Satisfaction–a Holserv Approach. In *AU Virtual International Conference on" Entrepreneurship & Sustainability in Digital Era" under the theme of" Challenges of Organizational & Business Management in Dynamic Digital Dimension"* (Vol. 3, No. 1, pp. 325-334).

Jeganathan, G. S., & Srinivasulu, Y. (2014). Growth Drivers of Tourism Industry in India. *International Journal of Business and Management*, 2(11), 100.

Kar, A. K., & Kushwaha, A. K. (2023). Facilitators and barriers of artificial intelligence adoption in business–insights from opinions using big data analytics. *Information Systems Frontiers*, 25(4), 1351–1374. 10.1007/s10796-021-10219-4

Khan, S., & Iqbal, M. (2020, June). AI-Powered Customer Service: Does it optimize customer experience? In *2020 8th International Conference on Reliability, Infocom Technologies and Optimization (Trends and Future Directions)(ICRITO)* (pp. 590-594). IEEE.

Kumar, P., Kumar, A., & Sankar, J. G. (2020). Service quality of health tourism in India: A structural equation modelling approach. *Solid State Technology*, 63(2), 1187–1191.

La Barbera, S. (2023). Insurtech Revolution in the Insurance Sector: A Comprehensive Review of the Transformational Impact and the Lemonade Case Study.

Lee, J. (2020). Access to finance for artificial intelligence regulation in the financial services industry. *European Business Organization Law Review*, 21(4), 731–757. 10.1007/s40804-020-00200-0

Mohanty, B., & Mishra, S. (2023). Role of Artificial Intelligence in Financial Fraud Detection. *Academy of Marketing Studies Journal*, 27(S4).

Odeyemi, O., Okoye, C. C., Ofodile, O. C., Adeoye, O. B., Addy, W. A., & Ajayi-Nifise, A. O. (2024). Integrating AI with blockchain for enhanced financial services security. *Finance & Accounting Research Journal*, 6(3), 271–287. 10.51594/farj.v6i3.855

Ooi, K. B., Tan, G. W. H., Al-Emran, M., Al-Sharafi, M. A., Capatina, A., Chakraborty, A., Dwivedi, Y. K., Huang, T.-L., Kar, A. K., Lee, V.-H., Loh, X.-M., Micu, A., Mikalef, P., Mogaji, E., Pandey, N., Raman, R., Rana, N. P., Sarker, P., Sharma, A., & Wong, L. W. (2023). The potential of generative artificial intelligence across disciplines: Perspectives and future directions. *Journal of Computer Information Systems*, 1–32. 10.1080/08874417.2023.2261010

Rani, Y. A., Balaram, A., Sirisha, M. R., Nabi, S. A., Renuka, P., & Kiran, A. (2024, April). AI Enhanced Customer Service Chatbot. In *2024 International Conference on Science Technology Engineering and Management (ICSTEM)* (pp. 1-5). IEEE.

Roh, T., Park, B. I., & Xiao, S. S. (2023). Adoption of AI-enabled Robo-advisors in Fintech: Simultaneous Employment of UTAUT and the Theory of Reasoned Action. *Journal of Electronic Commerce Research*, 24(1), 29–47.

Sabir, A. A., Ahmad, I., Ahmad, H., Rafiq, M., Khan, M. A., & Noreen, N. (2023). Consumer acceptance and adoption of AI robo-advisors in fintech industry. *Mathematics*, 11(6), 1311. 10.3390/math11061311

Sankar, G., & Naveenkumar, K. (2018). *Material Handling Management in Third Party Logistics Warehouse. International Journal for Research in Engineering Application & Management.*

Sankar, J. G. (2020a). Customer perception about innovative safety food delivery during lockdown. *Journal of Contemporary Issues in Business and Government*, 26(2).

Sankar, J. G. (2020b). Innovative celebrity endorsement and consumer purchase. *Journal of Contemporary Issues in Business and Government*, 26(2).

Sankar, J. G. (2020c). Innovative consumer behaviour towards sportswear. *Journal of Contemporary Issues in Business and Government*, 26(2).

Sankar, J. G. (2020d). Service Factors Influence on Customer Satisfaction in Innovative Ecommerce. *SANKAR, D.(2020). Service factors influence on customer satisfaction in innovative e-commerce.Journal of Contemporary Issues in Business and Government*, 26(2), 651–656.

Sankar, J. G. (2020e). Service quality of e-Commerce logistics services. *Journal of Contemporary Issues in Business and Government*, 26(2).

Sankar, J. G., & Kumar, G. (2020). Customer perception towards electric two-wheeler innovation. *Journal of Contemporary Issues in Business and Government*, 26(2).

Sankar, J. G. (2024a). AI-Driven Marketing Success Stories: A Case Note of Industry Pioneers. In *AI-Driven Marketing Research and Data Analytics* (pp. 48-66). IGI Global. 10.4018/979-8-3693-2165-2.ch003

Sankar, J. G. (2024b). Travel Redefined: Future Trends in AI-Enhanced Tourism Experiences. In *AI Innovations for Travel and Tourism* (pp. 135-162). IGI Global.

Sankar, J. G. (2024c). Travel Redefined: Future Trends in AI-Enhanced Tourism Experiences. In *AI Innovations for Travel and Tourism* (pp. 135-162). IGI Global.

Sankar, J. G., & David, A. (2023). Measuring the Service Quality of Artificial Intelligence in the Tourism and Hospitality Industry. In *Handbook of Research on Innovation, Differentiation, and New Technologies in Tourism, Hotels, and Food Service* (pp. 133-155). IGI Global. 10.4018/978-1-6684-6985-9.ch007

Sankar, J. G., & David, A. (2024a). A Comprehensive Examination of Mobile Augmented Reality in Tourism (MART) Adoption: Using the UTAUT2 Framework. In *Contemporary Trends in Innovative Marketing Strategies* (pp. 241-262). IGI Global.

Sankar, J. G., & David, A. (2024b). Transforming the Travel Landscape: Smart Contracts in Tourism Management. In *Decentralizing the Online Experience With Web3 Technologies* (pp. 246-266). IGI Global.

Sankar, J. G., David, A., & Ganesh Kumar, C. (2022). Adaptation of Blockchain Technology In HRM. *Available atSSRN* 4515408.

Sankar, J. G., David, A., & Ramasamy, R. (2023). Assessing Water and Sanitation Service Quality at Pilgrimage Sites After COVID-19: An Empirical Investigation. In *Prospects and Challenges of Global Pilgrimage Tourism and Hospitality* (pp. 160-179). IGI Global.

Sankar, J. G., David, A., & Shrutimeena, G. (2024). From Hesitation to Integration: Understanding Digital Healthcare Adoption. In *Multi-Sector Analysis of the Digital Healthcare Industry* (pp. 1-32). IGI Global.

Sankar, J. G., David, A., & Valan, P. (2023). Examining User Understanding and Perceptions of E-Commerce Data Privacy, Security, and Protection. In *Confronting Security and Privacy Challenges in Digital Marketing* (pp. 159–185). IGI Global. 10.4018/978-1-6684-8958-1.ch008

Sankar, J. G., & Devanand, K. (2020). Social media innovation on consumer buying behaviour. *SANKAR, JG (2020). Social media innovation on consumer buying behaviour.Journal of Contemporary Issues in Business and Government*, 26(2).

Sankar, J. G., & Kiruba Sagar, M, V. (2020). Examining the Risk Factor Associated with UTAUT Model. *Solid State Technology*, 63(2), 1196–1198.

Sankar, J. G., Rajeswari, M., & Dwarak, M. V. S. (2020). To Measure the Service Quality of Film and Television Technology. *Solid State Technology*, 63(2), 1192–1195.

Sankar, J. G., & Srinivasulu, Y. (2014a). A Study of Tourism Industry Impact on Macroeconomic Indicators. *GE-International Journal of Management Research*, 2(11), 2321–1709.

Sankar, J. G., & Srinivasulu, Y. (2014b). Contemporary Sustainable Development Practices in Indian Hospitality Sector: Triple Bottom Line Approach. *SSRN*, 2. 10.2139/ssrn.4204732

Sankar, J. G., Valan, P., & Siranjeevi, M. S. (2020). Various Models to Evaluate Quality in the Service Industry. In *Digital Transformation and Innovative Services for Business and Learning* (pp. 181–194). IGI Global.

Sasikala, J., & Jeganathan, G. S. (2017). A Study on Employee Engagement in Information Technology (IT) Industry. *SSRN*, 1(1), 233–239. 10.2139/ssrn.3536354

Shanmuganathan, M. (2020). Behavioural finance in an era of artificial intelligence: Longitudinal case study of robo-advisors in investment decisions. *Journal of Behavioral and Experimental Finance*, 27, 100297. 10.1016/j.jbef.2020.100297

Sheth, J. N., Jain, V., Roy, G., & Chakraborty, A. (2022). AI-driven banking services: The next frontier for a personalised experience in the emerging market. *International Journal of Bank Marketing*, 40(6), 1248–1271. 10.1108/IJBM-09-2021-0449

Simitha, S., Mugila, P., & Sankar, J. G. (2020). A Study on Customer Relationship Management in Siemens Healthineers. *Solid State Technology*, 63(2), 1199–1203.

Soori, M., Arezoo, B., & Dastres, R. (2023). Artificial intelligence, machine learning and deep learning in advanced robotics, a review. *Cognitive Robotics*, 3, 54–70. 10.1016/j.cogr.2023.04.001

Tan, G. K. S. (2021). Democratizing finance with Robinhood: Financial infrastructure, interface design and platform capitalism. *Environment and Planning A. Economy and Space*, 53(8), 1862–1878.

Tian, X., He, J. S., & Han, M. (2021). Data-driven approaches in FinTech: A survey. *Information Discovery and Delivery*, 49(2), 123–135. 10.1108/IDD-06-2020-0062

Truby, J., Brown, R., & Dahdal, A. (2020). Banking on AI: Mandating a proactive approach to AI regulation in the financial sector. *Law and Financial Markets Review*, 14(2), 110–120. 10.1080/17521440.2020.1760454

Velmurugan, T. A., & Sankar, J. G. (2017). A comparative study on motivation theory with Maslow's hierarchy theory and two factor theory in organization. *Indo-Iranian Journal of Scientific Research*, 1(1), 204–208.

Wong, E. L. (2021). Analysis of Wealthfront Generation Case Study.

Yalamati, S. (2023). Revolutionizing Digital Banking: Unleashing the Power of Artificial Intelligence for Enhanced Customer Acquisition, Retention, and Engagement. *International Journal of Management Education for Sustainable Development*, 6(6), 1–20.

Yusof, S. A. B. M., & Roslan, F. A. B. M. (2023). The Impact of Generative AI in Enhancing Credit Risk Modeling and Decision-Making in Banking Institutions. *Emerging Trends in Machine Intelligence and Big Data*, 15(10), 40–49.

KEY TERMS AND DEFINITIONS

Anti-Money Laundering (AML): Refers to a set of laws, regulations and procedures designed to prevent criminals from disguising illegally obtained funds as legitimate income. Its policies aim to detect and prevent money laundering activities, which can include transferring converting, or concealing money obtained through illegal means such as drug trafficking, terrorism, and corruption.

Decentralized Finance (DeFi): Refers to a financial system built on blockchain technology that aims to provide financial services without relying on traditional intermediaries like banks, brokers, or exchanges. DeFi utilizes smart contracts and decentralized applications to create an open, transparent, and permissionless financial ecosystem.

Digital Image Processing (DIP): Involves the use of computer algorithms to perform operations on digital images. The primary goal of digital image processing is to enhance images, extract useful information, and perform various analyses to achieve desired outcomes.

General Data Protection Regulation (GDPR): A comprehensive data protection law enacted by the European Union effective from May 25, 2018, which aims to give individuals greater control over their personal data and to harmonize data protection regulations across the European Union. It applies to any organization, regardless of location, that processes the personal data of individuals within the EU. Non-Compliance can result in fines and penalties.

High Frequency Trading (HFT): A type of algorithmic trading which involves many orders at extremely high speeds, often within milliseconds or microseconds. It uses sophisticated technological tools and computer algorithms to exploit minute price discrepancies in the financial markets.

Know Your Customer (KYC): A process used by financial institutions and other regulated companies to verify the identity of their clients and assess potential risks of illegal intentions for the business relationship. The primary purpose of KYC is to prevent identity theft, fraud, money laundering, and terrorist financing.

Machine Learning (ML): A branch of Artificial Intelligence whose focus is to develop Algorithms and Statistical models that enable computers to learn decision making based on the trained data.

Natural Language Processing (NLP): A field within Artificial Intelligence whose focus is to enable computers to understand interpret and generate human language in a way that is both meaningful and useful.

Chapter 8
Benefits and Challenges of Artificial Intelligence in FinTech

Mufaro Dzingirai
https://orcid.org/0000-0002-1518-8275
Midlands State University, Zimbabwe

Peterson K. Ozili
https://orcid.org/0000-0001-6292-1161
Central Bank of Nigeria, Nigeria

ABSTRACT

The proliferation of digital transactions in the financial sector when it comes to the 4th Industrial Revolution (41R) has allowed companies to use artificial intelligence. Worryingly, it appears that scant is known about artificial intelligence in the FinTech discourse especially when it comes to African economies. As such, this chapter aims to fill this gap by focusing on the role of artificial intelligence in FinTech. With the utilization of a comprehensive literature review methodology, it was observed that artificial intelligence is of utmost importance as it can augment accuracy, efficiency, fraud detection, effectiveness, human capabilities, and customer experiences; mitigate economic crimes; and accelerate regulatory compliance. Despite these benefits of artificial intelligence in FinTech, it brought to the fore some insurmountable challenges in the financial sector like ethical concerns, human rights issues, social engineering, and fraudulent data generation. The results of the current study are associated with theoretical and practical implications.

DOI: 10.4018/979-8-3693-5578-7.ch008

INTRODUCTION

Recently, it has been an open secret that artificial intelligence revolutionized the financial sector. With multiple sources of data, financial institutions are harnessing the benefits of artificial intelligence applications to gain valuable insights that are required in making evidence-based decisions. Notably, FinTerch refers to technology-based innovations when it comes to the financial sector. Interestingly, artificial intelligence has a notable potential to revolutionize a myriad of financial aspects in the contemporary financial industries in both developed and developing countries (Nica et al., 2024). With an exponential upsurge in the adoption of advanced technologies related to machine learning, deep learning, big data analytics, augmented reality, and mixed reality in the financial sector, it is not surprising to observe that artificial intelligence is a trending concept when it comes to financial technology (Biju, 2024; Farayola, 2024) With this in mind, it is crystal clear that traditional banking has been threatened given that disruptive FinTech firms are introducing fascinating innovative solutions with the aid of robotics and artificial intelligence. More interestingly, the confluence of mobile commerce and FinTech has been widely considered as a paradigm shift towards real-time transactional possibilities.

With the effective adoption of an approach based on artificial intelligence, FinTech can be transformed in a more engaging and personalized way for customers. By using big data and artificial intelligence to gain insights into customer preferences and needs, financial institutions are in a better position to deliver products and services that augment loyalty, customer satisfaction, and retention. This implies that the advent of artificial intelligence appears to be a game-changer as it is revolutionizing the way financial institutions invest, serve customers, and engage in risk management (Biju, 2024). It is worth highlighting that managers of financial institutions are demanded to have an appreciation of how artificial intelligence is transforming the FinTech sector with the aid of advanced machine learning and algorithms. More interestingly, machine learning, artificial intelligence, and deep learning technologies are transforming the once heavily regulated sectors like the financial sector (Biju, 2024; Kumari, 2024). As such, financial managers are expected to craft strategies to ensure the effective adoption of artificial intelligence in their organizations. Financial institutions that are algorithmically and artificial intelligence-based can be widely accepted as customer-centric institutions in the contemporary digital world.

Given an exponential upsurge in computational power and the breakthrough of machine learning, it is not surprising that artificial intelligence can adapt to unique and new situations in the financial sector (Nica et al., 2024). As such, there is a dire need for managers to understand the nexus between artificial intelligence and finance. While the financial sector has the deepest application of artificial intelligence, its actors do not include only technology companies that are associated with the provision of artificial technology but also traditional financial organizations that employ technology and financial supervisory authorities (Ahmad et al., 2024; Hidayah & Purnamasari, 2024). With robust artificial intelligence technologies, unique and innovative business models can be developed and applied in areas like intelligent customer service, intelligent marketing, intelligent investment advisory, and intelligent risk control.

Despite the fact that artificial intelligence technologies are here to stay and are game-changers in the corporate world, it is unfortunate that much is not known concerning the applicability of artificial intelligence in FinTech especially when it comes to financial inclusion. More worryingly, scanty attention has been paid to the challenges associated with artificial intelligence within the context of FinTech. Consequently, this study plugs these literature gaps by focusing on the benefits and challenges associated with artificial intelligence.

BACKGROUND

It has been observed that governments in developed and developing countries are considering the applicability of artificial intelligence as a strategic priority. According to Go et al. (2020), IBM and McKinsey predicted that the adoption of artificial intelligence is growing in leaps and bounds. In terms of the Russian financial sector, IA and Miglionico (2019) documented that the evolution of artificial intelligence is linked to technologies like robotics and automated mechanisms. As such, the Central Bank of Russia advocated for automation of payment systems. It is within this context that Russia is one of the leading players in the adoption of advanced digital transformation within the financial sector. In this respect, Russia is among the top 10 countries that have effectively adopted digital banking alongside Poland, Singapore, Spain, Japan, Belgium, Norway, Saudi Arabia, Turkey, and Qatar. More interestingly, Russia took 4th place in 2020 during the COVID-19 pandemic when it comes to effective non-cash payments transition (Argashokova et al., 2023). Nonetheless, some challenges have been witnessed in the Russian banking sector whereby banks faced regulatory problems when implementing artificial intelligence in retail banking payments (Rutskiy et al., 2022).

Moving forward, in the Indian financial sector, banks are confronted by a plethora of challenges related to increasing customer expectations, shifting demographics, changing regulations, and emerging global competition (Srivastava & Dhamija, 2022). In order to address these challenges, artificial intelligence provides solutions in terms of FinTech applications. More interestingly, the State Bank of India has adopted SBI Intelligent Assistant (SIA) which is an artificial-intelligent-powered chat assistant that can handle about 10,000 queries from customers per second (Umamaheswari & Valarmathi, 2023). In the same vein, ICICI Bank in India has applied robust software robotics covering over 200 business processes as it can handle approximately 2,000,000 transactions daily (Umamaheswari & Valarmathi, 2023). To this end, Andhra Bank in India adopted an artificial intelligence interactive assistant known as "ABHi" with the aim to address customer queries 24/7 at a faster rate than human beings.

Going forward, it is a fact that artificial intelligence technologies like chatbots, virtual assistants, bodily robots, and holograms are transforming FinTech. In this respect, the financial sectors in African economies are no exception. In South Africa, the government is lagging behind in terms of coming up with regulations related to the use of artificial intelligence within the context of the financial industry (Kgoale & Odeku, 2023). It is interesting to observe that South Africa is at the forefront when it comes to innovation on the African continent (Hanlin & Kelly, 2023). The adoption of artificial intelligence in South Africa demands the re-skilling of workers in the banking sector (Mamela et al., 2020). The performance of workers in the fourth industrial revolution (4IR) is affected by emerging technologies like blockchain, robotics, machine learning, and the Internet of Things (IoT).

In the Zimbabwean context, it has been observed that financial institutions adopted artificial intelligence in dealing with financial leakages like money laundering (Dzingirai, 2023). Moreover, financial institutions adopt customer churn prediction models that are powered by artificial intelligence in an attempt to predict dissatisfied customers (Chiurunge et al., 2024). More interesting, commercial banks in Zimbabwe are embracing digital transformation as a powerful turnaround strategy (Dzingirai, 2021a). From an internal auditor's perspective, Lloyd et al. (2024) argued that artificial intelligence and machine learning can be applied to detect early fraud among financial institutions. It must be noted that banks in Zimbabwe intensively adopted mobile and internet banking but the extent of the adoption of artificial intelligence is not known (Lloyd et al., 2024; Shambira, 2020). Moreover, there are limited studies on FinTech in African countries (Dzingirai, 2021b).

CRITICAL SUCCESS FACTORS FOR THE ADOPTION OF ARTIFICIAL INTELLIGENCE

It is necessary at this juncture to critically examine a myriad of critical success factors for the adoption of artificial intelligence in FinTech. The main thrust of artificial intelligence in FinTech is to augment service delivery in terms of efficiency and effectiveness. Nonetheless, the managers of financial institutions must have an in-depth understanding of the factors that underpin the adoption of artificial intelligence technologies in an attempt to outsmart their competitors. In this regard, leadership commitment to the adoption of artificial intelligence in FinTech is one of the critical success factors for the adoption of artificial intelligence (Rožman et al., 2023). Without a strong commitment from top management, it is cumbersome to effectively implement artificial intelligence technologies. The leadership establishes a compelling vision towards embedding artificial intelligence technologies in the processes and systems. Moreover, the sustainability of artificial intelligence initiatives depends on the vision set by the top managers and the objectives linked to the metrics of artificial intelligence (Hu et al., 2024).

Moreover, innovation culture can support the sustainability of artificial intelligence initiatives. It is a fact that FinTech operators are associated with a high affinity for advanced technology. With an innovation culture, employees can embrace and promote the effective use of artificial intelligence when delivering customer service (Goto, 2023; Jardim, 2024). As such, there will be no resistance to change when it comes to the implementation of artificial intelligence technologies. In addition, the availability of financial resources is another key success factor when it comes to the adoption of artificial intelligence (Ahmad et al., 2024). It is within this context that financial institutions with strong financial muscle can easily adopt artificial intelligence. In this respect, there is a need to set aside a budget for artificial intelligence technologies. The money can be used to purchase artificial intelligence technologies and train workers.

Going forward, data access is another key critical success factor for artificial intelligence adoption in FinTech. Artificial intelligence technology can be trained based on available data. In this respect, there is a dire need for big data so as to produce robust results. Data modeling is a key aspect of artificial intelligence (Baumgart, 2024). Therefore, both structured and unstructured data are a prerequisite when it comes to the effective adoption of artificial intelligence in the financial sector. Furthermore, internet connectivity is another factor that is necessary for the adoption of artificial intelligence. It is in this context that virtual assistants and chatbots depend on strong internet connectivity. As such, financial institutions must secure strong internet connectivity so as to avoid unnecessary disruptions.

It is also interesting to observe that the availability of human resources is a key requirement for the adoption of artificial intelligence in the financial sector. With the availability of artificial intelligence experts, financial institutions can effectively adopt artificial intelligence. Nonetheless, many developing countries face an insurmountable challenge of shortage of artificial intelligence experts as compared to developed countries (Vishwakarma, & Singh, 2023). This could be attributed to the poor remuneration of these experts in developing countries. To this end, they migrate to developed countries looking for greener pastures. This kind of human resources leakage can hinder the effective adoption of artificial intelligence within the financial sector.

BENEFITS OF ARTIFICIAL INTELLIGENCE IN THE FINANCIAL SECTOR

Following an in-depth discussion of the critical success factors for artificial intelligence adoption in FinTech, it appears to be necessary to survey some of the benefits linked to the adoption of artificial intelligence in the financial sector. With this in mind, it is worth mentioning that several benefits can be derived from artificial intelligence. Customer experience in the financial sector can be augmented by adopting artificial intelligence (Mhlanga, 2020). It is a fact that artificial intelligence-powered virtual assistants and chatbots are revolutionizing customer service by offering 24/7 service support across the globe. As such, customers can get reliable service at an alarming rate which fosters customer satisfaction. Following the outbreak of the COVID-19 pandemic, it appears that customers embrace the 'new normal" way of doing business online.

With the need to optimize business operations, financial institutions are embracing artificial intelligence technologies. This has been achieved by effectively and efficiently automating several operations and processes (Ochuba et al., 2024). With this in mind, it is not surprising to note that artificial intelligence-driven document automation can promote digital collaboration, reduce manual errors, streamline data entry, and simplify document verification in the financial sector. To this end, the automation of processes in the financial sector has liberated advisors from routine tasks which allows them to pay attention to advisory and strategic duties. Moving next, financial institutions that embraced artificial intelligence enjoyed a significant reduction in operation costs in the sense that labor-intensive tasks are minimized and human errors are eliminated. Notably, the paperwork-heavy process is a fertile ground for human errors that can lead to escalation of costs. To eliminate such costs, banking institutions are embracing robotic process automation. With the effective application of natural language processing, handwriting recognition, and other emerging artificial intelligence technologies, financial institutions can handle a plethora of financial workflows that were previously done by human beings.

It is worth mentioning that artificial intelligence technologies help financial institutions in promoting regulatory compliance. It is widely accepted that the financial sector is heavily regulated which implies that artificial intelligence can assist in automating compliance processes (Lee et al., 2018). This can pave the way for adherence to complex and cumbersome regulatory frameworks. By doing so, risks associated with non-compliance are eliminated. Pragmatically, financial institutions can incorporate artificial intelligence in detecting non-compliance and violations which can be depicted by a red flag in the system (Shoetan & Familoni, 2024). More interestingly, the adoption of artificial intelligence could assist in mitigating and managing investment risks associated with loans. Advanced artificial intelligence models can synthesize customer profiles in a few seconds and inform data-based loan decisions. This can go a long way in fostering optimum lending decisions to reduce non-performing loans. Financial institutions are applying artificial intelligence algorithms to synthesize big financial data, detect anomalies, and identify patterns that can offer insights into the prudent management of potential risks (Chaudhry et al., 2024).

Artificial intelligence has been hailed for aiding data-driven decisions in the financial sector (Apsilyam et al., 2024). It is a fact that artificial intelligence assists in the provision of instant data which enables quicker analysis and faster decision-making process. The interesting part relates to artificial intelligence-data analytics which is linked to descriptive and prescriptive analysis of financial data. Data analytics backed by artificial intelligence assist in identifying investment opportunities, assessing risks, and optimizing business strategies (Udo et al., 2024). The capabilities of the financial institution can be based on fast analysis of risk profiles, market trends, and historical data. This can be cemented by the artificial intelligence competencies of the workers and how they can draw insights to inform strategic decisions. Interestingly, artificial intelligence can analyze vast volumes of market and financial data at an alarming speed which can not be achieved by human beings (Maurya et al., 2024). In the contemporary business community, artificial intelligence helps in loan and creditworthiness assessments in the financial sector. In this regard, banks can use artificial intelligence to make reliable and profitable credit and loan decisions. This implies that machine learning algorithms can used to assess and predict customer patterns and behaviors. With an understanding of customer behavior, banks can ascertain the chance of default.

Given that artificial intelligence can automate the repetitive process, it must be noted that artificial intelligence can be applied to automating the investment process of financial institutions (Ochuba et al., 2024). Banks and other financial institutions are focusing on artificial intelligence as a smart approach to investment decisions. With artificial intelligence, bank managers identify untapped market opportunities provided by algorithmic trading systems. Although some expert judgments are necessary to be made by human beings, artificial intelligence technologies, and systems play an instrumental role in better market discovery and modeling in the financial sector. This is the reason why banks are embracing robo-advisors to assess portfolio management. With customer-specific models, chatbots, and robo-advisers, financial service companies can acquire high-quality strategic guidance on investment portfolios.

CHALLENGES ASSOCIATED WITH ARTIFICIAL INTELLIGENCE ADOPTION IN THE FINANCIAL SECTOR

Although there are many benefits of artificial intelligence adoption in the financial sector, there are some limitations that are worth the attention of managers. Firstly, the adoption of artificial intelligence in FinTech is associated with ethical concerns. Given that financial institutions are demanded to operate under strict regulations which can make it cumbersome to perform deep learning neural networks. Artificial intelligence systems pose a risk to data privacy. Using artificial intelligence systems to offer fintech services is risky because artificial intelligence systems are often allowed to access users' private information which they should not have access to (Cao et al, 2021). As a result, artificial intelligence systems may disclose customers' sensitive data to unauthorized persons who may use it for malicious purposes thereby leading to privacy and data protection concerns. Several data protection measures can be introduced to address privacy and data protection concerns such as encryption and two-factor authentication (Cao et al., 2021).

Secondly, there is a pressing issue of artificial intelligence bias as a major risk to be encountered by financial institutions. The machine learning models can have inherent bias which can lead to troubling results. It must be noted that once the machine learning model has been trained, inherent bias is very difficult to eliminate. The bias can be in the form of failure to consider societal inequalities when applying artificial intelligence tools. This suggests that there is inherent unjust discrimination in applying algorithmic decisions. Notably, such biases can be perpetuated by artificial intelligence models. It is worth mentioning that biases can take different forms in FinTech like gender-based discrimination, racial discrimination, and socioeconomic discrimination that can have a bearing on investment and credit decisions, customer service, and hiring practices. The dataset used to train the artificial intelligence systems used in the fintech sector may contain embedded bias or may be discriminatory in nature (Graham, 2021; Kelley et al., 2022). As a result, it could lead to incorrect or discriminatory lending and investment decisions. Also, the machine learning strategies used to reach artificial intelligence decisions may be biased and lead to incorrect decisions.

Thirdly, there is an element of mistrust from the customers. Oftentimes, the artificial intelligence tools embedded in fintech platforms such as artificial intelligence robo advisors, or artificial intelligence chatbots give inconsistent user experiences to customers. It leads to increasing frustration and customer complaints. This issue may be due to a bot in the artificial intelligence-based fintech platform or may be due to customers' lack of understanding of how the artificial intelligence-based fintech platform works. The prevalence of inconsistent user experiences is challenging and leads to customer dissatisfaction. When artificial intelligence technologies are deployed by financial institutions, some customers may lose trust especially those who are technologically handicapped. Many customers value the human touch in fintech service delivery. Customers want to be able to talk to a customer service representative who can help them solve their problems. As a result, customers may feel uncomfortable when artificial intelligence systems are being used to serve them especially when the artificial intelligence systems lack the traditional human touch that customers are used to when served by customer service representatives (Ashta & Herrmann, 2021).

Fourthly, deployment of artificial intelligence technologies is linked to a plethora of cybersecurity vulnerabilities. There is a growing concern related to malicious actors leveraging the power of artificial intelligence whereby the attackers use sophisticated artificial intelligence technology that can surpass those used by financial institutions. Cyberattacks are looming in the business community. The use of artificial intelligence for fintech services gives rise to cybersecurity risks. It can amplify or reinforce old risks, or it can give rise to new risks. For example, the artificial intelligence systems used for fintech services can increase the risks of identity theft, it increases the risk of fraud, and it could complicate regulatory compliance (Giudici, 2018). Increasing cybersecurity risks could make companies spend large amounts of money to protect themselves from hacking, and such huge spending may be unsustainable for many fintech firms.

Fifthly, the adoption of artificial intelligence in the FinTech is associated with unemployment. This kind of job displacement is connected to a lack of reskilling and upskilling to much the demands of artificial intelligence technologies. The use of artificial intelligence in the fintech industry could lead to better efficiency than human workers, but it could displace the workers who perform repetitive tasks such as logging customer complaints and receiving/processing customer requests (Zhang et al., 2021). As a result, artificial intelligence systems could lead to rising unemployment in the fintech industry. The workers that will be most affected are those in the customer service and financial analysis units.

Sixthly, there are some pressing data quality issues. The data fed into the artificial intelligence systems used in the FinTech sector need to be of good quality and complete. If the artificial intelligence systems use low-quality data, untrustworthy data, or unclear data to produce FinTech decisions, the decision reached would be unreliable, misleading, and incoherent (Ashta & Herrmann, 2021).

Seventhly, there is an element of regulatory ambiguity when deploying artificial intelligence in the financial sector. This implies that there is the risk of increasing regulatory ambiguity due to a lack of clear rules (Restoy, 2019; Yadav, 2020). Lack of clear artificial intelligence regulations is a challenge for the FinTech industry. The lack of clear rules means that FinTech firms may use artificial intelligence tools to serve customers in a manner that customers may not like, and regulators could penalize and sanction FinTech firms for doing so. Lack of clear rules also means that FinTech firms may unknowingly breach unwritten ethical rules and may receive legal or regulatory sanctions for doing so. There is a need for clear regulatory rules on how FinTech operators should use artificial tools to improve their processes and to serve customers better.

Eighthly, neglect of forward-looking data and over-reliance on historical data is another challenge. The artificial intelligence systems used in FinTech investment platforms do not rely on forward-looking data. Rather, they rely heavily on historical data to provide investment decisions (Ashta & Herrmann, 2021). The challenge is that the historical data may be outdated, or the data may be structurally different from the current realities of the investment climate, or the historical data may be impaired by frequent crises that occurred in the past; thereby making such historical data unfit for predicting future investment decisions.

Lastly, lack of requisite skills and shortage of artificial intelligence skills is a pressing challenge that is worth the attention of financial managers. Many FinTech firms do not have the requisite skills that are needed to develop, deploy, and manage the artificial intelligence systems used to offer FinTech services. For some FinTech firms, artificial intelligence skills may be in limited supply, and it may be too costly to hire employees who have the skills to develop, deploy, and manage the artificial intelligence systems used to offer fintech services (Almansour, 2023). As a result, they will rely on third-party providers who can embed their API into the business process of FinTech firms. But this also exposes the fintech firms to third-party risks due to interdependencies.

RECOMMENDATIONS

In light of the above-mentioned challenges linked to artificial intelligence adoption, the following solutions are proposed:

Upskilling and Reskilling: The African governments should provide financial support for training workers on artificial intelligence. This could assist in reducing massive job displacement since trained workers can be transferred to other sections of the organizations. With an understanding that artificial intelligence is here to stay, the government has to support training programs offered by financial institutions.

Updating Artificial Intelligence Models: Given the bias associated with machine learning models, financial institutions should continuously update these models so as to do away with some inherent biases like racial, gender, and socioeconomic discrimination. This implies that the new and updated dataset can be used to train the artificial intelligence models to suit the context of financial institutions.

Crafting Artificial Intelligence Regulatory Framework: To deal with ethical concerns associated with the application of artificial intelligence in the financial sector, it is prudent enough that government agencies should come up with a clear regulatory framework that stipulates how financial institutions should use artificial intelligence. This could bring sanity to the deployment of artificial intelligence without violating human rights.

Developing Artificial Intelligence Policy: To ensure transparency, financial institutions should come up with clear artificial intelligence policies. The policies could allow financial institutions to govern how employees can use artificial intelligence technologies in a transparent manner.

Investing in Online Security Measures: It is hereby recommended that the managers of financial institutions should put in place robust online security measures in an attempt to boost customer trust. This could be a strategic move to protect the privacy and confidentiality of customers. More interestingly, cyberattack vulnerabilities of financial institutions can be significantly reduced.

Supporting Artificial Intelligence Innovation Challenge: Both governments and financial institutions are recommended to fund higher education students when it comes to innovation related to artificial intelligence. Given that many state-owned universities in Zimbabwe have innovation hubs, designing artificial intelligence prototypes could be easily provided that there is a collaboration among government, industry, commerce, and non-governmental organizations.

CONCLUSION

This chapter has covered the benefits and challenges derived from the application of artificial intelligence in the financial sector from an African perspective. Given the proliferation of digital transactions in the financial sector, it has been observed that artificial intelligence is a game-changer that is worth the attention of players in the financial sector. It is a fact that artificial intelligence technologies like machine learning, deep learning, big data analytics, augmented reality, and mixed reality are essentials for sustainable finance technology. Unfortunately, it appears that scantly is known about generative artificial intelligence in the financial discourse especially when it comes to African economies. As such, this chapter aims to fill this gap by establishing the benefits and challenges linked to artificial intelligence adoption in the finance sector. It can be concluded that artificial intelligence can augment accuracy, efficiency, fraud detection, effectiveness, human capabilities, and customer experiences, mitigate economic crimes, and accelerate regulatory compliance. Despite these benefits of artificial intelligence in FinTech, it brought to the fore some insurmountable challenges in the financial sector like ethical concerns, human rights issues, social engineering, and fraudulent data generation. The results of the current study are associated with theoretical and practical implications. Looking forward, there is a dire need to put in place a clear regulatory framework that governs how artificial intelligence must be applied ethically in the financial sector to boost customer trust.

REFERENCES

Ahmad, A. Y. B., Tiwari, A., Nayeem, M. A., Biswal, B. K., Satapathy, D. P., Kulshreshtha, K., & Bordoloi, D. (2024). Artificial Intelligence Perspective Framework of the Smart Finance and Accounting Management Model. *International Journal of Intelligent Systems and Applications in Engineering*, 12(4s), 586–594.

Almansour, M. (2023). Artificial intelligence and resource optimization: A study of Fintech start-ups. *Resources Policy*, 80, 103250. 10.1016/j.resourpol.2022.103250

Apsilyam, N. M., Shamsudinova, L. R., & Yakhshiboyev, R. E. (2024). The application of artificial intelligence in the economic sector. *Central Asian Journal Of Education And Computer Sciences*, 3(1), 1–12.

Argashokova, S., Litvishko, O., & Novoselova, N. (2023). Digitalization of financial sector in Russia: Key components and concepts. In *E3S Web of Conferences* (Vol. 431, p. 05018). EDP Sciences. 10.1051/e3sconf/202343105018

Ashta, A., & Herrmann, H. (2021). Artificial intelligence and fintech: An overview of opportunities and risks for banking, investments, and microfinance. *Strategic Change*, 30(3), 211–222. 10.1002/jsc.2404

Baumgart, D. C. (2024). An intriguing vision for transatlantic collaborative health data use and artificial intelligence development. *NPJ Digital Medicine*, 7(1), 19. 10.1038/s41746-024-01005-y38263436

Biju, A. K. V. N., Thomas, A. S., & Thasneem, J. (2024). Examining the research taxonomy of artificial intelligence, deep learning and machine learning in the financial sphere—A bibliometric analysis. *Quality & Quantity*, 58(1), 849–878. 10.1007/s11135-023-01673-037359968

Cao, L., Yang, Q., & Yu, P. S. (2021). Data science and AI in FinTech: An overview. *International Journal of Data Science and Analytics*, 12(2), 81–99. 10.1007/s41060-021-00278-w

Chaudhry, R., Kaur, S., Singla, J., Mittal, R., & Malik, V. (2024). Fraud Detection and Prevention for a Secure Financial Future Using Artificial Intelligence. *In2024 International Conference on Emerging Smart Computing and Informatics (ESCI)* (pp. 1-6). IEEE. 10.1109/ESCI59607.2024.10497255

Chiurunge, P., Kandiero, A., & Chizwina, S. (2024). Customer Churn Prediction for Financial Institutions Using Deep Learning Artificial Neural Networks in Zimbabwe. In *Theoretical and Conceptual Frameworks in ICT Research* (pp. 227–265). IGI Global.

Dzingirai, M. (2021a). Demystifying Corporate Restructuring Strategy Through Digital Transformation: Lessons Learned From the Banking Sector of Zimbabwe. In Sandhu, K. (Ed.), *Emerging Challenges, Solutions, and Best Practices for Digital Enterprise Transformation* (pp. 164–181). IGI Global. 10.4018/978-1-7998-8587-0.ch009

Dzingirai, M. (2021b). Managerial Challenges Under FinTech: Evidence From Zimbabwean Commercial Banks. In Sghari, A., & Mezghani, K. (Eds.), *Influence of FinTech on Management Transformation* (pp. 141–166). IGI Global. 10.4018/978-1-7998-7110-1.ch007

Dzingirai, M. (2023, June). Effects of Artificial Intelligence on Money Laundering in Southern Africa. *InICABR Conference* (pp. 483-500). Cham: Springer Nature Switzerland.

Farayola, O. A. (2024). Revolutionizing banking security: Integrating artificial intelligence, blockchain, and business intelligence for enhanced cybersecurity. *Finance and Accounting Research Journal*, 6(4), 501–514. 10.51594/farj.v6i4.990

Giudici, P. (2018). Fintech risk management: A research challenge for artificial intelligence in finance. *Frontiers in Artificial Intelligence*, 1, 1. 10.3389/frai.2018.0000133733089

Go, E. J., Moon, J., & Kim, J. (2020). Analysis of the current and future of the artificial intelligence in financial industry with big data techniques. *Global Business and Finance Review*, 25(1), 102–117. 10.17549/gbfr.2020.25.1.102

Goto, M. (2023). Anticipatory innovation of professional services: The case of auditing and artificial intelligence. *Research Policy*, 52(8), 104828. 10.1016/j.respol.2023.104828

Graham, J. (2021). Risk of discrimination in AI systems: Evaluating the effectiveness of current legal safeguards in tackling algorithmic discrimination. *FinTechArtificial Intelligence and Law*, 211–229.

Hanlin, R., & Kelly, W. (2023). *Enhancing South Africa's Emerging Digital Technologies' Innovation Ecosystem.* https://edt.ubuntunet.net/wp-content/uploads/2023/09/Strengthening-of-Emerging-Digital-Technologies-Ecosystem-in-South-Africa-A-Policy-Brief-1.pdf

Hidayah, Z., & Purnamasari, P. (2024). Analysis Of The Impact Of The Application Of Artificial Intelligence (Ai) Based Technology And Digital Finance Knowledge In Improving Business Sustainability. *Jurnal Mantik*, 7(4), 3989–3996.

Hu, C., Din, Q. M. U., & Zhang, L. (2024). Short Empirical Insight: Leadership and Artificial Intelligence in the Pharmaceutical Industry. *Engineering. Technology and Applied Science Research*, 14(2), 13658–13664. 10.48084/etasr.7025

IA, G., & Miglionico, A. (2019). Artificial intelligence and automation in financial services: The case of russian banking sector. *Law and Economics Yearly Review*, 8(1), 125–147.

Jardim, J. (2024). Global Innovation Policies: Framework for Developing an Innovative Culture Based on Artificial Intelligence. In *Incorporating AI Technology in the Service Sector* (pp. 25–43). Apple Academic Press. 10.1201/9781003378068-2

Kelley, S., Ovchinnikov, A., Hardoon, D. R., & Heinrich, A. (2022). Antidiscrimination laws, artificial intelligence, and gender bias: A case study in nonmortgage Fintech lending. *Manufacturing & Service Operations Management*, 24(6), 3039–3059. 10.1287/msom.2022.1108

Kgoale, T. J., & Odeku, K. (2023). An analysis of legal accountability for artificial intelligence systems in the South African financial sector. *De Jure (Durban)*, 56(1), 191–205. 10.17159/2225-7160/2023/v56a14

Kumari, B., Kaur, J., & Swami, S. (2024). Adoption of artificial intelligence in financial services: A policy framework. *Journal of Science and Technology Policy Management*, 15(2), 396–417. 10.1108/JSTPM-03-2022-0062

Lee, K. Y., Kwon, H. Y., & Lim, J. I. (2018). Legal consideration on the use of artificial intelligence technology and self-regulation in financial sector: focused on robo-advisors. *In Information Security Applications: 18th International Conference, WISA 2017, Jeju Island, Korea, August 24-26, 2017, Revised Selected Papers 18* (pp. 323-335). Springer International Publishing.

Lloyd, C., Misheal, M. R., & Tavonga, N. (2024). *Harnessing Machine Learning and Artificial Intelligence for Ear-ly Fraud Detection Among Banks in Harare, Zimbabwe: Internal Auditors' Perspective.* https://www.researchgate.net/profile/Regis-Muchowe/publication/378862992_Harnessing_Machine_Learning_and_Artificial_Intelligence_for_Ear-_ly_Fraud_Detection_Among_Banks_in_Harare_Zimbabwe_Internal_Auditors'_Perspective/links/65eef7889ab2af0ef8aecd54/Harnessing-Machine-Learning-and-Artificial-Intelligence-for-Ear-ly-Fraud-Detection-Among-Banks-in-Harare-Zimbabwe-Internal-Auditors-Perspective.pdf

Mamela, T. L., Sukdeo, N., & Mukwakungu, S. C. (2020). Adapting to artificial intelligence through workforce re-skilling within the banking sector in South Africa. *In 2020 International Conference on Artificial Intelligence, Big Data, Computing and Data Communication Systems (icABCD)* (pp. 1-9). IEEE.

Maurya, S., Verma, R., Khilnani, L., Bhakuni, A. S., Kumar, M., & Rakesh, N. (2024). Effect of AI on the Financial Sector: Risk Control, Investment Decision-making, and Business Outcome. In *2024 11th International Conference on Reliability, Infocom Technologies and Optimization (Trends and Future Directions)(ICRITO)* (pp. 1-7). IEEE.

Mhlanga, D. (2020). Industry 4.0 in finance: The impact of artificial intelligence (ai) on digital financial inclusion. *International Journal of Financial Studies*, 8(3), 45. 10.3390/ijfs8030045

Nica, I., Delcea, C., & Chiri ă, N. (2024). Mathematical Patterns in Fuzzy Logic and Artificial Intelligence for Financial Analysis: A Bibliometric Study. *Mathematics*, 12(5), 782. 10.3390/math12050782

Ochuba, N. A., Adewunmi, A., & Olutimehin, D. O. (2024). The role of AI in financial market development: Enhancing efficiency and accessibility in emerging economies. *Finance and Accounting Research Journal*, 6(3), 421–436. 10.51594/farj.v6i3.969

Restoy, F. (2019). Regulating fintech: what is going on, and where are the challenges. *Bank for International Settlements*, 1-7.

Rožman, M., Oreški, D., & Tominc, P. (2023). Artificial-intelligence-supported reduction of employees' workload to increase the company's performance in today's VUCA Environment. *Sustainability (Basel)*, 15(6), 5019. 10.3390/su15065019

Rutskiy, V., Aljarbouh, A., Thommandru, A., Elkin, S., Amrani, Y. E., Semina, E., & Tsarev, R. (2022). Prospects for the Use of Artificial Intelligence to Combat Fraud in Bank Payments. In *Proceedings of the Computational Methods in Systems and Software* (pp. 959-971). Cham: Springer International Publishing.

Shambira, L. (2020). Exploring the adoption of artificial intelligence in the Zimbabwe banking sector. *European Journal of Social Sciences Studies*, 5(6), 110–124. 10.46827/ejsss.v5i6.942

Shoetan, P. O., & Familoni, B. T. (2024). Transforming fintech fraud detection with advanced artificial intelligence algorithms. *Finance and Accounting Research Journal*, 6(4), 602–625. 10.51594/farj.v6i4.1036

Srivastava, K., & Dhamija, S. (2022, May). FinTech: Application of Artificial Intelligence in Indian Banking. In *Proceedings of International Conference on Communication and Artificial Intelligence: ICCAI 2021* (pp. 601-613). Singapore: Springer Nature Singapore. 10.1007/978-981-19-0976-4_50

Udo, W. S., Ochuba, N. A., Akinrinola, O., & Ololade, Y. J. (2024). Theoretical approaches to data analytics and decision-making in finance: Insights from Africa and the United States. *GSC Advanced Research and Reviews*, 18(3), 343–349. 10.30574/gscarr.2024.18.3.0114

Umamaheswari, S., & Valarmathi, A. (2023). Role of artificial intelligence in the banking sector. *Journal of Survey in Fisheries Sciences*, 10(4S), 2841–2849.

Vishwakarma, L. P., & Singh, R. K. (2023). An analysis of the challenges to human resource in implementing artificial intelligence. In *The Adoption and Effect of Artificial Intelligence on Human Resources Management, Part B* (pp. 81–109). Emerald Publishing Limited. 10.1108/978-1-80455-662-720230006

Zhang, B. Z., Ashta, A., & Barton, M. E. (2021). Do FinTech and financial incumbents have different experiences and perspectives on the adoption of artificial intelligence? *Strategic Change*, 30(3), 223–234. 10.1002/jsc.2405

ADDITIONAL READING

Ahmad, A. Y. B., Tiwari, A., Nayeem, M. A., Biswal, B. K., Satapathy, D. P., Kulshreshtha, K., & Bordoloi, D. (2024). Artificial Intelligence Perspective Framework of the Smart Finance and Accounting Management Model. *International Journal of Intelligent Systems and Applications in Engineering*, 12(4s), 586–594.

Apsilyam, N. M., Shamsudinova, L. R., & Yakhshiboyev, R. E. (2024). The application of artificial intelligence in the economic sector. *Central Asian Journal Of Education and Computer Sciences*, 3(1), 1–12.

Biju, A. K. V. N., Thomas, A. S., & Thasneem, J. (2024). Examining the research taxonomy of artificial intelligence, deep learning and machine learning in the financial sphere—A bibliometric analysis. *Quality & Quantity*, 58(1), 849–878. 10.1007/s11135-023-01673-037359968

Hidayah, Z., & Purnamasari, P. (2024). Analysis Of The Impact Of The Application Of Artificial Intelligence (Ai) Based Technology And Digital Finance Knowledge In Improving Business Sustainability. *Jurnal Mantik*, 7(4), 3989–3996.

Huang, Z., Che, C., Zheng, H., & Li, C. (2024). Research on Generative Artificial Intelligence for Virtual Financial Robo-Advisor. *Academic Journal of Science and Technology*, 10(1), 74–80. 10.54097/30r2kk80

Kanaparthi, V. (2024). Transformational application of Artificial Intelligence and Machine learning in Financial Technologies and Financial services: A bibliometric review. *arXiv preprint arXiv*:2401.15710.

Kumari, B., Kaur, J., & Swami, S. (2024). Adoption of artificial intelligence in financial services: A policy framework. *Journal of Science and Technology Policy Management*, 15(2), 396–417. 10.1108/JSTPM-03-2022-0062

Sharma, P., & Manhas, S. (2024). The Future of Finance: Revolutionizing the Industry With Artificial Intelligence. In *Leveraging AI and Emotional Intelligence in Contemporary Business Organizations* (pp. 187–210). IGI Global.

Singh, C. (2024). Artificial intelligence and deep learning: Considerations for financial institutions for compliance with the regulatory burden in the United Kingdom. *Journal of Financial Crime*, 31(2), 259–266. 10.1108/JFC-01-2023-0011

Weber, P., Carl, K. V., & Hinz, O. (2024). Applications of explainable artificial intelligence in finance—A systematic review of finance, information systems, and computer science literature. *Management Review Quarterly*, 74(2), 867–907. 10.1007/s11301-023-00320-0

KEY TERMS AND DEFINITIONS

Artificial Intelligence: It refers to the robust imitation of human intelligence by machines, particularly computers.

Cybersecurity: It deals with security related to information technology with the sole purpose of defending servers, electronic systems, mobile devices, computers, data, and networks from malevolent attacks.

Data Analytics: It is a concept related to the systematic and methodological synthesis of raw data in order to inform evidence-based decision-making in an organization.

Financial Sector: It is a distinct sector of the economy that encompasses companies that offer financial services to different customers, especially retail and commercial clients.

FinTech: It describes the modern financial technology that can be incorporated into the automation of financial services with the aim of augmenting client service.

Machine Learning: It can be defined as the typical branch of artificial intelligence that deals with building computer systems that can learn from datasets.

Chapter 9
AI in Marketing

Serap Türkyilmaz
https://orcid.org/0000-0001-9847-4164
Beykent Üniversitesi, Turkey

ABSTRACT

In recent times, artificial intelligence (AI) has become an essential component in marketing, leading to the generation of large amounts of data and information, as well as advancements in management software and algorithms. The goal of artificial intelligence is to intelligently imitate human behavior. Artificial intelligence is a rapidly expanding technology, industry, and field of study. AI not only enhances existing marketing strategies, but also introduces innovative ways to deliver value to customers. AI also plays an important role in helping marketers manage marketing projects, support them, create content, and perform other tasks. Research shows that a lack of understanding of AI's capabilities and failed implementation efforts can create additional obstacles for organizations, including investment risks, ethical dilemmas, data issues, recruitment challenges, and negative environmental impacts. Despite being designed to reduce the workload of employees, human intervention is necessary in roles such as management, supervision, and innovation.

INTRODUCTION

In ancient times, symbols were believed to give intelligence to objects in Greek mythology, such as sculptures resembling robotic humans or the depiction of Greek and Egyptian gods by priests in various forms. Despite the relatively recent emergence of artificial intelligence (AI) in the market, its applications are already effective in various industries, especially in marketing. Recent advancements in AI technology and the increasing number of successful use cases have created enthusiasm among marketers. As AI continues to advance, the ability of marketers to implement and

DOI: 10.4018/979-8-3693-5578-7.ch009

manage it effectively has become a critical skill. As a result, AI is poised to revolutionize the field of marketing itself. The age of AI marketing requires fundamental changes in the way marketers interact with customers, as well as the strategies and tools they use to achieve their goals. Artificial intelligence (AI) is a rapidly developing technology with the potential to revolutionize many sectors, including marketing. Marketing seeks to understand customer needs, develop value propositions, and communicate effectively with target audiences and faces multiple challenges in the dynamic and complex business landscape, such as information overload, resource constraints, and evolving customer expectations. There is a huge demand for innovative solutions that can increase marketing performance and outcomes.

Artificial intelligence has been defined and utilized in various ways throughout history. The term "artificial intelligence" was first coined by (Chui et al. 2018), who described it as a field of engineering and the science of creating intelligent machines and programs. As time progressed, the definition of artificial intelligence became more specific, with many authors referring to it as a program, system, or machine that possesses human-like thinking and behavior. Nowadays, artificial intelligence encompasses different types, including systems, programs, algorithms, computers, and machines that exhibit intelligence. This intelligence represents various aspects of the human mind, such as learning, judging, inferring, reacting, and predicting. The implementation of artificial intelligence in marketing offers numerous opportunities for companies. However, there is still uncertainty among members of different departments regarding the benefits of such applications. It is important to approach the issue of AI in marketing with the understanding that it is not a one-size-fits-all solution for all marketing problems. Additionally, the advanced iterations and increased adoption of AI can have unintended consequences and undesirable outcomes. Despite the extensive use of advertising, the impact of AI on marketing is undeniably significant. 98% of marketing leaders express their anticipation of reaping the advantages of utilizing AI, as stated by Demand base in 2016. The evident interest among marketers in AI underscores the importance of comprehending the full potential of this technology before marketers are compelled to adapt. Surprisingly, only 28% of the aforementioned 98% of marketing leaders feel confident in their ability to utilize AI effectively. Even more concerning, 10% of them are currently making full use of this technology. It is imperative to bridge the gap between advertising and AI implementation in order to realize the daily benefits it offers and prepare for the ever-evolving landscape of marketing. Presently, consumers hold a mixed yet generally positive perception of artificial intelligence. The majority of consumers believe that AI will contribute to the betterment of society. According to a 2017 independent global survey conducted by ARM with Northstar Research Partners, 61% of consumers believe AI will have a positive impact on society, while only 22% believe it will have a negative impact. However, it is important to acknowledge that artificial intelligence is a complex and multifaceted subject. AI technologies have varying objectives and progress at different speeds, but their common aim is to replicate human intelligence in computers to enhance their functionality. AI can be categorized into two main groups: marketers who express interest in implementing AI in the near future, and those who have already integrated AI solutions into their business operations. Surprisingly, only a small fraction, 20%, of marketers have fully embraced AI as a core component of their business (Bughin et al. 2017). This disparity between enthusiasm and implementation suggests that there is still ample opportunity for marketers to adopt AI. However, the landscape of AI applications in marketing is rapidly evolving, with a wide range of advanced software and services available for brands to utilize. Over the past few years, several factors have contributed to the growing interest and feasibility of AI in marketing. These include improved computing capabilities that allow for cost-effective processing of AI algorithms, the emergence of big data and advancements in data management, a keen interest in cutting-edge technologies, and a large pool of highly skilled professionals eager to drive the industry forward. The recent surge in excitement surrounding AI has resulted in a substantial influx of venture capital, with AI startups receiving a lot of funding (Venture Scanner, 2018). In recent years, the interest and feasibility of AI technology in marketing have significantly increased, despite its presence in the industry for decades. The potential of AI technology in various marketing formats is becoming more evident as it becomes more feasible than ever before. While only a limited number of companies have implemented robust AI systems, many companies of different sizes are adopting smaller-scale solutions that require less involvement in setup and management. By implementing low-involvement AI solutions, companies can overcome barriers to entry, while those implementing high-involvement AI solutions can enjoy a wide range of benefits at the core of their operations. To determine the best solution for a company, a comprehensive analysis is necessary, and I will provide a framework for this evaluation later on. The topic of artificial intelligence in marketing is vast, but a logical starting point for discussion is the concept of personalization to make marketing more relevant to consumers. Personalization, in various forms, is a goal that many marketers strive for, as it is beneficial for brands and preferred by customers. Marketers recognize the significance of personalization in artificial intelligence marketing, yet they lack the necessary expertise to effectively implement it. The advantages of brands successfully delivering personalized marketing also benefit their customers. Artificial intelligence in marketing provides a range of capabilities that enhance marketers' understanding of their customers at both a comprehensive and individual level, allowing them to create and distribute personalized and relevant content to the right audience at the right time and place. The era of artificial intelligence marketing is rapidly approaching, with profound implications.

As AI becomes increasingly sophisticated and prevalent in marketing, marketers' ability to efficiently implement and oversee AI solutions becomes an even more crucial skill. Similarly, individuals must comprehend their role in contributing value in an AI-driven workplace, which is vital not only for their personal success but also for their company's success. With AI streamlining repetitive tasks, marketers can dedicate more attention to value-adding activities that enhance consumers' experiences, promote workplace satisfaction, and encourage innovative thinking for the betterment of society. A PwC report from 2017 forecasted that investing in artificial intelligence development could lead to a 14% increase in global GDP by 2030. Furthermore, AI is expected to generate $13 trillion by 2030 and boost global GDP by approximately 1.2% annually (Bughin et al. 2017). A recent survey of global marketers conducted in late 2020 revealed that 41% of participants experienced enhancements in revenue growth and overall performance by incorporating artificial intelligence into their marketing strategies. Over the past two decades, artificial intelligence has significantly transformed the marketing landscape, alongside fields like healthcare, finance, engineering, and education (Rust, 2020). The integration of artificial intelligence has led to substantial digital advancements, resulting in more personalized interactions between consumers and businesses. This trend has prompted organizations to increasingly invest in machine learning to improve their marketing efforts. Artificial intelligence plays a crucial role in digital marketing, paving the way for the creation of new business opportunities .This study explores the practical applications of artificial intelligence in marketing, particularly in the realm of digital marketing. Artificial intelligence involves the design and implementation of computer systems capable of performing tasks that typically require human intelligence. One promising application of artificial intelligence in marketing is data-driven project management. Project management is vital in marketing as it involves planning, executing, and monitoring projects to achieve specific objectives within set timeframes and budgets. While project management is a complex and uncertain process that relies on human judgment, creativity, and problem-solving skills, artificial intelligence can enhance human capabilities and provide valuable support in marketing project management (Nieto Rodriguez & Vargas, 2023). Artificial intelligence leverages data analytics, machine learning, natural language processing, and other advanced techniques to optimize marketing strategies.. British mathematician utilized an imitation game to assess whether machines could think, a technique that later became known as the Turing test (Turing, 1950). Computer scientists continue to utilize the Turing test and its various iterations to explore the inquiries that artificial intelligence seeks to address. ImageNet was established by AI researcher with the aim of enhancing and expanding existing data for training AI algorithms. ImageNet utilizes WordNet, a linguistic database, to categorize images into numerous groups and employs Amazon Mechanical Turk to label images. By understanding the history of artificial intelligence and the individuals who influenced it, we can gain a better grasp of how far artificial intelligence has progressed and the challenges it has encountered.

Advances in artificial intelligence are reshaping digital marketing and data analytics by providing new ways to meet customer needs and add value. Integrating AI into business practices can help organizations manage large amounts of data and information using machine learning and algorithms. Despite the benefits of AI in marketing processes, many companies are hesitant to implement these technologies due to concerns such as lack of awareness, uncertainties about AI-based solutions, and potential risks. This study focuses on understanding the barriers that prevent companies, particularly in the IT and software sectors, from adopting AI in their marketing processes. Through qualitative analysis and expert interviews, the study aims to explore marketers' concerns and perceptions of AI in marketing within these industries.

Research Gap

There is a research gap in the field of marketing project management when it comes to the role of artificial intelligence. Although there have been several studies on the application of artificial intelligence in project management, there is a lack of comprehensive research that specifically explores the impact of artificial intelligence on project management in the marketing field. Therefore, there is a need for more studies that delve into the challenges and opportunities that arise from the use of artificial intelligence in marketing project management.

Purpose of the Study

Marketing is a fast-paced and competitive industry that demands continuous adaptation and creativity. Utilizing data-driven marketing, which involves data analysis and artificial intelligence (AI) techniques, is crucial for optimizing marketing campaigns and strategies. This study aims to investigate the role of AI in enhancing various aspects of data-driven marketing project management, such as customer segmentation, predictive analytics, dynamic pricing, recommendation systems, and marketing automation. The primary research question focuses on how AI technology can enhance marketing project management performance.

Exploring the specific challenges and opportunities presented by AI in marketing, as well as the potential advantages of leveraging AI to enhance marketing project performance and drive business value, are key objectives of this research. Additionally, this study aims to identify critical factors that influence the successful integration of AI in marketing project management, including industry, organization size, and market characteristics. AI is a field that seeks to automate tasks typically requiring human intelligence, with machine learning (ML) and deep learning (DL) being specific AI methods. However, AI also encompasses non-learning methods, such as symbolic AI, which involves creating rules for various scenarios within a specific domain.

Informed decisions and new smart tools ensure competitive conditions. In general, this field of study refers to the following:

1. A comprehensive review of the latest developments in artificial intelligence (AI) and the marketing process.
2. Evaluating the impact of artificial intelligence on conversion rate, customer interaction, and customer satisfaction in the marketing process.
3. Examining challenges related to artificial intelligence and ML, data privacy concerns, ethical considerations, and algorithmic bias.
4. Examining and predicting future trends according to emerging technologies, such as deep learning, natural language processing, etc.
5. Forecasting the level of sales in management
6. Optimizing digital advertising campaigns
7. Deeper understanding of consumers in the market and communicating with them

Artificial intelligence methods improve data quality. With large amounts of data at their disposal, marketers use integrated data management software to prevent damage to these rich sources of information. As the customer experience improves, the bounce rate and irrelevant ads decrease. Initially, the cost of implementing this technology may be very high, so they should evaluate and check the return of the cost in advance. High costs can be an obstacle for companies to enter this field. In addition to constantly evolving, this system also requires skilled labor to upgrade. Therefore, implementing the system can be overwhelming.

Implementation of Artificial Intelligence in Digital Marketing

Artificial intelligence gained popularity in the late 2000s and was utilized by industry leaders like Amazon, Google, Apple, and Microsoft through machine learning and algorithmic tools. As a result, the demand has steadily risen over the years, leading to the expansion of these implementations across various business sectors. A recent study conducted by the commercial cloud platform revealed that internet users produce 2.5 quintillion bytes of data daily. Consequently, the provision of personal data and the focus on target customers are crucial for enhancing efficiency. Consequently, numerous companies dedicate significant resources and investments into digital marketing tools to target audiences.

The digitalization and technological advancements have revolutionized marketing strategies, making artificial intelligence an indispensable tool in digital marketing processes. Furthermore, AI applications have revolutionized operational processes and impacted sales channels in both B2B and B2C contexts (Paschen et al., 2020). Moreover, AI has introduced innovative solutions and methods for companies to enhance their brand appeal and target individual customers using various techniques and tools (Grover & Kar, 2017).

Thus, they possess the capability to generate data that supports future decision-making processes and the evolution of current and future marketing strategies (Mogaji et al. 2020). Marketing professionals have a plethora of AI applications in digital marketing at their disposal to boost performance, efficiency, operational effectiveness, and mitigate the risks of failure, complexity, and uncertainty. Professionals in the field of digital marketing utilize various AI applications such as machine learning approaches, algorithms, big data, personalization, and optimization tools (Wirth, 2018). The objective is to effectively analyze collected data, learn from it, and make predictions that can support future decision-making and strategic planning. These capabilities are crucial in driving companies to adopt artificial intelligence in their digital marketing operations, as it allows them to leverage big data, analytics, and gain valuable customer insights. By utilizing AI-based frameworks and implementations, marketers can gain a comprehensive understanding of their customers by analyzing feedback, tracking their preferences, and learning their behavior patterns. This enables them to optimize the use of digital marketing data and strengthen customer relationships.

Machine Learning

The concept of machine learning in artificial intelligence (AI) allows computers to analyze data independently, without human instruction. This enables machines to identify patterns and extract valuable information from the data they gather through their sensors. As a result, AI and machine learning continue to advance and overcome the limitations of traditional guidelines. It is crucial for marketing professionals to stay updated on future developments and emerging trends, as these will likely shape the future of AI and machine learning. Automations, which involve repetitive tasks and rely on low-level AI, follow a predetermined sequence. They assist users in the marketing process by incorporating chatbots, intelligent email systems, and interactive web design to align with business objectives. Customers benefit from this by having a more streamlined buying experience and placing trust in chatbots. This process is constantly improving, and optimizing the conditions leads to an enhanced overall experience. By utilizing these programs, individuals can engage in independent learning and generate content from various sources to cater to their audience. Search engine optimization (SEO) involves the use of on-page and off-page techniques to ensure that a website is effectively indexed and ranked by search engines like Google, Bing, and others. Achieving a successful and organic listing on the search engine results page requires significant effort (Dodson, 2016).

Machine learning, a subfield of artificial intelligence, focuses on automating conceptual modeling and analysis, enabling computers to adapt autonomously to new environments. According to Mahesh (2020), machine learning has been utilized to predict stock values, but its accuracy has been limited due to the influence of multiple variables on pricing. Mahesh (2020) categorizes developments in machine learning into three main types: supervised learning, unsupervised learning, and reinforcement learning. Each type has its own specific area of focus. However, this study found that reinforcement learning is the most effective and productive form of machine learning for predicting stock values (Mahesh, 2020).

This research contributes to the advancement of knowledge and practice in data-driven marketing optimization through the use of artificial intelligence. It offers a comprehensive and systematic framework for applying artificial intelligence techniques to various marketing aspects, providing practical guidelines and recommendations for marketing professionals. Additionally, it examines the benefits and challenges of artificial intelligence in marketing project management and explores the ethical and social implications of artificial intelligence for customers and society.

The field of marketing is increasingly recognizing the importance of artificial intelligence (AI) due to the availability of big data, reduced computational costs, and advancements in machine learning algorithms and models. Artificial intelligence is widely utilized across various marketing fields such as segmentation, advertising, customer relationship management, and project management. The influence of AI on marketing strategies and organizational culture is substantial, with predictions indicating that AI will revolutionize the future of marketing. Despite this, current academic research in marketing has not adequately addressed how to effectively harness AI benefits for marketing impact. Machine learning involves the use of computer algorithms to analyze and learn from data autonomously, without explicit programming. This process typically employs multiple algorithms in rapid succession to generate predictive outcomes.

Supervised Learning is a specific branch of machine learning that utilizes labeled datasets to train algorithms in order to classify or predict data. The primary objective of supervised learning is to enable the algorithm to understand the correlation between input and output data. The fundamental steps involved in supervised machine learning are as follows: (1) gathering a dataset and dividing it into distinct training, validation, and testing datasets; (2) employing the training and validation datasets to establish a model that captures the relationship between features and targets; and (3) assessing the model's performance using a test dataset to determine its ability to accurately predict unseen data. During each iteration, the algorithm's performance on the training data is compared to its performance on the validation data.

Unsupervised learning refers to a machine learning technique that utilizes unlabeled datasets to train models or algorithms. The primary objective of this algorithm is to comprehend the underlying structure of the data without any prior knowledge. Clustering and dimensionality reduction are two examples of unsupervised learning algorithms (Alpaydın, 2014). Unlike supervised learning, unsupervised learning aims to identify patterns within a dataset and assign individual samples to these categories. Common tasks in unsupervised learning include clustering, association, and anomaly detection. Clustering, as the name suggests, groups samples into distinct clusters based on specific combinations of features. In this particular case, the researchers applied a clustering algorithm to their dataset and identified three distinct clusters.

On the other hand, **reinforcement learning** is a type of machine learning algorithm where an agent learns to interact with the environment by taking actions and receiving rewards or penalties. The primary objective of this algorithm is to acquire an optimal policy that maximizes the cumulative reward over time (Alpaydın, 2014).

Deep Learning

Deep learning is a branch of machine learning that concentrates on neural networks and the algorithms used to train them. It encompasses various forms of neural networks. To construct deep learning models, a neural network with a minimum of two hidden layers is necessary, while very deep learning necessitates a neural network with at least 10 hidden layers. At a broader level, deep learning with supervised learning entails defining a model (commonly referred to as a neural network) and producing estimates for data points. Subsequently, the loss or error for each estimate is calculated, and gradient descent is employed to minimize these errors (Campesato, 2020).

General Reasoning of Artificial Intelligence

Artificial intelligence involves the transfer of human intelligence to machines, enabling them to perform tasks in an intelligent manner. AI has proven to be instrumental in enhancing various operations and services globally. (Wichert, 2020) highlights the potential of artificial intelligence in quantum computing and machine learning to swiftly address complex challenges.

General Marketing Argument

Marketing plays a crucial role within a company, focusing solely on the customer while other departments handle internal matters. Without customers, sales would not be possible, making marketing the most vital function. The essence of marketing lies in aligning a company's capabilities with the needs and wants of customers. Marketing management involves implementing strategies to achieve organizational goals, utilizing all available resources in the process. In business, marketing aims to attract new customers by showcasing the value of products or services, as customer acquisition requires proactive efforts from the company. Artificial intelligence is currently playing a crucial role in assisting experts in identifying opportunities, marketing strategies, market demands, target customers, and capabilities. The evolution of digitalization and technological advancements has reshaped marketing strategies, making artificial intelligence an essential tool in digital marketing processes. Furthermore, AI has introduced innovative solutions and methods for companies to enhance their brand appeal and effectively target individual customers through various tools. As a result, AI has the capacity to generate data that can support future decision-making processes and the advancement of current and future marketing strategies.

Digital Marketing

Digital marketing plays a crucial role in enhancing customer engagement and driving business growth. It allows companies to reach a wider audience, target specific demographics, track and analyze consumer behavior, and measure the effectiveness of marketing campaigns in real-time. By leveraging digital marketing strategies, businesses can create personalized and targeted marketing campaigns that resonate with their target audience, customer loyalty, leading to increased brand awareness, and ultimately, higher sales and revenue. In today's digital age, businesses that fail to embrace digital marketing risk falling behind their competitors and missing out on valuable opportunities to connect with consumers in a meaningful way. With the increasing adoption of digital technologies by offline customers and the influx of younger consumers, interactions are growing by over 20% annually, signifying a notable shift. To comprehend the crucial role of artificial intelligence in digital marketing strategies, it is imperative to assess the current landscape of digital marketing research and its alignment with industry trends. This evaluation will shed light on the extent to which digital marketing research is keeping pace with advancements in the business realm.

Obstacles, Challenges and Risks of Artificial Intelligence

The current state of the marketing industry has raised questions among users regarding certain concepts. Despite the perceived benefits of incorporating artificial intelligence (AI) into marketing strategies, its widespread adoption has yet to be achieved. Why hasn't AI become a standard practice in the business world? While there are numerous success stories showcasing the effectiveness of AI in digital marketing, the sector requires more practical examples to garner the full support of marketing professionals (Huang & Rust, 2021). Without such examples, many investors are hesitant to embrace these technologies due to potential problems, challenges, and risks (Turner, 2018). Additionally, the complexity of regulating AI is often attributed to a lack of understanding regarding its definition, which further exacerbates issues that can impact both the environment and companies. Characterizes artificial intelligence as a two-sided coin. Along with its positive aspects, these systems possess significant potential to introduce various challenges, risks, and hurdles for businesses and, more importantly, for society (Hermann, 2021). The challenges include increased consumption, investment risk, data privacy (Davenport et al. 2020), unemployment, cyber risks (Daugherty & Wilson, 2018), ongoing trends in current changes, inadequate IT infrastructure, lack of expertise, ethical regulations, and complexity (Canals & Heukamp, 2020) are just a few of these obstacles, challenges, and risks that can be observed in the field of artificial intelligence. Marketing professionals should always be mindful of these issues when utilizing artificial intelligence in their operations.

Artificial intelligence and machine learning algorithms have the capability to access concealed data and information without human intervention and assistance. They possess the ability to autonomously create complex structures and connections using this raw data. Furthermore, the deep learning approach can identify uncertain relationships between estimates or define specific features of images based on prior abstract concepts to uncover unknown contexts. Hence, it simplifies the complexity into an attainable task that surpasses human capabilities. These programs do not adapt or synchronize with the human model. Conversely, this partially controllable superpower of artificial intelligence may result in unforeseen negative repercussions for the user and their surroundings.

Moreover, with the emergence of new cutting-edge technologies, AI and ML tools are acquiring more effective capabilities like sentiment detectors. As users expect these programs to possess a range of skills that enable them to display empathy, they believe that customer trust and loyalty will also increase. However, these newfound abilities of machine learning tools can be easily exploited for illicit gains through AI capabilities. In such cases, these artificial emotional capabilities may create a false sense of connection between the company and customers, leading to significant ethical dilemmas (Canals & Heukamp, 2020). Therefore, the implementation of artificial intelligence in marketing also presents highly sensitive ethical challenges, as there are stringent ethical regulations governing the use of artificial intelligence and human rights (Pusztahelyi, 2020). This sensitive data can potentially result in catastrophic and inappropriate handling of private information, including data breaches, fraudulent use of confidential data, and mishandling of personal records. Despite the advanced capabilities of artificial intelligence and ML in marketing operations, such as emotional recognition and empathy, they are still not as efficient as they should be, and these machines are not yet capable of comprehending and experiencing human behaviors.

Hence, it can result in managers experiencing disappointment or misunderstanding due to high expectations. It is important for users to always be mindful that these types of adaptations will inevitably have limitations in functionality. Furthermore, conducting a thorough analysis and gathering crucial information plays a significant role in making informed decisions about the implementation of artificial intelligence and machine learning tools in marketing operations. Unfortunately, many individuals in top management positions often fail to think comprehensively and consider the potential negative impacts of AI on their operations prior to implementation. One of the potential obstacles that should not be overlooked and requires careful consideration is the investment risk (Domitriu & Popescu, 2020). These machine learning tools are a form of technological support application that necessitates continuous investment to remain up-to-date and function effectively, thus the organization must possess the financial capability to afford such ongoing investment (Huang & Rust, 2021). If this risk is not thoroughly examined and managers proceed with implementing AI and ML tools in operations without proper risk analysis, it could lead to disastrous consequences for the company.

Another challenge that companies encounter when applying ML in their marketing operations is the scarcity of qualified personnel in the market (Holtel, 2016). This barrier restricts the ability of AI tools to operate efficiently and prompts users to question the decision of utilizing these tools in the marketing process. Additionally, the scarcity of qualified personnel in the industry impacts the cost of hiring experts for the operation (Volkmar, 2020).

Increased Consumption

The primary objective of marketing concepts is to satisfy customers and boost sales by implementing effective strategies and tools (Huang & Rest, 2021). With the emergence of AI as a valuable tool in digital marketing, companies have started incorporating AI into their operations to enhance performance (Mogaji et al. 2020). However, alongside its supportive role, AI may also be increasingly utilized due to the uncontrollable nature of its applications (Hermann, 2021). Artificial intelligence and machine learning algorithms strive to achieve these goals without considering the consequences of overconsumption and environmental impacts. While these AI-supported operations are intended to enhance process performance, they often overlook the negative effects on society (de Bruin et al., 2020). It has been observed in numerous instances that successful AI applications in marketing processes have had detrimental effects on the social and natural environment. In addition to the financial benefits for companies, it leads to increased demand, sales, and unfortunately, waste generation . Amazon, being at the forefront of AI utilization in all aspects, including digital marketing, has scaled up its operations to meet the growing demand with the help of AI implementations. While this positive approach results in increased profits for the company, it unfortunately also leads to a rise in CO2 emissions. Amazon, as the largest e-commerce company, alone emits tons of carbon dioxide into the environment with its current multi-billion-dollar revenue (Amazon, 2020). However, Amazon is just one example of industry leaders that contribute to increased energy consumption and emissions. According to many experts, the development of artificial intelligence (AI) plays a significant role in excessive consumption by enhancing the speed and performance of marketing and other operations (Huang & Rust, 2021). In other words, AI has become a powerful tool for marketing, increasing demand for advertised products. Even though the primary goal of these applications is to create a sustainable demand process, they can lead to excessive demand and consumption. Specifically, AI has the capability to improve services and production operations by defining or suggesting the most sustainable features that are in demand and hold the highest value for customers. Furthermore, through analyzing customer behaviors, AI programs can predict future income and create personalized pricing to generate sustainable recommendations. Ultimately, after evaluating sustainable product proposals and customer segments, consumption becomes sustainable.

Investment Risk

It cannot be denied that the utilization of artificial intelligence in various operations has the potential to significantly increase revenue. This notion has been proven by numerous prominent companies, including their implementation of AI in marketing processes. The vast possibilities offered by AI undeniably hold the promise of substantial returns on investment (Jain & Aggarawal, 2020). However, it is crucial to acknowledge that sustaining such high returns necessitates substantial and ongoing investments in these programs. Consequently, the majority of successful AI adopters are large industry-leading companies that face no difficulty in securing the necessary funds for these endeavors. The emergence of new AI and machine learning concepts, driven by rapid technological advancements, often comes with a hefty price tag and requires a deep understanding of AI application. This poses challenges for small and medium-sized enterprises (SMEs) in adopting AI and ML, as their financial flexibility is not as robust as that of market leaders. SMEs must carefully consider whether the costs and investments associated with AI align with their company's interests. Moreover, smaller organizations typically struggle with making investment decisions that guarantee future returns, as sustainable investment is crucial for maintaining the performance of AI implementation.

The evaluation of the decision to incorporate artificial intelligence into operations is crucial for smaller companies in the market. It is essential to thoroughly analyze every aspect before proceeding. By implementing extensive artificial intelligence systems, these companies can benefit from affordable prices offered by various low-cost providers. This presents an opportunity for companies interested in enhancing their processes, including marketing with machine programs. However, it is important to note that cost-effectiveness should not lead companies to neglect future investments. It is crucial for companies to understand that utilizing artificial intelligence will bring forth additional obstacles and challenges in maintaining a competitive advantage. Artificial intelligence is not a disposable tool, and marketing managers must stay updated on the latest technological developments to survive in a competitive and rapidly changing environment. Therefore, experts are consistently concerned about the sustainable costs associated with implementing artificial intelligence in marketing operations. They may find themselves repeatedly requesting funding for a marketing tool that has already required significant investment for installation. The costs of having a machine-based marketing tool extend beyond its initial setup and maintenance. Organizations must also provide technical services and possess advanced skills to effectively manage artificial intelligence programs in digital marketing (Jain & Aggarwal, 2020). As mentioned earlier, the lack of qualified individuals to hire poses financial obstacles and challenges in finding suitable employees. This may result in an imbalance in salary distribution within the organization and increased competition for talent.

DIGITAL MARKETING TOOLS

Content Marketing

Content marketing involves creating and sharing valuable information about a brand to customers, potential customers, and specific groups through digital platforms or printed materials. In contrast to traditional advertising, which is typically described as a method of communication aimed at convincing or compelling the target audience to take action, either immediately or in the future, content marketing is centered on enhancing the audience's lives. For instance, by educating them, assisting them in problem-solving, bringing them joy, or aiding them in making well-informed decisions. The theoretical principle of social exchange posits that delivering relevant content from a company to the target audience results in reciprocal benefits in exchange for positive attitudes towards the organization. Considering that more than half of content recipients reject irrelevant content, marketers must exhibit creativity and innovation in their content creation if they wish to succeed in content marketing. An IBM study revealed that slightly over 70% of companies furnish a diverse array of impartial and helpful information to their clientele (Synovec, 2019). Personalization and appreciation of content are made feasible through the utilization of data.

An illustration of this is the use of data to suggest products and services based on previous purchases. Data that has been gathered over time can now be employed to provide content recommendations. Each individual possesses their own distinct preferences and interests. By leveraging this data, emails or social media advertisements can be customized to suit the preferences of each user. Consequently, achieving marketing objectives through intelligent content creation facilitated by artificial intelligence is attainable (Ellis-Chadwick & Chaffey, 2019). The creation of content with the assistance of artificial intelligence is more potent than it appears. It requires significant resources and financial investment to produce targeted information for a broad array of products and services. Alibaba stands out as a company that has developed an AI tool capable of generating millions of lines of text and producing 20,000 lines of ad copy within seconds. As a result, their platforms can generate content autonomously without human intervention. This tool, created as part of Alibaba's digital marketing division, streamlines the arduous and time-consuming tasks of retailers by extracting "millions" of authentic human sentences from the company's e-commerce platforms and interpreting them through product listings.

Marketing Strategies Based on Artificial Intelligence

Researchers asserts that marketing stands out as one of the professions integrating artificial intelligence. A crucial aspect of marketing involves grasping customer preferences, aligning them with suitable products and services, and ultimately persuading them to make a purchase. Implementing an AI-driven business and marketing approach has the potential to significantly boost sales. AI tracks customer sentiments, transactions, journeys, and other data to construct machine learning algorithms that forecast customer actions. Personalized information, offers, and communications are employed to devise customer engagement and retention strategies (Huang & Rust, 2021). AI aims to achieve objectives such as cost savings, revenue growth, and enhanced customer satisfaction (Huang & Rust, 2021). Despite lacking compassion or empathy, artificial intelligence (AI) is capable of performing a diverse array of tasks. By streamlining, optimizing, and offering data-driven insights on marketing campaigns, AI minimizes errors in digital marketing (Huang & Rust, 2021). A chatbot serves as a prime example of an artificial intelligence application that emulates human intelligence by interpreting and responding to customer inquiries and concerns, as well as facilitating online transactions. The utilization of chatbots is steadily gaining popularity, with numerous businesses incorporating them into their operations via meta messengers or their websites. Typically, the implementation of a chatbot aims to enhance the efficiency of the customer support department. However, the data acquired through Meta Messenger can also assist organizations in bolstering the effectiveness of their digital marketing strategies through the utilization of data analytics capabilities.

Figure 1. The conceptual model

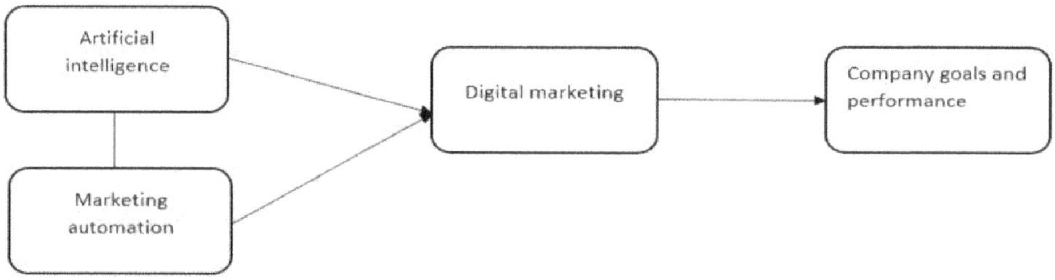

Artificial Intelligence Experts

The data collected revealed a certain level of adaptability in determining their proficiency in AI and their industry experience. However, when it comes to their perspectives on the relationship between AI and marketing, all participants share the same views. They unanimously believe that the current state of AI plays a crucial role in automating marketing efforts. Furthermore, the group argues that AI systems are designed in a manner that marketers are not required to comprehend the underlying architecture. While this can be advantageous and facilitate better understanding, they emphasize the importance of marketers being aware of the tool's true limitations. This entails understanding both its strengths and weaknesses. By doing so, marketers can utilize such solutions without any concerns of bias. Generally, AI experts hold moderate assumptions about marketers' practical infrastructure and technological knowledge. However, they believe that marketers possess a solid understanding of marketing automation. While they acknowledge the value of expanding marketers' knowledge of AI architecture, experts also emphasize that the most crucial aspect for marketers to learn is the system's behavior in action, as well as the impact of its outputs and inputs. In terms of marketing, AI experts suggest that this technology will significantly enhance the marketing system.

The Impact of Artificial Intelligence on Marketers' Responsibilities and Development Processes

Artificial intelligence technology has revolutionized the field of digital marketing. Numerous studies have demonstrated the multitude of advantages that stem from this technology, such as enhanced communication systems, a deeper understanding of customer preferences, and expedited product delivery. Furthermore, these studies, including the one at hand, have revealed that artificial intelligence enables marketers to obtain rapid feedback, enabling them to refine their products and ensure customer satisfaction. In the future, marketing campaigns and strategies can leverage data from previous campaigns and AI technology to effectively map the market and comprehend the whereabouts of individuals, as well as the type of information that garners the most attention. It is predicted that artificial intelligence will furnish marketers with insights into the emotional disposition of customers towards a product. This will provide marketers with a profound understanding of customer preferences from both a psychological and emotional standpoint. The ultimate objective of marketing is to attain customer satisfaction by precisely catering to their needs, and acquiring information about the customer is crucial for achieving this goal. Artificial intelligence technology is anticipated to sufficiently fulfill this requirement, thereby facilitating marketers in their endeavors.

The Value of Artificial Intelligence in Marketing

Artificial intelligence has been instrumental in saving time and enhancing learning from processed data, thereby unlocking growth potential. In the realm of modern marketing, a comprehensive understanding of customers' needs and interests is essential, along with the ability to promptly and effectively act on such information. Organizations that do not leverage AI in their marketing strategies often struggle to make real-time data-driven decisions. In addition to task automation, one of the key advantages of AI lies in the enhanced communication that marketers can establish with their customers. By harnessing personalization through vast data collection, businesses can gain deeper insights into consumer behavior and preferences across various platforms and touchpoints. This enables them to tailor content to match customer interests more effectively, ultimately driving sales. Marketers who do not incorporate artificial intelligence into their strategies may face challenges in swiftly integrating large volumes of customer data. Failing to follow up with customers at the right moment when they receive relevant information poses a risk of losing them. In today's information-rich environment, consumers may struggle to discern between truth and deception, underscoring the importance of marketers delivering accurate and pertinent content to optimize return on investment and operational efficiency. Enhanced decision-making capabilities can lead to improved efficiency, higher ROI, and increased revenue.

Providing tailored customer experiences poses a significant challenge for businesses operating in today's fiercely competitive market. Modern consumers highly value personalized interactions. To outshine their rivals, numerous enterprises are now delving into the realm of personalization. Crafting personalized experiences can be a time-consuming and labor-intensive endeavor, especially when dealing with copious amounts of data that make it arduous for a human to generate precise recommendations without scrutinizing the entire database. This is precisely where AI-driven product recommendation systems come into the picture. AI algorithms scrutinize user preferences regarding product attributes. Leveraging artificial intelligence aids marketers in tracking data, ascertaining real-time customer response rates, and fostering customer-centricity in the long run. Marketers who cater goods and services to consumers are viewed as partaking in a managerial process. It is imperative to utilize AI transparently and ethically, as when employed correctly, it can confer competitive advantages while delivering exceptional experiences.

Using artificial intelligence, businesses can determine the optimal price to attract customers at the most opportune moment. Additionally, smart tools offer the advantage of being constantly updated, providing value to customers and fostering motivation and creativity. By analyzing vast amounts of data, artificial intelligence equips marketers with actionable insights, ultimately enhancing business profitability and marketing effectiveness through customer engagement.

Throughout this process, artificial intelligence enables real-time acquisition of big data, leading to more precise and informed decision-making. The integration of artificial intelligence into business operations presents opportunities for improved marketing performance and streamlined processes.

Furthermore, the implementation of automation brings about various general benefits, such as error reduction, time and cost savings, personalized experiences, and intelligent workflows. By accurately identifying customer needs, businesses can tailor campaigns accordingly, resulting in increased profitability, return on investment (ROI), and reduced labor costs.

Artificial intelligence serves as a valuable tool in minimizing human errors and ensuring data protection by considering the security conditions within a business. Figure 2 provides a summary of the key reasons for combining AI and marketing.

Figure 2. Reasons for the interaction of marketing and artificial intelligence

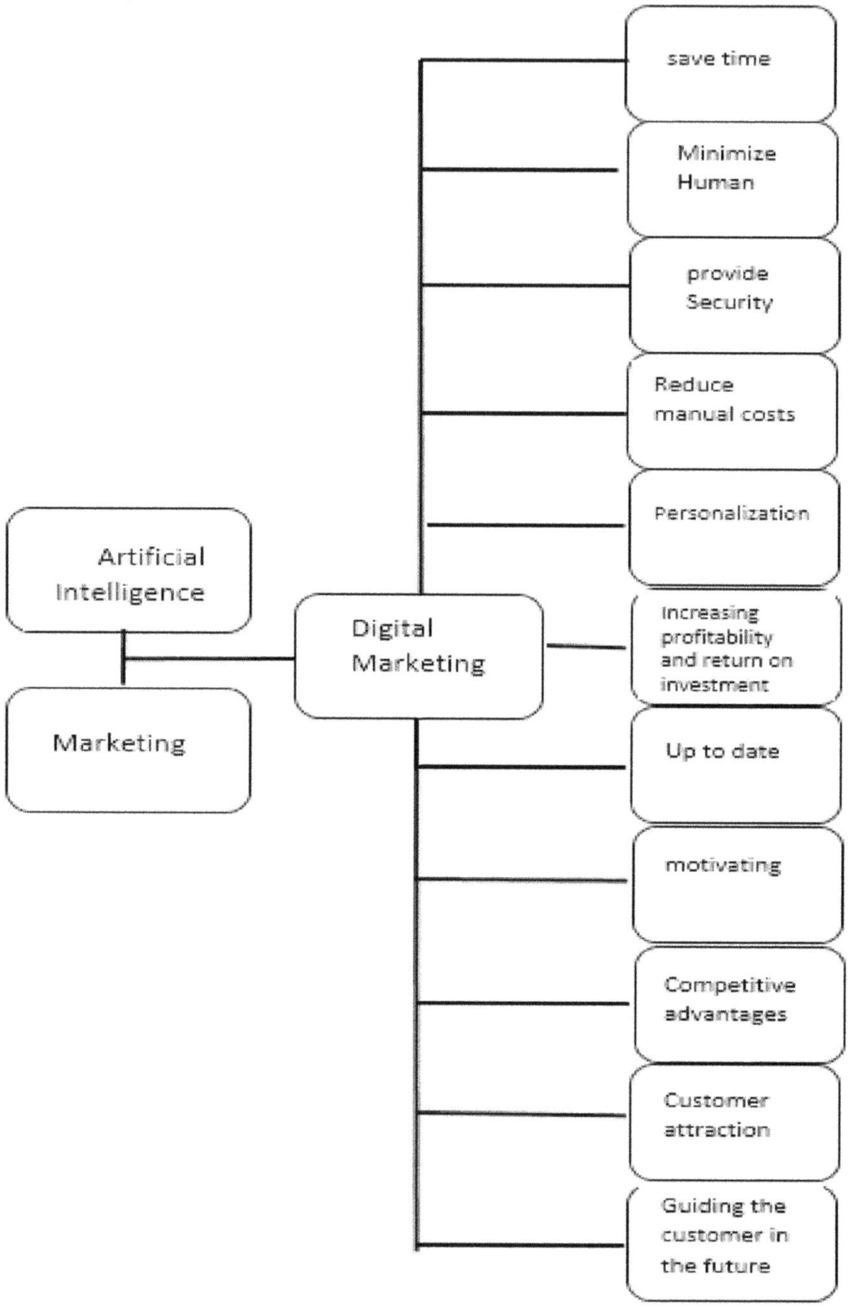

Reasons for Integrating Artificial Intelligence With Marketing

The findings indicate that technical expertise in artificial intelligence is not always necessary. The participants consider specialized skills to be of secondary importance. They believe that utilizing technology does not automatically require involvement in the machine's design. Both sides share the belief that AI systems are designed to be user-friendly, without the need for prior knowledge or understanding of AI. The interview results also highlight the significance of experience in artificial intelligence. Experts in AI assert that they have acquired their skills through continuous utilization of this technology. Furthermore, incorporating artificial intelligence technology into marketing activities enhances learning outcomes. Artificial intelligence technology relies on practical application to enhance knowledge and experience, particularly in the field of marketing. The participants have reported significant improvements in their marketing techniques and outcomes due to their expertise in machine learning and social media marketing. Businesses should incorporate artificial intelligence into their strategies. While it is crucial for consumers to comprehend the connection between advertising and data collection, it is equally important to understand how advertising is linked to data collection. The use of artificial intelligence technology holds great potential for the future of marketing, but appropriate regulations must be established to govern the data collected through its utilization.

THE FUTURE OF ARTIFICIAL INTELLIGENCE IN DIGITAL MARKETING

Artificial intelligence is increasingly being utilized in marketing operations, providing companies with a competitive edge across various industries. As this technology continues to advance, AI's learning capabilities become more efficient, potentially evolving into a more advanced form of action and acquiring the ability to learn (Davenport et al. 2020). Moreover, AI-based solutions in various fields offer a glimpse into the potential of future software and machines, encompassing goals such as compliance, specification, and contextual capabilities (Huang & Rest, 2021). Recent research on machine learning further demonstrates the continuous improvement of data training, analysis, mining, evaluation, and learning capabilities, surpassing the performance of recent programs (Davenport et al. 2020). Additionally, new technologies like artificial intelligence assistants, home appliances, biometric sensors, emotion detectors, and digital interaction facilitate personalization processes, enabling the collection of more customer data for analysis . The exponential growth of big data is also expected to provide marketing experts with larger datasets, enhancing the performance of evaluation processes and supporting future decision-making. Recent studies focusing on the development of artificial intelligence in marketing highlight its effects in areas such as continuous learning, refined content delivery, smarter calls, smarter advertising, and reliable bots (Yeğin, 2020). Continuous learning refers to a process in which the AI component not only discloses data but also utilizes the gathered information to create and execute more effective marketing campaigns, enhancing the interaction between the customer and the brand. Consequently, it is anticipated that programs will enhance decision-making processes. Moreover, the integration of artificial intelligence in marketing activities allows professionals to access pertinent data for identifying an appropriate and specific target customer segment, thereby improving overall performance. Furthermore, advancements in artificial intelligence and its components like machine learning, algorithms, and big data empower users to amalgamate these elements to deliver superior, more personalized, and pertinent content to their target audience. These programs, also referred to as digital optimization utilizing artificial intelligence (Cotter, 2019), play a crucial role in reducing costs and streamlining processes by leveraging the capabilities of robots. The integration of artificial intelligence not only helps in acquiring new customers and retaining existing ones but also proves to be essential for businesses to adapt and thrive in a dynamic environment. Artificial intelligence robots excel in data analysis, offer cost-effective solutions, and deliver superior performance compared to human-operated systems (Yeğin, 2020). Concerns about AI replacing human jobs and causing widespread unemployment are largely unfounded, as experts believe that AI will create new job opportunities (Davenport et al. 2020). However, these new roles are expected to be closely related to AI and evolve over time. AI implementations are designed to support human workers by minimizing errors and reducing operational time, thus minimizing the impact on human labor in the future (Yeğin, 2020). Looking ahead, the future of marketing will likely witness more innovative applications of artificial intelligence. AI-driven marketing strategies are already being used to forecast future actions, and we may soon witness AI-powered brand management where analytics play a central role in decision-making. Despite the remarkable progress in technology, the potential for even more advanced applications beyond our current imagination remains high for future generations (Yeğin, 2020).

Ethical Considerations

This segment demonstrates that participants possess a strong understanding of their ethical responsibilities and comply with the ethical standards outlined. Ethical dilemmas emerge during the research planning and design phases and vary depending on the nature of each study. Although there is no definitive blueprint for ethical conduct, research should aim to embody ethical principles and behaviors. Key principles encompass impartiality, honesty, fostering truthfulness, showing respect, and evaluating conduct to prevent harm to participants. Moreover, researchers must uphold confidentiality by safeguarding participants' privacy, informing them about the voluntary nature of the study, and obtaining informed consent. In figure 3, the state of the market over time is shown statistically.

Figure 3. Market value of artificial intelligence in marketing worldwide from 2020 to 2028 (Global AI in marketing revenue 2028, 2023)

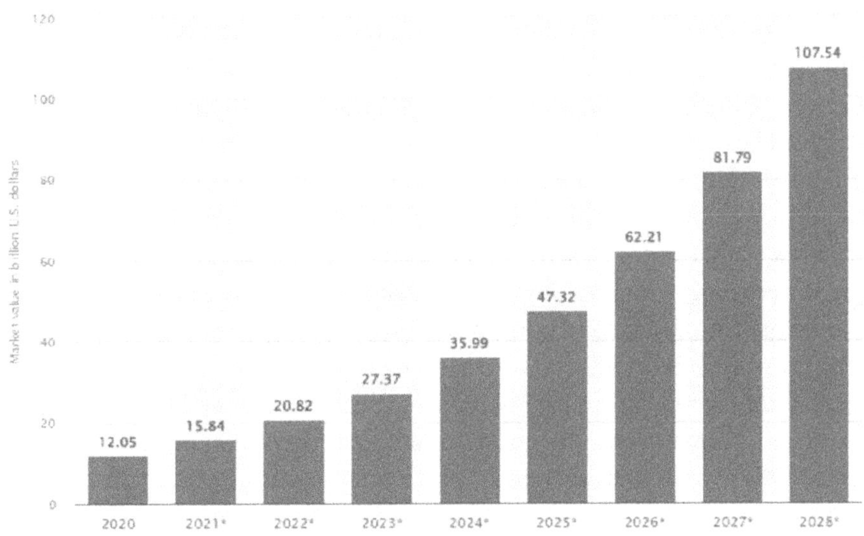

RECOMMENDATIONS

Integrating artificial intelligence into marketing project management is crucial for achieving success. AI offers valuable assistance in data analysis and automation, while human intuition, creativity, and critical thinking are indispensable for interpreting consumer sentiment and adjusting to market fluctuations. Marketers need to keep pace with AI advancements and adjust their strategies to fully leverage the benefits of this transformative technology to drive innovation, enhance decision-making, and boost overall marketing effectiveness.

Management Concept

This section has pinpointed the key competencies that will become essential for marketing professionals to develop in the future for better readiness. To grasp the utilization of artificial intelligence features, including the novel aspects and viewpoints for analyzing extensive data sets, marketing professionals need to possess the technical expertise to comprehend and assess this data. Furthermore, the creation of value propositions emerged as a crucial finding concerning the significance of the marketing management role. Since customer experience has consistently involved a technical element, as highlighted by a participant, the capacity to enhance customer experience through technological innovations is priceless. Marketing professionals must possess a deep understanding of how intelligent machines operate and how to effectively utilize the technology. In addition to technical skills, qualities related to emotional intelligence, such as social awareness and empathy, are crucial for success in the field. These attributes play a vital role in gathering valuable customer feedback for product development and innovation, as well as in determining the appropriate communication approach with customers and partners. Moreover, creativity is identified as a key factor in the marketing profession, influencing rational decision-making, driving innovation within the company, and shaping product features. The innovative aspect of the marketing role will continue to be essential, especially with the growing significance of artificial intelligence in marketing strategies. It is also important for marketing professionals to strike a balance between data-driven decisions and maintaining authenticity, as an excessive reliance on data may hinder creativity and increase risk aversion.

Offers

Assess marketing procedures to pinpoint areas where AI can tackle obstacles or enhance productivity. This may involve automating data analysis, enhancing customer segmentation, or simplifying project management workflows. For suitable AI tools or platforms that are in line with marketing objectives and requirements, while also offering customizable solutions tailored to specific demands. Verify that data utilized for AI analysis is precise, dependable, and complies with privacy regulations. Implement robust security measures to safeguard sensitive customer data and uphold data integrity. Establishing a specialized AI team or collaborating with AI specialists can aid in ensuring seamless integration and successful execution. Initiate AI projects on a small scale to assess the feasibility and efficacy of AI solutions. Collect insights, assess performance, and make necessary improvements. This iterative method enables continuous learning and enhancement. Collaboration among marketing, technology, and data teams is strongly encouraged in order to effectively harness the power of AI. Establish cross-functional teams that can collaborate to optimize AI strategies, share insights, and tackle challenges.

Key Performance Indicators (KPIs) are developed to monitor the impact of AI on marketing projects. Regularly review and measure results to evaluate the effectiveness of AI solutions.

Artificial intelligence is a rapidly evolving field. It stays up-to-date with the latest trends, research, and advancements in AI to continuously explore new possibilities and innovative ways to utilize AI in marketing. When utilizing artificial intelligence, it is crucial to prioritize ethical concepts such as privacy, impartiality, and transparency. Experiences are utilized to refine AI strategies and integrate AI as an ongoing learning process within the marketing function.

CONCLUSION

The marketing sector has been identified as one of the most promising sectors in the economy for improvement. It provides ample opportunities for growth, particularly through the utilization of technology. Marketing strategies have advanced with time, incorporating modern technology to enhance efficiency. The rise of digital marketing has the potential to significantly impact individuals, thanks to technological advancements that allow businesses to mass-produce goods and utilize digital platforms to expand their reach in promoting and selling products to consumers. Furthermore, the evolution of digital marketing is a result of the integration of big data and scientific research into innovative applications. This enables the collection of data on individual preferences for seamless use in marketing endeavors. This research aimed to explore the advantages of digital marketing, specifically focusing on the use of artificial intelligence and market automation to enhance marketing outcomes. Additionally, the study examined the influence of digital marketing on company performance. The findings of this study revealed a positive correlation between artificial intelligence, market automation, and digital marketing. Similar to other technological advancements, significant advancements were observed in the marketing firms under investigation, aligning with existing literature. Marketers anticipate that AI will continue to refine automation parameters, gradually assuming control over a majority of marketing processes. Present-day marketers are eager to enhance their digital marketing skills to effectively engage with each customer and address their needs comprehensively. Marketing professionals have expressed concerns about the level of control organizations will have over their efforts once AI automation is fully implemented. Those who are not familiar with AI technology may view it as expensive and unnecessary for their marketing systems. Some marketers believe that artificial intelligence cannot comprehend human intelligence, a sentiment shared by

AI experts. While automation is seen as a way to simplify tasks and solve problems, there is also apprehension about losing control over campaigns. Understanding AI capabilities is crucial for successful automation. Analyzing the application of AI in digital marketing and its impact can provide valuable insights into its benefits. As online businesses continue to grow, utilizing AI for marketing purposes is essential for reaching customers and achieving marketing objectives. The study highlights how AI enhances digital marketing processes and improves marketing strategies. Marketing managers must acquire AI skills to remain competitive and drive positive outcomes in their businesses. The advancement of marketing heavily relies on technological enhancements in marketing systems and structures. The marketing sector is anticipated to be completely taken over by artificial intelligence technology, which will enable the creation of personalized customer experiences and elevate marketing to new levels. Hence, it is imperative for every marketing manager to integrate artificial intelligence and marketing automation into their systems, as this technology is universally embraced. AI technology is projected to provide an economic boost by increasing GDP through investment returns. Gradually, this technology is replacing human functions in marketing, such as communication, making tasks easier to perform and enhancing overall efficiency. The virtual assistant mode ensures that each customer interacts with AI in the most human-like manner possible. While it is crucial to closely monitor this progress, it is evident that digital marketing is steadily advancing. Consequently, the role of artificial intelligence (AI) in marketing project management is becoming increasingly significant. AI technology has the potential to revolutionize the way marketing projects are planned, executed, and evaluated. By utilizing machine learning algorithms and natural language processing, artificial intelligence can assist marketers in identifying target audiences, optimizing marketing campaigns, and analyzing consumer behavior. By utilizing automated data analysis, artificial intelligence (AI) has the capability to provide marketers with valuable insights regarding customer preferences, behavioral patterns, and market trends. This, in turn, allows for more effective decision-making and the creation of personalized marketing strategies. Furthermore, AI-powered tools have the ability to automate repetitive tasks, thereby freeing up marketers' time to concentrate on more strategic activities.

Simultaneously, AI has the potential to enhance project management by streamlining workflows, optimizing resource allocation, and facilitating communication and collaboration among marketing teams. AI-based project management platforms can automate the allocation of tasks, scheduling, and tracking progress, resulting in improved efficiency and productivity.

REFERENCES

Alpaydın, E. (2014). *Introduction to Machine Learning*. The MIT Press.

Bughin, J., McCarthy, B., & Chui, M. (2017, August 28). A Survey of 3,000 Executives Reveals How Businesses Succeed with AI. Retrieved December 12, 2017, from https://hbr.org/2017/08/a-survey-of-3000-executives-reveals-how-businesses-succeed-with-ai

Campesato, O. (2020). Artificial Intelligence, Machine Learning and Deep Learning. Dulles: Mercury Learning and information.

Canals, J., & Heukamp, F. (2020). *The Future of Management in an AI World*. Springer International Publishing. 10.1007/978-3-030-20680-2

Chaffey, D., & Ellis-Chadwick, F. (2019). *Digital marketing* (7th ed.). Pearson.

Chui, M., Kamalnath, V., & McCarthy, B. (2018, March 12). An executive's guide to AI (Guide). Retrieved March 15, 2018, from McKinsey & Company website: https://www.mckinsey.com/business-functions/mckinsey-analytics/our-insights/an-executives-guide-to-ai

Cotter, K. (2019). Playing the visibility game: How digital influencers and algorithms negotiate influence on Instagram. *New Media & Society*, 21(4), 895–913. 10.1177/1461444818815684

Daugherty, P. R., & Wilson, H. J. (2018). *Human + Machine. Reimagining Work in the Age of AI*. Harvard Business Press.

Davenport, T., Guha, A., Grewal, D., & Bressgott, T. (2020). How artificial intelligence will change the future of marketing. *Journal of the Academy of Marketing Science*, 48(1), 24–42. 10.1007/s11747-019-00696-0

Dodson, I. (2016). *The Digital Marketing Playbook: The Definitive Guide to Creating Strategic, Targeted, and Measurable Online Campaigns*. John Wiley & Sons.

Dumitriu, D., & Popescu, M. A.-M. (2020). Artificial Intelligence Solutions for Digital Marketing. *Procedia Manufacturing*, 46, 630–636. 10.1016/j.promfg.2020.03.090

Grover, P., & Kar, A. K. (2017). Big Data Analytics: A Review on Theoretical Contributions and Tools Used in Literature. *Glob J Flex Syst Manag, 18*(3), 203–229. 10.1007/s40171-017-0159-3

Hermann, E. (2021): Artificial intelligence in marketing: friend or foe of sustainable consumption? In AI & Soc. 10.1007/s00146-021-01227-8

Holtel, S. (2016). Artificial Intelligence Creates a Wicked Problem for the Enterprise. *Procedia Computer Science*, 99, 171–180. 10.1016/j.procs.2016.09.109

How AI Is Pushing Man and Machine Closer Together. (Rep.). (2017, February). Retrieved January 16, 2018, from PwC website: https://www.pwc.in/assets/pdfs/consulting/digital-enablement-advisory1/pwc-botme-boo klet.pdf

Interest in AI Startups Exploded in 2017. (2018, January 19). Retrieved April 03, 2018, from https://www.venturescanner.com/blog/2018/interest-in-ai-startups-exploded-in-2017

Jain, P., & Aggarwal, K. (2020). Transforming Marketing with Artificial Intelligence.

Jamshed, S. (2014). Qualitative research method-interviewing and observation. *Journal of Basic and Clinical Pharmacy*, 5(4), 87. 10.4103/0976-0105.14194225316987

Mahesh, B. (2020). Machine learning algorithms-a review. International Journal of Science and Research, 9, 381-386.

Mogaji, E., Soetan, T. O., & Kieu, T. A. (2020): The implications of artificial intelligence on the digital marketing of financial services to vulnerable customers. Australasian Marketing Journal. 10.1016/j.ausmj.2020.05.003

Nieto-Rodriguez, A., & Vargas, R. V. (2023). How AI Will Transform Project Management. Retrieved from Harvard Business Review: https://hbr.org/2023/02/how-ai-will-transform-project-management

Paschen, J., Wilson, M., & Ferreira, J. J. (2020). Collaborative intelligence: How human and artificial intelligence create value along the B2B sales funnel. *Business Horizons*, 63(3), 403–414. 10.1016/j.bushor.2020.01.003

Rust, R. (2020). The future of marketing. *International Journal of Research in Marketing*, 37(1), 15–26. 10.1016/j.ijresmar.2019.08.002

Synovec, J. R. (2018). Making artificial intelligence real: How brands can use AI to supercharge their marketing stack.

Today, A. I., & Tomorrow, A. I. (Rep.). (2017, July). Retrieved January 16, 2018, from ARM with Northstar Research Partners website: http://pages.arm.com/rs/312-SAX-488/images/arm-ai-survey-report.pdf

Turner, J. (2018). Robot rules: Regulating artificial intelligence. Springer. Journal of Business Research.

Wichert, A. (2020). Principles of quantum artificial intelligence: quantum problem solving and machine learning.

Wirth, N. (2018). Hello marketing, what can artificial intelligence help you with? *International Journal of Market Research*, 60(5), 435–438. 10.1177/1470785318776841

Yeğin. (2020). The place and future of artificial intelligence in marketing strategies. 81st ed. 24 volumes: Ekev Akademi Dergisi. Available online at https://www.ekevakademi.org/makaleler/1000387091_25%20tugba%20yegın.pdf

KEY TERMS AND DEFINITIONS

Artificial Intelligence (AI): Artificial intelligence, or AI, is technology that enables computers and machines to simulate human intelligence and problem-solving capabilities.

Business to Business (B2B): Business-to-business (B2B) describes a transaction where one company sells a product or service to another company.

Business-to-Consumer (B2C): B2C e-commerce refers to the online transactions between businesses and individual consumers.

Deep Learning (DL): Deep learning is a subset of machine learning that uses multilayered neural networks, called deep neural networks, to simulate the complex decision-making power of the human brain.

Information Technology (IT): IT is a broad term that refers to jobs that involve technology in business.

Key Performance Indicators (KPIs): Key performance indicators (KPIs) are measurable and quantifiable metrics used to evaluate and assess the performance of your company or organization's activities.

Machine Learning (ML): Machine learning (ML) is a branch of artificial intelligence (AI) and computer science that focuses on the using data and algorithms to enable AI to imitate the way that humans learn, gradually improving its accuracy.

Search Engine Optimization (SEO): Search engine optimization (SEO) is the process of improving the quality and quantity of website traffic to a website or a web page from search engines

Small and Medium-Sized Enterprises (SMEs): Small and medium-sized enterprises (SMEs) or small and medium-sized businesses (SMBs) are businesses whose personnel and revenue numbers fall below certain limits.

Chapter 10
Generative AI for Customized Public Policy in Maritime Transport

Rupesh Kumar
https://orcid.org/0000-0002-3878-896X
Institute of Advanced Research, Gandhinagar, India

Chhote Lal Yadav
https://orcid.org/0000-0001-9982-4058
Institute of Law Nirma University, India

ABSTRACT

Maritime transport is crucial for global trade, transporting over 90% of global goods by volume and facing challenges such as environmental impacts and security threats. Public policy is the key to addressing these issues through regulations that enhance safety, security, and sustainability. Integrating this sector with generative AI can significantly improve predictive maintenance, route optimisation, and accident prevention. AI technologies can process vast amounts of data for real-time decision-making, which is vital for the efficiency and safety of maritime operations. AI can lead to autonomous ships, optimise logistics, and reduce human error. However, integrating AI poses technical barriers such as cybersecurity, significant initial costs, and social hurdles such as job displacement fears. Effective public policy must evolve to address these challenges and promote AI integration while considering ethical and legal implications.

DOI: 10.4018/979-8-3693-5578-7.ch010

INTRODUCTION

The maritime transport sector is pivotal in global trade and responsible for transporting over 90% of the world's goods by volume (Sirimanne et al., 2020). It offers a cost-effective means of moving large quantities of goods across great distances, making it indispensable for modern economies. However, this sector faces multiple challenges, including significant environmental impacts, as it contributes substantially to global greenhouse gas emissions. Moreover, the industry must navigate complex international regulatory environments and address security threats like piracy and maritime terrorism (Joung et al., 2020).

Public policy plays a crucial role in maritime transportation by establishing regulations that ensure safety, security, and environmental sustainability. Through international collaboration, policies aim to reduce the ecological footprint of maritime activities by enforcing stricter emission controls and encouraging the adoption of cleaner technologies (Stopford, 2009). Public policy also addresses security challenges by enhancing antipiracy measures and ensuring safe navigation in contentious waters. Furthermore, policies facilitate economic competitiveness by supporting technological advancements and infrastructure development, which are crucial for maintaining and enhancing the efficiency of global supply chains (Rodrigue, 2020). Generative AI refers to a subset of AI technologies that generate new content, from text and images to music and code, based on the patterns and information learned from large datasets. Unlike discriminative algorithms designed to recognise or classify data, generative AI actively creates and simulates novel outputs that plausibly mimic the original data (Goodfellow et al., 2016). The intersection of generative AI-customized public policy and maritime transport is a burgeoning area of study that seeks to leverage advanced AI technologies to address specific regulatory and operational challenges in the maritime sector. Generative AI is an algorithm that generates data and insights that mimic real-world phenomena, enabling policymakers to simulate and predict outcomes for better decision-making.

Maritime transport is critical to global trade and faces numerous challenges, including safety, efficiency, and environmental impact. The integration of generative AI can significantly enhance predictive maintenance, route optimisation, and accident prevention. For instance, Chaudhry et al. (2023) discussed a lightweight authentication protocol for maritime transport systems enhanced by 6G and IoT technologies to improve maritime operations' security and data integrity.

Customised public policy in maritime transport refers to tailored regulations and standards that dynamically respond to the sector's evolving needs. This approach is evident in the work of Malmborg (2023), who analyses advocacy coalitions in decarbonising maritime transport, highlighting the role of policy in steering sector-wide changes towards sustainability.

Integrating AI into public policy, particularly in a sector as complex as maritime transport, presents both challenges and opportunities. Security concerns, data privacy, and the need for a robust infrastructure are significant challenges. However, the ability to process large datasets for real-time decision-making presents a substantial opportunity to enhance efficiency and safety. The synergy between generative AI and customised public policy in maritime transport can redefine traditional approaches, making operations more efficient, secure, and environmentally friendly. Ongoing research and implementation in this field are crucial for realising AI's full potential to enhance public policy effectiveness in the maritime sector. Public policy is critical in maritime transportation, setting regulations that promote safety, security, and environmental sustainability. Through international cooperation, policies aim to minimise the environmental impact by enforcing stricter emission controls and promoting cleaner technologies. They also enhance security through improved antipiracy measures and ensure safe navigation in disputed waters. Moreover, public policy supports economic competitiveness by adopting technological advancements and infrastructure development, which are essential for maintaining and improving the efficiency of global supply chains.

GENERATIVE AI IN PUBLIC POLICY

Generative AI represents a paradigm shift in AI, moving beyond classification and prediction towards creating entirely new content. This section highlights the technical underpinnings of generative AI, exploring its core principles and the role of specific machine-learning models, particularly Generative Adversarial Networks (GANs).

Machine learning models have traditionally focused on discriminative tasks and learning to map inputs to desired outputs. For instance, an image recognition system may analyse an image and classify it as containing a cat. However, the generative AI flips this script. Instead of categorising existing data, it aims to generate new instances that adhere to the underlying patterns learned from a training dataset (Goodfellow et al., 2016). This empowers generative models to create realistic novel images, text, audio, or code. The concept of statistical modelling is at the heart of generative AI. The model captures the data's statistical properties by analysing vast training data. This knowledge can generate new data points that share the same statistical characteristics but represent entirely new entities. Generative AI leverages diverse machine learning models to achieve content creation goals. This section explores two prominent examples. VAEs compile input data into a latent representation, capturing its essence. This latent space acts as a compressed version of the original data, allowing the model to manipulate and generate new data points (Kingma &

Welling, 2013). By decoding these manipulated points, the VAE produces novel data instances that resemble the training data but have unique characteristics.

GANs introduce a fascinating twist in generative modelling. They are comprised of two neural networks: a generator and a discriminator. The generator acts as an artist and constantly strives to produce realistic and novel content. On the other hand, the discriminator plays the role of a discerning art critic, attempting to distinguish between actual data points from the training set and the creation of the generator (Isola et al., 2017). This adversarial training process pushes both networks to improve iteratively. The generator learns to create increasingly realistic content while the discriminator hones its ability to discern the real from the fake. The result is a powerful system capable of generating highly realistic and creative outputs.

APPLICATIONS OF GENERATIVE AI IN PUBLIC POLICY

AI's role in public policy has seen significant advancements, particularly in sectors where operational efficiency and safety are paramount. AI is instrumental in enhancing diagnostics, patient care, and data management in healthcare. A notable example is the use of machine-learning algorithms to predict hospital readmissions, which assists in improving patient outcomes and reducing costs. The potential of these technologies extends to maritime applications such as monitoring crew members' health and using predictive analytics to manage potential outbreaks on ships (Esteva et al., 2019). AI aids in urban planning by optimising traffic flow and enhancing the design of smart cities. AI applications in traffic management, for example, can also improve operations in port logistics, reduce congestion, and optimise the scheduling of shipments (Batty, 2013). AI significantly contributes to environmental monitoring by predicting climate phenomena and tracking wildlife populations. These technologies benefit maritime applications in route planning, risk assessment, and environmental protection (Rolnick et al., 2019).

Integrating AI into public policy has rapidly transformed these fields, particularly in the maritime, port, transportation, and shipping sectors. This literature review explores the current applications of AI across these domains, highlighting the key studies and findings that illustrate the role of AI in enhancing efficiency, safety, and sustainability. In the maritime industry, AI applications range from navigation support and traffic management to environmental monitoring and automated port operation. AI is critical for navigation and safety in maritime operations. Rani et al. (2022) We discuss using bio-inspired algorithms in maritime rescue, which enhance the accuracy of dynamic target node localisation in maritime search and rescue operations. AI algorithms achieve a 10% reduction in localisation errors compared to traditional methods. Ashraf et al. (2022) Present a survey on cyber security threats in the IoT-enabled maritime industry, highlighting AI's role in mitigating risks associated with digital transformation in maritime operations.

Ports are critical nodes in global supply chains where AI optimises operations and enhances security. The study by Wang et al. (2021) on attribute-based secure data aggregation for isolated IoT-enabled maritime transportation systems illustrates how AI can secure data flows in maritime ports, ensuring the reliability and integrity of operational data that are crucial for decision-making processes. Intelligent technologies and AI are being integrated into ports to manage resources and streamline logistics, significantly reducing operational downtimes and enhancing throughput efficiency.

AI applications in transportation and shipping range from route optimisation to predictive maintenance. Implementing AI in these sectors not only enhances operational efficiency but also contributes to significant reductions in carbon emissions and increased safety. A notable example is the use of AI in managing container shipping logistics, where AI algorithms help predict container storage and optimise ship-loading plans, reduce ship turnaround times, and improve port throughput. The current applications of AI in maritime, port, transportation, and shipping have demonstrated a significant positive impact on operational efficiency, safety, and environmental sustainability. As AI technology continues to evolve, its integration into public policy and operational frameworks is expected to deepen, offering even more significant benefits and transforming critical sectors.

AI dramatically transforms healthcare, maritime, urban planning, and transportation sectors by enhancing efficiency, safety, and sustainability. In healthcare, AI improves diagnostics and patient management, which parallels its application in maritime settings, where it monitors crew health and manages disease outbreaks. AI's capabilities extend to urban traffic management, optimising flow, and infrastructure design—similarly beneficial applications in port logistics, such as reducing congestion and optimising shipment schedules. AI supports crucial operations such as navigation, traffic management, and environmental monitoring. It enhances search and rescue missions through bio-inspired algorithms and mitigates cybersecurity risks in IoT-enabled maritime environments. In ports, AI ensures secure data flows and optimises operational processes, significantly reducing downtimes and increasing efficiency. AI is pivotal for route optimisation and predictive maintenance in transportation and shipping, contributing to lower carbon emissions and increased safety. Integrating AI into public policy continues to evolve, offering profound benefits across these interconnected domains.

GENERATIVE AI IN MARITIME TRANSPORT POLICY

The proliferation of generative AI has profoundly impacted various sectors, notably maritime transport. This section explores the integration of generative AI into maritime transport policy, highlighting its applications, advantages, challenges, and regulatory implications. Generative AI is emerging as a transformative force, influencing policy development and operational practices. Its applications in optimising logistics, enhancing safety, and improving decision-making necessitate reevaluating existing maritime policies. The maritime industry can achieve greater efficiency and sustainability by harnessing AI for route optimisation, predictive analytics, autonomous vessels, and environmental compliance. Consequently, policymakers must adapt regulations to leverage this advanced technology's benefits fully.

Generative AI subsumes a spectrum of technologies adept at synthesising new content from preexisting data. These technologies are pivotal for augmenting predictive analytics, decision-making capabilities, and operational efficiencies within maritime transport. A quintessential application involves using dual linear autoencoders to predict vessel trajectories and leveraging historical Automatic Identification System (AIS) data. This method significantly bolsters collision avoidance strategies, augments maritime safety, and underpins policy formulation through enhanced risk assessment tools in navigational practices. (Murray & Perera, 2020). Furthermore, generative AI was deployed to classify vessel types based on their movement patterns, a critical element for automated maritime surveillance. This capability substantially improves the efficiency of maritime traffic monitoring and ensures adherence to international maritime statutes. By enabling the automated surveillance and classification of vessels, generative AI facilitates the development of robust policy frameworks that efficiently oversee and regulate maritime activities (Li et al., 2020a).

The application of generative AI in processing extensive datasets from maritime operations provides policymakers with profound insights into the dynamics of marine traffic and its environmental impact. These insights are instrumental in formulating policies that harmonise developmental objectives with environmental preservation. However, integrating generative AI into maritime policies is not a challenge. Concerns such as the precision and dependability of AI-generated predictions, ethical issues surrounding autonomous decision-making, and the potential for data misappropriation or breaches necessitate the establishment of stringent regulatory frameworks. These frameworks are essential to ensure that AI technologies are safe, ethical, and adequate and to maintain a balance between innovation and regulation to safeguard privacy and safety. (Robards et al., 2016a).

Integrating generative AI into maritime transport policies substantially benefits navigational safety, operational efficiency, and environmental stewardship. While generative AI promises to significantly enhance maritime transport's efficacy, safety, and sustainability, its adoption must be coupled with careful policy considerations that address potential risks and ethical dilemmas. Aligning technological advancements with comprehensive regulatory frameworks enables the maritime sector to fully leverage the capabilities of generative AI while mitigating associated risks. Generative AI is revolutionising maritime transport policy by enhancing predictive analytics and decision-making capabilities. This technology synthesises new content from existing data, significantly improving operational efficiencies. A notable application is using dual linear autoencoders to predict vessel trajectories based on historical Automatic Identification System data, enhancing collision avoidance and maritime safety.

Generative AI aids in classifying vessel types from their movement patterns, improving maritime surveillance and compliance with international statutes. While offering substantial benefits in maritime safety and environmental stewardship, integrating generative AI into maritime policies raises concerns about AI predictions' accuracy, ethical issues, and data security. These challenges necessitate robust regulatory frameworks to ensure AI's safe and ethical use, balancing innovation with regulation to protect privacy and safety.

Route Optimization: Generative AI analyses extensive datasets, including historical shipping routes, weather patterns, and market conditions, to optimise vessel routes and improve fleet management. This not only boosts operational efficiency but also reduces fuel consumption and emissions (Munim et al., 2020).

Predictive Analytics for Safety: AI-driven predictive analytics help maritime stakeholders forecast potential accidents and security threats like piracy and illegal fishing. This proactive safety approach can lead to stronger safety regulations and response strategies (Heilig & Voß, 2017).

Autonomous Vessels: Developing autonomous ships powered by generative AI introduces new challenges and opportunities for maritime policy. These vessels operate with minimal human intervention, requiring updated regulations for their operation, safety standards, and liability issues (Tijan et al., 2021).

Enhanced Communication: AI-driven chatbots facilitate communication between crew managers and port agents, streamlining operations and reducing human error. This improvement can lead to more efficient decision-making processes in maritime logistics (Kumar, 2023).

Sustainability and Environmental Compliance: Generative AI helps monitor compliance with environmental regulations by analysing emissions and fuel consumption data. This supports the development of policies aimed at promoting sustainability in maritime transport (Lee & Yang, 2018).

CHALLENGES ADDRESSED BY AI

AI in the maritime, seaport, and shipping sectors addresses various challenges, leading to significant transformations in these fields. These advancements highlight the critical role of AI in transforming maritime and shipping operations, enhancing safety, efficiency, and sustainability while addressing the complex challenges posed by modern maritime activities. We identified some key challenges tackled by AI technologies:

AI contributes significantly to maritime safety by improving navigation and collision avoidance systems. By analysing historical and real-time data, AI models can predict vessel trajectories and enhance route planning, preventing accidents and ensuring smooth operations (Murray & Perera, 2020). AI helps maritime companies adhere to environmental regulations, such as those imposed by the International Maritime Organization (IMO), by optimising fuel usage and reducing emissions. Advanced AI applications monitor and adjust fuel consumption and engine performance to meet stringent environmental standards, promoting sustainability in shipping practices (Ceyhun, 2019). In seaports, AI facilitates the management of cargo handling and storage operations, significantly improving operational efficiency. AI-driven systems analyse patterns in container traffic, optimise loading and unloading operations, predict equipment maintenance needs, minimise downtime, and reduce operational costs. (Kontzinos et al., 2022).

Cybersecurity has become a paramount concern with the increasing digitalisation of maritime operations. AI is crucial for detecting and mitigating cyber threats and ensuring the integrity and security of navigational and operational data. AI systems can identify unusual patterns that may indicate cyberattacks, thereby protecting sensitive information and maintaining the security of maritime operations. (Androjna et al., 2020).

AI significantly transforms the maritime, seaport, and shipping sectors by enhancing safety, efficiency, and sustainability. It improves navigation and collision avoidance by predicting vessel trajectories and optimising routes, ensuring safer maritime operations. Additionally, AI helps companies meet environmental regulations by optimising fuel usage and reducing emissions. AI optimises cargo handling and predicts seaport maintenance needs, boosting operational efficiency. Moreover, AI is crucial in cybersecurity, detecting threats, and protecting data integrity in increasingly digital maritime environments. Despite its potential benefits, integrating generative AI into policy development presents several challenges that must be addressed to maximise its effectiveness.

Data Privacy and Security Concerns: Generative AI relies heavily on data, raising concerns about privacy and security. Policymakers must ensure that data used in AI systems is collected and managed ethically, adhering to privacy regulations and protecting sensitive information (Tian et al., 2017). Establishing robust data governance frameworks is essential to mitigate data breaches and misuse risks. Additionally, policymakers need to address the potential biases inherent in AI algorithms. If generative AI systems are trained on biased data, they may produce skewed insights that could lead to unfair or ineffective policies. Ensuring diversity in training data and implementing bias detection mechanisms are critical steps in promoting fairness in AI-driven policy development (Kuhlemann & Tierney, 2020).

Regulatory Adaptation: The rapid evolution of generative AI technologies necessitates adaptive regulatory frameworks that can keep pace with advancements. Existing regulations may not adequately address the unique challenges posed by AI, leading to gaps in oversight and accountability (Woo & Yang, 2018). Policymakers must engage with AI experts and industry stakeholders to develop regulations that forward innovation while ensuring safety and ethical standards. For example, regulations governing autonomous vessels in maritime transport must consider the implications of AI-driven navigation systems and the potential for human oversight failures. Policymakers must establish clear guidelines for the operation of autonomous vessels, including safety protocols and liability frameworks (Tijan et al., 2021).

The Need for Adaptive Frameworks: To effectively harness the potential of generative AI in policy development, adaptive frameworks are essential. These frameworks should prioritize flexibility, collaboration, and continuous learning.

Collaborative Policy Development: Collaboration among stakeholders is crucial for effective policy development in the context of generative AI. Policymakers should engage with industry experts, researchers, and civil society organizations to gather diverse perspectives and insights. This collaborative approach raises a more comprehensive understanding of the implications of AI technologies and promotes the development of well-informed policies (Leong, 2019).

Continuous Learning and Adaptation: Policymakers must embrace a culture of continuous learning to keep pace with advancements in generative AI. This involves investing in training and education for policymakers to enhance their understanding of AI technologies and their implications for policy development (Handayani et al., 2021) By encouraging a culture of learning, policymakers can better navigate the complexities of AI and make informed decisions that benefit society as a whole.

GENERATIVE AI IMPACT ON POLICY DEVELOPMENT

Generative AI represents a significant advancement in artificial intelligence, characterized by its ability to create new content and insights based on learned data patterns. This capability is transforming various sectors, including maritime transport, logistics, and supply chain management. The implications of generative

AI extend beyond operational efficiencies; they are reshaping policy development across industries. This paper explores how generative AI impacts policy development, focusing on its applications, challenges, and the need for adaptive regulatory frameworks. Generative AI can enhance policy development through its applications in data analysis, predictive modeling, and decision-making support. These applications are critical in sectors where data-driven decisions are paramount.

Data-Driven Decision Making: Generative AI systems can analyze vast amounts of data from diverse sources, providing policymakers with insights that inform their decisions. In the maritime industry, generative AI can optimize shipping routes and predict global trade patterns by analyzing historical data, weather conditions, and market dynamics. This capability allows for more informed policy decisions regarding trade regulations and environmental compliance. In logistics, generative AI can streamline supply chain operations by predicting demand and optimizing inventory levels. This predictive capability enables policymakers to develop regulations that encourage efficiency and sustainability in supply chains (Zhao et al., 2023). By leveraging AI-generated insights, policymakers can create frameworks that promote best practices in resource management and environmental stewardship.

Predictive Modeling for Risk Assessment: Generative AI enhances risk assessment processes by providing predictive models that simulate various scenarios. In maritime transport, AI can predict potential accidents or security threats, allowing policymakers to implement proactive measures (Heilig & Voß, 2017). This predictive capability is essential for developing safety regulations and emergency response strategies. Moreover, generative AI can assist in modeling the economic impacts of policy changes, enabling policymakers to assess the potential outcomes of their decisions before implementation. By simulating different scenarios, policymakers can identify the most effective strategies for achieving desired outcomes while minimizing risks (Munim et al., 2020).

Enhancing Communication and Collaboration: Generative AI facilitates improved communication and collaboration among stakeholders involved in policy development. AI-driven tools can automate information sharing and streamline communication processes, making it easier for policymakers to engage with industry experts, researchers, and the public (Kumar, 2023). This enhanced communication advances a collaborative environment where diverse perspectives can inform policy decisions. AI chatbots, for instance, can gather feedback from stakeholders on proposed regulations, allowing policymakers to refine their approaches based on real-time input. This level of engagement can lead to more effective and inclusive policy development processes (Tijan et al., 2021). The integration of generative AI into maritime transport necessitates significant changes in policy frameworks. Regulatory adaptation is essential, as policymakers must update existing regulations to align with the operational realities of AI technologies, particularly for autonomous vessels and AI-driven decision-making processes (Kuhlemann & Tierney, 2020). Furthermore, robust data governance policies are crucial, given the reliance on big data for AI applications. These policies must address privacy, security, and data-sharing issues among stakeholders to ensure the responsible use of AI-generated data (Tijan et al., 2021).

Workforce development is vital as AI technologies transform job roles within the maritime sector. Policies should focus on training and upskilling employees to prepare them for new technologies and ensure a smooth transition to AI-enhanced operations (Handayani et al., 2021). Encouraging collaboration between technology providers, shipping companies, and regulatory bodies is also crucial for innovation. Policies that support research and development in AI applications can lead to more effective solutions tailored to industry needs (Leong, 2019).

ECONOMIC BENEFITS OF AI IN MARITIME TRANSPORT

Maritime transport is a crucial component of global trade, and the economic impact of implementing AI in this sector is significant. AI technologies enhance efficiency, safety, and environmental sustainability in maritime operations. The integration of AI in maritime transport not only reshapes operational efficiencies but also has profound social implications, particularly affecting employment, skill requirements, and public perception.

AI integrates with systems like the Automatic Identification System (AIS) to enhance maritime navigation, traffic management, and vessel tracking, leading to more efficient route planning and logistics management. This reduction in travel time and increased predictability in ship arrivals can significantly lower operational costs and enhance service reliability (Pan et al., 2021; Robards et al., 2016b). AI applications in maritime transport help predict vessel trajectories, which is crucial for collision avoidance and risk management. The use of deep learning models, such as the RNN-LSTM, improves the accuracy of these predictions, thereby enhancing maritime safety (Xiao et al., 2022). AI-driven systems can automate many aspects of maritime operations, including cargo handling and fleet management. This automation reduces the need for human intervention, lowers labour costs, and minimises human error, further boosting economic efficiency. (Ceyhun, 2020).

AI aids in optimising fuel usage and reducing emissions by providing more efficient vessel routing and better speed management. This not only helps in complying with international environmental standards but also reduces the costs associated with fuel consumption and potential environmental penalties. (Ceyhun, 2020). AI's ability to analyse AIS data enables better decision-making regarding vessel positioning and port operations. This strategic use of data supports the improvement of throughput and resource allocation, thereby increasing the overall profitability of maritime transport entities. (Miler & Bujak, 2013). Introducing AI in maritime operations may lead to displacing specific jobs, especially those involving routine tasks susceptible to automation. This shift can reduce the demand for traditional roles while increasing the need for tech-savory professionals who can manage and maintain AI systems. The maritime sector must navigate these changes carefully to prevent significant disruptions in employment. (Morandini et al., 2023).

As AI transforms maritime operations, there is a growing need to reskill the workforce to handle new technologies. Skills in digital literacy, AI management, and data analysis become crucial. This shift requires maritime education systems to adapt, ensuring that current and future workers have the necessary skills to operate alongside advanced AI technologies. Establishing continuous learning and development programs is essential for facilitating this transition. (Mohamed & Elnoury, 2023). The adoption of AI in maritime transport also influences public perception. While AI can significantly improve efficiencies and safety, there can be concerns about job losses and the reliability of automated systems. Building public trust in AI applications involves transparent communication of the benefits and safeguards against potential failures. Ensuring that AI systems are reliable and that their roles in safety and efficiency are well understood by the public is crucial for acceptance (Millefiori et al., 2021).

The social dynamics of AI in maritime transport point towards a future where technology and human skills coalesce to a safer, more efficient, and sustainable industry. While the transformation brings challenges, particularly in employment and skills development, it also opens up opportunities for significant advancements in maritime operations. The sector's stakeholders must address these changes proactively, ensuring the workforce is prepared and public confidence in AI-integrated maritime systems is vital. Integrating AI into maritime transport streamlines operations and enhances economic outcomes through increased efficiency, safety, and cost-effectiveness. As AI technologies evolve, their deployment in maritime transport is expected to revolutionise the industry further, providing substantial economic benefits and reinforcing the sector's contribution to global trade.

Integrating AI in maritime transport enhances global trade efficiency, safety, and sustainability, reshaping operations and social dynamics. AI improves navigation, traffic management, and route planning, reducing costs and improving safety through precise trajectory predictions. Automation in cargo handling and fleet management boosts economic efficiency and reduces labour costs. However, AI also necessitates workforce reskilling and raises public concerns about job security and system reliability. Successful AI integration requires balancing technological advancements with strategic workforce development and public engagement to ensure a sustainable and responsible sector evolution.

CUSTOMIZING PUBLIC POLICY

Big data are instrumental in informing maritime transport policies by enabling a comprehensive analysis of diverse aspects that impact maritime operations. These data are critical for enhancing operational efficiency, safety, and environmental sustainability in the maritime sector. (Murray & Perera, 2020).

Big data encompasses a wide range of information types in the maritime context, including but not limited to weather patterns, vessel traffic, cargo logistics, port operations, and environmental data. These data help stakeholders understand and optimise the complex logistics involved in maritime transport. For instance, analysing historical shipping data helps to reveal traffic trends, common navigation routes, and potential operational bottlenecks. Similarly, weather data are crucial for predicting adverse conditions affecting maritime safety and efficiency and guiding preemptive measures to mitigate potential risks (Kontzinos et al., 2022). Moreover, data on port congestion levels can inform strategies to enhance port throughput and reduce turnaround times, which is essential for improving maritime gateways' economic viability and operational efficiency (Li et al., 2020a).

Big Data Analysis for Maritime Policy: Generative AI, a subset of AI technologies that generate new data based on existing datasets, offers extensive data analysis capabilities in maritime transport. It provides sophisticated tools for predicting and simulating various maritime conditions that are invaluable for policy development. Generative AI models can simulate complex weather systems to predict their impacts on shipping routes and schedules, offering predictive insights that are vital for planning safer and more efficient maritime operations (Murray & Perera, 2020). By analyzing historical data on ship arrivals and cargo volumes, generative AI can forecast future port congestion, allowing for better scheduling and resource allocation, reduced delays, and increased port efficiency (Kontzinos et al., 2022).

Generative AI's capability extends to route optimization, where it can analyze historical shipping data, weather information, and real-time maritime traffic to identify the optimal shipping routes. These routes optimize fuel consumption, reduce transit time, and enhance shipping efficiency (Li et al., 2020a). Generative AI can simulate the potential outcomes of various policy decisions, helping policymakers understand the possible impacts of new regulations before implementation. This capability is crucial for assessing the effectiveness of policy measures aimed at reducing environmental impact, improving safety, and enhancing operational efficiency (Ceyhun, 2019).

By identifying patterns from past incidents, such as collisions or environmental violations, generative AI can predict future risks and suggest preventive measures. This predictive capability is essential for crafting robust safety regulations and effective emergency response strategies (Androjna et al., 2020). Integrating big data and generative AI provides a robust framework for maritime transport policy development. Leveraging these technologies enables policymakers to make informed decisions that significantly enhance the safety, efficiency, and sustainability of maritime operations.

LOCALIZED POLICY ADJUSTMENTS

Customised public policy in maritime transport focuses on adapting regulations and initiatives to meet the unique needs and characteristics of different regions and shipping routes. This approach recognises that maritime activities vary globally and even within countries, necessitating policies that can adapt to regional variations, such as economic conditions, environmental challenges, and social demands.

Generative AI, an advanced form of AI capable of generating new content based on training data, is beneficial for analysing regional variations within the maritime industry. For example, generative AI can process vast amounts of data from maritime activities such as commercial shipping, fishing, and recreational activities and identify patterns and specifics for different regions. This capability allows for in-depth analysis of maritime traffic and activities, facilitating the development of precisely tailored public policies for specific areas or routes (Miola et al., 2011; Pelot et al., 2009). In regions such as Maluku Province, Indonesia, generative AI helps customise policies by providing insights from data-driven models. These models can help optimise the maritime transportation system to enhance regional development through better logistics and transportation solutions that cater to the region's geographic and socio-economic contexts (Gaspersz, 2007).

Generative AI can also be employed to develop models that simulate the impacts of various policy decisions on maritime transport efficiency and environmental sustainability. Such models can incorporate regional environmental data, shipping traffic patterns, and economic indicators to predict potential policy outcomes. By simulating different scenarios, policymakers can better understand the implications of their decisions before implementation, ensuring that policies are effective and sustainable (Miola et al., 2011). Moreover, generative AI in maritime policymaking extends to the legal domain, where it helps analyse the effects of maritime law and regulations across different regions. This is particularly valuable in countries such as Indonesia, where maritime transport is integral to national infrastructure, and legal frameworks must be adapted to the unique conditions of various archipelagic regions (Kusnan, 2020).

Integrating generative AI into maritime transport analysis can significantly enhance the capability of developing customised public policies. By leveraging AI-driven insights into regional variations, governments and authorities can formulate targeted strategies to address different maritime regions' distinct needs and challenges, promoting more efficient, sustainable, and equitable maritime transport systems.

IMPLEMENTATION STRATEGIES

Implementing AI-driven public policy in maritime transport requires the active engagement of all relevant stakeholders, including government authorities, private sector entities, non-governmental organisations (NGOs), and communities affected by such policies. The inclusiveness of the policymaking process ensures that the developed policies are comprehensive and cater to all parties' diverse needs and expectations. Engaging stakeholders in the early stages of policy development facilitates the exchange of ideas and information, which is crucial for the acceptance and success of AI-driven initiatives (Pelot et al., 2009).

The deployment of generative AI in maritime transport policy requires robust technological infrastructure. This includes advanced data analytics capabilities, secure and scalable computing resources, and reliable data collection mechanisms from diverse sources, such as satellite imagery, port operations, and shipborne sensors. The infrastructure must also support interoperability among different technological systems to facilitate seamless data exchange and integration, which are essential for the practical application of AI technologies (Miola et al., 2011). As AI technologies become integral to maritime public policy, there is a growing need for training and capacity building in the human workforce. This training should focus on the technical skills required to operate and manage AI systems and understand how AI can enhance decision-making processes in maritime transport. Such initiatives help build an adaptable and equipped workforce to work alongside AI, thus ensuring that AI technologies are effectively and ethically used in public policy settings (Gaspersz, 2007).

Implementing AI-driven public policy in maritime transport involves multiple stakeholders, including government bodies, private sector entities, NGOs, and affected communities, to ensure inclusive policies address diverse needs. This engagement promotes information exchange, which is vital for policy acceptance. Robust infrastructure, including advanced data analytics, secure computing resources, and interoperability among systems, is crucial for applying AI effectively. As AI technologies become central to maritime policy, workforce training in technical skills and AI applications is essential to ensure AI's ethical and effective utilisation in decision-making processes.

ETHICAL AND REGULATORY CONSIDERATIONS

Biases in AI can stem from skewed data or flawed algorithm design, potentially leading to discriminatory policies that unfairly affect specific groups. Inclusivity and stakeholder awareness are crucial for mitigating ethical risks and protecting vulnerable societies from harm (Yapo & Weiss, 2018). The extensive data required to train AI models raises significant privacy issues. The handling, storage, and processing of such data must comply with data protection laws to prevent breaches and misuse (Hickok, 2021). AI and automation in maritime operations could lead to job displacement, necessitating strategies to manage the transition for affected employees and re-skill them for new roles in the industry (Jaiswal et al., 2023).

Integrating AI into maritime policy must align with current legal frameworks, posing challenges to harmonising new technology-driven approaches with established regulations (Addis & Kutar, 2019).

There is a need for AI-specific regulations in maritime transport to address unique challenges, such as algorithmic transparency, accountability, and the ethical use of AI. These regulations should further ethical AI practices while ensuring safety and efficacy (Jobin et al., 2019). Policymakers must ensure that AI systems are understandable to stakeholders, maintain trust, and allow for informed discussions of AI-driven decisions (Hoffmann et al., 2018). Establishing clear lines of responsibility for decisions made with the aid of AI is critical. This includes defining who is accountable for outcomes and ensuring that mechanisms are in place to address any negative impacts arising from AI decisions (Koene, 2017).

AI biases stemming from skewed data or flawed designs risk discriminatory outcomes and emphasise the need for inclusivity and stakeholder awareness. The extensive data needed for AI also poses privacy concerns, requiring strict adherence to data protection laws. AI's integration into maritime operations could displace jobs, necessitating re-skilling efforts. Legal challenges include aligning AI with existing frameworks and developing AI-specific regulations to ensure transparency, accountability, and ethical usage. Establishing clear accountability for AI-driven decisions is crucial to maintaining trust and addressing potential negative impacts.

The emergence of generative artificial intelligence (AI) can significantly impact maritime public policy by enhancing decision-making processes, optimising operations, and improving safety. However, its implementation also raises critical ethical and regulatory concerns that must be addressed to ensure responsible usage. This paper explores the ethical considerations and regulatory frameworks necessary to effectively apply generative AI in maritime public policy.

Transparency and Accountability: One of the primary ethical concerns surrounding generative AI is the need for transparency in its operations. AI systems often function as "black boxes," making it challenging to understand how decisions are made. This lack of transparency can lead to accountability issues, especially in high-stakes environments like maritime transport, where decisions can impact safety and environmental sustainability (Paul & Sarkar, 2023). To mitigate these concerns, it is essential to implement mechanisms that ensure AI systems are interpretable and that their decision-making processes are transparent to stakeholders.

Bias and Fairness: Generative AI systems can perpetuate existing biases in the data they are trained on, leading to unfair outcomes. In maritime contexts, this could manifest in biased decision-making regarding port operations, vessel inspections, or regulatory compliance (Kumar Jaiswal et al., 2023). To address these issues, developing guidelines that promote fairness and equity in AI applications is crucial, including regular audits of AI systems to identify and mitigate biases.

Human Oversight: Deploying generative AI in maritime policy should not replace human judgment but rather augment it. Ethical frameworks must emphasise the importance of human oversight in AI decision-making processes. This is particularly important in scenarios where AI systems are used to make safety-critical decisions, such as navigation or emergency response (Tijan et al., 2021). Ensuring trained personnel can intervene and override AI decisions when necessary is vital for maintaining accountability and safety.

Establishing Clear Regulations: As generative AI technologies evolve, there is a pressing need for regulatory frameworks that govern their use in maritime contexts. Current regulations may not adequately address the unique challenges posed by AI, necessitating the development of specific guidelines tailored to the maritime industry (Chen et al., 2024). These regulations should encompass data privacy, security, and ethical AI development practices.

Data Governance: Generative AI relies heavily on data, making data governance a critical regulatory consideration. Policymakers must establish regulations that ensure the ethical collection, storage, and usage of data, particularly sensitive information related to maritime operations (Paul & Sarkar, 2023). This includes implementing measures to protect personal data and ensuring compliance with international data protection standards.

Collaboration with Stakeholders: Effective regulation of generative AI in maritime policy requires collaboration among various stakeholders, including government agencies, industry representatives, and civil society organisations. Engaging these groups in the regulatory process can help identify potential risks and develop comprehensive policies that address the multifaceted nature of AI technologies (Kuhlemann & Tierney, 2020). This collaborative approach looks after trust and ensures that regulations reflect all stakeholders' diverse interests and concerns.

OPPORTUNITIES AND CHALLENGES

Generative AI holds transformative potential for numerous sectors, including maritime transport. By generating new content based on existing data, these technologies can offer significant advancements in creating customised public policies to enhance maritime safety, efficiency, and sustainability. However, the integration of generative AI in maritime transport policy also presents several challenges. Opportunities and challenges associated with employing generative AI for customised public policy in maritime transport are as follows:

Opportunities: Generative AI offers substantial advancements in maritime transport, particularly in predictive analytics, vessel classification, and environmental sustainability. Generative models enhance predictive analytics by analysing historical AIS data, allowing for accurate vessel trajectory predictions. This improves collision avoidance and route optimisation, leading to more efficient traffic management and reduced operational costs (Han & Yang, 2020; Murray & Perera, 2020).

GANs play a crucial role in vessel classification and surveillance. These models can identify vessel types and detect out-of-class vessels, which is essential for enhancing maritime security and preventing illegal activities (Li et al., 2020b). Furthermore, AI-driven policies support environmental sustainability by optimising vessel operations to reduce emissions and energy consumption. Machine learning models can predict environmental impacts and suggest measures to mitigate pollution, promoting greener maritime practices (Mansoursamaei et al., 2023).

Generative AI also aids in data-driven policy development and proactive safety measures. Generative AI facilitates the creation of effective, data-driven public policies by synthesising large volumes of maritime data into actionable insights. This empowers policymakers to design regulations and interventions based on comprehensive real-time and historical data analysis (Kontzinos et al., 2022). Moreover, generative AI enhances proactive safety measures by predicting potential hazards and vessel behaviours. This capability includes forecasting high-risk areas for piracy and other maritime threats, allowing for preemptive actions and better resource allocation (Dabrowski & de Villiers, 2015). These applications of generative AI improve the safety and efficiency of maritime transport and support sustainable and secure maritime operations.

Challenges: Data quality and availability significantly influence generative AI models' effectiveness in maritime transport. Incomplete or inaccurate AIS data can result in flawed predictions and misguided policy recommendations, jeopardising maritime safety and operational efficiency. Accurate and comprehensive data collection ensures that AI models provide policymakers with reliable insights. However, the maritime industry often faces challenges in maintaining data quality and consistency, highlighting the need for robust data management practices and infrastructure (Lorenz et al., 2023).

Implementing generative AI models in maritime transport also requires substantial computational resources and expertise. The complexity of these models demands advanced technological capabilities that may not be readily available to all maritime organisations. This can lead to disparities in the implementation of AI-driven policies, with technologically advanced organizations benefiting more than those with limited resources. To ensure equal access to technological capabilities, overcoming these challenges necessitates significant investment in computational infrastructure and training programs to build the necessary expertise within the industry. (Huang et al., 2020).

Ethical and legal concerns present another significant challenge in deploying generative AI in maritime policy. Issues such as data privacy, security, and the potential for unauthorised use of data must be carefully navigated to ensure compliance with legal frameworks and ethical standards. Moreover, generative AI models can perpetuate biases in their training data, leading to unfair or discriminatory outcomes. Ensuring fairness and mitigating bias requires rigorous validation and continuous monitoring of AI systems. Additionally, resistance to adoption from stakeholders accustomed to traditional decision-making processes can impede the integration of AI in maritime policy. Addressing this resistance involves comprehensive training and clear demonstrations of the benefits that AI-driven approaches can offer (Park, 2023; Russo, 2024; Shah, 2023).

Generative AI presents numerous opportunities for advancing customised public policy in maritime transport, from enhancing predictive analytics to promoting environmental sustainability. However, successfully integrating these technologies also involves addressing significant challenges related to data quality, computational complexity, ethical concerns, bias, and stakeholder resistance. Policymakers must balance these opportunities and challenges to harness the full potential of generative AI to create safer, more efficient, and sustainable maritime transport systems.

FUTURE DIRECTIONS

AI paves the way for fully autonomous ships, which could revolutionise logistics and reduce human errors in maritime transport (Bradley, 2022). AI-driven predictive analytics can significantly enhance maintenance strategies, reduce downtime, and extend the lifespan of maritime assets (Huriye, 2023). AI models help monitor and ensure compliance with environmental regulations and optimise routes to minimise emissions and environmental impacts (Gupta, 2023).

Integrating AI with legacy systems and the need for robust cybersecurity measures are significant technical barriers (Koene, 2017). High initial investment costs and uncertainty about return on investment deter many stakeholders from fully committing to AI solutions (Jobin et al., 2019). Workforce resistance due to the fear of job displacement and the need for significant upskilling and reskilling initiatives are major social hurdles (Jaiswal et al., 2023). Encourage partnerships between governments, industry leaders, and academic institutions to share knowledge, resources, and best practices (Addis & Kutar, 2019). Develop targeted education and training programs to prepare the current and future workforce for the shifts brought about by AI technologies (Hickok, 2021). Establish regulatory frameworks addressing AI's ethical, legal, and social implications to build trust and facilitate adoption (Jobin et al., 2019).

AI's ability to process vast amounts of data can lead to highly customised policy solutions that are both efficient and scalable, addressing specific challenges within the maritime industry (Bradley, 2022). Although AI introduces advantages, it also brings challenges like potential biases and privacy concerns. Ethical and regulatory frameworks must evolve to address these issues effectively (Jobin et al., 2019). AI in maritime transport promises economic benefits through optimised operations and reduced costs; however, it requires substantial initial investments and presents economic hurdles that must be navigated (Addis & Kutar, 2019). The integration of AI will transform the maritime workforce, necessitating significant efforts in education and training to prepare workers for new roles within a more automated industrial framework (Jaiswal et al., 2023).

AI will transform maritime transport with prospects for autonomous ships, enhancing logistics and reducing human errors. It offers advanced predictive analytics for better maintenance and compliance with environmental standards, optimising routes to minimise emissions. However, challenges include integrating AI with legacy systems, ensuring robust cybersecurity, and overcoming high initial costs and ROI uncertainties. Socially, workforce resistance and the need for substantial reskilling present hurdles. Addressing these challenges requires partnerships among governments, industry, and academia, targeted training programs, and developing regulatory frameworks to manage AI's ethical and social implications. These efforts are crucial for realising AI's potential in maritime transport.

CONCLUSION

The maritime transport sector, responsible for over 90% of global trade, is transforming by integrating generative AI into public policy. This transformation is more than a technological upgrade; it is a strategic reinvention addressing environmental, security, and regulatory challenges. Generative AI's predictive maintenance, route optimisation, and accident prevention capabilities revolutionise maritime logistics, enhancing efficiency and safety. Public policy is critical in aligning AI advancements with societal goals, including safety, security, and environmental sustainability. Policies advocating for decarbonisation emphasise AI-driven approaches to promote sustainable practices. These policies aim to make the maritime sector contribute positively to global environmental goals rather than just complying with new standards.

Generative AI moves beyond simple data analysis to create realistic simulations of complex scenarios. This ability helps policymakers forecast potential outcomes, develop proactive strategies, and seize emerging opportunities. Collaboration between generative AI and maritime policy can significantly improve operational efficiency, establishing a safer and more environmentally friendly industry. Continuous research and practical application are essential for meeting the dynamic needs of the maritime sector and realising AI's full potential.

AI significantly enhances maritime operations by improving safety, efficiency, and compliance. It optimises route planning and collision avoidance, leading to safer navigation. Port operations benefit from AI through better cargo handling, storage optimisation, predictive maintenance, and increased throughput, which reduces downtime. Generative AI models contribute to monitoring maritime traffic by predicting vessel trajectories and classifying ships, enhancing safety and operational efficiency—AI aids in environmental compliance by optimising fuel consumption and reducing emissions, helping companies meet regulatory requirements.

Despite its advantages, deploying AI in maritime operations faces several challenges. Ensuring the accuracy of AI-generated data and addressing the ethical implications of autonomous decision-making necessitates stringent regulation and active stakeholder engagement. It is essential to mitigate biases in datasets and algorithm designs to avoid discriminatory practices. Economically, while AI boosts operational efficiency and reduces costs, it also poses social challenges by potentially displacing jobs. Therefore, it is critical to implement proactive workforce development and education strategies to address these impacts and prepare the workforce for an AI-driven industry. Future policies must leverage big data and generative AI to promote data-driven decision-making. By simulating future scenarios, policymakers can anticipate the impact of regulations and develop targeted policies for different maritime industry regions. The synergy between AI and human expertise will yield an efficient, profitable, resilient, and adaptable maritime sector, capable of responding to challenges like climate change and geopolitical shifts.

Successful AI integration into public policy demands a comprehensive strategy. Engaging stakeholders from government, industry, academia, and civil society is vital for creating well-rounded and widely accepted AI policies. This integration requires substantial investments in advanced data analytics, secure computing resources, and robust data integration systems to support technological infrastructure. Ethical and regulatory frameworks are essential to ensure responsible AI use, focusing on privacy and data protection. Additionally, workforce development through training programs and educational initiatives is crucial to equip maritime professionals with the skills needed for new roles emerging from AI advancements.

The journey toward a fully integrated AI-driven maritime sector is complex and challenging. However, it promises to redefine global trade and transport with the right policies and frameworks. Generative AI can revolutionise policy development by enhancing data-driven decision-making, improving risk assessment, and facilitating stakeholder communication. Policymakers must prioritise collaboration, continuous learning, and adaptive regulatory approaches to maximise the benefits of generative AI and create compelling, equitable policies that address modern complexities.

REFERENCES

Addis, C., & Kutar, M. (2019). AI Management An Exploratory Survey of the Influence of GDPR and FAT Principles. *2019 IEEE SmartWorld, Ubiquitous Intelligence & Computing, Advanced & Trusted Computing, Scalable Computing & Communications, Cloud & Big Data Computing, Internet of People and Smart City Innovation (SmartWorld/SCALCOM/UIC/ATC/CBDCom/IOP/SCI)*, 342–347. 10.1109/SmartWorld-UIC-ATC-SCALCOM-IOP-SCI.2019.00102

Androjna, A., Brcko, T., Pavic, I., & Greidanus, H. (2020). Assessing Cyber Challenges of Maritime Navigation. *Journal of Marine Science and Engineering*, 8(10), 776. 10.3390/jmse8100776

Ashraf, I., Park, Y., Hur, S., Kim, S. W., Alroobaea, R., Zikria, Y., & Nosheen, S. (2022). A Survey on Cyber Security Threats in IoT-Enabled Maritime Industry. *IEEE Transactions on Intelligent Transportation Systems*, 1–14. 10.1109/TITS.2022.3164678

Batty, M. (2013). Big data, smart cities and city planning. *Dialogues in Human Geography*, 3(3), 274–279. 10.1177/2043820613513390

Bradley, F. (2022). Representation of Libraries in Artificial Intelligence Regulations and Implications for Ethics and Practice. *Journal of the Australian Library and Information Association*, 71(3), 189–200. 10.1080/24750158.2022.2101911

Ceyhun, G. Ç. (2019). *Recent Developments of Artificial Intelligence in Business Logistics: A Maritime Industry Case*. 10.1007/978-3-030-29739-8_16

Ceyhun, G. Ç. (2020). *Recent Developments of Artificial Intelligence in Business Logistics: A Maritime Industry Case*. 10.1007/978-3-030-29739-8_16

Chaudhry, S. A., Irshad, A., Khan, M. A., Khan, S. A., Nosheen, S., Alzubi, A. A., & Zikria, Y. Bin. (2023). A Lightweight Authentication Scheme for 6G-IoT Enabled Maritime Transport System. *IEEE Transactions on Intelligent Transportation Systems, 24*, 2401–2410. https://api.semanticscholar.org/CorpusID:245442072

Chen, X., Ma, D., & Liu, R. W. (2024). Application of Artificial Intelligence in Maritime Transportation. *Journal of Marine Science and Engineering*, 12(3), 439. 10.3390/jmse12030439

Dabrowski, J. J., & de Villiers, J. P. (2015). Maritime piracy situation modelling with dynamic Bayesian networks. *Information Fusion*, 23, 116–130. 10.1016/j.inffus.2014.07.001

Esteva, A., Robicquet, A., Ramsundar, B., Kuleshov, V., DePristo, M., Chou, K., Cui, C., Corrado, G., Thrun, S., & Dean, J. (2019). A guide to deep learning in healthcare. *Nature Medicine*, 25(1), 24–29. 10.1038/s41591-018-0316-z30617335

Gaspersz, B. (2007). *Pemodelan transportasi laut di propinsi maluku*. https://api.semanticscholar.org/CorpusID:114714448

Goodfellow, I., Bengio, Y., & Courville, A. (2016). *Deep learning*. MIT Press.

Gupta, N. (2023). Artificial Intelligence Ethics and Fairness: A study to address bias and fairness issues in AI systems, and the ethical implications of AI applications. *Revista Review Index Journal of Multidisciplinary*, 3(2), 24–35. 10.31305/rrijm2023.v03.n02.004

Han, P., & Yang, X. (2020). Big data-driven automatic generation of ship route planning in complex maritime environments. *Acta Oceanologica Sinica*, 39(8), 113–120. 10.1007/s13131-020-1638-5

Handayani, D., Sediono, W., & Shah, A. (2021). Anomaly detection in vessel tracking – A Bayesian networks (BNs) approach. *International Journal of Maritime Engineering*, 157(A3). Advance online publication. 10.5750/ijme.v157iA3.956

Heilig, L., & Voß, S. (2017). Information systems in seaports: A categorization and overview. *Information Technology and Management*, 18(3), 179–201. 10.1007/s10799-016-0269-1

Hickok, M. (2021). Lessons learned from AI ethics principles for future actions. *AI and Ethics*, 1(1), 41–47. 10.1007/s43681-020-00008-1

Hoffmann, A. L., Roberts, S. T., Wolf, C. T., & Wood, S. (2018). Beyond fairness, accountability, and transparency in the ethics of algorithms: Contributions and perspectives from LIS. *Proceedings of the Association for Information Science and Technology*, 55(1), 694–696. 10.1002/pra2.2018.14505501084

Huang, Y., Li, Y., Zhang, Z., & Liu, R. W. (2020). GPU-Accelerated Compression and Visualization of Large-Scale Vessel Trajectories in Maritime IoT Industries. *IEEE Internet of Things Journal*, 7(11), 10794–10812. 10.1109/JIOT.2020.2989398

Huriye, A. Z. (2023). The Ethics of Artificial Intelligence: Examining the Ethical Considerations Surrounding the Development and Use of AI. *American Journal of Technology*, 2(1), 37–45. 10.58425/ajt.v2i1.142

Isola, P., Zhu, J.-Y., Zhou, T., & Efros, A. A. (2017). Image-to-image translation with conditional adversarial networks. *Proceedings of the IEEE Conference on Computer Vision and Pattern Recognition*, 1125–1134.

Jobin, A., Ienca, M., & Vayena, E. (2019). The global landscape of AI ethics guidelines. *Nature Machine Intelligence*, 1(9), 389–399. 10.1038/s42256-019-0088-2

Joung, T.-H., Kang, S.-G., Lee, J.-K., & Ahn, J. (2020). The IMO initial strategy for reducing Greenhouse Gas (GHG) emissions, and its follow-up actions towards 2050. *Journal of International Maritime Safety, Environmental Affairs, and Shipping*, 4(1), 1–7. 10.1080/25725084.2019.1707938

Kingma, D. P., & Welling, M. (2013). Auto-encoding variational bayes. *ArXiv Preprint ArXiv:1312.6114.*

Koene, A. (2017). Algorithmic Bias: Addressing Growing Concerns [Leading Edge]. *IEEE Technology and Society Magazine*, 36(2), 31–32. 10.1109/MTS.2017.2697080

Kontzinos, C., Kanellou, I., Michalakopoulos, V., Mouzakitis, S., Tsapelas, G., Kapsalis, P., Kormpakis, G., & Askounis, D. (2022, November 8). State-of-the-art analysis of artificial intelligence approaches in the maritime industry. *Proceedings of the International Conferences on Applied Computing 2022 and WWW/Internet 2022*. 10.33965/AC_ICWI2022_202208C029

Kuhlemann, S., & Tierney, K. (2020). A genetic algorithm for finding realistic sea routes considering the weather. *Journal of Heuristics*, 26(6), 801–825. 10.1007/s10732-020-09449-7

Kumar, D. B. (2023). *Harnessing the Power of Generative AI: Transforming the Maritime Industry*. Https://Www.Linkedin.Com/Pulse/Harnessing-Power-Generative-Ai-Transforming-Maritime-Kumar-Ph-d--5orqc

Kumar Jaiswal, R., Sundar Sharma, S., & Kaushik, R. (2023). Ethics in AI and machine learning. *Journal of Nonlinear Analysis and Optimization, 14*(01), 08–12. 10.36893/JNAO.2023.V14I1.0008-0012

Kusnan, K. (2020). Penggunaan hukum sebagai instrumen kebijakan publik dalam pengangkutan laut nasional. *Jurnal Widya Publika*, 8(2), 176–192. 10.47329/widyapublika.v8i2.648

Lee, P. T.-W., & Yang, Z. (Eds.). (2018). *Multi-Criteria Decision Making in Maritime Studies and Logistics* (Vol. 260). Springer International Publishing., 10.1007/978-3-319-62338-2

Leong, L. K. (2019). *AI Revolution: 6 steps to prepare your business*. Https://Maritimefairtrade.Org/Ai-Revolution-6-Steps-to-Prepare-Your-Business/

Li, D., Liu, H., & Ng, S.-K. (2020). VC-GAN: Classifying Vessel Types by Maritime Trajectories using Generative Adversarial Networks. *2020 IEEE 32nd International Conference on Tools with Artificial Intelligence (ICTAI)*, 923–928. 10.1109/ICTAI50040.2020.00144

Lorenz, P., Perset, K., & Berryhill, J. (2023). *Initial policy considerations for generative artificial intelligence.*

Malmborg, F. V. (2023). Advocacy coalitions and policy change for decarbonisation of international maritime transport: The case of FuelEU maritime. *Maritime Transport Research.* https://api.semanticscholar.org/CorpusID:259497857

Mansoursamaei, M., Moradi, M., González-Ramírez, R. G., & Lalla-Ruiz, E. (2023). Machine Learning for Promoting Environmental Sustainability in Ports. *Journal of Advanced Transportation*, 2023, 1–17. 10.1155/2023/2144733

Miler, R. K., & Bujak, A. (2013). *exactEarthSatellite – AIS as One of the Most Advanced Shipping Monitoring Systems* (pp. 330–337). 10.1007/978-3-642-41647-7_40

Millefiori, L. M., Braca, P., Zissis, D., Spiliopoulos, G., Marano, S., Willett, P. K., & Carniel, S. (2021). COVID-19 impact on global maritime mobility. *Scientific Reports*, 11(1), 18039. 10.1038/s41598-021-97461-734508144

Miola, A., Marra, M., & Ciuffo, B. (2011). Designing a climate change policy for the international maritime transport sector: Market-based measures and technological options for global and regional policy actions. *Energy Policy*, 39(9), 5490–5498. 10.1016/j.enpol.2011.05.013

Mohamed, E. A., & Elnoury, A. (2023). Technological Innovations in the Maritime Sector: A Comprehensive Analysis of Intelligence Knowledge and Industry Dynamics for Graduates Adaptation. *AIN Journal*, 2(46). Advance online publication. 10.59660/467315

Morandini, S., Fraboni, F., De Angelis, M., Puzzo, G., Giusino, D., & Pietrantoni, L. (2023). The Impact of Artificial Intelligence on Workers' Skills: Upskilling and Reskilling in Organisations. *Informing Science: The International Journal of an Emerging Transdiscipline, 26*, 039–068. 10.28945/5078

Munim, Z. H., Dushenko, M., Jimenez, V. J., Shakil, M. H., & Imset, M. (2020). Big data and artificial intelligence in the maritime industry: A bibliometric review and future research directions. *Maritime Policy & Management*, 47(5), 577–597. 10.1080/03088839.2020.1788731

Murray, B., & Perera, L. P. (2020). A dual linear autoencoder approach for vessel trajectory prediction using historical AIS data. *Ocean Engineering*, 209, 107478. 10.1016/j.oceaneng.2020.107478

Pan, N., Ding, Y., Fu, J., Wang, J., & Zheng, H. (2021). Research on Ship Arrival Law Based on Route Matching and Deep Learning. *Journal of Physics: Conference Series*, 1952(2), 022023. 10.1088/1742-6596/1952/2/022023

Park, S. H. (2023). Use of Generative Artificial Intelligence, Including Large Language Models Such as ChatGPT, in Scientific Publications: Policies of *KJR* and Prominent Authorities. *Korean Journal of Radiology*, 24(8), 715. 10.3348/kjr.2023.064337500572

Paul, R. K., & Sarkar, B. (2023). Generative AI and ethical considerations for trustworthy AI implementation. *Journal ID, 2157*, 0178.

Pelot, R., Eng, P., Lin, D., Wu, C., & Hilliard, D. (2009). Spatial Analysis of Maritime Traffic for Maritime Security.

Rani, S., Babbar, H., Kaur, P., Alshehri, M. D., & Shah, S. H. A. (2022). An Optimized Approach of Dynamic Target Nodes in Wireless Sensor Network Using Bio Inspired Algorithms for Maritime Rescue. *IEEE Transactions on Intelligent Transportation Systems*, 1–8. 10.1109/TITS.2021.3129914

Robards, M., Silber, G., Adams, J., Arroyo, J., Lorenzini, D., Schwehr, K., & Amos, J. (2016). Conservation science and policy applications of the marine vessel Automatic Identification System (AIS)—A review. *Bulletin of Marine Science*, 92(1), 75–103. 10.5343/bms.2015.1034

Rodrigue, J.-P. (2020). *The geography of transport systems*. Routledge. 10.4324/9780429346323

Rolnick, D., Donti, P. L., Kaack, L. H., Kochanski, K., Lacoste, A., Sankaran, K., Ross, A. S., Milojevic-Dupont, N., Jaques, N., Waldman-Brown, A., Luccioni, A., Maharaj, T., Sherwin, E. D., Mukkavilli, S. K., Kording, K. P., Gomes, C., Ng, A. Y., Hassabis, D., Platt, J. C., … Bengio, Y. (2019). *Tackling Climate Change with Machine Learning*. Academic Press.

Russo, D. (2024). Navigating the complexity of generative ai adoption in software engineering. *ACM Transactions on Software Engineering and Methodology*, 33(5), 1–50. 10.1145/3652154

Shah, C. (2023). Generative AI and the Future of Information Access. *Proceedings of the 32nd ACM International Conference on Information and Knowledge Management*, 3–3. 10.1145/3583780.3615317

Sirimanne, S. N., Hoffman, J., Juan, W., Asariotis, R., Assaf, M., Ayala, G., Ayoub, A., Benamara, H., Chantrel, D., & Hoffmann, J. (2020). Review of maritime transport 2020. *United Nations Conference on Trade and Development.*

Stopford, M. (2009). *Maritime Economics. Routledge.*

Tian, Z., Liu, F., Li, Z., Malekian, R., & Xie, Y. (2017). The Development of Key Technologies in Applications of Vessels Connected to the Internet. *Symmetry*, 9(10), 211. 10.3390/sym9100211

Tijan, E., Jović, M., Aksentijević, S., & Pucihar, A. (2021). Digital transformation in the maritime transport sector. *Technological Forecasting and Social Change*, 170, 120879. 10.1016/j.techfore.2021.120879

Wang, C., Shen, J., Vijayakumar, P., & Gupta, B. B. (2021). Attribute-Based Secure Data Aggregation for Isolated IoT-Enabled Maritime Transportation Systems. *IEEE Transactions on Intelligent Transportation Systems*, 1–10. 10.1109/TITS.2021.3127436

Xiao, Y., Li, X., Yao, W., Chen, J., & Hu, Y. (2022). Bidirectional Data-Driven Trajectory Prediction for Intelligent Maritime Traffic. *IEEE Transactions on Intelligent Transportation Systems*, 1–13. 10.1109/TITS.2022.3219998

Yapo, A., & Weiss, J. (2018). *Ethical Implications of Bias in Machine Learning*. 10.24251/HICSS.2018.668

Zhao, L., Zuo, Y., Li, T., & Chen, C. L. P. (2023). Application of an Encoder–Decoder Model with Attention Mechanism for Trajectory Prediction Based on AIS Data: Case Studies from the Yangtze River of China and the Eastern Coast of the U.S. *Journal of Marine Science and Engineering*, 11(8), 1530. 10.3390/jmse11081530

KEY TERMS AND DEFINITIONS

Automatic Identification System (AIS): A tracking system used on ships and by vessel traffic services to identify and locate vessels in real-time, enhancing maritime safety and efficiency by transmitting data such as vessel identity, position, course, and speed.

Autonomous Ships: Vessels equipped with AI systems capable of navigating and operating without human intervention, potentially increasing efficiency and reducing human error.

Ethical and Legal Implications: The consideration of moral principles and legal frameworks in the integration of AI into maritime transport, addressing issues like job displacement and data privacy.

Generative Adversarial Networks (GANs): A class of machine learning frameworks consisting of two neural networks, a generator and a discriminator, that work against each other to create realistic synthetic data, which can be used to simulate maritime scenarios and improve predictive models in public policy and maritime transport.

Generative AI: A subset of artificial intelligence that can create new content, such as data, designs, or solutions, through algorithms trained on existing data, enhancing decision-making processes.

Internet of Things (IoT): A network of interconnected devices equipped with sensors, software, and other technologies to collect and exchange data, enhancing the efficiency and safety of maritime operations through real-time monitoring and management.

Long Short-Term Memory (LSTM): A variant of RNNs capable of learning long-term dependencies, addressing the vanishing gradient problem, and effectively processing and predicting time-series data in maritime transport for applications like predictive maintenance and demand forecasting.

Maritime Transport: Crucial for global trade, maritime transport involves the movement of goods and people by sea, handling over 90% of global trade by volume.

Public Policy: A set of regulations and guidelines issued by governments to address societal issues and development, ensuring safety, security, and sustainability in various sectors, including maritime transport.

Recurrent Neural Networks (RNNs): A type of artificial neural network designed for sequential data, where connections between nodes form a directed graph along a temporal sequence, useful in time-series prediction and anomaly detection in maritime operations.

Chapter 11
Revolutionizing Tourism: The Power of Generative AI

Jaswanth Atluri
https://orcid.org/0009-0004-9405-6570
Amity University, Dubai, UAE

Reena George
https://orcid.org/0000-0002-2956-6142
Amity University, Dubai, UAE

ABSTRACT

This chapter aims to explore the potential of generative (AI) in improving aspects of tourism experiences. Areas focused on include personalized recommendation systems, content generation for marketing purposes, virtual tour guides, and adaptive travel planning within the tourism industry. It focuses on customization approaches, incorporation of AR and VR technologies, and creation of real-time decision support systems. Moreover, its objective is to understand the ethical utilization of AI in the tourism industry, concerns regarding data privacy, and the incorporation of AI into current tourism infrastructure. It helps to delineate forthcoming research paths and emerging patterns, highlighting the possible influence of AI on the tourism sector and its future. Furthermore, it seeks to elucidate the socio-economic impacts of using AI in the tourist industry, examining its capacity to transform employment patterns, visitor characteristics, and methods for developing destinations. Finally, it promotes interdisciplinary discussion in influencing the future of tourism.

INTRODUCTION

Generative artificial intelligence (GAI) is a type of machine learning algorithm that is specifically created to independently generate new content in different forms

DOI: 10.4018/979-8-3693-5578-7.ch011

such as text, graphics, and code. This is achieved by analyzing current datasets and understanding the patterns within them. GAI, in contrast to standard AI models, does not depend on predetermined rules or analysis of past data. Instead, it generates new material by extrapolating from learnt patterns (Akshay Kulkarni, Applied Generative AI for Beginners Practical Knowledge on Diffusion Models, ChatGPT, and Other LLMs, 2023). GAI models, like OpenAI's Generative Pre-trained Transformer (GPT), have the ability to generate coherent and contextually relevant text in response to input inquiries. These models, typically trained on large collections of text data, have the ability to generate text ranging from brief sentences to long tales, showcasing their capacity to imitate human-like language skills (Hetler, 2023). In addition to text and images, GAI demonstrates its potential to generate various types of material, such as code, music, and artistic pieces. These systems utilize acquired patterns to automatically generate output that is influenced by the input parameters and the data they were trained on (Stefan Feuerriegel, 2023). The difference between AI and machine learning is that machine learning is a form of artificial intelligence. Machine learning is a process where experts create artificial intelligence by using models that can autonomously learn from patterns in data without human guidance (McKinsey & Company, 2024). When we focus specifically on the tourism industry, the potential for significant change is just as profound. Envision tailored marketing efforts that specifically target individual travelers, automated customer support that is accessible around the clock, and dynamic pricing tactics that maximize income in real-time. GAI holds the potential to enhance productivity and generate novel sources of revenue (Susann Almasi, 2023). In a research conducted in September 2023 online travel agencies (OTAs) in the United States, it was found that approximately 40 percent of destination marketing businesses anticipated that GAI may have a significant impact on the personalization of marketing content (statista, 2024). A study revealed that implementing GAI at a company employing 5,000 customer care workers resulted in a 14 percent increase in issue resolution per hour and a 9 percent reduction in the time required to handle each issue. Additionally, it decreased the rate of agent attrition and the number of requests to talk to a management by 25 percent (Michael Chui, 2023). In the United States, more than 60 percent of respondents used GAI on mobile devices for trip planning, while in India, the percentage was about 40 percent. However, in the United Kingdom and Japan, less than 10 percent of respondents used GAI on mobile devices for travel planning. This implies that comprehending how to cater to specific area requirements, as well as effectively attracting diverse age demographics, appears to be the subsequent crucial phase of an ongoing transformation in the travel industry (Statista, 2024). Conversations regarding the utilization of GAI in the travel and tourism industry commenced well in advance of the public debut of ChatGPT in November 2022. Nevertheless, the implementation of GAI inside the sector became a tangible potential when OpenAI's tool attracted 1 million users within just five days of its launch. According to a Statista analysis on the utilization of GAI in the European housing sector, 20% of enterprises in Germany and Austria had already implemented GAI by August 2023. Meanwhile, over 25% of lodging establishments in Spain have intentions to do so during the upcoming six months (Statista, 2024). McKinsey cautioned that an astonishing 800 million workers may face displacement as a result of technology by the year 2030. Furthermore, according to the Global Economics Analyst Report, GAI has the potential to automate approximately 300 million jobs. However, it is important to note that this technology also has the capacity to create new employment and give rise to new occupations (Keng-Boon Ooi, 2023). The ability of GAI to create original content in several fields has significant implications for creative and inventive pursuits. The capabilities of GAI represent a major change in the combination of machine learning and creativity. It can assist in content creation, design processes, and software development, opening up new possibilities for exploration and application in academic and practical settings.

History of GAI in Tourism

The actual historical development of GAI in the tourism industry is distinguished by a slow progression that is defined by significant achievements, novel ideas, and effective executions. Although the incorporation of GAI into the tourism sector is a relatively new occurrence, its origins may be traced back to the initial investigations of AI technologies in many fields. With a concise summary of the factual chronology of GAI in the tourism industry, Initial Implementations can be seen during the early 2000s, when the tourist sector-initiated trials with rudimentary types of AI, such as rule-based chatbots and recommendation systems, in order to improve customer service and simplify the booking procedures by handling basic queries (Nechaeva, 2023). Further in an effort to personalize and stand out in a competitive market, accommodation providers such as Airbnb have utilized AI-driven recommendation systems to offer personalized suggestions for rooms, places, and experiences based on individual interests and travel histories (Tiernan, 2023). Going forward GAI has gained popularity in content generation and storytelling by creating travel material such as destination descriptions, blog pieces, and social media captions. Tourism organizations and destination marketing companies utilize AI-generated content to captivate passengers, advertise locations, and stimulate tourism by means of immersive storytelling and persuasive tales (Team, 2023). To summarize, the actual historical development of GAI in the tourist industry demonstrates a process of creativity and adjustment, as AI technologies consistently transform the methods by which travelers explore, organize, and encounter their trips. The future of GAI in tourism has significant potential to enhance personalization, immersion, and engagement in the travel industry as the discipline continues to develop.

GAI: SHAPING MODERN TOURISM

The tourism industry is facing a surge in interest in artificial intelligence (AI). There has been a noticeable increase in interest in incorporating (AI) technologies into the tourism business in recent years as shown in Figure 1. The growing interest in AI is due to the acknowledgment of its capacity to transform different aspects of the tourist ecosystem, including customer service, marketing, destination management, and experience development (Sun, 2023). The tourist industry, known for its dynamic nature and need on customized experiences, is increasingly adopting AI-powered solutions to meet changing customer needs and overcome business obstacles. An area of particular interest involves the application of AI-driven customization methods to customize travel experiences based on individual preferences and behavioral patterns. In response to the growing need for personalized and immersive travel experiences, many involved in the tourism industry are investigating the use of AI-powered recommender systems and predictive analytics tools. These technologies aim to forecast and meet the specific needs and preferences of individual visitors. Additionally, AI technologies are being utilized to optimize pricing tactics, simplify booking processes, and improve client engagement through focused marketing efforts. Furthermore, the rise of AI-powered chatbots and virtual assistants has become a central focus in the tourist sector, providing cutting-edge solutions for customer service and assistance. These conversational assistants, powered by artificial intelligence, have the ability to offer immediate support, respond to questions, and aid with making reservations. This improves the efficiency of operations and increases client satisfaction. In addition, progress in natural language processing (NLP) has empowered chatbots to participate in more intricate exchanges, providing customized suggestions and travel guidance that is specifically tuned to individual interests (Singh, 2023).

Figure 1. GAI in Tourism

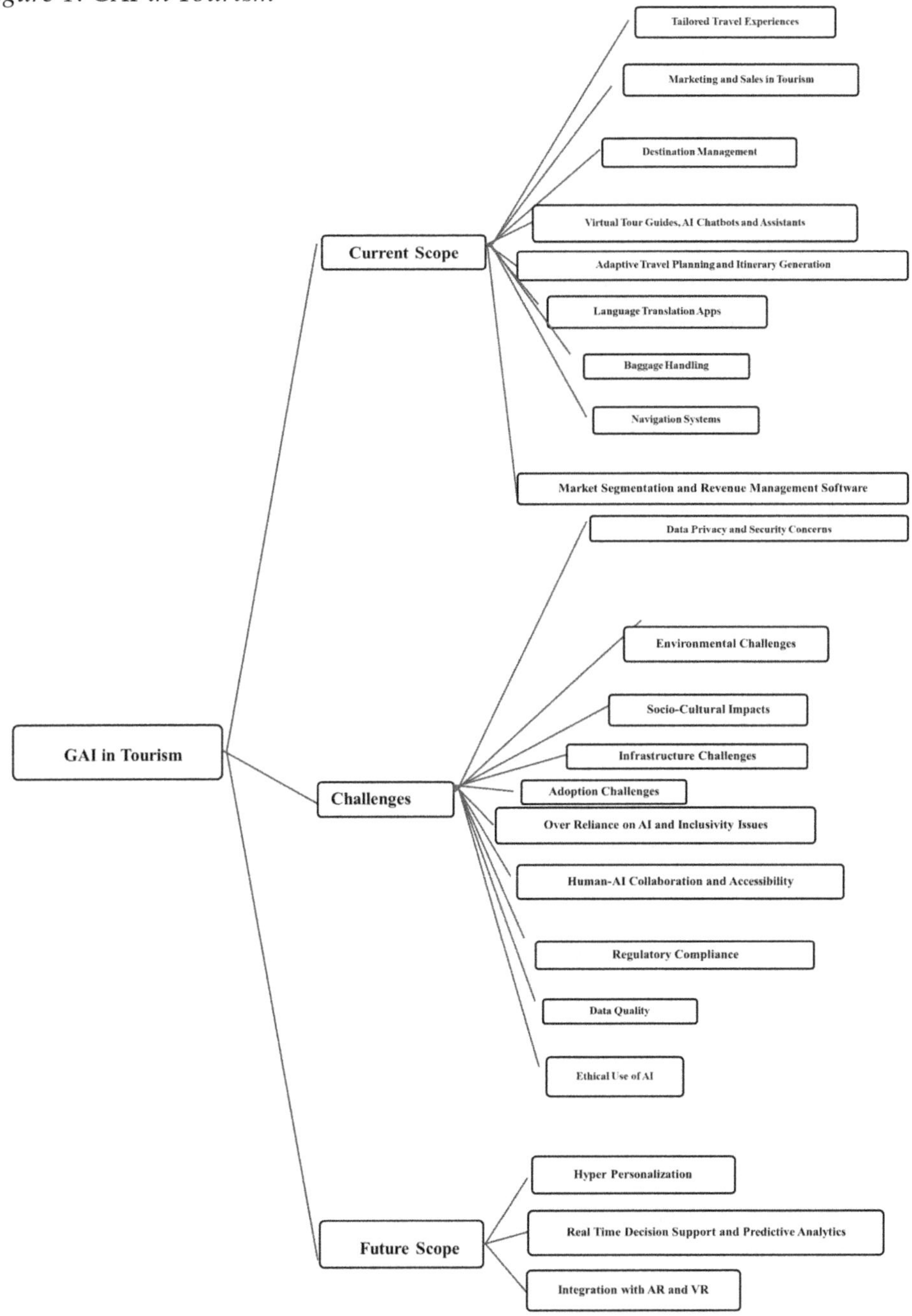

GAI for Tailored Travel Experiences

Over the past few years, the tourist sector has experienced a significant and fundamental change due to the combination of technological advancements and changing consumer preferences. This change has created an increased need for travel experiences that go beyond the ordinary and embrace the uniqueness of each visitor. The integration of GAI is leading the way in this transformation. GAI is a subset of AI techniques that has the remarkable ability to autonomously create new content. This offers unprecedented opportunities for personalization and immersion in the field of tourism. GAI, known for its capacity to create original content by analyzing established datasets, is a transformative power that has the potential to change the tourism industry. This disruption is emphasized by its capacity to surpass traditional frameworks of travel planning and content creation, introducing a novel age of customized and immersive travel experiences designed to suit the distinct tastes and interests of individual travelers. A notable example of how GAI can have a significant impact is its ability to create personalized travel plans that respond to the unique preferences and interests of travelers (GREAT CHAT, 2024.). Historically, creating a trip schedule has been a time-consuming and frequently stressful task, filled with logistical difficulties and an excessive amount of information. Nevertheless, with the introduction of itinerary planners powered by GAI, passengers now have the ability to create customized trip experiences with remarkable simplicity and effectiveness. Travelers can utilize GAI to receive customized itineraries that are optimized for their preferences, including activities, attractions, culinary tastes, and budget limitations. This computational technology ensures that the itineraries are painstakingly tuned to maximize enjoyment and reduce logistical challenges. These AI-generated travel plans utilize advanced algorithms to examine various aspects such as weather conditions, local events, and historical tourism statistics. The result is individualized itineraries that cater to the specific preferences and interests of each traveler. An example of implementation of AI in giving tailored travel experiences is a tourism recommender system incorporated with AI which uses reasoning processes, such as rule-based systems to infer the tourist's choices and preferences (likes and dislikes) (Joan Borràs, 2014). In addition, GAI is positioned to completely transform the field of trip content creation, introducing a new era of highly tailored narratives and captivating storytelling experiences. Conventional travel information, although helpful, frequently lacks a deep comprehension of the unique interests of individual travelers, leading to a standardized approach that fails to fascinate and engage various audiences. GAI-powered content generators utilize machine learning and natural language processing to create personalized narratives that align with the specific interests and preferences of individual travelers. Through the examination of extensive amounts of user data, such as previous travel experiences, social media engagement, and online habits, these content generators powered by artificial intelligence extract tailored insights to create compelling travel material that goes beyond the limitations of generic narrative (Keng-Boon Ooi, 2023). GAI enables content creators to engage audiences with tales that are as varied and complex as the travelers themselves, whether through vivid descriptions of destinations, insightful travel blogs, or immersive travel guides. Furthermore, the emergence of AI-driven travel companions or chatbots represents a new era in tailored travel support and direction. These AI-powered virtual concierges act as intelligent and ever-present companions, providing personalized suggestions, travel advice, and logistical assistance during the traveler's trip. Using sophisticated machine learning algorithms and natural language processing, these virtual assistants have meaningful and contextually appropriate conversations with travelers. They answer questions, give information about destinations, and give personalized recommendations based on individual preferences and interests. AI-powered travel companions enhance the travel experience by providing recommendations for unique attractions, assisting with bookings and reservations, and offering ease and confidence in navigating the complexity of travel. This fosters a sense of autonomy and empowerment for travelers. AI is being used in museums to enhance the traditional exhibition design by providing personalized alternatives to visitors, such as allowing them to identify themselves with a museum painting. In addition, RAISA has been utilized in the field of heritage management. AI software products are utilized for the purpose of verifying the authenticity of paintings (Webster, Robots, Artificial Intelligence and Service Automation in Travel, Tourism and Hospitality, 2022).

GAI for Marketing and Sales in Tourism

In the always changing domain of the tourism industry, the techniques and principles of marketing and sales strategies play a crucial role in determining the success and long-term viability of firms in this dynamic sector. Tourism stakeholders are increasingly required to use new strategies that go beyond traditional marketing methods in order to address the problems of the digital era and meet the expectations of modern tourists. The integration of GAI is a key aspect of this transformative journey. GAI is an emerging field that excels in creating targeted marketing campaigns, dynamic travel packages, and captivating content with a unique combination of precision and creativity. Through the use of GAI, brands can elevate their marketing and sales efforts to a higher standard and provide genuinely individualized experiences that cannot be achieved by humans alone. The use of GAI offers advantages such as the ability to provide tailored messages to customers at the optimal moment, utilizing personalization techniques and utilizing comprehensive and important data. For example, the use of up-to-date visual representations, tailored written content, and anticipatory suggestions might facilitate the expansion of personalized experiences on significant occasions in a cost-efficient manner (Nir Kshetri, 2023). GAI is a mysterious component of the larger field of AI that has the special capability to create new content on its own by utilizing patterns it has learnt from enormous amounts of current data. Tour Operators make dynamic tour packages which incorporates artificial intelligence in the process of making the package. In addition, other AI-powered software applications use customer travel history, preferences, and past experiences to identify specific customers and suggest personalized offers (Webster, Robots, Artificial Intelligence and Service Automation in Travel, Tourism and Hospitality, 2022).

The mysterious capacity of GAI makes it a powerful force in the field of tourism marketing and sales, with the potential to disrupt conventional methods and provide new opportunities for interaction and conversion. GAI has the potential to create tailored marketing efforts that go beyond standard segmentation, which is one of its most exciting possibilities. In today's advertising landscape, traditional standardized methods are no longer effective. GAI enables marketers to explore the complex and detailed patterns of passenger demographics and behavior, uncovering the unique tastes and tendencies of each individual. By utilizing a variety of data sources, including demographic profiles and past purchasing behavior, GAI empowers marketers to create narratives that strongly connect with the distinct preferences of each audience segment. This injects campaigns with a newfound level of relevance and resonance that has not been witnessed before (Jacques Bulchand-Gidumal, 2023). Furthermore, GAI has the potential to completely transform the traditional process of creating travel packages by adding a new level of energy and customization that was previously considered impossible to achieve. Historically, the task of creating vacation packages has been filled with complications, ranging from manual selection to inflexible pricing systems. However, with the introduction of GAI-powered package generators, a new era arises, defined by flexibility and ability to adjust. GAI utilizes machine learning algorithms and real-time data analysis to enable tourism stakeholders to create customized travel packages that adapt to market trends. This includes adjusting prices and inclusions in response to the changing preferences of travelers (Elisa, Navigating New Horizons - How AI Will Transform the Tourism Industry, 2024). This additional flexibility gives travel packages a sense of surprise and attractiveness, capturing audiences and increasing conversions with unparalleled enthusiasm.

Moreover, the incorporation of GAI holds the potential to provide an element of unpredictability and liveliness into the field of content marketing, reshaping the limits of innovation and audience interaction. In a day marked by an overwhelming amount of content and short attention spans, the challenge of captivating people's emotions and thoughts with engaging stories has become extremely difficult. However, GAI is able to meet the issue by utilizing the immense capabilities of natural language processing to extract valuable information from large amounts of data and create engaging and inspiring narratives. GAI enhances content by infusing it with spontaneity and vitality, allowing brands to captivate travelers through lyrical travel descriptions, engaging social media posts, and persuasive ad copy. This propels brands to the forefront of the traveler's imagination and encourages them to take action. AI models provide hospitality and tourism SMEs with increased autonomy in creative pursuits and the option to handle more tasks internally, if desired (Tuomi, 2023).Ultimately, the incorporation of GAI ushers in a fresh era of opportunities and potential in the tourism sector, enabling hitherto unattainable avenues for innovation, engagement, and conversion. As tourism industry participants navigate the challenges of the digital environment and compete for the attention of discerning travelers, the use of GAI technologies becomes crucial. These technologies provide a pathway to a future where marketing and sales efforts are characterized by complexity, unpredictability, and limitless creativity.

The Impact of GAI on Destination Management

GAI can be utilized by both individual firms and destinations. At the level of deciding to travel, It may enhance every step of the journey, starting with the phase of looking forward to and organizing the trip, to the actual travel to the destination, the experience at the destination, and the phase of reflecting on the trip afterwards. During the destination development phase, GAI may facilitate the creation of highly immersive and tailored tourist offerings, such as personalized travel guides that are customized according to individual tastes (Tarik Dogru-Dr. True, 2023). Effective destination management has become a crucial requirement in the constantly changing and sometimes chaotic world of global tourism, not just as a strategic necessity but also as a moral duty. It serves as the foundation for achieving sustainable growth, preserving culture, and ensuring tourist happiness. Nevertheless, as destinations confront the intricacies of handling tourist influx, forecasting upcoming patterns, and providing tailored experiences, the incorporation of GAI has emerged as a promising solution—a revolutionary power that vows to overhaul destination management practices and introduce a fresh era of innovation and effectiveness. GAI, a fascinating branch of AI approaches that may autonomously create new material, has great potential for the field of destination management. GAI, utilizing machine learning algorithms and predictive analytics, equips destination managers with the computational capabilities to address complex difficulties in a very accurate and innovative manner, this technology allows managers to adapt their methods based on traveler behavior (Lalli, 2024). Imagine a vibrant metropolis filled with visitors from all over the world, each one contributing to the diverse fabric of international tourism. However, in the midst of the overwhelming variety of visual and auditory stimuli, there is a significant problem that needs to be addressed—the effective control of tourist numbers and the reduction of overcrowding at major tourist spots. The issue of overcrowding poses a significant threat to the local infrastructure and environmental sustainability, akin to a persistent obstacle hindering progress. Introducing GAI, the often overlooked champion of crowd control, it enables destination administrators to design dynamic crowd management plans by analyzing extensive data sets, such as visitor demographics, historical visitation patterns, and real-time crowd data (www.baeventures.com, 2024). By utilizing predictive analytics and machine learning algorithms, GAI can effectively predict high visitor periods, detect possible congestion points, and suggest specific interventions, such as staggered entry times, alternate routes, or crowd dispersal strategies, to reduce congestion and restore balance to the urban environment. However, there is more to it. GAI is a tool that can forecast future outcomes in an unpredictable world. Conventional approaches to predicting tourism demand and distributing resources are frequently like trying to navigate a maze while blindfolded, with restrictions on data and personal biases acting as significant challenges. However, with the introduction of GAI-powered predictive models, destination managers are now free from the constraints of uncertainty. Equipped with sophisticated algorithms that assess various elements, such as economic data, social trends, and geopolitical events, GAI empowers destination managers to gain exceptional insight into the future. GAI enables destination managers to enhance the competitiveness and resilience of their destinations by combining insights from different data sources and using scenario planning techniques.

Virtual Tour Guides, AI Chatbots, and Assistants

Virtual Tour Guides, AI Chatbots and Assistants represent a significant change in the tourism industry, going beyond conventional models to rethink the fundamental nature of exploration. Utilizing complex GAI algorithms, these digital companions act as knowledgeable guides, curating immersive adventures that are enriched with up-to-date advice, contextual knowledge, and personalized recommendations that cater to the specific preferences of each traveler (Kamath, 2022). The core of Virtual Tour Guides, AI Chatbots and Assistants rests in their exceptional skill to create customized tales, skillfully combining a variety of experiences carefully selected from the large amount of data they have access to. Chatbots utilizing ChatGPT technology have the capability to offer round-the-clock customer support, addressing inquiries on bookings, facilities, and other pertinent details. According to the chat, Chatbots can also offer information about local tourist sites, available tourism facilities, and suggest transportation options to clients. Chatbots can also offer tailored suggestions for activities and attractions, taking into account individual customer preferences and behavior (Utpal Chakraborty, Rise of GAI and ChatGPT Understand how GAI and ChatGPT are transforming and reshaping the business world, 2023). Using advanced algorithms, these digital experts analyze vast amounts of historical data, user preferences, and real-time information to create personalized travel plans that cater to the unique desires of each traveler. However, their importance goes beyond just being a suggestion; they act as channels of independence and empowerment, freeing tourists from the restrictions of tradition and giving them the liberty to explore destinations at their own speed and will. Using user-friendly interfaces and engaging conversations, these skilled digital experts guide tourists into a world of limitless inquiry, where every question is answered with a personalized response and every curiosity is enthusiastically satisfied. ChatGPT may provide valuable guidance to travelers when it comes to selecting places for their itinerary, as well as making judgments about routes, transit options, accommodation, and pricing factors (Hong Chuong Pham, 2024). GAI utilizes natural language processing and machine learning algorithms to analyze extensive data and provide personalized recommendations for attractions, activities, and dining options to travelers. These recommendations can be delivered through mobile apps, websites, or virtual assistants, enhancing the visitor experience significantly. Pelago is an AI chatbot that uses generative technology to engage in goal-oriented discussions, providing responses to open-ended inquiries such as "Plan a trip to Dubai". It facilitates the booking of flight tickets and accommodations for potential consumers and tourists, enables the creation of personalized itineraries, provides recommendations for transportation, and even assists with submitting complaints. Additionally, it enables them to conveniently make any payments associated with the journey through their mobile application. Utilizing Natural Language Processing (NLP), Pelago possesses the ability to comprehensively comprehend the customer's requirements and effectively aid in addressing inquiries pertaining to airplane departure schedules, package enhancements, and daily tasks. Having a virtual assistant is advantageous for travel organizations and enterprises in the hospitality sector due to the high expense and complexity of providing round-the-clock support, which can have a negative impact on client happiness and confidence (yellow.ai, n.d.).

Hopper is a platform that use machine learning and extensive historical flight data to forecast the optimal timing for purchasing flights using a mobile application. Hopper developed and educated its initial predictive algorithms by acquiring data from operators of global distribution systems. Users specify their desired travel destination and provide a general timeframe, and Hopper provides the most competitive prices available. Hopper's search for flights is more extensive and likely to yield better deals when the consumer is open to a wider range of dates and destinations. At first glance, this may seem similar to how traditional price comparison services operate. However, Hopper sets itself apart by providing users with a prediction in addition to the usual information. Customers will receive information regarding whether the price offered is the most advantageous option available, or if it would be more beneficial for them to wait for a more favorable bargain in the future. This may appear peculiar - essentially, akin to entering a store and being convinced not to make a purchase immediately, but rather to hold off until costs decrease. However, it is the predictive model that sets Hopper apart from numerous price comparison sites that also earn money from referral fees charged to the airlines for ticket sales (Ward, Artificial Intelligence in Practice: How 50 Successful Companies Used AI and Machine Learning to Solve Problems, 2019). Integrating ChatGPT into customer service systems is a strategic decision for firms seeking to provide timely responses to client inquiries. A retail organization has the option to integrate a ChatGPT-powered chatbot on its website and customer care channels. This technology not only enhances customer happiness by offering immediate response, but also enables human customer service agents to allocate more time to complex client issues that necessitate a personalized approach and thorough problem-solving (Publications, 2024). Trip.com became the pioneer in the online travel agency industry by incorporating GAI into its app through the introduction of its TripGen chatbot in February 2023. Shortly thereafter, Trip.com introduced their enhanced AI vacation planning assistance, TripGenie. The TripGenie, which utilizes GAI technology, ensures that the journey planning procedure for consumers is smooth, easy to use, and captivating (Hines, 2024).

Adaptive Travel Planning and Itinerary Generation

Adaptive Travel Planning and Itinerary Generation are two important components in the field of AI-infused exploration. In traditional trip planning, the process involved extensive research and strict itineraries, lacking the flexibility and spontaneity that are fundamental to travel. Nevertheless, with the emergence of GAI, this story experiences a significant transformation, as computers utilize data to shape flexible and responsive travel plans that change in sync with the traveler's desires and preferences. GAI algorithms play a crucial role in planning and executing the traveler's experience, coordinating a harmonious balance between optimization and serendipity. These algorithms create personalized trip plans by combining various inputs such as traveler preferences, time limitations, budget restraints, and current environmental conditions (Takyar, n.d.). The plans are designed to go beyond conventional experiences and offer amazing ones. TripIt's Smart Itinerary Planner is a highly regarded artificial intelligence-powered travel companion that offers several benefits such as generating a detailed itinerary for the entire journey (Olson, 2023). Current commercial travel planners include distinct options for flight planning and lodging planning, requiring customers to manually locate and book accommodations after finalizing their flight schedule. Rather than approaching flight and accommodation arrangements as distinct tasks, a research study proposed an AI travel itinerary planner "VacAItionary" which can create a trip schedule that optimizes the benefits of both. It considers a synthesis of flights, destinations, and accommodations while strictly sticking to the limitations and requirements of the traveler (Wang, 2020).Tripify is a trip manager that uses artificial intelligence to make itinerary planning easier for both busy professionals and leisure travelers. The system produces personalized travel plans by taking into account the preferences, schedules, and financial limitations of the users. Tripify's real-time adaptability allows for seamless alterations to accommodate schedule changes, ensuring stress-free and effective trip planning. In addition, the application offers local knowledge, safety suggestions for individuals traveling alone, and timely alerts to improve the overall travel experience (Kailash Sharma, 2024).

AI-Powered Language Translation Apps

Within the field of tourism, artificial intelligence (AI) proves to be a valuable asset in overcoming language barriers. It provides a diverse range of solutions to enhance smooth communication across different languages. AI-based Translation apps developed with the help of Machine Learning and Natural Language Processing are at the forefront of technology, enabling travelers to easily understand foreign languages by providing quick translations of spoken or written information while on the move (Bulchand-Gidumal, 2022). Real-time speech translation extends this power, facilitating seamless communications between individuals who speak different languages. In addition to these developments, there are multilingual chatbots that have been cleverly built to interact with travelers in their preferred language. These chatbots offer support and information with exceptional efficiency and accuracy. Interpretation devices are used during face-to-face contacts to provide live translation, enabling meaningful communication even when there are language barriers. Furthermore, text recognition algorithms have a crucial function in converting text from photos, allowing visitors to understand signs, menus, or other written material in new languages. Together, these artificial intelligence-powered solutions not only improve the effectiveness of communication but also encourage cultural interchange and inclusiveness, enhancing the tourism experience for travelers around the globe.

AI-Powered Baggage Handling and RMS

Each year, airports manage millions of luggage. SITA, the airport IT specialist, is utilizing artificial intelligence (AI) to optimize airport baggage handling systems.

In the future, airports have the potential to become completely automated through the use of robotics and artificial intelligence. This advancement will allow for more efficient handling of lost luggage. Several airports have previously used AI technology through experimental programs. As an example, the Eindhoven Airport has effectively implemented artificial intelligence (AI) based luggage handling technologies that do not require baggage labels (Izchak, 2024). Due to the proliferation of online travel companies and websites, manually completing bookings has become unfeasible due to the overwhelming volume of data generated on a daily basis. Revenue Management Systems (RMS) gather and process vast quantities of intricate data in real-time, which is then analyzed using models to generate simply comprehensible insights and determine the optimal room rate. An appropriately trained system can efficiently analyze the signals obtained from market variables, identify patterns and anomalies, and subsequently utilize this information to predict guest arrivals and determine optimal prices in response to market fluctuations (Prashant Balodi, 2022).

AI-Powered Navigation Systems

Google Maps utilized GPS technology to provide travelers with real-time directions. The implementation of Artificial Intelligence technology in Google Maps enhanced the provision of information by providing real-time updates to travelers regarding accidents and traffic congestion. Google Maps use Artificial Intelligence to offer a real-time depiction of the physical environment. The latest addition to Google Maps initiates the camera function and promptly scans the surroundings in search of visual cues such as buildings and stores. Travelers can activate the Google Maps application to determine their precise location and get the real-time display of Google Maps. The information would encompass details regarding various establishments such as shops, companies, hotels, malls, cinema theatres, restaurants, canteens, recreational zones, and more, hence facilitating location-specific experiences. By utilizing the live view, tourists navigate in a precise route, without any ambiguity (Nagaraj Samala, 2020). Uber employs artificial intelligence (AI) to facilitate its primary operation of assigning drivers to clients and determining the most optimal routes for reaching their destinations. Additionally, it fuels the company's “surge pricing” strategy, which raises fees during periods of high demand in order to incentivize additional drivers to start working, hence decreasing client waiting times. Uber utilizes artificial intelligence (AI) in its marketing endeavors by employing machine learning algorithms to categorize and target clients. Uber utilizes machine learning technology in its Uber Eats food delivery business as well. The objective is to forecast with utmost accuracy the anticipated duration for the delivery of a customer's food (Ward, Artificial Intelligence in Practice: How 50 Successful Companies Used AI and Machine Learning to Solve Problems, 2019).

NAVIGATING GAI CHALLENGES IN TOURISM

The incorporation of AI in the tourism industry has raised numerous ethical concerns, highlighting the complicated relationship between innovation and accountability. With the increasing integration of AI in the tourism industry, stakeholders are faced with complex ethical dilemmas. These dilemmas revolve around issues such as prejudice, transparency, and the potential loss of jobs. Bias is a central concern in ethical discussions, as it has the potential to corrupt AI-based decision-making. AI algorithms, albeit appearing objective, are still susceptible to biases present in the datasets used to train them. Without careful curation and algorithmic auditing, AI systems are at risk of perpetuating and magnifying existing prejudices, including racial and gender discrepancies as well as socioeconomic inequalities. Within the expansive realm of the tourism industry, characterised by its abundant variety, the risks and rewards are exceptionally elevated. Ensuring equitable and unbiased representation in AI-driven systems is not just an ethical concern, but a moral obligation that requires proactive steps to eliminate biases before they undermine justice and inclusivity. However, openness serves as a source of optimism and guidance among the complex realm of decision-making influenced by artificial intelligence. With the growing impact of AI algorithms on the production and distribution of travel information, travelers are demanding more openness and authority over their online travel experiences. They insist on being informed about the presence of AI systems operating covertly, moulding their experiences and impacting their decisions. They desire the ability to have control over the AI-generated information they come across—to modify preferences, refine recommendations, and offer feedback in an effort to regain ownership of their digital identities. Transparency is essential for establishing trust, ensuring responsibility, and empowering individuals in the AI-mediated environment.

Data Privacy and Security Concerns

Data privacy and security concerns arise due to the careful management of large and varied information while integrating AI technology into the tourism business. As AI-driven applications become more prevalent, the tourism sector faces the challenge of protecting sensitive visitor information from potential breaches and unauthorized access. In addition, dealing with the complicated network of global data protection legislation, such as the strict General Data Protection Regulation (GDPR) in the European Union, further complicates data management methods in the tourism industry (Ng, 2018). To address these concerns effectively, it is necessary to adopt a comprehensive strategy that includes strong encryption techniques, strict access controls, and strict adherence to evolving regulatory requirements. This will help to strengthen the security and confidentiality of tourist data in the rapidly growing digital environment.

Ethical Use of AI

The incorporation of AI in the tourism industry raises significant ethical concerns, as stakeholders navigate the complex relationship between technical advancement and ethical obligations. An important issue revolves with the unintentional spread of societal biases in AI systems, which might worsen existing inequalities and perpetuate systemic injustices (Elisa, Opportunities and Challenges of Artificial Intelligence in the Tourism Industry, 2023). The ethical dilemma surrounding the creation and use of AI presents itself in various ways, ranging from the hidden presence of biased algorithms to the urgent need for transparency and accountability in decision-making processes driven by AI. Moreover, when it comes to dealing with the complex issues of permission, autonomy, and responsible usage of AI in the tourism industry, there is a strong requirement for well-developed ethical frameworks to support the integration of AI. Although Gen AI presents numerous thrilling prospects, it also gives rise to significant ethical inquiries. The capacity of artificial intelligence (AI) to produce authentic content, be it in the form of text, photographs, or videos, can be exploited, resulting in the dissemination of false information, manipulation, and apprehensions regarding privacy. Deepfakes have the capability to generate deceptive videos that manipulate the appearance of individuals, causing them to appear as if they are saying or doing things that they have not actually done. Likewise, text generated by artificial intelligence can be utilized to create large amounts of false information or unsolicited content (Almeida, Artificial Intelligence Fundamentals for Business Leaders: Up to Date with GAI, 2023).

Data Quality

The crucial issue at the center of AI-driven advancements in tourism is the matter of data quality, which is a complex problem filled with nuances and difficulties. The effectiveness of AI applications depends heavily on the accuracy, level of detail, and reliability of the underlying datasets, which presents significant challenges for tourism stakeholders who are trying to take use of the transformative capabilities of AI technologies (Ng, 2018). The complex and intricate nature of the terrain, which is marked by diverse data types, inconsistencies, and missing information, makes the challenging process of combining, preparing, and analyzing different data sources accurately and reliably. Moreover, the hidden and harmful presence of data bias and isolated datasets worsens the difficulty of ensuring data quality in the tourism industry. The European Commission's Ethics Guidelines for Trustworthy AI outline a framework that is grounded in four ethical principles: respect for human autonomy, harm prevention, fairness (unbiased), and explicability (Pauline A. Milwood, 2023). To effectively tackle these challenges, it is necessary to establish and follow strict data management protocols. This includes thorough validation, cleansing, and standardization practices to create a collection of high-quality data that can be used effectively by AI algorithms in tourism applications.

Regulatory Compliance

The incorporation of AI technology into the tourism industry creates a complex situation where stakeholders must navigate through a complicated network of compliance duties and legal restrictions. The rapid increase in the number of regional and international regulations for data protection, exemplified by the extensive requirements of laws like the General Data Protection Regulation (GDPR) and the California Consumer Privacy Act (CCPA), creates a complex and unclear landscape for compliance (Secure Privacy, 2023). Tourism enterprises are faced with complex and strict regulations that require them to implement rigorous data governance practices, transparent privacy policies, and vigilant oversight mechanisms. These measures are necessary to ensure compliance with regulations and avoid penalties. To successfully navigate the complex regulations surrounding the integration of AI in the tourism industry, one must possess a deep understanding of the legislative landscape, take a proactive approach to compliance, and demonstrate a strong commitment to ethical data management.

Human-AI Collaboration and Accessibility

The merging of human creativity and artificial intelligence signifies a significant change in the tourist industry, creating a diverse range of opportunities and problems. Tourism firms are currently undergoing a process of integrating AI into their operations. However, this integration involves dealing with the complex and uncertain nature of human-AI collaboration. Although AI-powered chatbots and virtual assistants have enhanced customer service in some aspects, they can also pose obstacles for travelers who lack proficiency in technology or have disabilities. Ensuring the accessibility and inclusivity of AI applications for all travelers continues to be a major concern. The convergence involves complex interactions between trust dynamics, communication modalities, and skill paradigms (Joseph, 2023). Achieving harmonic collaboration between human agents and AI-driven systems requires careful balance. Various difficulties, including worries about job loss and retraining, as well as concerns about the transparency and interpretability of algorithms, hinder the progress towards a harmonious coexistence between humans and robots in the tourism industry. To tackle these challenges, it is necessary to take a comprehensive approach that includes initiatives to improve skills, efforts to engage stakeholders, and the application of ethical principles in designing AI systems. This will help create a mutually beneficial relationship between humans and AI systems, leading to positive outcomes in the tourism industry.

Over-Reliance on AI and Inclusivity Issues

The increasing dependence on AI technology in the tourism industry brings about a complex combination of opportunities and problems, adding subtle nuances and dilemmas to the environment. As tourism businesses navigate the unfamiliar territory of incorporating AI, they face a complex set of existential dilemmas, with the most important one being the intricate relationship between technology advancement and human-centered approaches. The steady progression towards AI-powered automation and algorithmic decision-making creates a noticeable feeling of unease, as those involved struggle with the inevitable decline of human interaction and individualized experiences that define the essence of tourism (Santos, n.d.). Furthermore, the issue of digital divide is a significant concern that threatens the equal and fair principles of AI-driven tourism projects. Marginalized groups face the risk of being excluded from the privileged realm of AI-enhanced travel experiences. While AI undeniably improves tourist experiential services, it cannot transcend the indispensable human touch, which is a crucial factor in determining the quality of experiential tourism (Nagaraj Samala, 2020). To navigate this complex situation, it is important to have a clear understanding of the future, the ability to understand and share the feelings of others, and the responsibility to make ethical decisions. Tourism businesses need to find a balance between using AI-driven automation and providing personalized human service. This will create an environment where technology enhances, rather than replaces, the unique value of human interaction and expertise in the tourism industry.

Adoption Challenges

Challenges in AI adoption within the tourism industry are complex and difficult to navigate. They are characterized by a wide range of obstacles that are unclear and confusing, making it challenging for even the most determined stakeholders. Tourism firms have numerous complex challenges when adopting AI, including technological difficulties, limited resources, organizational resistance, and cultural barriers (Joseph, 2023). The progress towards integrating AI faces numerous obstacles, as those involved struggle with the immense challenge of coordinating a successful combination of technological advancements, organizational changes, and gaining support from stakeholders in order to achieve a smooth transition towards AI-driven operational models. Also, the workforce of a tourism enterprise might struggle to adopt AI technologies due to varying levels of skillset, so in order to attain a superior level of professional proficiency, individuals working in the tourism sector must possess the requisite knowledge to comprehensively comprehend the desires and emotions of customers or guests. Additionally, they must possess the capability to effectively utilize digital equipment specific to the tourism industry, thereby necessitating the attainment of a high level of digital competence (Adrid Indaryanto, 2023). In addition, the issue of algorithmic opacity and interpretability creates widespread concerns about the deployment of AI, leading to existential worries about trust, responsibility, and regulatory compliance. To successfully navigate this complex maze, one must possess a deep awareness of the underlying social and technological dynamics, a strong dedication to change management concepts, and a determined mindset to overcome the numerous challenges that arise while using AI in the tourism industry.

Infrastructure Challenges

The process of integrating AI into the tourism industry involves a wide range of sophisticated infrastructure requirements and obstacles. These challenges include logistical subtleties and technical difficulties that even experienced stakeholders find difficult to navigate. As tourism firms use AI technology, they face complex challenges related to outdated systems, difficulties in connecting different systems, limited internet capacity, and risks to cybersecurity (Ng, 2018). The complex and intricate nature of preparing infrastructure requires a coordinated effort to overcome the numerous challenges that arise while transitioning to AI-driven operating models. This involves utilizing resources, experience, and strategic planning to navigate the roadblocks along the way. Furthermore, the need for infrastructure preparedness is influenced by several socio-economic factors, making the task of improving infrastructure within the tourism industry more complicated. To successfully navigate this complex situation, it is essential to adopt a comprehensive strategy that includes making strategic investments, collaborating across different sectors, and implementing rigorous risk mitigation measures. These actions are crucial for strengthening the fundamental aspects of integrating AI technology in the tourism industry.

Socio-Cultural Impacts

The integration of AI into the tourism industry brings about a diverse range of cultural influences, resulting in a complex and transformative effect on society. Tourism enterprises are currently facing the challenge of adapting to the unstoppable progress of AI-driven automation and algorithmic decision-making. This presents them with numerous existential challenges related to the preservation of cultural authenticity, history, and identity in a world that is becoming more and more computerized (Management, 2023).The constant progress towards technology advancement creates a noticeable feeling of unease, as those involved grapple with the fear of cultural sameness and commercialization caused by AI-powered tourism projects. Stakeholders must carefully balance technological advancements with the preservation of cultural heritage. The goal is to create a fair and balanced approach where AI-driven innovations enhance, rather than replace, the distinct cultural aspects that define tourism experiences. To navigate the complex web of sociocultural dynamics in tourism, one must possess a wide range of empathy, cultural sensitivity, and ethical responsibility. Tourism businesses must strive to find a harmonious balance between technological advancements and the preservation of local culture.

Environmental Challenges

Environmental sustainability is being greatly influenced by the integration of AI in the tourism industry. This is causing a significant change in the way things are done and raising important questions that affect society as a whole. Tourism enterprises are faced with a complex set of issues as they strive to prioritize environmental stewardship and sustainability. These challenges include reducing carbon footprint, minimizing waste, conserving biodiversity, and preserving ecosystems. The unstoppable progress towards AI-driven innovation creates a noticeable feeling of unease, as those involved struggle with the looming threat of environmental damage caused by unsustainable tourist practices and the exploitation of resources. Furthermore, the process of integrating AI creates a complex situation with many ethical challenges. Stakeholders must carefully balance the advancement of technology with the need to protect the environment. They aim to create a fair combination where AI-driven innovations promote sustainable tourism practices and minimize negative environmental effects. To successfully navigate the complex field of environmental sustainability in tourism, it is crucial to have a deep understanding of ecology, collaborate with stakeholders, and act as responsible stewards. This will help tourism businesses move towards a more sustainable and resilient future.

GAI TRANSFORMING TOURISM'S TOMORROW

Within the dynamic realm of tourism, the revolutionary capabilities of GAI present themselves as an enticing illusion on the far horizon, offering the prospect of customized, engaging, and environmentally-friendly travel encounters. As the tourist sector faces the challenges of innovation, sustainability, and authenticity, the use of GAI emerges as a significant opportunity to transform the travel experience and introduce a new era of exploration and enjoyment. Leading the way in this change is the exciting potential of AI-driven travel simulations and virtual experiences—a digital frontier where the distinctions between reality and imagination blend into a multitude of possibilities. By harnessing the limitless creativity of GAI, those involved in the tourist industry are in a position to access a wealth of immersive experiences that go beyond the limitations of time and space. Imagine a reality where explorers navigate through simulated environments, fully immersed in the visual, auditory, and tactile experiences of faraway places and historical periods. AI-driven simulations provide a captivating preview of many worldwide travel experiences, ranging from ancient ruins to futuristic cityscapes, crowded marketplaces to serene landscapes. These simulations entice adventurers to go on grand journeys without having to leave the comfort of their homes. By combining the artistic abilities of GAI with advanced technologies like AR and VR, tourism industry participants may create more immersive and interactive experiences, transforming the way travelers are inspired and explore. Imagine a traveler wearing augmented reality glasses, experiencing a world that has been turned into a captivating digital display. In this world, every street corner has secret riches and every landmark tells exciting stories of exploration. Guided by GAI, tourists embark on explorations that beyond the limitations of guidebooks and brochures, creating a unique fabric of tailored experiences that emerge in the present moment, adjusting and developing with each action performed.

Integration of AR and VR With GAI

The combination of GAI with Augmented Reality (AR) and Virtual Reality (VR) represents a significant change in immersive travel experiences. It allows passengers to go beyond the limits of physical reality and into a world of limitless exploration and sensory immersion. The seamless integration of generative algorithms, immersive technology, and experiential narrative at the center of this convergence creates virtual travel experiences that are filled with wonder, presence, and authenticity. An example of integration of GAI with AR and VR is the use of GAI, particularly large language models (LLMs) can enable individuals without technical expertise to express a concept using simple written language in order to construct an augmented or virtual reality encounter. The integration of these technologies to the workforce will likely result in a significant change in expectations around training and experience (Barry, 2023).

AR is a technology that integrates virtual information into the physical world. The technical methods employed by the system include multimedia, 3D modeling, real-time tracking and registration, intelligent interaction, sensing, and other advanced techniques. The core concept of augmented reality is to overlay computer-generated virtual information, including text, photos, 3D models, music, video, etc., over the real world after a simulation (Yunqiang Chen, 2019). AR is a revolutionary technology that enhances the travel experience by adding digital information and interactive features to the actual world. It provides contextual insights, historical tales, and interactive points of interest to enrich real-world landscapes. By incorporating GAI algorithms, AR applications have the ability to create contextual content, offer personalized recommendations, and provide immersive storytelling experiences. These features enhance the traveler's comprehension of their environment and encourage a more profound connection with the local culture, heritage, and attractions.

VR refers to the utilization of a computer-generated three-dimensional (3D) environment, known as a 'Virtual Environment' (VE), which allows users to travel and perhaps interact with it, so creating a real-time replica of one or more of the user's five senses. The term 'navigate' pertains to the capability of moving and exploring the VE, whereas 'interact' pertains to the capability of selecting and manipulating items within the VE (Guttentag, 2010). VR allows users to experience otherworldly regions and simulated landscapes, providing an unmatched level of immersion and presence that goes beyond the limitations of physical space and time. By utilizing GAI algorithms, VR experiences may be created, customized, and adjusted in real-time to match the unique preferences and interests of passengers. Travel and Hospitality enterprises can showcase various tourist attractions and hotel rooms using these technologies. This allows for the creation of tailored journeys that appeal to a wide range of tastes, aspirations, and learning styles. As GAI can produce detailed and realistic images, sounds, and even 3D models of places based on photographs, videos, and other data inputs, travel companies can serve virtual tours as a powerful marketing tool to showcase the potential of their offerings. To boost tourism, Saudi Arabia leveraged VR technology to allow digital tourists to explore the ancient city of Hengra, the country's first UNESCO World Heritage Site (R, 2024).

Real-time Decision Support and Predictive Analytics

Real-time decision support systems are the most advanced form of GAI for tourism. They provide stakeholders with the ability to predict future events and analyze data, allowing them to negotiate the intricacies of current travel dynamics with exceptional accuracy and effectiveness. Machine learning algorithms are fundamental components of real-time decision support systems. The sources can include weather patterns, transportation schedules, social media sentiment, and consumer feedback. Machine learning algorithms facilitate the adaptation and evolution of decision support systems by continuously learning from new data inputs and refining prediction models. This allows them to respond to changing market conditions, consumer preferences, and competitive dynamics (Swetaseal, 2023). Predictive analytics is crucial in predicting future trends, detecting developing patterns, and anticipating changes in traveler behavior. This allows decision support systems to proactively manage risks, take advantage of opportunities, and optimize the allocation of resources in real-time. Predictive analytics enables tourism stakeholders to anticipate future trends and make informed decisions by examining historical data and projecting them forward. This allows them to optimize pricing strategies, adapt marketing campaigns, and efficiently manage inventory to meet changing demand patterns (Chatterjee, 2024).

Hyper Personalization

The utilization of customization and personalization approaches within the realm of GAI for tourism represents the extensive study of data-driven insights to create unique travel experiences that are specifically tuned to the individual interests and behaviors of visitors. The heart of this project involves the complex understanding of the behavioral analysis of each traveler. This helps to uncover the subtle details of traveler preferences, past interactions, and contextual factors. This information is then used to create highly personalized travel experiences. Behavioral analysis is the foundation of tailored travel experiences. It involves studying the complex details of traveler behavior, psychographics, and decision-making processes to discover hidden preferences and unfulfilled requirements. Behavioral analysis in the tourism industry utilizes sentiment analysis, natural language processing (NLP), and user profiling techniques to decipher the underlying motivations and aspirations that influence traveler behavior (Santos, 2024.).This allows tourism stakeholders to create highly personalized and emotionally impactful travel experiences. To put it simply, hyper personalization methods utilize data-driven insights and behavioral analysis to create highly personalized travel experiences that align with the specific preferences and aspirations of travelers. This leads to a new era of customized exploration and immersive discovery.

GAI GUIDELINES FOR TOURISM INDUSTRY

With rising demand for tourist needs the tourism industry is in a continuous push to adopt dynamic tools and policies to retain and justify the satisfactory pre and post travel feedback. As the technology sector is growing in all sectors the tourism sector shouldn't be left behind in pathway to hold and sustain its GDP share. Below Fig 2.0 highlights are some key pointers to enhance the industry further.

Figure 2. GAI Guidelines for Tourism Industry

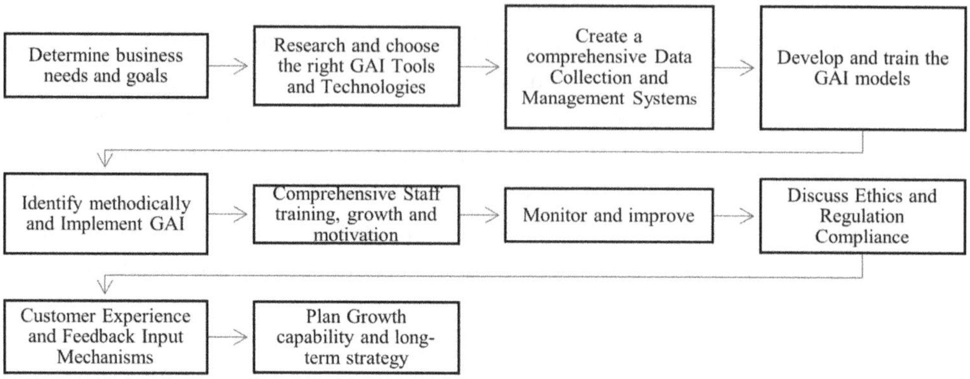

CONCLUSION

To summarise, the use of GAI in the tourism industry marks the beginning of a revolutionary period, fundamentally altering the way travel experiences are conceived, provided, and controlled. Currently, GAI is causing significant changes in the tourism sector by utilizing its powers in personalized recommendation systems, advanced content production for marketing purposes, virtual tour guides, and adaptable vacation planning. These advancements are enhancing the customization and involvement of travel experiences, resulting in unprecedented unique and customized encounters for travelers. Nevertheless, this technological revolution is accompanied by numerous problems. Significant ethical quandaries, specifically pertaining to the protection of data privacy and the presence of inherent biases, are of great concern. Integrating AI into the current tourism infrastructure requires substantial investment and technical expertise, which can be challenging for smaller organisations. Furthermore, it is imperative to maintain openness and accountability in AI systems, which requires continuous supervision and control. When considering the future, the potential of GAI in the tourism industry seems limitless and full of potential. The integration of emerging technologies, such as augmented and virtual reality, with real-time decision support systems is poised to bring about a further transformation in the industry. These developments are positioned to provide more engaging and dynamic travel experiences, improve operational effectiveness, and encourage sustainable behaviours. The potential of AI in optimising resources and decreasing environmental effect aligns perfectly with the growing focus on sustainable tourism. In order to achieve successful integration of GAI in the tourism industry, it is crucial to tackle existing obstacles, maintain ethical guidelines, and promote strong interdisciplinary cooperation. As the industry rapidly evolves, the combination of AI developments with tourism will create new models, propelling a future where technology and human experiences not only exist together but also blend seamlessly to generate more significant and environmentally-friendly travel experiences. The future holds a landscape where the digital and physical worlds merge effortlessly, providing unparalleled possibilities for discovery and interaction.

REFERENCES

Adrid Indaryanto, B. D. (2023, December). The growing use and impact of artificial intelligence technologies in the tourism industry. *Sustainable Engineering and Innovation, 5*(2), 189–204. DOI: 10.37868/sei.v5i2.id238

Akshay Kulkarni, A. S. (2023). *Applied Generative AI for Beginners Practical Knowledge on Diffusion Models, ChatGPT, and Other LLMs*. Apress. DOI: 10.1007/978-1-4842-9994-4

Almeida, I. (2023). *Artificial Intelligence Fundamentals for Business Leaders: Up to Date With Generative AI*. Now Next Later AI.

Barry, D. (2023, May 31). Retrieved April 19, 2024, from reworked: https://www.reworked.co/digital-workplace/what-vr-ar-and-generative-ai-will-make-possible-in-the-digital-workplace/

Bulchand-Gidumal, J. (2022, September 2). Impact of Artificial Intelligence in Travel, Tourism, and Hospitality. *Handbook of e-Tourism*, 1943–1962.

Chatterjee, M. (2024, May 6). Retrieved May 11, 2024, from Great Learning: https://www.mygreatlearning.com/blog/what-are-the-use-cases-for-the-predictive-analytics-in-the-travel-industry/

Elisa, M. T. (2023, December 18). Opportunities and Challenges of Artificial Intelligence in the Tourism Industry. *Global Journal of Tourism, Leisure and Hospitality Management, 1*(1).

Great Chat. (n.d.). Retrieved April 4, 2024, from GreatChat: https://www.greatchat.ai/en-blog/ai-in-the-travel-industry-how-is-ai-creating-personalized-itineraries-and-enhancing-concierge-services

Guttentag, D. (2010, October 1). Virtual reality: Applications and implications for tourism. *Tourism Management, 31*(5), 637–651. DOI: 10.1016/j.tourman.2009.07.003

Hetler, A. (2023, December). Retrieved May 1, 2024, from TechTarget: https://www.techtarget.com/whatis/definition/ChatGPT

Hines, M. (2024, February 29). Retrieved April 27, 2024, from PhocusWire: https://www.phocuswire.com/ai-check-in-tripcom-tripgenie

Hong Chuong Pham, C. D. (2024, February 9). What drives tourists' continuance intention to use ChatGPT for travel services? A stimulus-organism-response perspective. *Journal of Retailing and Consumer Services, 78*, 1–13.

iWebScraping. (2024, April 11). Retrieved April 21, 2024, from Medium: https://medium.com/@seo_14803/big-data-analytics-for-the-tourism-industry-cda451149d58

Izchak, O. E. (2024, February 15). Retrieved April 25, 2024, from mize: https://mize.tech/blog/6-examples-of-how-ai-is-used-in-the-travel-industry

Jacques Bulchand-Gidumal, E. W. (2023, June 30). Artificial intelligence's impact on hospitality and tourism marketing: Exploring key themes and addressing challenges. *Current Issues in Tourism*, 1–18.

Joan Borràs, A. M. (2014, June 9). Intelligent tourism recommender systems: A survey. *Expert Systems with Applications*, *41*(16), 7370–7389. DOI: 10.1016/j.eswa.2014.06.007

Joseph, A. (2023, September 19). Retrieved April 12, 2024, from Medium: https://medium.com/publishfive/artificial-intelligence-in-travel-top-7-challenges-f860702acb05

Kailash Sharma, N. S. (2024, May 2). Retrieved May 11, 2024, from DEVPOST: https://devpost.com/software/k-2bl1ch

Kamath, P. (2022, August 25). Retrieved April 7, 2024, from itilite: https://www.itilite.com/blog/virtual-travel-assistant-benefits/

Keng-Boon Ooi, G. (2023, October 5). The Potential of Generative Artificial Intelligence Across Disciplines: Perspectives and Future Directions. *Journal of Computer Information Systems*, 1–32.

Lalli, M. (2024, March 18). *datadrivendestinations.com*. Retrieved April 5, 2024, from Data Driven Destinations: https://datadrivendestinations.com/2024/03/ai-and-generative-ai-transforming-destination-management

Management, J. F. (2023, October 27). Retrieved April 13, 2024, from Medium: https://james-francis-paradigm.medium.com/unraveling-the-ethical-implications-artificial-intelligences-impact-on-cultural-appropriation

McKinsey & Company. (2024, April 2). Retrieved April 25, 2024, from McKinsey & Company: https://www.mckinsey.com/featured-insights/mckinsey-explainers/what-is-generative-ai

Michael Chui, R. R. (2023, June 14). Retrieved July 7, 2024, from Mckinsey & Company: https://www.mckinsey.com/capabilities/mckinsey-digital/our-insights/the-economic-potential-of-generative-ai-the-next-productivity-frontier#business-value

Nagaraj Samala, B. S. (2020, April 24). Impact of AI and robotics in the tourism sector: A critical insight. *Journal of Tourism Futures*, *8*(1), 73–87. DOI: 10.1108/JTF-07-2019-0065

Nechaeva, A. (2023, August 17). Retrieved April 3, 2024, from solimarInternational: https://www.solimarinternational.com/the-impact-of-ai-on-the-travel-industry/

Ng, B. (2018, April 12). Retrieved April 10, 2024, from rezdy: https://rezdy.com/blog/pros-cons-artificial-intelligence-travel-industry/

Nir Kshetri, Y. K. (2023, October 18). Generative artificial intelligence in marketing: Applications, opportunities, challenges, and research agenda. *International Journal of Information Management*, *75*(6), 71–75.

Olson, G. (2023, March 13). Retrieved April 10, 2024, from Thrifty Traveler: https://thriftytraveler.com/guides/travel/tripit-review/

Pauline A. Milwood, S. H.-C. (2023, January 15). A Scoping Study of Ethics in Artificial Intelligence Research in Tourism and Hospitality. *Information and Communication Technologies in Tourism*, *2023*, 243–254.

Prashant Balodi, A. T. (2022, December). Role of artificial intelligence in the travel and hospitality industry. *International Journal of Food and Nutritional Sciences*, *11*(3), 3138–3149.

Publications, M. (2024). *Generative AI & ChatGPT for Beginners Made Easy 2-Books-in-1: Master Artificial Intelligence Fundamentals, Elevate Your Skills, and Unlock Money-Making Strategies with Conversational AI*. ModernMind Publications.

R, P. (2024, March 4). Retrieved April 25, 2024, from intuz: https://www.intuz.com/blog/generative-ai-in-travel-tourism

Santos, C. (n.d.). Retrieved April 12, 2024, from Stippl.: https://stippl.io/blog/ai-travel-what-are-the-pros-and-cons-for-travelers

Secure Privacy. (2023, October 4). Retrieved April 11, 2024, from Secure Privacy: https://secureprivacy.ai/blog/ai-personal-data-protection-gdpr-ccpa-compliance

Singh, L. (2023, November 18). Retrieved April 3, 2024, from yellow.ai: https://yellow.ai/blog/chatbot-for-travel/

Statista. (n.d.). Retrieved July 7, 2024, from statista: https://www.statista.com/topics/10887/artificial-intelligence-ai-use-in-travel-and-tourism/

Stefan Feuerriegel, J. H. (2023, September 12). Generative AI. *Business & Information Systems Engineering*, *66*(1), 111–126. DOI: 10.1007/s12599-023-00834-7

Sun, J. (2023, December 19). Retrieved April 26, 2024, from World Economic Forum: https://www.weforum.org/agenda/2023/12/how-is-ai-reshaping-the-travel-tourism/

Susann Almasi, A. C. (2023, September 27). Retrieved July 7, 2024, from Mckinsey and Company: https://www.mckinsey.com/industries/travel-logistics-and-infrastructure/our-insights/the-promise-of-travel-in-the-age-of-ai

Swetaseal. (2023, January 15). Retrieved April 20, 2024, from Medium: https://medium.com/@swetaseal/machine-learning-use-cases-in-tourism-f580d2f14c5b

Takyar, A. (n.d.). Retrieved April 9, 2024, from LeewayHertz: https://www.leewayhertz.com/generative-ai-in-travel/

Tarik Dogru-Dr. True, T. N. (2023, July). Generative Artificial Intelligence in the Hospitality and Tourism Industry: Developing a Framework for Future Research. *Journal of Hospitality & Tourism Research (Washington, D.C.).*

Team, 1. (2023, September 20). Retrieved May 2, 2024, from 10xDS: https://10xds.com/blog/transforming-the-travel-and-tourism-industry-with-generative-ai-and-llm/

Tiernan, K. (2023, August 28). Retrieved April 1, 2024, from BDO Digital: https://www.bdodigital.com/insights/analytics/airbnb-artificial-intelligence-transform-business

Tuomi, A. (2023, January 15). AI-Generated Content, Creative Freelance Work and Hospitality and Tourism Marketing. *Information and Communication Technologies in Tourism, 2023*, 323–328. DOI: 10.1007/978-3-031-25752-0_35

Utpal Chakraborty, S. R. (2023). *Rise of Generative AI and ChatGPT Understand how Generative AI and ChatGPT are transforming and reshaping the business world*. BPB Online.

Wang, L. Z. (2020, June). VacAItionary: AI Travel Itinerary Planning Based on Ant Colony Optimization.

Ward, B. M. (2019). *Artificial Intelligence in Practice: How 50 Successful Companies Used AI and Machine Learning to Solve Problems*. Wiley.

Webster, S. I. (2022). *Robots, Artificial Intelligence and Service Automation in Travel, Tourism and Hospitality*. Emerald Publishing Limited.

yellow.ai. (n.d.). Retrieved April 8, 2024, from yellow.ai: https://yellow.ai/case-study/pelago-reimagines-customer-experience-with-gen-ai-powered-conversational-ai-agents/#solution

Yunqiang Chen, Q. W. (2019, June 1). An overview of augmented reality technology. *Journal of Physics: Conference Series*, *1237*(2), 022082. DOI: 10.1088/1742-6596/1237/2/022082

KEY TERMS AND DEFINITIONS

Artificial Intelligence (AI): AI, a fascinating branch of computer science, develops systems that can perform human tasks. Complex problem-solving, precision decision-making, flexible learning, and high natural language comprehension are required for these tasks. AI systems are carefully designed to watch their environment, evaluate and grasp information, and take actions that maximize their chances of success, giving computers some cognitive ability.

Augmented Reality (AR): AR is an interactive experience that enhances the real world with computer-generated perceptual information. Using software, apps, and hardware such as AR glasses, AR overlays digital content onto real-life environments and objects.

Blockchain: The unique and decentralized blockchain technology employs a distributed ledger to precisely and securely record transactions on several computers, preventing tampering. Each chain block has a detailed transaction record and is tightly related to the previous block, ensuring transparency and integrity. Blockchain is used in supply chain management, digital identity verification, and smart contracts in addition to cryptocurrencies like Bitcoin. It establishes digital transaction trust and accountability.

Generative AI (GAI): GAI uses complicated patterns from pre-existing data to create new content including text, images, audio, and video. This technology is led by Generative Adversarial Networks (GANs) and transformers like GPT-4. These models may replicate and reinvent their training data's style and structure. This opens up new creative domains and automated content generation, ushering in a new digital creativity era.

Generative Pre-Trained Transformer (GPT): GPT is a cutting-edge big language model that uses transformer architecture to perform a variety of natural language processing tasks. OpenAI GPT models are pre-trained unsupervised using a large dataset. They then refine their performance in translation, summarization, and question answering. The two-step process gives GPT models a deep understanding of language, which is then tuned to excel in specific applications, making them powerful and versatile.

Internet of Things (IoT): The Internet of Things (IoT) is a network of gadgets, automobiles, appliances, and other items with sensors, software, and other technologies that connect and exchange data via the internet. This connectivity provides remote object sensing and control, integrating the physical world and computer-based systems for better efficiency, accuracy, and economic benefits.

Large Language Model (LLM): LLM is a strong AI model that learned to understand, interpret, and synthesize human language from massive textual data. Due to thorough training on diverse datasets, these models can effectively foresee and provide contextually relevant and logically connected content. LLMs, or Language Models, use deep learning to represent human language's various nuances. LLMs like OpenAI's GPT series and Google's BERT have raised natural language processing standards.

Machine Learning (ML): ML is a dynamic discipline of AI that creates methods for computers to learn from data and make predictions or judgments. ML algorithms use training data to make data-driven predictions and judgments instead of writing explicit instructions for each operation. This paradigm change allows systems to dynamically adjust and improve, revealing new intelligence and automation.

Natural Language Processing (NLP): NLP studies how computers perceive, interpret, and generate human language. NLP is a fascinating AI field that handles computer-human language interaction. NLP creates algorithms and models to help computers understand, interpret, and produce human language. Language translation, sentiment analysis, speech recognition, and conversational robots have been revolutionized by NLP. This has greatly changed computer-human interaction.

Virtual Reality (VR): VR is a computer-generated environment with scenes and objects that appear to be real, making the user feel they are immersed in their surroundings. This environment is perceived through a device known as a VR headset or helmet. VR allows us to immerse ourselves as if we were one of the characters.

Chapter 12
The Improvements in Significance of AI in Experiential and Medical Tourism

Ranjit Barua
https://orcid.org/0000-0003-2236-3876
Indian Institute of Engineering Science and Technology, India

Sudipto Datta
https://orcid.org/0000-0003-2161-6878
Indian Institute of Science, Bangalore, India

ABSTRACT

By enhancing specific experiences, simplifying healthcare services, and guaranteeing patient and travel safety, AI integration has completely changed these industries. Artificial intelligence (AI)-powered virtual assistants and recommendation systems in experiential tourism respond to individual preferences by providing personalized recommendations and seamless support during the trip. In the meantime, artificial intelligence (AI) in medical tourism makes it easier to obtain high-quality remote healthcare services by enabling precise diagnosis, customized treatment programs, and virtual healthcare platforms. AI also helps with risk assessment and preventative safety measures, which improves patients' and tourists' overall pleasure and peace of mind. This chapter promises more developments and innovation in the future by highlighting the critical role AI is playing in changing the face of medical and experience tourism.

DOI: 10.4018/979-8-3693-5578-7.ch012

INTRODUCTION

Understanding how artificial intelligence impacts an organization's performance helps stakeholders create the right strategies and leverage those new opportunities (Samala et al., 2020) (Barua et al., 2023). Bulchand-Gidumal et al., 2023 explore the impact of artificial intelligence on marketing for hotels across three interlinked phases: also, questionnaire-based surveys, in focus groups and in-depth interviews. According to the data, based on the characteristics of each attribute, ten trends of AI affecting hotel marketing are summarized into four aspects (Saulat., 2018). AI disrupts the internal organization's functioning by training the augmented worker, using data and content as competitive enablers, performing a vast-scale personalization and customization (Jiang et al., 2021) (Barua et al., 2023). AI also play in stakeholders' engagements since it controls legal and ethical aspects of data usage, promotes sustainability, and determines ROI. The functions of the networks to which the organizations belong are enabled by AI-based concentration and integration of organizations and transformation of distribution patterns (Overgoor et al., 2019). By offering consumers smart and wanted treatment and by positing better help to customers and services, artificial intelligence (AI) alters customer procedures and processes (Prentice et al., 2020). The investigation builds an research plan and opens up conversation topics across business and academic professionals, thus, by showing the changes which artificial intelligence is anticipated to introduce to the particular ad of both tourism and hospitality (Samala et al., 2020). Experiential tourism has a high association with AI since it has a central mandate of improving the experience of an individual while travelling (Zhang et al., 2019) (Barua., 2024). This study from He et al. in 2023 follows the inspiration transmission approach with the aim of evaluating the antecedent and consequences of visitor inspiration within the well-being tourism context.

i. **Personalized References:**

Programs implemented in the AI rely on the user's preferences, habits, and previous choices and histories to suggest certain travelling locations, activities, and places of lodging (Prentice et al., 2020).

Since, AI can have detailed analysis of the details provided by the travelers, it can plan a proper itinerary, and can suggest proper experiences that can be a traveler's interest (Bulchand-Gidumal et al., 2023).

ii. **Virtual Chatbots and Assistants:**

- The key features of AI artificially intelligent assistants & chat programs include appearance of ready to help 24/7 to provide travelers with local attractions, weather conditions, language translations, and travel directions (Antonova., 2022).

- Such virtual companions improve the general trip through the facilitation of fast and precise information gathering and responding to inquiries alongside assistance during the trip (Omoge et al., 2022).

iii. **Augmented Reality (AR) and Virtual Reality (VR):**

- It is apparent that with the help of Augmented reality (AR) and Virtual Reality (VR) combined use of Artificial intelligence (AI) optimizes the traveling experience. This includes the concepts such as, virtual visitation, augmented reality guidelines, then navigational maps which help in the searching of historical places or regions (Wei et al., 2022) (Barua et al., 2022).
- AR and VR may also be used in mode experiences this means that a tourist can be able to feel the events or place that he or she has not been to (Thilagavathy et al., 2019).

iv. **Predictive Analytics for Crowd Management:**

- Convention centers, museums, and theme parks are among the numerous application areas of AI for crowd analysis that can be used to forecast and control crowds in such areas (Singh et al., 2020) (Barua., 2024). This assists in coming up with close times of visits as this will not be crowded making it enjoyable for travellers.

v. **Language Translation Services:**

- The language translation services provided by artificial intelligence greatly helps to enhance the interaction between the tourists and the residents as well as easing language barriers in providing tourists with appropriate experiences that would enhance their cultural experience (Kasneci et al., 2023).

vi. **Personalized Marketing Campaigns:**

- The AI helps travel companies understand what offer may be of interest to an individual and use this to promote the travel destination or activity they should try (Di Salvo et al., 2020).

vii. **Facial Recognition for Seamless Services:**

- Biometric identity, such as face identification, may be used for seamless authorization, safety, and personalized offerings (Barua., 2024). This increases the effectiveness of journeys and gives travelers additional options for experiencing and learning (Gupta et al., 2023).

viii. **Data-Driven Insights for Destination Management:**

ix. • AI analyzes large amounts of data to offer insights into visitor choices, behavior, and patterns. This knowledge can help organizations that manage destinations make better choices about facility growth and advertising initiatives (Neubig et al., 2022).

x. **Enhanced Safety and Security Measures:**

AI-powered detection and tracking technologies improve visitor safety by recognizing possible dangers and reacting proactively to crises (Vignesh Saravanan et al., 2023).

AI is essential in revolutionizing and enhancing the sensory tourist industry by providing customized suggestions, engaging encounters, effective amenities, and data-driven conclusions that improve people's journeys.

Figure 1. AI Technology Ecosystem (Aldoseri et al., 2023)

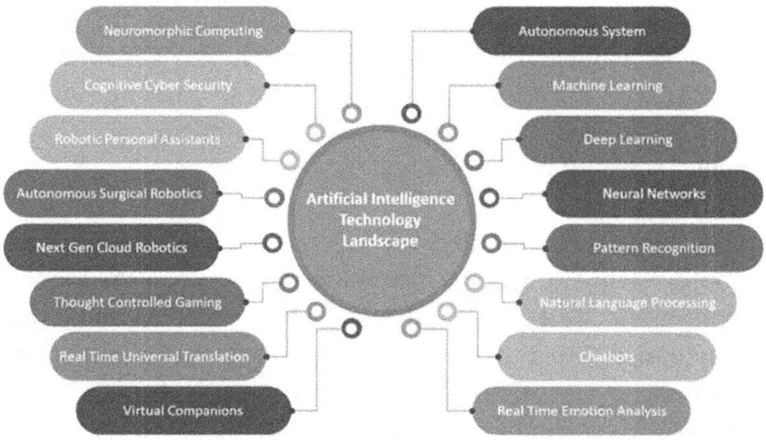

APPLICATION OF ARTIFICIAL INTELLIGENCE IN THE TRAVELING AND TOURISM SECTOR

AI technology is now accelerating the travel and hospitality business, especially in the concept of experiential travel. Immersion tourism is a specialized type of traveling where the presence is based only on first-hand, without any limits inherent in most touring, where tourists go specialized trips to create unique experiences. In this paper, we present the evidence that uses Artificial Intelligence in the sphere of tourism positively affects the aspects of security, effectiveness and flexibility of the experience tourism. The other huge contribution of AI in experiential tourism is that it may present activities and other recommendations after filtering. AI then processes one tonne of data consisting of the customers' preferences, past and real time data and generates highly personalized itineraries through the use of multiparameter algorithms and sophisticated artificial intelligence such as machine learning algorithms. Thus, it will make such guests able to do something that he/she wants to do while in the area, which will indeed make the vacation more satisfying and entertaining. This is attained by employing artificial intelligence (AI) chatbots or assistants with a view of improving the relation between the customers and the system. Thus, the travelers could make dedicated decisions and find ways through such regions effectively and efficiently since these technologies would allow the travelers to get first-hand information about the specific areas of interest such as attractions and shows as well as the restaurants and coffee shops. Thus, travel is not only made easy, but is also made enjoyable by the interface with these artificial intelligence assistants. This paper is centered on application and integration of ICT that is inherently connected to AI in the focal industry of experiential tourism influenced by AR and VR (Barua., 2024). Regular and accurate connections of AR applications are used to geo-reference location information concerning historical places, landmarks or a local wildlife and then superimpose that information on the regular view of the world in real time. VR at the same time can come in handy when it comes to travel experiences, meaning people can go to certain places without going there or can provide an illusion of being physically present for people who cannot travel. Of all the aspects of experiential tourism, AI proves especially valuable in improving the businesses' processes. They also use artificial intelligence in several aspects of travel such as in specific features as well as choices of accommodation and options of travel destinations. This is as an important area where the use of predictive analytics is useful because it aids the business in forecasting the periods in which many people will come to the business; therefore, it can help regulate a high flow of people and serve customers better. This efficiency does not only pertain to the direct benefit of the traveler as it also applies to the preservation of touristic environments and the structures of social context associated with tourism. Security cannot be overlooked when it comes to tourism and, of course, when speaking about AI and other related advancements, tourism security is essential for visitors. An AI surveillance system also has the capability to watch the packed zones observe the threat and give the signal toward probable threat. It also improves security measures in airports among other common places of interest to ensure that travelers are always safe. Thus, taking into account that the concept of tourism and integration of artificial intelligence into the circulation of the economy is increasing, how people interact with the world will change. Experience tourism can also be enhanced by, suggestions, AR, and procedural effectiveness and security. This is because the travel industry can meet the current consumer need and wants in its totality by embracing the use of AI to support sustainable tourism. AI makes experience tourism much more enjoyable and easier for those people who are worried about the actuality of the kinds of experiences that can be offered. Tourism is one of the many fields where AI can be applied as it is anticipated to revolutionaries several segments of the industry. The manner in which customers are dealt with in real-time, manner in which recommendation are handled as being unique increases the effectiveness of the use of chatbots for AI interaction. Pricing and demand management is all about how the resources should be utilized in terms of what has been collected and analyzed to forecast the total demand (Barua., 2024). With services being embedded in virtual assistants, this implies that services are preprogrammed and embedded and Artificial intelligence translation ensures that language becomes a non-issue when one is travelling between different countries. This practice of using big data processing and analysis through such models of predictive analytics as the best practice for segmentation and creating advertising campaigns. To start with, self-driving cars prevent the rate of accidents while on the same note enhancing the transport system supported by AI. Therefore, in the consideration of the Tourism sector, AI integration is helpful for customers, operations, and business approaches within the Tourism sector. However, it is imperative to appreciate the fact that it is now part of the society and this is why it has been incorporated into the travel, tourism and hospitality sector because of these interesting findings. Similarly, application of AI and other related techniques and tools in the travel, tourism and hospitality industries by the companies like Google Travel, Trip Advisor, Tata Consultancy Services, etc have only surfaced in the literature in very recent times (Viglia et al., 2014). The consequences of these researches are as follows and these are significant in travel and tourism industries. From the interview conducted to the different firms that comes under travel and hospitality service sector and as per the information shared by TATA consultancy services it was found that 85 percent of the service organization companies are already using Artificial Intelligence into their working (Sharma et al., 2023). It can also be because, the digital travel products have been selling at a higher rate and are expected to be $ 800 billion in 2020 (Chawla, 2019).

According to Google Travel & Trip Advisor surveys Consumers rely on the internet when planning for a vacation with 48% of these consumers using a mobile phone (Ahren, 2019). In other studies, what is discovered for instance is that 85 percent of the consumers decide on travelling the moment they arrive at the destination (thinkwithgoogle. com, 2016). As per the survey done by Peranzo in 2019, From the selected facts we can forecast that 80% of the consumers will appreciate self-service technology more than the conventional service and 36% of the consumers will like the self-service interactive booking process than the normal one. According to ThinkwithGoogle. Regarding traveling, according to the survey that was carried out by Statista in 2016, 90% of the passengers wished to be provided with related information of the trip. Thus, AI is an innovative solution for numerous industries, and tourism industry cannot be an exception. AI has revealed several possibilities in developing the expectation for tourism such as the modularity of business strategy and the sovereignty of the consumer. There are numerous opportunities that are provided by AI in the tourism domain, ranging from recommenders to predictive analytical tools, virtual assistants, self-driving cars, etc.

i. Customer Interaction and Engagement:

Chatbots powered by AI and virtual assistants are important in altering relationships with customers in the tourist business. These smart solutions offer actual time support, asking questions and directing passengers during their journey (Liu et al., 2021). Natural Language Processing (NLP) allows chatbots to comprehend and reply to customer requests more efficiently. This not only improves client happiness but also simplifies the entire booking procedure, providing passengers with an easier time.

ii. Personalized Recommendations:

Other benefits that have been associated with the use of AI in the tourism industry include the generation of facts and capability of analyzing them with a view of coming up with passenger-specific solutions. Proposals for the reform of machine learning to help clients select proper vacation routes, modify the schedules, and look for recreational activities make use of customer data, behaviours, and experience (Tavakoli et al., 2022). It also enhances every activity associated with travelling and yet it equally contributes to the enhancement of customer loyalty since it tries to address some interests.

iii. Predictive Analytics for Pricing and Demand Forecasting:

When it comes to more specific strategies such as the financial and price management, as well as in demand estimations in the sphere of tourism, the benefit of AI in terms of working with data sets is being utilized. It is evidenced by machine learning algorithms dealing with previous data, timetables and market data samples to reflect demands in the future. In turn, this assists an institution to improve on the pricing strategies where competition and revenues are key factors. Furthermore, forecasting help in right staff distribution in order to predict the busy periods of the year to ensure availability of enough staff (Antonopoulos et al., 2020).

iv. Revolutionizing Marketing Campaigns:

The tourism industry has seen an incredible opportunity to enhance the marketing industry in their line of work with the help of advances in Artificial Intelligence. The machine learning algorithms function for the big information wherein they identify the pattern, customers preference and their behaviours (Barua., 2024). It is used in depicting strategies of marketing which, though aligned on a strategic level, entail tactical approaches. Marketing applied through AI, promotion ends up being placed where it gets a chance and reach intended targets without the possibility of inconveniences people with messages they do not need. AI in marketing outreach enhances marketing messages like email, social media advertising and others making marketing promotions resulting in enhanced customer interaction (Alin et al., 2019).

v. Overcoming Language Barriers:

AI-powered translators tackle a major issue in the global tourism industry: language barriers Language. Translation algorithms are an artificial asset that ensures real-time translation, making communication between tourists and inhabitants smooth. This helps in intercultural exchange; there is a better understanding; and this will in one way or another contribute to a more enjoyable and satisfying trip for international visitors (Xiao., 2021).

vi. Smart Destination Management:

Applicable to the development of the tourism industry and useful in the organization of tourist destinations, both in terms of the tourism industry itself, and in terms of municipal needs. The data collected through SNS, tourism polls and especially footfall monitoring is quite informative in quantitative terms only in term of absolute difference but is quite informative in term of qualitative difference. Such findings can also be used for exercising the quantitative assessment of tourist's choice, acknowledging recognized locations and accurate distribution of services' and facilities' formation (Barua., 2024). In this way, AI smart destinations contribute to the notion of environmentally sustainable tourism policies because they verify that it is possible to arrange the efficient use of resources in order to solve the management of goal-oriented historical and natural sites (Ivars-Baidal et al., 2019).

vii. Enhancing Operational Efficiency:

Robotics and artificial intelligence help tourism businesses enhance their operational efficiency significantly. From motel check-ins to immigration examinations, AI-powered technologies improve activities, lowering waiting periods and increasing overall effectiveness. Robotic Process Automation (RPA) is used to automate regular and routine tasks, allowing human resources to focus on more complicated and added-value tasks (Kumari, 2021).

viii. Augmented Reality (AR) and Virtual Reality (VR) Experiences:

The combination of AI-powered AR and VR technology improves tourists' full immersion. Virtually excursions, Augmented Reality directs, and AI-powered simulators give passengers a taste of locations and activities before their visit. This not just helps with trip preparation, but it also makes for an additional educated and interesting vacation (Barua et al., 2022).

ix. Autonomous Vehicles for Transportation:

AI has paved the path for self-driving cars, which will have an impact on mobility in the tourism sector. Algorithms using artificial intelligence enable automated cars as well as other automated forms of travel, resulting in more secure and more efficient transport. The use of this technology additionally improves the overall safety of tourists, but it also helps to optimize routes for transportation & costs. (Ma et al., 2020).

x. Facilitating Sustainable Tourism:

As the following typology particularly underscores, the potential for supporting sustainability in the tourism sector at the environmental level pertains to AI. What are examples of how AI reduces the impact of travel and tourism on the environment: I also like the idea of cutting down on accommodation energy expenditure or providing an environment-friendly solution for flying. Furthermore, the results of the data could be in managing and directing the tourist traffic flow areas to make such places to address some of the issues such as traffic congestions and adding more pressure on the environment.

AI in Tourism encompasses various elements and presence in the business: nature of knowledge management, customer communications, organizational functioning and management, and problem solving. Picking holes in such a statement remains very hard especially knowing that, with new technologies that improve the integration capacity of artificial intelligence technology, the travel sector will be among the main beneficiaries (Samala et al., 2020). Continuing with individualization or overcoming international trends related to language multiculturalism or shifting to the existing issue of the viability of the AI in tourist industry AI is transforming the environment of the tourist sector and offers unmatched prospects for modernization. As for applied artificial intelligence business and places used for touristic destinations, it is possible to unveil an additional further, efficient and more enriching aspect towards all people of the whole wide world (Rane et al, 2023).

ARTIFICIAL INTELLIGENCE'S IMPACT ON ASPECTS RELATING TO TRAVEL, TOURISM, AND HOSPITALITY

The elements developed under the Technological criteria of the travel, tourism, and hospitality industries are being 'alervised' with the use of Artificial Intelligence (AI). In their review done in 2021, Koo et al posited that clients' fulfillment, business-related processes, and change through Artificial Intelligence have been made possible through AI technologies. There is an electric network that combines customer care services through the use of bots and assistants while self-developed AI programs yielded an average find of general customer satisfaction that is (Antonova., 2022) (Barua., 2024). It means that they should be able to or at least are supposed to be able to respond to simple answers, book, and guide travelers. This is therefore a mutual benefit gamble where organizations offering the services benefit from an enhanced social relation with customers since the latter benefits from improved services offered to him or her. AI utilizes big data in spectacular volumes of calculation per-ceived by individuals in their choice and actions (Ivanov et al., 2019). This is beneficial for firms as it allows them to fashion highly unique travelling experiences or it may even help in the formula for how the travelling will be formed as well as which particular hotel may be preferred. The arithmetic used in this paper shows that it is achievable to realize this advantage of customization and get customer satisfaction and a further degree of loyalty by-the-bye improving the total travel experience. Specific examples of such AI algorithms and technologies include the following; The use of practical applications in the kind of work that integrates the use of practical applications such as the use of Predictive Supply Analytics because of its functionality of forecasting requirements; The use of dynamic pricing techniques as postulated by Viglia and his team (2014). In this respect, it is sure that the firms have the capability to think on the changes in the conditions of the market to fix the price levels that generate for the optimal revenues on the composite travel market place (Overgoor & Van der Veen, 2019). Marketing Tools and Automation Benefits: Since there are Machines for the marketing strategy it is beneficial to know the buying behavior of the customers to target the audience. Promotional Communication and its effectiveness of an AI application Marketing application of artificial intelligence Some of the fields taking marketing applications of artificial intelligence in promotional communication include Companies with direct customer contact; Online newsletters Advertisements in forms and special offers; Social businesses. Translations serve a pivotal role in enhancing the relationship between the community and the tourists since language is not an obstructing factor facilitated by artificial intelligence. Some of the mobile applications and home appliances that can help in real time translation include; A number of mobile applications and home appliances about,, real time translation help in making communication more friendly, accessible, and nondiscriminatory therefore enhancing the quality of travel experience of tourists and visitor from other countries (Viglia et al ., 2014). With regard to this, automation that has embraced artificial intelligence enhance a variety of matters concerning operations within the hospitality industry. This encompasses contactless, self-service, technological, checking on the rooms, and even have a technological though mechanical butler. This listing is not all positive since it can predict a tremendous increase in functionality, warding off costs and most importantly an improvement in the lot of guests in the treatment side. We do acknowledge that the AI is applied in improving the security niche of the travelling as well as the hotel agentage entrepreneurship. They are as follows; Face recognition whereby there is an instance in airports, and hotels that have had a tight secure check replacing conventional methods of identification (Antonopoulos et al., 2020). These technologies are useful in improving the aspects of safety and security concerning the domain of traveling as well as the roads that connect to this particular domain. Artificial Intelligences make possible virtual or augmented world tourisms put at the disposal of the tourists first contacts with countries, lodging places, and points of interest. In Van et al., 2020 they pointed out that video centered tours, augmented reality assistants and games that mimic virtual visits help in encouraging better decisions and experiences when travelling. Self-driving cars is a feature that is associated with AI to push change to infrastructure type resembles a generalized business implication since it directly affects the tourism business. Self-driving cars or artificial intelligence in the automation of routes and other services with the smart mobility could be safer, as well as, promising and efficient means of transport thus reducing or limiting the use of conventional modes of transport. It is essential to combine the obtained data with a set of analytics supported by artificial intelligence, which assists various companies and places for tourism in decision-making. From the cross-sectional study by Overgoor et al., (2019), it is postulated that through application of big data, the industry entities are able to gain the wide endogenous views of the consumer tendencies and preferences, the market, and the organizational performances. It is also important to note that the approach enables the organisation to arrive at a much improved and shifted decision primarily based on the situations (Viglia et al., 2014). AI is also employed in rationalizing resource use and providing measures of addressing the environmental concerns that tourists encounter making tourism eco-friendly. They assist in controlling the number of tourists in order to share management of tourists within and out of the territories to prevent any incidences of overcrowding or degradations within crowded received areas often modified and developed by tourists. Fluctuations that are happening at the moment in relation to offering work and relationship between the ability to work from home and including traveling. Technological innovation in this case specifically aids in supporting telecommuting and the prospect of artificial intelligence in this aspect particularly enhances real-time access and other services to boost it. It has been reported that a large number of service sectors including the hospitality industry follows some of the trends in the market today such as Services for the Growing Population of Digitalk Nomads — By Van et al., 2020; AI is the process of transforming and upgrading the travel and hospitality industry through enhancing the quality of services for travelers and streamlining organizational processes. Technology also has future campuses, and thus it also shows that the AI element shall also be a primary component for evolving or impacting these sectors in the future as well as in the shaping of campuses for travelers as well as business as a more agile as well as informed solution to match requirements.

AI'S SIGNIFICANCE IN MEDICAL AND TOURISM EXPERIENCES

AI today signifies fresh growth in more fields than every other technology; its existence extends unendingly… even in the fields that it did not affect before (Barua et al., 2023) (Datta et al., 2019). Among all these domains, the domains of experiential, and medical tourism were among those which changed radically while the AI technologies & applications appeared in the industry. In recent years, AI became an inherent part of these sectors – it not only enhanced the efficiency and efficacy of the services provided but also raised the level of personalization and security that had impact on the transformation of the experience of travelling and carrying for the consumers (Overgoor et al., 2019). A new type of tourism involving explorations where tourists come across the indigenous people, their habitat, and culture or their art have hugely benefited from a paradigm shift through the practice of Artificial Intelligence. Lack of equal emphasis on innovation and improvement is seen in the following domains: The most noteworthy hopeful frontier in meeting changes is Recommendation systems emerging from Artificial Intelligence Algorithms (Barua et al., 2023). Through AI, complex data regarding travelling habits, activeness, and prior choices could be analyzed and integrated properly followed by suggesting recommendation regarding the actual preferences of a patient to the administrators (Ivanov et al., 2019) (Barua et al., 2024). It makes the whole goal of travelling much more satisfying and meaningful because, at its core, it is designed to ensure that the travelers engage in things that they would otherwise want to do or expect to do while travelling. Moreover, when it comes to the slogan AI as the key elements for effective organization of successful travels, it should be noted that virtual assistants have become a necessity for tourists (Antonova., 2022). This kind of virtual assistants are dependent on voice query recognition technologies, natural language processing and machineries and learning algorithms to listen and understand and respond by recommending services or answers to questions and all inquiries in a very efficient way. Consequently, the experiential tourism providers will originate much from employing the different AI based solutions to allow customers and travelers to get support that will make traveling less tiring (Kumari., 2021). Furthermore, and most importantly, the emergence of AI in the healthcare domain has influenced and altered the existence of medical tourism and the conventional systems of the health care delivery structures with better patients' results. As for the issue of implementing the higher form of artificial intelligence into the banking system, one of the most exclusive areas is related to the medical diagnosis. The latest developments in Computer Science: deep machine learning prove to be very efficient in the assessment of such pictures like the X-ray images, MRI, and CT scans as unveiled by Barua et al in their study in the year 2024. AI diagnostics assist in early identification of abnormality or existing but last known health conditions that might require the attention of the medical professionals and enable the initiation of appropriate actions or treatment procedures translating into minimal expansive diagnostics (Ivanov et al., 2019) (Jain et al., 2024). Thirdly, another significant component of the medical tourism industry is the appointment of artificial neural networks and big data analysis to assist in the evaluation of the treatment courses of action and probable outcomes for the patients. With the help of Big Data, programs can understand the complex information of a patient's history and general or hereditary health, and how specifically the body responds to the treatment that can be beyond the clinician's vision (Rane et al., 2023). This enables the healthcare provider to design one-of-a-kind practices for each patient to support them in indicating the correct dosages that would effectively cure their illnesses without causing deleterious effects. Besides, it can reveal the chances of any adversity or delay for the patient or possibly a relapse of the disease, so the preventive precaution measures required to protect the life of the patient can be arranged before medical tourism is opted (Ivars-Baidal et al., 2019).

Another concept that has received a boost from the use if AI in medical tourism is virtual healthcare care solutions. They also convey telemedicine technologies and artificial intelligent diagnostic tools for distant consultation and other (Samala et al., 2020; Singh et al., 2020). This appears helpful for medical tourists since they could have complications with the required health care in their home countries or precisely are comfortable with online communications as opposed to face-to-face consultations. People can even get doctor recommendations, be prescribed with medications, or even get remote check-ups; this removes spatial barriers to healthcare while at the same time increasing access to good healthcare (Barua., 2024) . Moreover, Artificial Intelligence integrated in robotics has improved the Surgical procedures which in practical sense, make medical tourism a noble success. Mechanized surgical frameworks combined with AI applications can be valuable in improving getting it done delicacy amid expressive surgeries; it can reduce the possibility of failure and improve patient's healing period (Ivanov et al., 2019). Besides, the use of Artificial Intelligence in robotics enables surgeries to be done via small incisions hence reduce on the potential of injuring the body tissues, not mentioning the pains that the patients may be forced to go through especially those who come from different countries for plastic surgery, cosmetic surgery and related procedures (Barua., 2024).

Along with enhancing the nature and accessibility of the medical services for the medical tourists, AI has also been employed in augmenting the safety measures present in such situations (Samala et al., 2020). Artificial intelligence-based risk assessment applications that perform a risk calculation can determine various probabilities and provide an analysis of the risks of travel, health, and possible risks from travel destinations (Kumari., 2021). Medical tourists can be more careful when approaching their travel destination and design their trips in a manner that would prevent any negative impact on their health; this will add to their safety and security during their travels (Ivanov et al., 2019). Nevertheless, the reality of the use of artificial intelligence in such applications as chatbots and virtual assistants can be very useful for medical tourists as they will receive necessary information and assistance at the moment. These devices powered by AI can provide such relevant information of the medical facilities, contact telephone numbers, local traffic information to the medical tourist who might not be conversant with the environment. Besides, with the application of the AI chatbots, the patients can get support in multiple languages hence they are not restricted by language when interacting with the care giving team and therefore the quality of care given to the clients is enhanced. Finally, based on the discussion above, it would be important to state that the roles that AI plays in both the experiential and medical tourism context are quite significant (Samala et al., 2020). Self-organized recommendation platforms and smart assistants in the field of experiential tourism, diagnostics and prognosis and virtual Health care in Medical Tourism field are clear evidence for the usage of next generation AI in a new paradigm transformation. Therefore, engaging in the implementation of the aforementioned AI technologies by the stakeholders of these industries will improve the quality, safety and availability of service to enhance global travel and health care experiences for people (Overgoor et al. 2019). Since the two domains of experiment and medical tourism have not embraced the application of AI up to the present time, the enhancement of AI in the future for the two fields is unmeasurable and is therefore expected to change the two fields positively.Top of Form

ARTIFICIAL INTELLIGENCE CHALLENGES IN THE TRAVEL INDUSTRY

Challenges that Artificial Intelligence poses to the travel industry are; Data security challenges, loss of employment as most jobs will be done by Artificial Intelligence and High capital investment is required during the initial stage of Artificial Intelligence. Still, the policies aimed at improving the protection of the client data that is considered so crucial with the increase in the use of information remains a moot issue as a policy concern. Hence, it could disturb the employee's working pattern and would require people to be trained for reskilling. To address these challenges, it is required to achieve a harmonization of the positive work of AI and address the ethical, social, and economic implications together with the coordination of AI planning and the principal strategies and ethical considerations given continuous shifts occurring in the context of the travel industry environment. Admittedly artificial intelligence is changing day by day but those who are not educated properly cannot take the best utilization of it (Reddy, 2006). Yet these restrictions have to be met and they shall be when called for by new technologies and solutions together with transforming regulatory environments. Nevertheless, the consequence of this outcome is the general alienation of man and labor with the development of AI and evoking the sentiment that AI will supplant human intellect following the emergence of many issues in various commercial domains. The major disadvantage of such services being managed by software is if there is a small occurrence of malware it brings a lot of havoc through the software as well as the service providers being affected. Indeed, they might be introduced as modern technology, as the next big thing that lots of people can adhere to, but small service providers can simply afford it because the given system significantly requires a major investment (Murphy et al., 2017). The last type of threat that prevents the setting up of the application of artificial intelligence is that of data security and safety. However, there are some factors or key issues that still emerge for example in what is considered very sensitive industries such as the military industry and the banking industries. This is why the following nations have not accepted the use of facial recognition technology due to privacy and data security complications even though they have adopted Blockchain technologies in the use of facial recognition software on data protection and security (Bowyer, 2004). On the one hand, chatbots and hotel services store prior buying and traveling history thus raising issues on data security and privacy breaches. That results in data security and privacy issues (Kannan and Bernoff, 2019). Therefore, it can be safely stated that the application of AI in the traveling business has unveiled new frontiers to the traveling business regarding efficiency, productivity, and customer satisfaction as well as the utilities of the business. However, at the same time, it is crucial to underline here that these advances in technology are not without challenges. Speaking of the challenges that the travel industry has to deal with, it is possible to distinguish the following ones: They are the things that cannot be left aside while speaking about ethical disputes about the travel industry unlike the financial or healthcare services to name a few; Apart from that, the impact on the workforce disruptions as the implementation of new technologies results in the creation of new position then firing the previous workforce

i. Data Privacy and Security:

That is why it is appropriate to outline several crucial questions that are being raised in connection with the gradual improvement of the application of AI in the sphere of the travel industry and data security. However, remembering that many aspects are gathered regarding individuals for personalized products and sales forecasts, it is necessary to pay close attention to data security. Its unwanted uses as well as leakage of client information necessitates the application of stringent computer security in travel companies (Elliott., 2022). Other steps in relation to these concerns are important and cover the promotion and endorsement of the correct implementation of the data rules and being compliant with the GDPR.

ii. Ethical Considerations:

The impact of these applications of artificial intelligence in moral terms, greatly affects the situated tourism industry. This is because computerized decision-making techniques have a bias that the program may have during its programming and the data that the computer uses or was trained on might not be fair hence reaching unfair and discriminating conclusions. AI effectiveness brings gains; therefore, in relation to making it fairly and equally for every gender to have a seamless experience and quality life, the situation must be observed, and ethical rules and modification of algorithms must be implemented (Mujtaba et al., 2019). The overall policies concerning artificial intelligence in the industry must radically embrace equity, accountability and transparency of the technology.

iii. Job Displacement and Workforce Reskilling:

The application of appropriate technologies in daily work involving the use of artificial intelligence (AI) evokes concerns on job threats specifically in the tourism industry. Organization work on customers services representatives, or data entry functions can become automated, may imply changes in the skills of workers. Industry and workplace need to continue to offer enough training and developmental opportunities in the place to ensure that people remain valuable in a future with advanced technologies (George et al. 2023). The implementation of CCSS is going to require the activism of both labor and cooperation from organizations such as companies, schools, and authorities.

iv. Initial Implementation Costs:

The implementation of AI into the tourism industry entails the commitment of rather-heavy capital investment on both physical assets, human resources, as well as the organisational culture that is inclined to technology innovation. Smaller and medium organizations experience various issues with the implementation of AI due to limited resources when attempting to incorporate AI into the organization's processes. It is significant to evaluate the benefits of the AI application that could turn into gross in the long run, and measure them against the initial costs of deploying AI (Tsolakis et al., 2023). This problem may be solved by launching collaborations campaigns and government grants to come up with affordable low-cost AI solutions.

v. User Trust and Acceptance:

AI deployment takes considerably huge capital investment on infrastructure, training and technology acceptance in the context of tourism. Issues like limited capital to implement the use of AI in the conduct of business transactions may be experienced by mid-sized firms. There is need to achieve stability in the characteristics that are exhibited by AI systems in the long run and the expenses of implementing the systems (Tsolakis et al., 2023). With the help of partnership initiatives, the support of authorities, as well as the creation of user-friendly AI tools, this problem can be tackled.

vi. Integration With Legacy Systems:

There is also a list of some popular industries in the tourism sector that utilize old equipment that cannot support the modern AI technology. The incorporation of said technologies into existing structures could prove to be cumbersome and potentially even problematic. Companies require the upgrading or replacement of ageing infrastructure which makes the integration of AI easier. When addressing the issue of integration and capitalizing on the AI functionality, one must think about the future and cooperate with the technology providers (Singh et al., 2023).

vii. Regulatory Compliance:

Future developments of the AI environment in the tourism sector cause questions concerning laws and norms. While the use of AI remains still far, authorities and regulators are in the process of building regulation regarding the application of AI in various spheres, especially the sphere of travelling. The requirements needed in the business must be achieved as the business community faces a dynamic cost environment and fulfils the present and new standards. To ensure compatibility of technology, moral issues and to formulate the necessary regulations, there must be a symbiosis of business interests and the government (Adams et al., 2020).

viii. Managing Overdependence on AI:

However, concerning being positive to AI and possibilities made available by it, there is a great danger to develop over dependence on the Internet and barely consume people's discretion and search for better solutions than such systems offer. Stark from the analysis is the assertion that the business community must take an active role not to have a dilution of relations with clients in aspiration to output efficiencies when engaging newer technologies such as AI to perform their tasks. Just as important, it accepts that these are utilized so that improving human capabilities is facilitated rather than diminished AI's role, as such, for adopting a positive and selective approach to the tourism sector (Glikson et al., 2020). Some of the impacts which are associated with adoption of Artificial Intelligence technologies in the tourism industry are the following; Since the challenges of adopting Artificial Intelligence technologies in the tourism industry are numerous, we can regard them as part of the big picture. Issues such as data privacy, ethical issues, and employment issues can only be addressed through intervention, by the major stakeholders which comprise industries, government, and employees (Choung et al., 2023). These challenges are as follows: On this perspective, the tourism sector can address these challenges in the following ways: Proper use of AI technology for its activities, employee training for these sectors and use of AI technology was more transparent to its users.

AI'S POTENTIAL USES IN TRAVEL AND TOURISM AND FUTURE PERSPECTIVES

The future in the increasing automation of processes is AI which can become the reality in the travel and tourism industry where they can maybe implement the positive effects in traveling and in acquiring tourism services. Hence, in the same way, it remains an object of continuing focus as a relatively recent development; it shall gradually become a larger participant in the making of the industries' future. Individual trips as an application in the future is an application that has not been seen in the market before and was newly created by the further development of individual offers (Barua., 2024). It means that to create specific learning experiences for every single travel customer, these utilitarian experiences have to be worked with, such as the prior customer itineraries, the needs, and the circumstances of the customers. This means that lodges, suggestions for places that one has been to before, new places that none of us have been to before, places to play, and places to stay are three things that AI is going to transform. Each time facial recognition technologies are rerouted because of matters of concern causing some insecurity of data, then these matters might in later days be handled by reliable blockchain characteristics likely to improve the security of data (Leong, 2019). Therefore, cleaning robots may welcome the visitors of hotels and lead them to their rooms, carry their belongings, offer the abovementioned, etc, However, only a dozen hotels around the world use such solutions today (Barua et al., 2022) (Yang et al., 2020).

Some of the reasons that are provided by some people are the following: another argument could be made that the virtual assistants that are AI-based are also projected to become even more complex for managing the travel arrangements process and are required to use fluent natural language in all phases. Nearly all of these assistants shall assist in booking and response to such questions; In addition, they shall decide in real time depending on the types of travelers, the weather, and the events in the destination country. Such a highly active type of assistance will go a long way in ensuring that even the basic processes such as the one involved in traveling are brought back to what they are, natural. Also, we consider the fact that, with the proposed AI algorithms, the impact on the efficiency of the pricing strategies and the demand forecast will remain high. Any other intricate ML algorithm, say, for instance, would capture multiple such data signals and business cycles, demand & supply patterns, etc., as necessary to exercise optimal control over the price mechanism and, thus, achieve the best value addition and resource mobilization (Barua., 2024). Thus, such usage of said predictive capability will play a major role in helping the industry respond or adapt relatively fast to any change that may happen in market or consumer characteristics.

The AI-assisted self-learning chatbots will naturally operate in the environment of customs services and will be expected to mimic humans. AI Interpretation; The interpretation of the technical aspect of AI; Enhanced NLP techniques will impact the functionality of the chatbots to include elaborative and complex queries of support thus enhancing customer care services. In addition, the forms of interpreting services are to be improved and enhanced by AI while translating between individuals in different fields, traveling, and dwelling. It will also continue to develop or evolve in other spheres or facets of Artificial Intelligence popularly known as AI like augmented reality or Virtual Reality (Barua., 2024). It is such technologies that will give persons in their journeys a feel of what such places look like and some of the likely incidents on the move. For example, instead of using pictures and descriptions to display the features of guestrooms, the hotels will develop AR & VR applications to be named walk through the guestrooms while instead of coming up with a detailed description of the form of culture, the latter will give the customer a reality of culture events.

Thus, it can be stated that the further evolution of applying artificial intelligence in the TR & T context is quite stable: new and enhanced concepts appear and are to recast the industry even further, increasing customization, activating smart conversation, and ensuring more innovative solutions. In the future, AI will still be present in the background to bring even more efficiency to various companies and travelers, increasing the level of efficiency in the travel market more than it are already present today. All these are certain to be established as their implementation is likely to define the competitively of the market other than giving vacationing enthusiasts an idea of how to have it best shortly.

CONCLUSION

The future in the continuously developing automated processes is AI which can be a reality for the travel and tourism industry where they can perhaps use the positive aspect of traveling and getting the tourism services. Therefore, similar to this, they would remain an object of continuing interest being a subject of rather recent emergence; it shall play a proportionately larger role in writing the future of the industries. This, individual trips as an application in the future is an application that has not been existing in the market nowadays and was developed based on the individual applications from the existing offers. It means that to ensure and generate specific learning-travel learning experiences for any individual travel customer the organization has to work with these utilitarian experiences some of which include; the prior customer itineraries, their needs, and circumstances. This implies that things such as lodges suggestions of places that one has visited before, places that none of us have visited before places of play, and places to stay are three things where AI is going to reshape. Every time facial recognition technologies are rerouted due to matters of concern that give some measure of insecurity to data, then such matters might in later days be managed by secure blockchain characteristics, which are most likely to enhance the security of data (Leong, 2019). Thus, it means that the cleaning robots could greet the visitors of the hotel and lead them to their rooms and carry their things, offering all the above mentioned, etc., However, to date, only twelve hotels use such solutions in the whole world (Barua et al., 2022) (Reddy., 2006) (Yang et al., 2020).

Some of the reasons that are provided by some people are the following: another perspective could be argued that the other kind of virtual assistants that are based on artificial intelligence is expected to get even more sophisticated regarding the travel arrangements process and to employ the fluent natural language in all the stages. Almost all these assistants shall help in the booking and the response to such questions as which; Moreover, they should 'book' and decide depending on the type of travelers, the weather, or events in the destination country, all in real time. A highly active type like this will contribute to a large extent in helping to lessen the complexity of executing the simplest of traveling processes down to their very essence, natural. However, it is also worth noting that compared to an initial assessment, the proposed AI algorithms as well as their pace when it comes to further penetration and their effects on the form and efficiency of the aforementioned pricing strategies and the aggregate demand forecast are still rather high. Any other complex ML algorithm, for example, would be able to extract multiple such data signals and business cycles, demand and supply patterns, etc., if required for its further control over the pricing mechanism to achieve the maximum value addition and resource realization. Therefore, usage of said predictive capability within such a context will be a key factor towards ensuring that the industry responds, or adapts, rather fast to any change that may occur with regards to either market or consumer characteristics.

The concept of self-learning chatbots that are helped by AI will logically work within the sphere of customs services, and as such will be expected to behave in the same way as humans. AI Translation; The translation of the technical feature of AI and improved NLP features will affect the capabilities of the chatbots to extend them up to elaborate and naïve inquiries of support therefore promoting customer-client relations services. Second, the forms of interpreting services must be evolved and upgraded by AI when and if interpreting between people in different fields, during traveling and dwelling. It will also continue to be developed or expand in other spheres or facets of Artificial Intelligence fussy referred to as AI such as augmented reality or Virtual Reality. It is such technologies that will enable the persons on their journeys to have a mere glimpse of such places and some of the likely incidences on the move. For instance, instead of using pictures and descriptions of the guestrooms' features, the hotels will create an AR & VR application – virtual tour of the guestrooms while instead of the hotel providing a detailed description of the form of culture, the latter offer the customer reality of culture events.

Thus, it can be stated that the further evolution of applying artificial intelligence in the TR & T context is quite stable: New and more superior ideas emerge and are to reshape the industry even further, raise individualization, incite smart talk, and guarantee more creative solutions. In the future AI will still operate in the background thus contributing to enhancing the efficiency of various companies as well as the travelers resulting in an even higher efficiency level in the travel industry than is already witnessed currently. All these are sure to be set with certainty as it is anticipated that their implementation will present the competitively of the market other than providing vacationing enthusiasts an insight on how to have it best in the near future.

CONFLICTS OF INTEREST

The authors declare that there are no conflicts of interest regarding the publication of this chapter.

FUNDING

No funding has been provided for this work.

ETHICAL APPROVAL

Not required.

ACKNOWLEDGMENT

The authors would like thanks to Mrs. Nibedita Bardhan for language proof reading.

REFERENCES

Adams, J., & Hagras, H. (2020, July). A type-2 fuzzy logic approach to explainable AI for regulatory compliance, fair customer outcomes and market stability in the global financial sector. In *2020 IEEE international conference on fuzzy systems (FUZZ-IEEE)* (pp. 1-8). IEEE. 10.1109/FUZZ48607.2020.9177542

Aldoseri, A., Al-Khalifa, K., & Hamouda, A. (2023). Re-Thinking Data Strategy and Integration for Artificial intelligence: Concepts, opportunities, and challenges. *Applied Sciences (Basel, Switzerland)*, 13(12), 7082. 10.3390/app13127082

Alin, L., & Hasan, A. (2019). The impact of industrial revolution to marketing. *Electronic Research Journal of Social Sciences and Humanities*, 1(4), 114–122.

Antonopoulos, I., Robu, V., Couraud, B., Kirli, D., Norbu, S., Kiprakis, A., Flynn, D., Elizondo-Gonzalez, S., & Wattam, S. (2020). Artificial intelligence and machine learning approaches to energy demand-side response: A systematic review. *Renewable & Sustainable Energy Reviews*, 130, 109899. 10.1016/j.rser.2020.109899

Antonova, A. (2022). How do chatbots affect customer satisfaction within Russian banks? (Doctoral dissertation, Dublin, National College of Ireland).

Barua, R. (2024a). Advanced Biomimetic Compound Continuum Robot for Minimally Invasive Surgical Applications. In T. Choudhury, A. Mary X., S. Chowdhury, C. Karthik, & C. Evangeline (Eds.), Modeling, Simulation, and Control of AI Robotics and Autonomous Systems (pp. 213-231). IGI Global. 10.4018/979-8-3693-1962-8.ch013

Barua, R. (2024b). An In-Depth Exploration of AI and Humanoid Robotics' Role in Contemporary Healthcare. In V. Grover, B. Balusamy, N. M.K., V. Anand, & M. Milanova (Eds.), *Approaches to Human-Centered AI in Healthcare* (pp. 42-61). IGI Global.

Barua, R. (2024c). The Emerging Role of Artificial Intelligence in Organ-on-a-Chip (OOAC) Biomedical Devices. In Reshaping Healthcare with Cutting-Edge Biomedical Advancements (pp. 369-381). IGI Global.

Barua, R. (2024d). Exploring Artificial Intelligence in Evolving Healthcare Environments: A Comprehensive Analysis. In Shah, I., & Sial, Q. (Eds.), *Advances in Computational Intelligence for the Healthcare Industry 4.0* (pp. 123–138). IGI Global. 10.4018/979-8-3693-2333-5.ch006

Barua, R. (2024e). An Investigation of AI Techniques for Detecting Kidney Stones in CT Scan Images Through Advanced Image Processing. In Sharma, A., Chanderwal, N., Tyagi, S., Upadhyay, P., & Tyagi, A. (Eds.), *Enhancing Medical Imaging with Emerging Technologies* (pp. 133–150). IGI Global. 10.4018/979-8-3693-5261-8.ch008

Barua, R., Das, D., & Biswas, N. (2024). Revolutionizing Drug Discovery With Artificial Intelligence: Enhancing Efficiency, Addressing Ethical Concerns, and Overcoming Limitations. In V. Grover, B. Balusamy, N. M.K., V. Anand, & M. Milanova (Eds.), *Approaches to Human-Centered AI in Healthcare* (pp. 62-85). IGI Global.

Barua, R., & Das, S. (2022). Improvements of virtual and augmented reality for advanced treatments in urology. In *Emerging Advancements for Virtual and Augmented Reality in Healthcare* (pp. 117–131). IGI global. 10.4018/978-1-7998-8371-5.ch008

Barua, R., Das, S., &Mondal, J. (2023). Emerging Applications of Artificial Intelligence (AI) and Machine Learning (ML) in Modern Urology. *Exploring the Convergence of Computer and Medical Science Through Cloud Healthcare*, 117-133.

Barua, R., & Datta, S. (2023). Artificial intelligence in modern medical science: A promising practice. In *Recent Developments in Machine and Human Intelligence* (pp. 1–12). IGI Global. 10.4018/978-1-6684-9189-8.ch001

Barua, R., & Datta, S. (2024). An Extensive Evaluation of New Federated Learning Approaches for COVID-19 Identification. In Hassan, A., Prasad, V., Bhattacharya, P., Dutta, P., & Damaševičius, R. (Eds.), *Pioneering Smart Healthcare 5.0 with IoT, Federated Learning, and Cloud Security* (pp. 246–257). IGI Global.

Barua, R., Datta, S., Datta, P., & Roychowdhury, A. (2022). Study and application of machine learning methods in modern additive manufacturing processes. In *Applications of Artificial Intelligence in Additive Manufacturing* (pp. 75–95). IGI Global. 10.4018/978-1-7998-8516-0.ch004

Barua, R., Datta, S., & Sarkar, A. (2023). Artificial intelligence and robotics-based minimally invasive surgery: Innovations and future perceptions. In *Contemporary Applications of Data Fusion for Advanced Healthcare Informatics* (pp. 350–368). IGI Global. 10.4018/978-1-6684-8913-0.ch015

Barua, R., & Mondal, J. (2023). Study of the Current Trends of CAD (Computer-Aided Detection) in Modern Medical Imaging. *Machine Learning and AI Techniques in Interactive Medical Image Analysis*, 35-50.

Bowyer, K. W. (2004). Face recognition technology: Security versus privacy. *IEEE Technology and Society Magazine*, 23(1), 9–19. 10.1109/MTAS.2004.1273467

Bulchand-Gidumal, J., William Secin, E., O'Connor, P., & Buhalis, D. (2023). Artificial intelligence's impact on hospitality and tourism marketing: Exploring key themes and addressing challenges. *Current Issues in Tourism*, 1–18.

Chawla, S. (2019). 7 Successful applications of AI & machine learning in the travel industry.

Choung, H., David, P., & Ross, A. (2023). Trust in AI and Its Role in the Acceptance of AI Technologies. *International Journal of Human-Computer Interaction*, 39(9), 1727–1739. 10.1080/10447318.2022.2050543

Datta, S., Barua, R., & Das, J. (2019). Application of artificial intelligence in modern healthcare system. *Alginates-recent uses of this natural polymer*.

Di Salvo, A., & Arcoraci, A. (2020). Human connections. Design interactive artefacts through narration and speculation. *AGATHÓN| International Journal of Architecture. Art and Design*, 8, 254–261.

Elliott, D., & Soifer, E. (2022). AI technologies, privacy, and security. *Frontiers in Artificial Intelligence*, 5, 826737. 10.3389/frai.2022.82673735493613

George, A. S., George, A. H., & Martin, A. G. (2023). ChatGPT and the Future of Work: A Comprehensive Analysis of AI's Impact on Jobs and Employment. *Partners Universal International Innovation Journal*, 1(3), 154–186.

Glikson, E., & Woolley, A. W. (2020). Human trust in artificial intelligence: Review of empirical research. *The Academy of Management Annals*, 14(2), 627–660. 10.5465/annals.2018.0057

Gupta, S., Modgil, S., Lee, C. K., & Sivarajah, U. (2023). The future is yesterday: Use of AI-driven facial recognition to enhance value in the travel and tourism industry. *Information Systems Frontiers*, 25(3), 1179–1195. 10.1007/s10796-022-10271-835529102

He, M., Liu, B., & Li, Y. (2023). Tourist inspiration: How the wellness tourism experience inspires tourist engagement. *Journal of Hospitality & Tourism Research (Washington, D.C.)*, 47(7), 1115–1135. 10.1177/10963480211026376

Ivanov, S., & Webster, C. (Eds.). (2019). *Robots, artificial intelligence, and service automation in travel, tourism and hospitality*. Emerald Publishing Limited. 10.1108/9781787566873

Ivars-Baidal, J. A., Celdrán-Bernabeu, M. A., Mazón, J. N., & Perles-Ivars, Á. F. (2019). Smart destinations and the evolution of ICTs: A new scenario for destination management? *Current Issues in Tourism*, 22(13), 1581–1600. 10.1080/13683500.2017.1388771

Jain, N., Barua, R., Waidi, Y. O., & Datta, S. (2024). Nanowires for Bio-Sensing Applications. In Kulkarni, S., Kharisov, B., Haghi, A., & Srivastava, V. (Eds.), *Next Generation Materials for Sustainable Engineering* (pp. 205–219). IGI Global. 10.4018/979-8-3693-1306-0.ch010

Jiang, C., Xv, X., & Zhu, Z. (2021, September). Research on the Construction of Chinese Hotel Experiential Marketing Model Under the Background of AI. In *2021 International Conference on Financial Management and Economic Transition (FMET 2021)* (pp. 470-475). Atlantis Press. 10.2991/aebmr.k.210917.071

Kannan, P. V., & Bernoff, J. (2019). The future of customer service is AI-Human collaboration. *MIT Sloan Management Review*.

Kasneci, E., Seßler, K., Küchemann, S., Bannert, M., Dementieva, D., Fischer, F., Gasser, U., Groh, G., Günnemann, S., Hüllermeier, E., Krusche, S., Kutyniok, G., Michaeli, T., Nerdel, C., Pfeffer, J., Poquet, O., Sailer, M., Schmidt, A., Seidel, T., & Kasneci, G. (2023). ChatGPT for good? On opportunities and challenges of large language models for education. *Learning and Individual Differences*, 103, 102274. 10.1016/j.lindif.2023.102274

Koo, C., Xiang, Z., Gretzel, U., & Sigala, M. (2021). Artificial intelligence (AI) and robotics in travel, hospitality and leisure. *Electronic Markets*, 31(3), 473–476. 10.1007/s12525-021-00494-z35603226

Kumari, S. (2021). Interplay of AI-Driven Maritime Logistics: An In-Depth Research into Port Management, Advanced Operations Automation, and CRM Integration for Optimized Performance and Efficiency. *ESP Journal of Engineering and Technology Advancements*, 1(1), 1–5.

Leong, B. (2019). Facial recognition and the future of privacy: I always feel like… somebody's watching me. *Bulletin of the Atomic Scientists*, 75(3), 109–115. 10.1080/00963402.2019.1604886

Liu, X., Shin, H., & Burns, A. C. (2021). Examining the impact of luxury brand's social media marketing on customer engagement: Using big data analytics and natural language processing. *Journal of Business Research*, 125, 815–826. 10.1016/j.jbusres.2019.04.042

Ma, Y., Wang, Z., Yang, H., & Yang, L. (2020). Artificial intelligence applications in the development of autonomous vehicles: A survey. *IEEE/CAA Journal of AutomaticaSinica, 7*(2), 315-329.

Mujtaba, D. F., & Mahapatra, N. R. (2019, November). Ethical considerations in AI-based recruitment. In *2019 IEEE International Symposium on Technology and Society (ISTAS)* (pp. 1-7). IEEE.

Murphy, J., Hofacker, C., & Gretzel, U. (2017). Dawning of the age of robots in hospitality and tourism: Challenges for teaching and research. *European Journal of Tourism Research*, 15, 104–111. 10.54055/ejtr.v15i.265

Neubig, S., Baecker, J., Gehring, N., Hein, A., Weking, J., &Krcmar, H. (2022). Data-driven Initiatives of Destinations Supporting Sustainable Tourism.

Omoge, A. P., Gala, P., & Horky, A. (2022). Disruptive technology and AI in the banking industry of an emerging market. *International Journal of Bank Marketing*, 40(6), 1217–1247. 10.1108/IJBM-09-2021-0403

Overgoor, G., Chica, M., Rand, W., & Weishampel, A. (2019). Letting the computers take over: Using AI to solve marketing problems. *California Management Review*, 61(4), 156–185. 10.1177/0008125619859318

Peranzo, P. (2019). *AI assistant: the future of travel industry with the increase of artificial intelligence*. Imaginovation. Imagination Turns to Innovation.

Prentice, C., Weaven, S., & Wong, I. A. (2020). Linking AI quality performance and customer engagement: The moderating effect of AI preference. *International Journal of Hospitality Management*, 90, 102629. 10.1016/j.ijhm.2020.102629

Rane, N., Choudhary, S., & Rane, J. (2023). Sustainable tourism development using leading-edge Artificial Intelligence (AI), Blockchain, Internet of Things (IoT), Augmented Reality (AR) and Virtual Reality (VR) technologies. *Blockchain, Internet of Things (IoT), Augmented Reality (AR) and Virtual Reality (VR) technologies.*

Reddy, R. (2006). Robotics and intelligent systems in support of society. *IEEE Intelligent Systems*, 21(3), 24–31. 10.1109/MIS.2006.57

Samala, N., Katkam, B. S., Bellamkonda, R. S., & Rodriguez, R. V. (2020). Impact of AI and robotics in the tourism sector: a critical insight. *Journal of Tourism Futures, 8*(1), 73-87.

Saulat, A. (2018). Four ways AI is re-imagining the future of travel. Mindtree. com.

Sharma, S., Rawal, Y. S., Soni, H., & Batabyal, D. (2023, February). Technological Impacts of AI on Hospitality and Tourism Industry. In *Proceedings of International Conference on Data Science and Applications: ICDSA 2022,* Volume 1 (pp. 71-78). Singapore: Springer Nature Singapore. 10.1007/978-981-19-6631-6_6

Singh, N., & Adhikari, D. (2023). Challenges and Solutions in Integrating AI with Legacy Inventory Systems. *International Journal for Research in Applied Science and Engineering Technology*, 11(12), 609–613. 10.22214/ijraset.2023.57376

Singh, S. K., Rathore, S., & Park, J. H. (2020). Blockiotintelligence: A blockchain-enabled intelligent IoT architecture with artificial intelligence. *Future Generation Computer Systems*, 110, 721–743. 10.1016/j.future.2019.09.002

Tavakoli, M., Faraji, A., Vrolijk, J., Molavi, M., Mol, S. T., & Kismihók, G. (2022). An AI-based open recommender system for personalized labor market driven education. *Advanced Engineering Informatics*, 52, 101508. 10.1016/j.aei.2021.101508

Thilagavathy, R., Veeramani, T., & Ramakrishna, B. (2019, March). Role of Augmented Reality and Virtual Reality in Digital World. In *2019 Fifth International Conference on Science Technology Engineering and Mathematics (ICONSTEM)* (Vol. 1, pp. 179-186). IEEE. 10.1109/ICONSTEM.2019.8918727

Tsolakis, N., Schumacher, R., Dora, M., & Kumar, M. (2023). Artificial intelligence and blockchain implementation in supply chains: A pathway to sustainability and data monetisation? *Annals of Operations Research*, 327(1), 157–210. 10.1007/s10479-022-04785-235755830

Van, N. T. T., Vrana, V., Duy, N. T., Minh, D. X. H., Dzung, P. T., Mondal, S. R., & Das, S. (2020). The role of human–machine interactive devices for post-COVID-19 innovative sustainable tourism in Ho Chi Minh City, Vietnam. *Sustainability (Basel)*, 12(22), 9523. 10.3390/su12229523

Viglia, G., Furlan, R., & Ladron-de-Guevara, A. (2014). Please, talk about it! When hotel popularity boosts preferences. *International Journal of Hospitality Management*, 42, 155–164. 10.1016/j.ijhm.2014.07.001

VigneshSaravanan, K., JothiThilaga, P., Kavipriya, S., &Vijayalakshmi, K. (2023). Data Protection and Security Enhancement in Cyber-Physical Systems Using AI and Blockchain. In *AI Models for Blockchain-Based Intelligent Networks in IoT Systems: Concepts, Methodologies, Tools, and Applications* (pp. 285-325). Cham: Springer International Publishing.

Wei, J., & Wang, R. (2022, December). Application of Artificial Intelligence in the Development of Media Integration under the Background of Smart Media. In *2022 International Symposium on Advances in Informatics, Electronics and Education (ISAIEE)* (pp. 360-364). IEEE. 10.1109/ISAIEE57420.2022.00081

Xiao, T. (2021, December). Research on Overcoming about Language Barriers of AI Machine Translation replacing Interpreting under Information Technology. In *2021 International Conference on Aviation Safety and Information Technology* (pp. 12-20). 10.1145/3510858.3510865

Yang, L., Henthorne, T. L., & George, B. (2020). Artificial intelligence and robotics technology in the hospitality industry: Current applications and future trends. *Digital transformation in business and society: Theory and cases*, 211-228.

Zhang, Y., & Qi, S. (2019). User experience study: the service expectation of hotel guests to the utilization of ai-based service robot in full-service hotels. *HCI in Business, Government and Organizations. eCommerce and Consumer Behavior: 6th International Conference, HCIBGO 2019, Held as Part of the 21st HCI International Conference, HCII 2019, Orlando, FL, USA, July 26-31, 2019Proceedings*, 21(Part I), 350–366.

KEY TERMS AND DEFINITIONS

AI: Computer programs that learn from data, spot patterns, and make judgments are referred to as artificial intelligence (AI) systems. It includes natural language processing, machine learning, and problem-solving skills. By empowering machines to carry out tasks, anticipate outcomes, and adjust to new data, it promotes progress in a variety of industries.

Chatbots: Some information systems known as are friendly, created, and coded to communicate with the users through natural language processes. Another way that employers use artificial intelligence is in the complementary of various actions, addressing questions together with communication via the web in social networks, native applications, and sites. In the present days, chatbots are expected to improve the selling activities, the degree of the customers' and users' satisfaction in various types of enterprises.

Customized: "Customized" is used to point when goods, services, or experiences are modified or made unique in accordance with the need or want of an individual. It is obvious that in matching products and solutions with customers, customer satisfaction levels will be higher since customers will have found something that is meaningful for their lives. Personalization is widely practiced in various industries, technology, fashion sectors, services, etc.

Marketing: Marketing profession is a managerial activity aimed at creating awareness among the consumers, generating interest among the target market, creating a base of loyal customers and facilitating sales of products and service. As much as it is a concept, marketing mix also includes activities such as branding, market analysis, advertisement, and communication strategy. The best way in which marketing can be done is by identifying and meeting the customer needs, augmenting the sales and building a brand image.

Tourism: Temporary migration which can be defined as the movement of people to other places for holidays, business purposes or any other related reason for they stay in other accommodations, commute or engage in other activities instead of in their home environments.

Compilation of References

Abdulwahid, A. H., Pattnaik, M., Palav, M. R., Babu, S. T., Manoharan, G., & Selvi, G. P. (2023, April). Library Management System Using Artificial Intelligence. In *2023 Eighth International Conference on Science Technology Engineering and Mathematics (ICONSTEM)* (pp. 1-7). IEEE.

Abrokwah-Larbi, K. (2023). The role of generative artificial intelligence (GAI) in customer personalisation (CP) development in SMEs: A theoretical framework and research propositions. *Industrial Artificial Intelligence*, 1(1), 11. 10.1007/s44244-023-00012-4

Adams, J., & Hagras, H. (2020, July). A type-2 fuzzy logic approach to explainable AI for regulatory compliance, fair customer outcomes and market stability in the global financial sector. In *2020 IEEE international conference on fuzzy systems (FUZZ-IEEE)* (pp. 1-8). IEEE. 10.1109/FUZZ48607.2020.9177542

Addis, C., & Kutar, M. (2019). AI Management An Exploratory Survey of the Influence of GDPR and FAT Principles. *2019 IEEE SmartWorld, Ubiquitous Intelligence & Computing, Advanced & Trusted Computing, Scalable Computing & Communications, Cloud & Big Data Computing, Internet of People and Smart City Innovation (SmartWorld/SCALCOM/UIC/ATC/CBDCom/IOP/SCI)*, 342–347. 10.1109/SmartWorld-UIC-ATC-SCALCOM-IOP-SCI.2019.00102

Addy, W. A., Ajayi-Nifise, A. O., Bello, B. G., Tula, S. T., Odeyemi, O., & Falaiye, T. (2024). Transforming financial planning with AI-driven analysis: A review and application insights. *World Journal of Advanced Engineering Technology and Sciences*, 11(1), 240–257. 10.30574/wjaets.2024.11.1.0053

Addy, W. A., Ajayi-Nifise, A. O., Bello, B. G., Tula, S. T., Odeyem, O., & Falaiye, T. (2024). Algorithmic Trading and AI: A Review of Strategies and Market Impact. *World Journal of Advanced Engineering Technology and Sciences*, 11(1), 258–267. 10.30574/wjaets.2024.11.1.0054

Adetayo, A. J. (2024). Reimagining learning through AI art: The promise of DALL-E and MidJourney for education and libraries. *Library Hi Tech News*. Advance online publication. 10.1108/LHTN-01-2024-0005

Adrid Indaryanto, B. D. (2023, December). The growing use and impact of artificial intelligence technologies in the tourism industry. *Sustainable Engineering and Innovation*, 5(2), 189–204. 10.37868/sei.v5i2.id238

Adula, M., & Kant, S. (2022). Interpretative Phenomenological Perceptional Study of Women Entrepreneurs Facing Challenges in Entrepreneurial Activity in the Horn of Africa. *Journal of Entrepreneurship, Management, and Innovation*, 4(2), 321–335.

Adula, M., Kant, S., & Birbirsa, Z. A. (2022). Systematic Literature Review on Human Resource Management Effect on Organization Perceived organizational support. *Annals of Human Resource Management Research*, 2(2), 131–146.

Adula, M., Kant, S., & Birbirsa, Z. A. (2023). Qualitative Analysis with MAXQDA Approach: HRM Practices effect on Organization Perceived organizational support with Mediation of Employee Work Attitude in Textile Industries of Ethiopia. *Advanced Qualitative Research*, 1(1), 1–14.

Agarwal, A. (2022). AI adoption by human resource management: A study of its antecedents and impact on HR system effectiveness. *Foresight*, 67–81.

Aggarwal, N., & Singh, K. B. (2024). Evolution and Adoption of Conversational Artificial Intelligence in the Banking Industry. *Conversational Artificial Intelligence*, 85-93.

Ahmad, A. Y. B., Tiwari, A., Nayeem, M. A., Biswal, B. K., Satapathy, D. P., Kulshreshtha, K., & Bordoloi, D. (2024). Artificial Intelligence Perspective Framework of the Smart Finance and Accounting Management Model. *International Journal of Intelligent Systems and Applications in Engineering*, 12(4s), 586–594.

Akmaeva, R., Arykbaev, R., Epifanova, N., & Glinchevskiy, E. 2020. Influence of digitalization upon formation of corporate strategy and new business models of modern organizations. In SHS Web of Conferences (Vol. 89, p. 03003). *EDP Sciences*. DOI: 10.1051/shsconf/20208903003

Akpamah, P., & Matkó, A. (2021). Information Technology deployment in Human Resource Management: A case study in deprived regions. *International Review of Applied Sciences and Engineering*, 13(1), 1–10. 10.1556/1848.2021.00278

Akshay Kulkarni, A. S. (2023). *Applied Generative AI for Beginners Practical Knowledge on Diffusion Models, ChatGPT, and Other LLMs*. Apress. 10.1007/978-1-4842-9994-4

Al-Amin, M., Shazed Ali, M., Salam, A., Khan, A., Ali, A., Ullah, A., Alam, N., & Chowdhury, S. K. (2024). History of generative Artificial Intelligence (AI) chatbots: past, present, and future development.

Al-Awar, M. S., Al-Habeet, A., & Gafer, A., Al-Amery, B., Edrees, W. H., & Al-Asbahi, A. (2022). Job satisfaction at clinical laboratories in Sana'a hospitals, Yemen, using the application of Herzberg's two-factor theory of motivation. *Al- Razi University. Journal for Medical Sciences*, 6(1).

Al-Dmour, R. H. (2020). The influence of HRIS usage on employee performance and mediating effects of employee engagement in five-star hotels in Jordan. *International Journal of Information Systems in the Service Sector*, 12(3), 1–18. 10.4018/IJISSS.2020070101

Aldoseri, A., Al-Khalifa, K., & Hamouda, A. (2023). Re-Thinking Data Strategy and Integration for Artificial intelligence: Concepts, opportunities, and challenges. *Applied Sciences (Basel, Switzerland)*, 13(12), 7082. 10.3390/app13127082

Alex Rajesh G., & Florence Sheeba J. (2022). A Study on Exploring Perceptions of Emotional Intelligence among Educators. *IJFANS International Journal of Food and Nutritional Sciences*, ISSN PRINT 2319-1775 Online 2320-7876.

Ali Quaosar, G. M. A., & Rahman, M. (2021). Human Resource Information Systems (HRIS) of Developing Countries in 21st Century: Review and Prospects. *Journal of Human Resource and Sustainability Studies*, 09(03), 470–483. 10.4236/jhrss.2021.93030

Ali, I., Mughal, N., Khan, Z. H., Ahmed, J., & Mujtaba, G. (2022). Resume Classification System using Natural Language Processing and Machine Learning Techniques. *Mehran University Research Journal of Engineering and Technology*, 41(1), 65–79. 10.22581/muet1982.2201.07

Alin, L., & Hasan, A. (2019). The impact of industrial revolution to marketing. *Electronic Research Journal of Social Sciences and Humanities*, 1(4), 114–122.

Almansour, M. (2023). Artificial intelligence and resource optimization: A study of Fintech start-ups. *Resources Policy*, 80, 103250. 10.1016/j.resourpol.2022.103250

Almeida, I. (2023). *Artificial Intelligence Fundamentals for Business Leaders: Up to Date With Generative AI*. Now Next Later AI.

Alpaydın, E. (2014). *Introduction to Machine Learning*. The MIT Press.

Alqurayn, A., Kulendran, N., & Ihalanayake, R. (2024). An event study of potential insider trading in the Saudi stock market. *Cogent Economics & Finance*, 12(1), 2367368. 10.1080/23322039.2024.2367368

Alwahedi, F., Aldhaheri, A., Ferrag, M. A., Battah, A., & Tihanyi, N. (2024). Machine learning techniques for IoT security: Current research and future vision with generative AI and large language models. *Internet of Things and Cyber-Physical Systems*.

Alzahrani, R. A., & Aljabri, M. (2022). AI-based techniques for Ad click fraud detection and prevention: Review and research directions. *Journal of Sensor and Actuator Networks*, 12(1), 4. 10.3390/jsan12010004

Anderson, D., Lees, B., & Avery, B. 2015, June. Reviewing the literature using the Thematic Analysis Grid. In European Conference on Research Methodology for Business and Management Studies. Valetta, Malta: *Academic Conferences and Publishing International* (pp. 455-457).

Androjna, A., Brcko, T., Pavic, I., & Greidanus, H. (2020). Assessing Cyber Challenges of Maritime Navigation. *Journal of Marine Science and Engineering*, 8(10), 776. 10.3390/jmse8100776

Antonopoulos, I., Robu, V., Couraud, B., Kirli, D., Norbu, S., Kiprakis, A., Flynn, D., Elizondo-Gonzalez, S., & Wattam, S. (2020). Artificial intelligence and machine learning approaches to energy demand-side response: A systematic review. *Renewable & Sustainable Energy Reviews*, 130, 109899. 10.1016/j.rser.2020.109899

Antonova, A. (2022). How do chatbots affect customer satisfaction within Russian banks? (Doctoral dissertation, Dublin, National College of Ireland).

Apsilyam, N. M., Shamsudinova, L. R., & Yakhshiboyev, R. E. (2024). The application of artificial intelligence in the economic sector. *Central Asian Journal Of Education And Computer Sciences*, 3(1), 1–12.

Arenas-Torres, F., Bustamante-Ubilla, M., & Campos-Troncoso, R. (2021). The incidence of social responsibility in the adoption of business practices. *Sustainability (Basel)*, 13(5), 2794. 10.3390/su13052794

Argashokova, S., Litvishko, O., & Novoselova, N. (2023). Digitalization of financial sector in Russia: Key components and concepts. In *E3S Web of Conferences* (Vol. 431, p. 05018). EDP Sciences. 10.1051/e3sconf/202343105018

Arun, C. (2020). AI and the Global South: Designing for other worlds. In The Oxford Handbook of Ethics of AI. Oxford Academic. 588–606. https://papers.ssrn. com/sol3/papers.cfm?abstract_id=3403010

Ashiq, V. M., Fredrik, E. T., Kumar, N. K., Torres-Cruz, F., Colque, J. P. B., & Manoharan, G. (2023, September). A Deep Learning Approaches for Natural Language Processing and Sentiment Analysis in Social Media. In 2023 6th International Conference on Contemporary Computing and Informatics (IC3I) (Vol. 6, pp. 1746-1750). IEEE.

Ashraf, I., Park, Y., Hur, S., Kim, S. W., Alroobaea, R., Zikria, Y., & Nosheen, S. (2022). A Survey on Cyber Security Threats in IoT-Enabled Maritime Industry. *IEEE Transactions on Intelligent Transportation Systems*, 1–14. 10.1109/TITS.2022.3164678

Ashta, A., & Herrmann, H. (2021). Artificial intelligence and fintech: An overview of opportunities and risks for banking, investments, and microfinance. *Strategic Change*, 30(3), 211–222. 10.1002/jsc.2404

Attard-Frost, B., De los Ríos, A., & Walters, D. R. (2023). The ethics of AI business practices: A review of 47 AI ethics guidelines. *AI and Ethics*, 3(2), 389–406. 10.1007/s43681-022-00156-6

Awotunde, J. B., Adeniyi, E. A., Ogundokun, R. O., & Ayo, F. E. (2021). Application of big data with fintech in financial services. In *Fintech with artificial intelligence, big data, and blockchain* (pp. 107–132). Springer Singapore. 10.1007/978-981-33-6137-9_3

Aydin, Ö. (2023). Google Bard Generated Literature Review: Metaverse. *Journal of AI, 1*(7). doi:https://bard.google.com

Babelova, Z. G., Vranakova, N., & Starecek, A. (2023). *The Integration of HR Information Systems Utilization in Industrial Enterprises*. Mm Science Journal.

Bai-Ngern, K., & Tubtiang, A. 2020. Leadership in the Digital Era. In 2020 *5th International STEM Education Conference* (iSTEM-Ed) (pp. 127-130). IEEE. DOI: 10.1109/iSTEM-Ed50324.2020.9332712

Bali, S. A. (2019). An analytical study of human resource information system applications in modern human resources management. *Int. J. Sustainable Agricultural Management and Informatics, 5*(4).

Bandari, V. (2019). Exploring the transformational potential of emerging technologies in human resource analytics: a comparative study of IoT, AI, and cloud computing applications. *Journal of Humanities and Applied Science Research*, 15-27.

Bandyopadhyay, I. (2024). Implementation Of An Artificial Intelligence And Machine Learning Powered Financial Decision-Support System For Stock Market Speculators. *Educational Administration: Theory and Practice*, 30(4), 203–209.

Ban, G. Y., El Karoui, N., & Lim, A. E. (2018). Machine learning and portfolio optimization. *Management Science*, 64(3), 1136–1154. 10.1287/mnsc.2016.2644

Banh, L., & Strobel, G. (2023). Generative artificial intelligence. *Electronic Markets*, 33(1), 63. 10.1007/s12525-023-00680-1

Bao, Y., Hilary, G., & Ke, B. (2022). Artificial intelligence and fraud detection. *Innovative Technology at the Interface of Finance and Operations*, I, 223–247. 10.1007/978-3-030-75729-8_8

Barry, D. (2023, May 31). Retrieved April 19, 2024, from reworked: https://www.reworked.co/digital-workplace/what-vr-ar-and-generative-ai-will-make-possible-in-the-digital-workplace/

Barua, R. (2024a). Advanced Biomimetic Compound Continuum Robot for Minimally Invasive Surgical Applications. In T. Choudhury, A. Mary X., S. Chowdhury, C. Karthik, & C. Evangeline (Eds.), Modeling, Simulation, and Control of AI Robotics and Autonomous Systems (pp. 213-231). IGI Global. 10.4018/979-8-3693-1962-8.ch013

Barua, R. (2024b). An In-Depth Exploration of AI and Humanoid Robotics' Role in Contemporary Healthcare. In V. Grover, B. Balusamy, N. M.K., V. Anand, & M. Milanova (Eds.), *Approaches to Human-Centered AI in Healthcare* (pp. 42-61). IGI Global.

Barua, R. (2024c). The Emerging Role of Artificial Intelligence in Organ-on-a-Chip (OOAC) Biomedical Devices. In Reshaping Healthcare with Cutting-Edge Biomedical Advancements (pp. 369-381). IGI Global.

Barua, R., & Mondal, J. (2023). Study of the Current Trends of CAD (Computer-Aided Detection) in Modern Medical Imaging. *Machine Learning and AI Techniques in Interactive Medical Image Analysis*, 35-50.

Barua, R., Das, D., & Biswas, N. (2024). Revolutionizing Drug Discovery With Artificial Intelligence: Enhancing Efficiency, Addressing Ethical Concerns, and Overcoming Limitations. In V. Grover, B. Balusamy, N. M.K., V. Anand, & M. Milanova (Eds.), *Approaches to Human-Centered AI in Healthcare* (pp. 62-85). IGI Global.

Barua, R., Das, S., &Mondal, J. (2023). Emerging Applications of Artificial Intelligence (AI) and Machine Learning (ML) in Modern Urology. *Exploring the Convergence of Computer and Medical Science Through Cloud Healthcare*, 117-133.

Barua, R. (2024d). Exploring Artificial Intelligence in Evolving Healthcare Environments: A Comprehensive Analysis. In Shah, I., & Sial, Q. (Eds.), *Advances in Computational Intelligence for the Healthcare Industry 4.0* (pp. 123–138). IGI Global. 10.4018/979-8-3693-2333-5.ch006

Barua, R. (2024e). An Investigation of AI Techniques for Detecting Kidney Stones in CT Scan Images Through Advanced Image Processing. In Sharma, A., Chanderwal, N., Tyagi, S., Upadhyay, P., & Tyagi, A. (Eds.), *Enhancing Medical Imaging with Emerging Technologies* (pp. 133–150). IGI Global. 10.4018/979-8-3693-5261-8.ch008

Barua, R., & Das, S. (2022). Improvements of virtual and augmented reality for advanced treatments in urology. In *Emerging Advancements for Virtual and Augmented Reality in Healthcare* (pp. 117–131). IGI global. 10.4018/978-1-7998-8371-5.ch008

Barua, R., & Datta, S. (2023). Artificial intelligence in modern medical science: A promising practice. In *Recent Developments in Machine and Human Intelligence* (pp. 1–12). IGI Global. 10.4018/978-1-6684-9189-8.ch001

Barua, R., & Datta, S. (2024). An Extensive Evaluation of New Federated Learning Approaches for COVID-19 Identification. In Hassan, A., Prasad, V., Bhattacharya, P., Dutta, P., & Damaševičius, R. (Eds.), *Pioneering Smart Healthcare 5.0 with IoT, Federated Learning, and Cloud Security* (pp. 246–257). IGI Global.

Barua, R., Datta, S., Datta, P., & Roychowdhury, A. (2022). Study and application of machine learning methods in modern additive manufacturing processes. In *Applications of Artificial Intelligence in Additive Manufacturing* (pp. 75–95). IGI Global. 10.4018/978-1-7998-8516-0.ch004

Barua, R., Datta, S., & Sarkar, A. (2023). Artificial intelligence and robotics-based minimally invasive surgery: Innovations and future perceptions. In *Contemporary Applications of Data Fusion for Advanced Healthcare Informatics* (pp. 350–368). IGI Global. 10.4018/978-1-6684-8913-0.ch015

Baswardono, W., Cahyana, R., Rahayu, S., & Nashrulloh, M. R. (2019). Design of human resource information system for micro, small, and medium enterprises. *Journal of Physics: Conference Series*, 1402(6), 066056. Advance online publication. 10.1088/1742-6596/1402/6/066056

Batty, M. (2013). Big data, smart cities and city planning. *Dialogues in Human Geography*, 3(3), 274–279. 10.1177/204382061351339029472982

Baumgart, D. C. (2024). An intriguing vision for transatlantic collaborative health data use and artificial intelligence development. *NPJ Digital Medicine*, 7(1), 19. 10.1038/s41746-024-01005-y38263436

Belhadi, A., Kamble, S., Fosso Wamba, S., & Queiroz, M. M. (2022). Building supply-chain resilience: An artificial intelligence-based technique and decision-making framework. *International Journal of Production Research*, 60(14), 4487–4507. 10.1080/00207543.2021.1950935

Bendel, O. (2023). Image synthesis from an ethical perspective. *AI & Society*. Advance online publication. 10.1007/s00146-023-01780-4

Bhattacharyya, D. S., Shafique, S., Akhter, S., Rahman, A., Islam, M. Z., Rahman, N., & Anwar, I. (2020). Challenges and facilitators of implementing an information communication and technology (ICT)-based human resources management tool in the government health sector in Bangladesh: Protocol for an exploratory qualitative research study. *BMJ Open*, 10.33318122

Biju, A. K. V. N., Thomas, A. S., & Thasneem, J. (2024). Examining the research taxonomy of artificial intelligence, deep learning and machine learning in the financial sphere—A bibliometric analysis. *Quality & Quantity*, 58(1), 849–878. 10.1007/s11135-023-01673-037359968

Bi, Q. (2023). Analysis of the Application of Generative AI in Business Management. *Advances in Economics and Management Research*, 6(1), 36–36. 10.56028/aemr.6.1.36.2023

Borji, A. (2023). Mohammadian, M. Battle of the Wordsmiths: Comparing ChatGPT, GPT-4, Claude, and Bard. Available online: https://papers.ssrn.com/sol3/papers.cfm?abstract_id=4476855

Bowyer, K. W. (2004). Face recognition technology: Security versus privacy. *IEEE Technology and Society Magazine*, 23(1), 9–19. 10.1109/MTAS.2004.1273467

Bradley, F. (2022). Representation of Libraries in Artificial Intelligence Regulations and Implications for Ethics and Practice. *Journal of the Australian Library and Information Association*, 71(3), 189–200. 10.1080/24750158.2022.2101911

Brindha, S., & Rhytheema, D. (2023). Predictive HR Analytics: Pioneering Innovation in the Workplace. *European Chemical Bulletin*, 820–835.

Budhwar, P., Chowdhury, S., Wood, G., Aguinis, H., Bamber, G. J., Beltran, J. R., Boselie, P., Lee Cooke, F., Decker, S., DeNisi, A., Dey, P. K., Guest, D., Knoblich, A. J., Malik, A., Paauwe, J., Papagiannidis, S., Patel, C., Pereira, V., Ren, S., . . . Varma, A. (2023). Human resource management in the age of generative artificial intelligence: Perspectives and research directions on ChatGPT. *In Human Resource Management Journal, 33*(3), 606–659.

Bughin, J., McCarthy, B., & Chui, M. (2017, August 28). A Survey of 3,000 Executives Reveals How Businesses Succeed with AI. Retrieved December 12, 2017, from https://hbr.org/2017/08/a-survey-of-3000-executives-reveals-how-businesses-succeed-with-ai

Bulchand-Gidumal, J. (2022, September 2). Impact of Artificial Intelligence in Travel, Tourism, and Hospitality. *Handbook of e-Tourism*, 1943–1962.

Cacicio, S., & Riggs, R. (2023). Bridging Resource Gaps in Adult Education: The Role of Generative AI. *Adult Literacy Education: The International Journal of Literacy, Language, and Numeracy*, 5(3), 80–86. 10.35847/SCacicio.RRiggs.5.3.80

Campesato, O. (2020). Artificial Intelligence, Machine Learning and Deep Learning. Dulles: Mercury Learning and information.

Canals, J., & Heukamp, F. (2020). *The Future of Management in an AI World.* Springer International Publishing. 10.1007/978-3-030-20680-2

Cao, L. (2022). Ai in finance: Challenges, techniques, and opportunities. *ACM Computing Surveys*, 55(3), 1–38. 10.1145/3502289

Cao, L., Yang, Q., & Yu, P. S. (2021). Data science and AI in FinTech: An overview. *International Journal of Data Science and Analytics*, 12(2), 81–99. 10.1007/s41060-021-00278-w

Cardon, P., Getchell, K., Carradini, S., Fleischmann, A. C., & Stapp, J. (2023). Generative AI in the Workplace: Employee Perspectives of ChatGPT Benefits and Organizational Policies. Available online: https://osf.io/preprints/socarxiv/b3ezy10.31235/osf.io/b3ezy

Ceyhun, G. Ç. (2019). *Recent Developments of Artificial Intelligence in Business Logistics: A Maritime Industry Case.* 10.1007/978-3-030-29739-8_16

Chaffey, D., & Ellis-Chadwick, F. (2019). *Digital marketing* (7th ed.). Pearson.

Chakraborty, M., & Khan, A. M. K. (2019). A case study on the importance of Human Resource Information System in the Healthcare sector of a corporate Hospital in India. IEEE 2019 International Conference on Digitization (ICD). 10.1109/ICD47981.2019.9105864

Chatterjee, M. (2024, May 6). Retrieved May 11, 2024, from Great Learning: https://www.mygreatlearning.com/blog/what-are-the-use-cases-for-the-predictive-analytics-in-the-travel-industry/

Chaudhry, S. A., Irshad, A., Khan, M. A., Khan, S. A., Nosheen, S., Alzubi, A. A., & Zikria, Y. Bin. (2023). A Lightweight Authentication Scheme for 6G-IoT Enabled Maritime Transport System. *IEEE Transactions on Intelligent Transportation Systems, 24*, 2401–2410. https://api.semanticscholar.org/CorpusID:245442072

Chaudhry, R., Kaur, S., Singla, J., Mittal, R., & Malik, V. (2024). Fraud Detection and Prevention for a Secure Financial Future Using Artificial Intelligence. *In2024 International Conference on Emerging Smart Computing and Informatics (ESCI)* (pp. 1-6). IEEE. 10.1109/ESCI59607.2024.10497255

Chawla, S. (2019). 7 Successful applications of AI & machine learning in the travel industry.

Chen, Y. (2023). Designing an Investment Research System for Asset Management Based on Natural Language Processing (Doctoral dissertation, Massachusetts Institute of Technology).

Chen, X., Ma, D., & Liu, R. W. (2024). Application of Artificial Intelligence in Maritime Transportation. *Journal of Marine Science and Engineering*, 12(3), 439. 10.3390/jmse12030439

Chiurunge, P., Kandiero, A., & Chizwina, S. (2024). Customer Churn Prediction for Financial Institutions Using Deep Learning Artificial Neural Networks in Zimbabwe. In *Theoretical and Conceptual Frameworks in ICT Research* (pp. 227–265). IGI Global.

Chopra, R., & Sharma, G. D. (2021). Application of artificial intelligence in stock market forecasting: A critique, review, and research agenda. *Journal of Risk and Financial Management*, 14(11), 526. 10.3390/jrfm14110526

Choudhary, S. (2022). AI in Organizations a Helping hand of HR. ResearchGate.

Choung, H., David, P., & Ross, A. (2023). Trust in AI and Its Role in the Acceptance of AI Technologies. *International Journal of Human-Computer Interaction*, 39(9), 1727–1739. 10.1080/10447318.2022.2050543

Chowdhary, K., & Chowdhary, K. R. (2020). Natural language processing. *Fundamentals of artificial intelligence*, 603-649.

Chuang, Y. H., Kang, T. C., Chang, W. C., & Chen, P. J. (2020). Creative Design Ltd.: The path to youth entrepreneurship. *Emerald Emerging Markets Case Studies*, 10(2), 1–17. 10.1108/EEMCS-07-2019-0182

Chui, M., Kamalnath, V., & McCarthy, B. (2018, March 12). An executive's guide to AI (Guide). Retrieved March 15, 2018, from McKinsey & Company website: https://www.mckinsey.com/business-functions/mckinsey-analytics/our-insights/an-executives-guide-to-ai

Chuma, E. L., & de Oliveira, G. G. (2023). Generative AI for business decision-making: A case of ChatGPT. *Management Science and Business Decisions*, 3(1), 5–11. 10.52812/msbd.63

Cohen, G. (2022). Algorithmic trading and financial forecasting using advanced artificial intelligence methodologies. *Mathematics*, 10(18), 3302. 10.3390/math10183302

Cohen, G. (2022). Artificial Intelligence in Trading the Financial Markets. *International Journal of Economics & Business Administration*, 10(1), 101–110. 10.35808/ijeba/751

Ćormarković, T., Dražeta, L. and Njeguš, A., 2022. The levels of artificial intelligence application in human resource systems. *The European Journal of Applied Economics*, 19(2). DOI: .10.5937/EJAE19-39535

Cotter, K. (2019). Playing the visibility game: How digital influencers and algorithms negotiate influence on Instagram. *New Media & Society*, 21(4), 895–913. 10.1177/1461444818815684

Dabrowski, J. J., & de Villiers, J. P. (2015). Maritime piracy situation modelling with dynamic Bayesian networks. *Information Fusion*, 23, 116–130. 10.1016/j.inffus.2014.07.001

Dakalbab, F., Talib, M. A., Nassir, Q., & Ishak, T. (2024). Artificial intelligence techniques in financial trading: A systematic literature review. *Journal of King Saud University. Computer and Information Sciences*, 36(3), 102015. 10.1016/j.jksuci.2024.102015

Danilwan, Y., & Dirhamsyah, I. P. (2022). The Impact of The Psychological intrinsic reward on The Organizational Perceived organizational support: Does Ethical Climate Matter? *Journal of Positive School Psychology*, 6(3), 1–16.

Datta, S., Barua, R., & Das, J. (2019). Application of artificial intelligence in modern healthcare system. *Alginates-recent uses of this natural polymer*.

Daugherty, P. R., & Wilson, H. J. (2018). *Human + Machine. Reimagining Work in the Age of AI*. Harvard Business Press.

Davenport, T., Guha, A., Grewal, D., & Bressgott, T. (2020). How artificial intelligence will change the future of marketing. *Journal of the Academy of Marketing Science*, 48(1), 24–42. 10.1007/s11747-019-00696-0

David, A., Chandirasekaran, G., & Sankar, J. G. (2023, November). Blockchain and Artificial Intelligence in Food Industry-Case Analysis of Ripe. Io Firm. In *Proceedings of the 5th International Conference on Information Management & Machine Intelligence* (pp. 1-6).

David, A., Jeganathan, G. S., Sikandar, M. D., & Azam, S. A. (2023, May). Internet Users Top Concerns Ensuring Data Privacy, Security, and Protection. In *Arokiaraj David, Jeganathan Gomathi Sankar & Md Sikandar Azam, —Internet Users Top Concerns Ensuring Data Privacy, Security, and Protection , 10th International Conference on Multidisciplinary Research and Modern Education, ISBN* (No. 978-920, pp. 5-20241).

David, A., Ahmed, R. R., Ganesh Kumar, C., & Sankar, J. G. (2020). Consumer purchasing process of organic food product: An empirical analysis. *Journal of Management Systems. Quality - Access to Success*, 21(177), 128–132.

David, A., Maheswari, M., Sankar, G., Christy, F., Karuppannan, A., & Banumathi, M. (2023). Mental illness of Pregnant Women determined by Covid-19: An Empirical Analysis of Pre-and- Post Delivery. *The Saybold Report Journal*, 18(03), 1706–1721.

Delbufalo, E., Di Bernardo, M., & Risso, M. (2022). Human-Machine Interaction and AI for Competitive Business in the Digital Era. *Symphonya*, (2), 134–143. 10.4468/2022.2.12delbufalo.dibernardo.risso

Dessain, J., Bentaleb, N., & Vinas, F. (2023, July). Cost of Explainability in AI: An Example with Credit Scoring Models. In *World Conference on Explainable Artificial Intelligence* (pp. 498-516). Cham: Springer Nature Switzerland. 10.1007/978-3-031-44064-9_26

Deviprasad, S., Madhumithaa, N., Vikas, I. W., Yadav, A., & Manoharan, G. (2023). The Machine Learning-Based Task Automation Framework for Human Resource Management in MNC Companies. *Engineering Proceedings*, 59(1), 63.

Dhir, S., & Chakraborty, T. (2021). Does the perceived efficiency of the HR department matter in influencing satisfaction and employee perceived organizational support? *International Journal of Productivity and Perceived organizational support Management*, (ahead-of-print).

Di Salvo, A., & Arcoraci, A. (2020). Human connections. Design interactive artefacts through narration and speculation. *AGATHÓN| International Journal of Architecture. Art and Design*, 8, 254–261.

Dobre, R., Bulin, D., Iorgulescu, M.C. & Oehler-Sincai, I.M. (2020). Artificial Intelligence Sector: The Next Technology Bubble? A Comparative Analysis with Dotcom Based on Stock Market Data. *Romanian Economic Journal*, (76).

Dodson, I. (2016). *The Digital Marketing Playbook: The Definitive Guide to Creating Strategic, Targeted, and Measurable Online Campaigns*. John Wiley & Sons.

Dong, Z., Xin, Z., Liu, D., & Yu, F. (2024). The impact of artificial intelligence application on company environmental investment in Chinese manufacturing companies. *International Review of Financial Analysis*, 95, 103403. 10.1016/j.irfa.2024.103403

Dumitriu, D., & Popescu, M. A.-M. (2020). Artificial Intelligence Solutions for Digital Marketing. *Procedia Manufacturing*, 46, 630–636. 10.1016/j.promfg.2020.03.090

Durai, S., Manoharan, G., & Ashtikar, S. P. (2024). *Harnessing Artificial Intelligence: Pioneering Sustainable Solutions for a Greener Future. Social and Ethical Implications of AI in Finance for Sustainability*. IGI Global. 10.4018/979-8-3693-2881-1.ch003

Durai, S., Manoharan, G., Priya, T. S., Jayanthi, R., Razak, A., & Ashtikar, S. P. (2024). It is quantifying the Impacts of Artificial Intelligence Implementations in Marketing. In *Smart and Sustainable Interactive Marketing* (pp. 120–144). IGI Global. 10.4018/979-8-3693-1339-8.ch008

Dwivedi, Y. K., Hughes, L., Ismagilova, E., Aarts, G., Coombs, C., Crick, T., Duan, Y., Dwivedi, R., Edwards, J., Eirug, A., Galanos, V., Ilavarasan, P. V., Janssen, M., Jones, P., Kar, A. K., Kizgin, H., Kronemann, B., Lal, B., Lucini, B., & Williams, M. D. (2021). Artificial Intelligence (AI): Multidisciplinary perspectives on emerging challenges, opportunities, and agenda for research, practice, and policy. *International Journal of Information Management*, 57, 101994. 10.1016/j.ijinfomgt.2019.08.002

Dzingirai, M. (2023, June). Effects of Artificial Intelligence on Money Laundering in Southern Africa. *InICABR Conference* (pp. 483-500). Cham: Springer Nature Switzerland.

Dzingirai, M. (2021a). Demystifying Corporate Restructuring Strategy Through Digital Transformation: Lessons Learned From the Banking Sector of Zimbabwe. In Sandhu, K. (Ed.), *Emerging Challenges, Solutions, and Best Practices for Digital Enterprise Transformation* (pp. 164–181). IGI Global. 10.4018/978-1-7998-8587-0.ch009

Dzingirai, M. (2021b). Managerial Challenges Under FinTech: Evidence From Zimbabwean Commercial Banks. In Sghari, A., & Mezghani, K. (Eds.), *Influence of FinTech on Management Transformation* (pp. 141–166). IGI Global. 10.4018/978-1-7998-7110-1.ch007

Eisenstadt, V., Althoff, K. D., & Langenhan, C. (2020). Student Graduation Projects in the Context of Framework for AI-Based Support of Early Conceptual Phases in Architecture. *In LWDA* (pp. 174-179).

Elisa, M. T. (2023, December 18). Opportunities and Challenges of Artificial Intelligence in the Tourism Industry. *Global Journal of Tourism, Leisure and Hospitality Management, 1*(1).

Elita, Y., & Sinthia, R. (2021). Knowledge Sharing Behavior Reviewed From a Social Exchange Perspective. *International Conference on Educational Sciences and Teacher Profession (ICETeP 2020)* (pp. 509-512). Atlantis Press.

Elliott, D., & Soifer, E. (2022). AI technologies, privacy, and security. *Frontiers in Artificial Intelligence*, 5, 826737. 10.3389/frai.2022.82673735493613

El-Namaki, M.S.S. (2016). How Companies are Applying AI to the Business Strategy Formulation. DOI: */JOURNAL.SIJBPG05080110*.19085

ElZomor, M., Pradhananga, P., Santi, G., & Vassigh, S. (2020, June). Preparing the future workforce of architecture, engineering, and construction for robotic automation processes. *2020 ASEE Virtual Annual Conference ContentAccess*. 10.18260/1-2--35082

Emmanuel, N., & Nwuzor, J. (2021). Employee and Organisational Perceived organizational support: Employees Perception of Intrinsic and Extrinsic Psychological intrinsic rewards System. *Applied Journal of Economics. Management and Social Sciences*, 2(1), 26–32.

Emmanuel, N., & Nwuzor, J. (2021). Employee and Organizational Perceived organizational support: Employees Perception of Intrinsic and Extrinsic Psychological intrinsic rewards System. *Applied Journal of Economics. Management and Social Sciences*, 2(1), 26–32.

Esen, M. F., Bilgic, E., & Basdas, U. (2019). How to detect illegal corporate insider trading? A data mining approach for detecting suspicious insider transactions. *International Journal of Intelligent Systems in Accounting Finance & Management*, 26(2), 60–70. 10.1002/isaf.1446

Esqueda, M. D., & Melo, B. C. (2020). The uncharted territory in Uncharted 3: Expectancy vs. Professional norms in translated games. *Belas Infiéis*, 9(4), 173–199. 10.26512/belasinfieis.v9.n4.2020.26449

Esteva, A., Robicquet, A., Ramsundar, B., Kuleshov, V., DePristo, M., Chou, K., Cui, C., Corrado, G., Thrun, S., & Dean, J. (2019). A guide to deep learning in healthcare. *Nature Medicine*, 25(1), 24–29. 10.1038/s41591-018-0316-z30617335

Falletta, S. (2014). In search of HR intelligence: Evidence-based HR analytics practices in high performing companies. *People and Strategy*, 36(4), 28.

Fanni, S. C., Febi, M., Aghakhanyan, G., & Neri, E. (2023). Natural language processing. In *Introduction to Artificial Intelligence* (pp. 87–99). Springer International Publishing. 10.1007/978-3-031-25928-9_5

Farayola, O. A. (2024). Revolutionizing banking security: Integrating artificial intelligence, blockchain, and business intelligence for enhanced cybersecurity. *Finance and Accounting Research Journal*, 6(4), 501–514. 10.51594/farj.v6i4.990

Fenwick, M., Vermeulen, E. P., & Corrales, M. (2018). Business and regulatory responses to artificial intelligence: Dynamic regulation, innovation ecosystems and the strategic management of disruptive technology. In Robotics, AI and the Future of Law (pp. 81–103). Springer Singapore., 1007/978-981-13-2874-9_4. 10.1007/978-981-13-2874-9_4

Fernández Pérez, I., Prieta, F. D. L., Rodríguez-González, S., Corchado, J. M., & Prieto, J. (2022, July). Quantum AI: achievements and challenges in the interplay of quantum computing and artificial intelligence. In *International Symposium on Ambient Intelligence* (pp. 155-166). Cham: Springer International Publishing.

Ferreira, F. G., Gandomi, A. H., & Cardoso, R. T. (2021). Artificial intelligence applied to stock market trading: A review. *IEEE Access : Practical Innovations, Open Solutions*, 9, 30898–30917. 10.1109/ACCESS.2021.3058133

Feuerriegel, S., Hartmann, J., Janiesch, C., & Zschech, P. (2023). Generative AI. *Business & Information Systems Engineering*, 66(1), 111–126. 10.1007/s12599-023-00834-7

Fezari, M., Al-Dahoud, A., & Al-Dahoud, A. (2023). Augmenting Reality: The Power of Generative AI. https://www.spaceo.ai/wp-content/uploads/2023/02/OpenAI-GPT-3-Architecture.jpg

Frost, M., Jeske, T., & Ottersböck, N. (2020). Leadership and corporate culture as key factors for thriving digital change. In Advances in Human Factors and Systems Interaction: Proceedings of the AHFE 2020 Virtual Conference on Human Factors and Systems Interaction, July 16-20, 2020, USA (pp. 55-61). *Springer International Publishing*. 10.1007/978-3-030-51369-6_8

Ganeshkumar, C., Sankar, J. G., & David, A. (2023). Impact of Artificial Intelligence on Agriculture Value Chain Performance: Agritech Perspective. In *Blockchain, IoT, and AI Technologies for Supply Chain Management* (pp. 71-98). CRC Press.

Ganeshkumar, C., David, A., & Sankar, J. G. (2024). Blockchain Technology Acceptance in Agribusiness Industry. In Idrees, S. M., & Nowostawski, M. (Eds.), *Blockchain Transformations. Signals and Communication Technology*. Springer., 10.1007/978-3-031-49593-9_15

Ganeshkumar, C., David, A., Sankar, J. G., & Saginala, M. (2023). Application of Drone Technology in Agriculture: A Predictive Forecasting of Pest and Disease Incidence. In *Applying Drone Technologies and Robotics for Agricultural Sustainability* (pp. 50–81). IGI Global.

Ganeshkumar, C., Sankar, J. G., & David, A. (2023). Adoption of Big Data Analytics: Determinants and Performances Among Food Industries. *International Journal of Business Intelligence Research*, 14(1), 1–17. 10.4018/IJBIR.317419

Gao, Z. (2020). The application of artificial intelligence in stock investment. *Journal of Physics: Conference Series*, 1453(1), 012069. 10.1088/1742-6596/1453/1/012069

Gaspersz, B. (2007). *Pemodelan transportasi laut di propinsi maluku*. https://api.semanticscholar.org/CorpusID:114714448

George, A. S., George, A. H., & Martin, A. G. (2023). ChatGPT and the Future of Work: A Comprehensive Analysis of AI's Impact on Jobs and Employment. *Partners Universal International Innovation Journal*, 1(3), 154–186.

Gigante, G., & Zago, A. (2023). DARQ technologies in the financial sector: Artificial intelligence applications in personalized banking. *Qualitative Research in Financial Markets*, 15(1), 29–57. 10.1108/QRFM-02-2021-0025

Gina, B., & Budree, A. (2020). A review of literature on critical factors that drive the selection of business intelligence tools. *In 2020 International Conference on Artificial Intelligence, Big Data, Computing and Data Communication Systems (icABCD)* (pp. 1-7). IEEE. 10.1109/icABCD49160.2020.9183852

Giudici, P. (2018). Fintech risk management: A research challenge for artificial intelligence in finance. *Frontiers in Artificial Intelligence*, 1, 1. 10.3389/frai.2018.0000133733089

Glikson, E., & Woolley, A. W. (2020). Human trust in artificial intelligence: Review of empirical research. *The Academy of Management Annals*, 14(2), 627–660. 10.5465/annals.2018.0057

Go, E. J., Moon, J., & Kim, J. (2020). Analysis of the current and future of the artificial intelligence in financial industry with big data techniques. *Global Business and Finance Review*, 25(1), 102–117. 10.17549/gbfr.2020.25.1.102

Gonçalves, R., Dias, Á., Costa, R., Pereira, L., Bento, T., & Rosa, Á. (2022). Gaining competitive advantage through artificial intelligence adoption. *International Journal of Electronic Business*, 1(1), 386–406. 10.1504/IJEB.2022.10044363

Goodfellow, I., Bengio, Y., & Courville, A. (2016). *Deep learning*. MIT Press.

Goto, M. (2023). Anticipatory innovation of professional services: The case of auditing and artificial intelligence. *Research Policy*, 52(8), 104828. 10.1016/j.respol.2023.104828

Govori, A., & Sejdija, Q. (2023). Future prospects and challenges of integrating artificial intelligence within the business practices of small and medium enterprises. *J. Gov. Regul.*, 12(2), 176–183. 10.22495/jgrv12i2art16

Gozalo-Brizuela, R., & Garrido-Merchán, E. C. (2023). A survey of Generative AI Applications. doi:http://arxiv.org/abs/2306.02781

Graham, J. (2021). Risk of discrimination in AI systems: Evaluating the effectiveness of current legal safeguards in tackling algorithmic discrimination. *FinTechArtificial Intelligence and Law*, 211–229.

Great Chat. (n.d.). Retrieved April 4, 2024, from GreatChat: https://www.greatchat.ai/en-blog/ai-in-the-travel-industry-how-is-ai-creating-personalized-itineraries-and-enhancing-concierge-services

Grover, P., & Kar, A. K. (2017). Big Data Analytics: A Review on Theoretical Contributions and Tools Used in Literature. *Glob J Flex Syst Manag, 18*(3), 203–229. 10.1007/s40171-017-0159-3

Gunjan, A., & Bhattacharyya, S. (2023). A brief review of portfolio optimization techniques. *Artificial Intelligence Review*, 56(5), 3847–3886. 10.1007/s10462-022-10273-7

Gupta, N. (2023). Artificial Intelligence Ethics and Fairness: A study to address bias and fairness issues in AI systems, and the ethical implications of AI applications. *Revista Review Index Journal of Multidisciplinary*, 3(2), 24–35. 10.31305/rrijm2023.v03.n02.004

Gupta, S., Modgil, S., Lee, C. K., & Sivarajah, U. (2023). The future is yesterday: Use of AI-driven facial recognition to enhance value in the travel and tourism industry. *Information Systems Frontiers*, 25(3), 1179–1195. 10.1007/s10796-022-10271-835529102

Guttentag, D. (2010, October 1). Virtual reality: Applications and implications for tourism. *Tourism Management*, 31(5), 637–651. 10.1016/j.tourman.2009.07.003

Hacker, P., Engel, A., & Mauer, M. (2023). Regulating ChatGPT and other Large Generative AI Models. *ACM International Conference Proceeding Series*, 1112–1123. 10.1145/3593013.3594067

Haddadian, H., Baky Haskuee, M., & Zomorodian, G. (2022). A hybrid artificial intelligence approach to portfolio management. *Iranian Journal of Finance*, 6(1), 1–27. 10.30699/ijf.2021.287131.1237

Hadi, M. U., Al-Tashi, Q., Qureshi, R., Shah, A., Muneer, A., Irfan, M., Zafar, A., Shaikh, M., Akhtar, N., Wu, J., ... (2023). Large Language Models: A Comprehensive Survey of Its Applications, Challenges, Limitations, and Future Prospects. Available online: https://www.techrxiv.org/users/618307/articles/682263-large-language-models-a-comprehensive-survey-of-its-applications-challenges-limitations-and-future-prospects

Hadi, M., & Najm, M. (2023). Introduction to ChatGPT: A new revolution of artificial intelligence with machine learning algorithms and cybersecurity. *Sci. Arch.*, 4, 276–285. 10.47587/SA.2023.4406

Hamilton, R., & Davison, H. (2022). Legal and Ethical Challenges for HR in Machine Learning. *Employee Responsibilities and Rights Journal*, 34(1), 19–39. Advance online publication. 10.1007/s10672-021-09377-z

Handayani, D., Sediono, W., & Shah, A. (2021). Anomaly detection in vessel tracking – A Bayesian networks (BNs) approach. *International Journal of Maritime Engineering*, 157(A3). Advance online publication. 10.5750/ijme.v157iA3.956

Hanlin, R., & Kelly, W. (2023). *Enhancing South Africa's Emerging Digital Technologies' Innovation Ecosystem*. https://edt.ubuntunet.net/wp-content/uploads/2023/09/Strengthening-of-Emerging-Digital-Technologies-Ecosystem-in-South-Africa-A-Policy-Brief-1.pdf

Han, P., & Yang, X. (2020). Big data-driven automatic generation of ship route planning in complex maritime environments. *Acta Oceanologica Sinica*, 39(8), 113–120. 10.1007/s13131-020-1638-5

Hao, J., Zhang, G., Liu, W., Zou, H., & Wang, Y. (2022). Autotune control algorithm based on relay feedback and adaptive neural network for attitude tracking of nonlinear AUG system. *Ocean Engineering*, 250, 111051.

Harshvardhan, G. M., Gourisaria, M. K., Pandey, M., & Rautaray, S. S. (2020). A comprehensive survey and analysis of generative models in machine learning. *Computer Science Review*, 38, 100285. 10.1016/j.cosrev.2020.100285

Hassani, H., Huang, X., Silva, E., & Ghodsi, M. (2020). Deep learning and implementations in banking. *Annals of Data Science*, 7(3), 433–446. 10.1007/s40745-020-00300-1

Hearn, A. (2023). The collateralized personality: Creditability and resistance in the age of automated credit-scoring and lending. *Cultural Studies*, 37(1), 123–148. 10.1080/09502386.2022.2042576

Heilig, L., & Voß, S. (2017). Information systems in seaports: A categorization and overview. *Information Technology and Management*, 18(3), 179–201. 10.1007/s10799-016-0269-1

He, M., Liu, B., & Li, Y. (2023). Tourist inspiration: How the wellness tourism experience inspires tourist engagement. *Journal of Hospitality & Tourism Research (Washington, D.C.)*, 47(7), 1115–1135. 10.1177/10963480211026376

Hermann, E. (2021): Artificial intelligence in marketing: friend or foe of sustainable consumption? In AI & Soc. 10.1007/s00146-021-01227-8

Hetler, A. (2023, December). Retrieved May 1, 2024, from TechTarget: https://www.techtarget.com/whatis/definition/ChatGPT

Hickok, M. (2021). Lessons learned from AI ethics principles for future actions. *AI and Ethics*, 1(1), 41–47. 10.1007/s43681-020-00008-1

Hidayah, Z., & Purnamasari, P. (2024). Analysis Of The Impact Of The Application Of Artificial Intelligence (Ai) Based Technology And Digital Finance Knowledge In Improving Business Sustainability. *Jurnal Mantik*, 7(4), 3989–3996.

Hidayat, M., Defitri, S. Y., & Hilman, H. (2024). The Impact of Artificial Intelligence (AI) on Financial Management. *Management Studies and Business Journal Productivity*, 1(1), 123–129. 10.62207/s298rx18

Hines, M. (2024, February 29). Retrieved April 27, 2024, from PhocusWire: https://www.phocuswire.com/ai-check-in-tripcom-tripgenie

Hoffmann, A. L., Roberts, S. T., Wolf, C. T., & Wood, S. (2018). Beyond fairness, accountability, and transparency in the ethics of algorithms: Contributions and perspectives from LIS. *Proceedings of the Association for Information Science and Technology*, 55(1), 694–696. 10.1002/pra2.2018.14505501084

Holtel, S. (2016). Artificial Intelligence Creates a Wicked Problem for the Enterprise. *Procedia Computer Science*, 99, 171–180. 10.1016/j.procs.2016.09.109

Hong Chuong Pham, C. D. (2024, February 9). What drives tourists' continuance intention to use ChatGPT for travel services? A stimulus-organism-response perspective. *Journal of Retailing and Consumer Services*, 78, 1–13.

How AI Is Pushing Man and Machine Closer Together. (Rep.). (2017, February). Retrieved January 16, 2018, from PwC website: https://www.pwc.in/assets/pdfs/consulting/digital-enablement-advisory1/pwc-botme-boo klet.pdf

Huang, K., Huang, J., & Catteddu, D. (2024). GenAI Data Security. In *Generative AI Security: Theories and Practices* (pp. 133–162). Springer Nature Switzerland. 10.1007/978-3-031-54252-7_5

Huang, S. Y., & Lee, C. J. (2022). Predicting continuance intention to fintech chatbot. *Computers in Human Behavior*, 129, 107027. 10.1016/j.chb.2021.107027

Huang, Y., Li, Y., Zhang, Z., & Liu, R. W. (2020). GPU-Accelerated Compression and Visualization of Large-Scale Vessel Trajectories in Maritime IoT Industries. *IEEE Internet of Things Journal*, 7(11), 10794–10812. 10.1109/JIOT.2020.2989398

Huang, Z., Che, C., Zheng, H., & Li, C. (2024). Research on Generative Artificial Intelligence for Virtual Financial Robo-Advisor. *Academic Journal of Science and Technology*, 10(1), 74–80. 10.54097/30r2kk80

Hu, C., Din, Q. M. U., & Zhang, L. (2024). Short Empirical Insight: Leadership and Artificial Intelligence in the Pharmaceutical Industry. *Engineering. Technology and Applied Science Research*, 14(2), 13658–13664. 10.48084/etasr.7025

Hung, M. C., Hsia, P. H., Kuang, X. J., & Lin, S. K. (2024). Intelligent portfolio construction via news sentiment analysis. *International Review of Economics & Finance*, 89, 605–617. 10.1016/j.iref.2023.07.103

Huriye, A. Z. (2023). The Ethics of Artificial Intelligence: Examining the Ethical Considerations Surrounding the Development and Use of AI. *American Journal of Technology*, 2(1), 37–45. 10.58425/ajt.v2i1.142

IA, G., & Miglionico, A. (2019). Artificial intelligence and automation in financial services: The case of russian banking sector. *Law and Economics Yearly Review*, 8(1), 125–147.

Ilieva, R., Ivanova, M., Peycheva, T., & Nikolov, Y. (2021). Modelling in support of decision making in business intelligence. In *Integration Challenges for Analytics, Business Intelligence, and Data Mining* (pp. 115–144). IGI Global. 10.4018/978-1-7998-5781-5.ch006

Indrani, M.W., Naidoo, M. & Wickremasinghe, G. (2020). Comparative analysis of pricing decisions made by listed companies representing different industry sectors: evidence from Sri Lanka. DOI: */IJABF.V6I1.53*.4038

Interest in AI Startups Exploded in 2017. (2018, January 19). Retrieved April 03, 2018, from https://www.venturescanner.com/blog/2018/interest-in-ai-startups -exploded-in-2017

Isensee, C., Griese, K. M., & Teuteberg, F. (2021). Sustainable artificial intelligence: A corporate culture perspective. In Sustainability Management Foruml Nachhaltigkeits Management Forum(Vol. 29, No. 3-4, pp. 217-230). Berlin/Heidelberg: *Springer Berlin Heidelberg*. 10.1007/s00550-021-00524-6

Ismael, F., Hussein, B., Ibrahim, M. S., & Akoye, S. (2022). The mediation role of organization citizenship behavior among employee motivation and productivity: Analysis of Pharmaceutical Industries in KRG. *International Journal of Humanities and Education Development*, 4(1), 10–22.

Ismael, F., Hussein, B., Ibrahim, M. S., & Akoye, S. (2022). The mediation role of organization citizenship behaviour between employee motivation and productivity: Analysis of Pharmaceutical Industries in KRG. *International Journal of Humanities and Education Development*, 4(1), 10–22.

Isola, P., Zhu, J.-Y., Zhou, T., & Efros, A. A. (2017). Image-to-image translation with conditional adversarial networks. *Proceedings of the IEEE Conference on Computer Vision and Pattern Recognition*, 1125–1134.

Ivanov, S., & Webster, C. (Eds.). (2019). *Robots, artificial intelligence, and service automation in travel, tourism and hospitality*. Emerald Publishing Limited. 10.1108/9781787566873

Ivars-Baidal, J. A., Celdrán-Bernabeu, M. A., Mazón, J. N., & Perles-Ivars, Á. F. (2019). Smart destinations and the evolution of ICTs: A new scenario for destination management? *Current Issues in Tourism*, 22(13), 1581–1600. 10.1080/13683500.2017.1388771

iWebScraping. (2024, April 11). Retrieved April 21, 2024, from Medium: https://medium.com/@seo_14803/big-data-analytics-for-the-tourism-industry-cda451149d58

Izchak, O. E. (2024, February 15). Retrieved April 25, 2024, from mize: https://mize.tech/blog/6-examples-of-how-ai-is-used-in-the-travel-industry

Jacques Bulchand-Gidumal, E. W. (2023, June 30). Artificial intelligence's impact on hospitality and tourism marketing: Exploring key themes and addressing challenges. *Current Issues in Tourism*, 1–18.

Jagwani, V., Meghani, S., Pai, K., & Dhage, S. (2023). Resume Evaluation through Latent Dirichlet Allocation and Natural Language Processing for Effective Candidate Selection. doi:arXiv:2307.15752v1.

Jain, P., & Aggarwal, K. (2020). Transforming Marketing with Artificial Intelligence.

Jain, N., Barua, R., Waidi, Y. O., & Datta, S. (2024). Nanowires for Bio-Sensing Applications. In Kulkarni, S., Kharisov, B., Haghi, A., & Srivastava, V. (Eds.), *Next Generation Materials for Sustainable Engineering* (pp. 205–219). IGI Global. 10.4018/979-8-3693-1306-0.ch010

Jain, R., Prajapati, D., & Dangi, A. (2023). Transforming the financial sector: A review of recent advancements in FinTech. *Available atSSRN* 4380348.

Jammalamadaka, K. R., & Itapu, S. (2023). Responsible AI in automated credit scoring systems. *AI and Ethics*, 3(2), 485–495. 10.1007/s43681-022-00175-3

Jamshed, S. (2014). Qualitative research method-interviewing and observation. *Journal of Basic and Clinical Pharmacy*, 5(4), 87. 10.4103/0976-0105.14194225316987

Jardim, J. (2024). Global Innovation Policies: Framework for Developing an Innovative Culture Based on Artificial Intelligence. In *Incorporating AI Technology in the Service Sector* (pp. 25–43). Apple Academic Press. 10.1201/9781003378068-2

Jebadurai, D. J., Sheela, M. V., Rajeshkumar, L., Soundarya, M., Meena, R., Manickam, T., . . . Manikandan, M. (2024). AI-Driven Decision-Making and Optimization in Modern Agriculture Sectors. In Using Traditional Design Methods to Enhance AI-Driven Decision Making (pp. 269-288). IGI Global.

Jeganathan, G. S., David, A., & Ilangovan, K. (2022). Determination of Hospitality Services Quality and Customer Satisfaction–a Holserv Approach. In *AU Virtual International Conference on" Entrepreneurship & Sustainability in Digital Era" under the theme of" Challenges of Organizational & Business Management in Dynamic Digital Dimension"* (Vol. 3, No. 1, pp. 325-334).

Jeganathan, G. S., & Srinivasulu, Y. (2014). Growth Drivers of Tourism Industry in India. *International Journal of Business and Management*, 2(11), 100.

Jiang, Z., Gao, W., Tang, F., Wang, L., Xiong, X., Luo, C., Lan, C., Li, H., & Zhan, J. (2021). Hpc ai500 v2. 0: The methodology, tools, and metrics for benchmarking hpc ai systems. In *IEEE International Conference on Cluster Computing* (CLUSTER) (pp. 47-58). IEEE. 10.1109/Cluster48925.2021.00022

Jiang, C., Xv, X., & Zhu, Z. (2021, September). Research on the Construction of Chinese Hotel Experiential Marketing Model Under the Background of AI. In *2021 International Conference on Financial Management and Economic Transition (FMET 2021)* (pp. 470-475). Atlantis Press. 10.2991/aebmr.k.210917.071

Joan Borràs, A. M. (2014, June 9). Intelligent tourism recommender systems: A survey. *Expert Systems with Applications*, 41(16), 7370–7389. 10.1016/j.eswa.2014.06.007

Jobin, A., Ienca, M., & Vayena, E. (2019). The global landscape of AI ethics guidelines. *Nature Machine Intelligence*, 1(9), 389–399. 10.1038/s42256-019-0088-2

Johnson, J. A., Coggburn, J. D., & Valcik, N. A. (2022). Artificial Intelligence and Public Human Resource Management: Questions for Research and Practice. *Public Personnel Management*, 51(4), 539–560. 10.1177/00910260221126498

Joseph, A. (2023, September 19). Retrieved April 12, 2024, from Medium: https://medium.com/publishfive/artificial-intelligence-in-travel-top-7-challenges-f860702acb05

Joseph, J. (2023). Conceptual Framework of Open and Distance Learning (ODL) for Studio-Based Architectural Design Courses Assessing the Potential of Laboratory Instructional Tool through Synthesia AI: A Case Study on Student Learning Outcome.

Jospin Jeya, J., & Raja Ratna, S. (2023). *G.* Generative AI Boosts Business Productivity.

Joung, T.-H., Kang, S.-G., Lee, J.-K., & Ahn, J. (2020). The IMO initial strategy for reducing Greenhouse Gas (GHG) emissions, and its follow-up actions towards 2050. *Journal of International Maritime Safety, Environmental Affairs, and Shipping*, 4(1), 1–7. 10.1080/25725084.2019.1707938

Junça Silva, A., & Coelho, N. (2022). The moderating role of organizational culture on the association among workers' attitudes towards telework and happiness. *Kybernetes.*

Junça Silva, A., & Coelho, N. (2022). The moderating role of organizational culture on the relationship between workers' attitudes towards telework and happiness. *Kybernetes.*

Júnior, S. H. D. L., Silva, F. Í. C., Albuquerque, G. S. G., de Medeiros, F. P. A., & Lira, H. B. (2020). Enterprise Architecture in Healthcare Systems: A systematic literature review. *arXiv preprint arXiv:2007.06767.* 10.17632/44bygxg8w3.1

Kailash Sharma, N. S. (2024, May 2). Retrieved May 11, 2024, from DEVPOST: https://devpost.com/software/k-2bl1ch

Kamath, P. (2022, August 25). Retrieved April 7, 2024, from itilite: https://www.itilite.com/blog/virtual-travel-assistant-benefits/

Kannan, P. V., & Bernoff, J. (2019). The future of customer service is AI-Human collaboration. *MIT Sloan Management Review.*

Kant, S., Belay, B., & Dabaso, A. (2023). Coffee Logistics Operation Knowledge Effect on Cooperative Associations Functionalism in Ethiopia with Mediation of Cybernetics and Local People Knowledge Base. *Journal of Production, Operations Management and Economics, 3*(1), 21-33.

Kar, A. K., & Kushwaha, A. K. (2023). Facilitators and barriers of artificial intelligence adoption in business–insights from opinions using big data analytics. *Information Systems Frontiers*, 25(4), 1351–1374. 10.1007/s10796-021-10219-4

Kasneci, E., Seßler, K., Küchemann, S., Bannert, M., Dementieva, D., Fischer, F., Gasser, U., Groh, G., Günnemann, S., Hüllermeier, E., Krusche, S., Kutyniok, G., Michaeli, T., Nerdel, C., Pfeffer, J., Poquet, O., Sailer, M., Schmidt, A., Seidel, T., & Kasneci, G. (2023). ChatGPT for good? On opportunities and challenges of large language models for education. *Learning and Individual Differences*, 103, 102274. 10.1016/j.lindif.2023.102274

Kassa, A. G., & Tsigu, G. T. (2022). Corporate entrepreneurship, employee engagement and innovation: A resource-based view and a social exchange theory perspective. *The International Journal of Organizational Analysis*, 30(6), 1694–1711.

Kaur, M. (2021). Adoption of Artificial Intelligence in Human Resource Management: A Conceptual Model. *Indian Journal of Industrial Relations*, 57, 331.

Kaur, M., & Gandolfi, F. (2023). Research on Artificial Intelligence in Human Resource Management: Trends and Prospects. *Global Journal of Management and Business Research*, 23(1).

Kelley, S., Ovchinnikov, A., Hardoon, D. R., & Heinrich, A. (2022). Antidiscrimination laws, artificial intelligence, and gender bias: A case study in nonmortgage Fintech lending. *Manufacturing & Service Operations Management*, 24(6), 3039–3059. 10.1287/msom.2022.1108

Kgoale, T. J., & Odeku, K. (2023). An analysis of legal accountability for artificial intelligence systems in the South African financial sector. *De Jure (Durban)*, 56(1), 191–205. 10.17159/2225-7160/2023/v56a14

Khan, S., & Iqbal, M. (2020, June). AI-Powered Customer Service: Does it optimize customer experience? In *2020 8th International Conference on Reliability, Infocom Technologies and Optimization (Trends and Future Directions)(ICRITO)* (pp. 590-594). IEEE.

Kimseng, T., Javed, A., Jeenanunta, C., & Kohda, Y. (2020). Applications of Fuzzy Logic to Reconfigure Human Resource Management Practices for Promoting Product Innovation in Formal and Non-Formal R&D Firms. *Journal of Open Innovation*, 6(2), 38. Advance online publication. 10.3390/joitmc6020038

Kingma, D. P., & Welling, M. (2013). Auto-encoding variational bayes. *ArXiv Preprint ArXiv:1312.6114.*

Kiran, R. G. R., Manoharan, G., Durai, S., Ashtikar, S. P., & Kunchala. (2024). Higher Education in India and the Influence of Online Certification Programs. Evaluating Global Accreditation Standards for Higher Education. IGI Global.

Kitsios, F., & Kamariotou, M. (2021). Artificial intelligence and business strategy towards digital transformation: A research agenda. *Sustainability (Basel)*, 13(4), 2025. 10.3390/su13042025

Koene, A. (2017). Algorithmic Bias: Addressing Growing Concerns [Leading Edge]. *IEEE Technology and Society Magazine*, 36(2), 31–32. 10.1109/MTS.2017.2697080

Konstantinidis, T., Farres, A. B., Xu, Y. L., Constantinides, T. G., & Mandic, D. P. (2023, June). Financial News Classification Model for NLP-based Bond Portfolio Construction. In 2023 24th International Conference on Digital Signal Processing (DSP) (pp. 1-5). IEEE.

Kontzinos, C., Kanellou, I., Michalakopoulos, V., Mouzakitis, S., Tsapelas, G., Kapsalis, P., Kormpakis, G., & Askounis, D. (2022, November 8). State-of-the-art analysis of artificial intelligence approaches in the maritime industry. *Proceedings of the International Conferences on Applied Computing 2022 and WWW/Internet 2022*. 10.33965/AC_ICWI2022_202208C029

Koo, C., Xiang, Z., Gretzel, U., & Sigala, M. (2021). Artificial intelligence (AI) and robotics in travel, hospitality and leisure. *Electronic Markets*, 31(3), 473–476. 10.1007/s12525-021-00494-z35603226

Korzynski, P., Mazurek, G., Altmann, A., Ejdys, J., Kazlauskaite, R., Paliszkiewicz, J., Wach, K., & Ziemba, E. (2023). Generative artificial intelligence as a new context for management theories: Analysis of ChatGPT. *Central European Management Journal*, 31(1), 3–13. 10.1108/CEMJ-02-2023-0091

Kreines, M. G., & Kreines, E. M. (2019). Artificial Intelligence Tools for Business Applications: Objective Map of Science and Analysis of Texts. *In 2019 IEEE 21st Conference on Business Informatics (CBI)* (Vol. 1, pp. 445-451). IEEE. 10.1109/CBI.2019.00058

Kuhlemann, S., & Tierney, K. (2020). A genetic algorithm for finding realistic sea routes considering the weather. *Journal of Heuristics*, 26(6), 801–825. 10.1007/s10732-020-09449-7

Kumar Jaiswal, R., Sundar Sharma, S., & Kaushik, R. (2023). Ethics in AI and machine learning. *Journal of Nonlinear Analysis and Optimization, 14*(01), 08–12. 10.36893/JNAO.2023.V14I1.0008-0012

Kumar, C. S., Vani, D. D., Damodar, K., Manoharan, G., & Veerapaga, N. (2024). Climate Change Mitigation Through AI Solutions. In Gastronomic Sustainability Solutions for Community and Tourism Resilience (pp. 37-59). IGI Global. 10.4018/979-8-3693-4135-3.ch003

Kumar, D. B. (2023). *Harnessing the Power of Generative AI: Transforming the Maritime Industry*. Https://Www.Linkedin.Com/Pulse/Harnessing-Power-Generative-Ai-Transforming-Maritime-Kumar-Ph-d--5orqc

Kumari, B., Kaur, J., & Swami, S. (2024). Adoption of artificial intelligence in financial services: A policy framework. *Journal of Science and Technology Policy Management*, 15(2), 396–417. 10.1108/JSTPM-03-2022-0062

Kumari, S. (2021). Interplay of AI-Driven Maritime Logistics: An In-Depth Research into Port Management, Advanced Operations Automation, and CRM Integration for Optimized Performance and Efficiency. *ESP Journal of Engineering and Technology Advancements*, 1(1), 1–5.

Kumar, P., Kumar, A., & Sankar, J. G. (2020). Service quality of health tourism in India: A structural equation modelling approach. *Solid State Technology*, 63(2), 1187–1191.

Kusnan, K. (2020). Penggunaan hukum sebagai instrumen kebijakan publik dalam pengangkutan laut nasional. *Jurnal Widya Publika*, 8(2), 176–192. 10.47329/widyapublika.v8i2.648

La Barbera, S. (2023). Insurtech Revolution in the Insurance Sector: A Comprehensive Review of the Transformational Impact and the Lemonade Case Study.

Lalli, M. (2024, March 18). *datadrivendestinations.com.* Retrieved April 5, 2024, from Data Driven Destinations: https://datadrivendestinations.com/2024/03/ai-and-generative-ai-transforming-destination-management

Larsen, G. (2023). Boutique Staffing Firm Internship: How AI is Changing the Staffing Boutique Staffing Firm Internship: How AI is Changing the Staffing Industry. Retrieved from https://scholarworks.uark.edu/finnuht/113

Lee, K. Y., Kwon, H. Y., & Lim, J. I. (2018). Legal consideration on the use of artificial intelligence technology and self-regulation in financial sector: focused on robo-advisors. *In Information Security Applications: 18th International Conference, WISA 2017, Jeju Island, Korea, August 24-26, 2017, Revised Selected Papers 18* (pp. 323-335). Springer International Publishing.

Lee, J. (2020). Access to finance for artificial intelligence regulation in the financial services industry. *European Business Organization Law Review*, 21(4), 731–757. 10.1007/s40804-020-00200-0

Lee, P. T.-W., & Yang, Z. (Eds.). (2018). *Multi-Criteria Decision Making in Maritime Studies and Logistics* (Vol. 260). Springer International Publishing., 10.1007/978-3-319-62338-2

Leong, L. K. (2019). *AI Revolution: 6 steps to prepare your business.* Https://Maritimefairtrade.Org/Ai-Revolution-6-Steps-to-Prepare-Your-Business/

Leong, B. (2019). Facial recognition and the future of privacy: I always feel like… somebody's watching me. *Bulletin of the Atomic Scientists*, 75(3), 109–115. 10.1080/00963402.2019.1604886

Li, D., Liu, H., & Ng, S.-K. (2020). VC-GAN: Classifying Vessel Types by Maritime Trajectories using Generative Adversarial Networks. *2020 IEEE 32nd International Conference on Tools with Artificial Intelligence (ICTAI)*, 923–928. 10.1109/ICTAI50040.2020.00144

Li, L., Lassiter, T., Oh, J., & Lee, M. K. (2021). Algorithmic Hiring in Practice: Recruiter and HR Professional's Perspectives on AI Use in Hiring. Proceedings of the 2021 AAAI/ACM Conference on AI, Ethics, and Society. Association for Computing Machinery, 166–176. Retrieved from 10.1145/3461702.3462531

Lin, C.-C. & Chang, S.-F. (2021). Using AI to Improve Corporate Governance. 10.1051/e3sconf/202124503063

Lin, W.-K., Lin, S.-J., & Yang, T.-N. (2017). Integrated Business Prestige and Artificial Intelligence for Corporate Decision Making in Dynamic Environments. 10.1080/01969722.2017.1284533

Liu, X., Shin, H., & Burns, A. C. (2021). Examining the impact of luxury brand's social media marketing on customer engagement: Using big data analytics and natural language processing. *Journal of Business Research*, 125, 815–826. 10.1016/j.jbusres.2019.04.042

Lloyd, C., Misheal, M. R., & Tavonga, N. (2024). *Harnessing Machine Learning and Artificial Intelligence for Ear-ly Fraud Detection Among Banks in Harare, Zimbabwe: Internal Auditors' Perspective.*https://www.researchgate.net/profile/Regis-Muchowe/publication/378862992_Harnessing_Machine_Learning_and_Artificial_Intelligence_for_Ear-_ly_Fraud_Detection_Among_Banks_in_Harare_Zimbabwe_Internal_Auditors'_Perspective/links/65eef7889ab2af0ef8aecd54/Harnessing-Machine-Learning-and-Artificial-Intelligence-for-Ear-ly-Fraud-Detection-Among-Banks-in-Harare-Zimbabwe-Internal-Auditors-Perspective.pdf

Lorenz, P., Perset, K., & Berryhill, J. (2023). *Initial policy considerations for generative artificial intelligence.*

Lourens, M., Sharma, S., Pulugu, R., Gehlot, A., Manoharan, G., & Kapila, D. (2023, May). Machine learning-based predictive analytics and big data in the automotive sector. In 2023 3rd International Conference on Advance Computing and Innovative Technologies in Engineering (ICACITE) (pp. 1043-1048). IEEE. 10.1109/ICACITE57410.2023.10182665

Lozie, D. R., Omasa, R., Hesami, S., Zaman, S., Kajbaf, M., & Malik, A. R. (2024). Examining the impact of generative artificial intelligence on work dynamics. *Human Resources Management and Services*, 6(2), 3420. Advance online publication. 10.18282/hrms.v6i2.3420

Lund, B., & Wang, T. (2023). Chatting about ChatGPT: How may AI and GPT impact academia and libraries? *Library Hi Tech News*, 40(3), 26–29. 10.1108/LHTN-01-2023-0009

Lu, Y. (2019). Artificial intelligence: A survey on evolution, models, applications and future trends. *Journal of Management Analytics*, 6(1), 1–29. 10.1080/23270012.2019.1570365

Ma, Y., Wang, Z., Yang, H., & Yang, L. (2020). Artificial intelligence applications in the development of autonomous vehicles: A survey. *IEEE/CAA Journal of AutomaticaSinica, 7*(2), 315-329.

Madanchian, M., Taherdoost, H., & Mohamed, N. (2023). AI-Based Human Resource Management Tools and Techniques; A Systematic Literature Review. *Procedia Computer Science*, 229, 367–377. 10.1016/j.procs.2023.12.039

Mahesh, B. (2020). Machine learning algorithms-a review. International Journal of Science and Research, 9, 381-386.

Mai, K. N., & Nguyen, A. K. T. (2021). The Impact of Corporate Social Responsibility Performance on Competitive Advantage and Business Success: A Case of Vietnamese Enterprises. *International Journal of Asian Business and Information Management*, 12(3), 1–15. 10.4018/IJABIM.294095

Makedon, V., Mykhailenko, O., & Vazov, R. (2021). Dominants and Features of Growth of the World Market of Robotics. *European Journal of Management Issues*, 29(3), 133–141. 10.15421/192113

Malik, A., Thevisuthan, P., & Sliva, T. (2022). Artificial Intelligence, Employee Engagement, Experience, and HRM. In Malik, A. (Ed.), *Strategic Human Resource Management and Employment Relations* (pp. 171–184). Springer. 10.1007/978-3-030-90955-0_16

Malmborg, F. V. (2023). Advocacy coalitions and policy change for decarbonisation of international maritime transport: The case of FuelEU maritime. *Maritime Transport Research*. https://api.semanticscholar.org/CorpusID:259497857

Mamela, T. L., Sukdeo, N., & Mukwakungu, S. C. (2020). Adapting to artificial intelligence through workforce re-skilling within the banking sector in South Africa. *In 2020 International Conference on Artificial Intelligence, Big Data, Computing and Data Communication Systems (icABCD)* (pp. 1-9). IEEE.

Management, J. F. (2023, October 27). Retrieved April 13, 2024, from Medium: https://james-francis-paradigm.medium.com/unraveling-the-ethical-implications-artificial-intelligences-impact-on-cultural-appropriation

Mannuru, N. R., Shahriar, S., Teel, Z. A., Wang, T., Lund, B. D., Tijani, S., Pohboon, C. O., Agbaji, D., Alhassan, J., Galley, J., Kousari, R., Ogbadu-Oladapo, L., Saurav, S. K., Srivastava, A., Tummuru, S. P., Uppala, S., & Vaidya, P. (2023). Artificial intelligence in developing countries: The impact of generative artificial intelligence (AI) technologies for development. *Information Development*, 1–19. 10.1177/02666669231200628

Manoharan, G., Ashtikar, S. P., & Nivedha, M. (2024). Harnessing the Power of Artificial Intelligence in Reinventing the Manufacturing Sector. In Using Real-Time Data and AI for Thrust Manufacturing (pp. 113-137). IGI Global. 10.4018/979-8-3693-2615-2.ch007

Manoharan, G., Ashtikar, S. P., & Nivedha, M. (2024). Integrating Artificial Intelligence in Library Management: An Emerging Trend. AI-Assisted Library Reconstruction, 144-157.

Manoharan, G., Durai, S., Ashtikar, S. P., & Kumari, N. (2024). Artificial Intelligence in Marketing Applications. In Artificial Intelligence for Business (pp. 40-70). Productivity Press.

Manoharan, G., Durai, S., Rajesh, G. A., & Ashtikar, S. P. (2023). A Study on the Application of Natural Language Processing Used in Business Analytics for Better Management Decisions: A Literature Review. Artificial Intelligence and Knowledge Processing, 249-261.

Manoharan, G., Durai, S., Rajesh, G. A., & Ashtikar, S. P. (2024). A Study on the Application of Expert Systems as a Support System for Business Decisions: A Literature Review. Artificial Intelligence and Knowledge Processing, 279-289.

Manoharan, G., Jalaja, V., Sathe, M. A., Lourens, M., & Suresh, K. (2023, December). Machine Learning and Data Privacy in Human Resource Management. In 2023 4th International Conference on Computation, Automation and Knowledge Management (ICCAKM) (pp. 1-6). IEEE. 10.1109/ICCAKM58659.2023.10449576

Manoharan, G., Rao, C. G., Ashtikar, S. P., Kumar, S., & Nivedha, M. (2024). Voyage Virtuoso: Artificial Intelligence in Transforming Tourism. In Utilizing Smart Technology and AI in Hybrid Tourism and Hospitality (pp. 79-97). IGI Global.

Manoharan, G., Razak, A., Rajchandar, K., Nithya, G., Durai, S., & Ashtikar, S. P. (2024). Digital Learning for Professional Development in Varied Fields of Service Sectors: Embracing Technological Advancements. In Embracing Technological Advancements for Lifelong Learning (pp. 111-137). IGI Global.

Manoharan, G., Razak, A., Rao, B. S., Singh, R., Ashtikar, S. P., & Nivedha, M. (2024). Navigating the Crescendo of Challenges in Harnessing Artificial Intelligence for Disaster Management. In Predicting Natural Disasters With AI and Machine Learning (pp. 64-94). IGI Global. 10.4018/979-8-3693-2280-2.ch003

Manoharan, G., Razak, A., Rao, C. G., Ashtikar, S. P., & Nivedha, M. (2024). Artificial Intelligence at the Helm: Steering the Modern Business Landscape Toward Progress. In The Ethical Frontier of AI and Data Analysis (pp. 72-99). IGI Global.

Mansoursamaei, M., Moradi, M., González-Ramírez, R. G., & Lalla-Ruiz, E. (2023). Machine Learning for Promoting Environmental Sustainability in Ports. *Journal of Advanced Transportation*, 2023, 1–17. 10.1155/2023/2144733

Mao, J., Chen, B., & Liu, J. (2023). Generative Artificial Intelligence in Education and Its Implications for Assessment. *TechTrends*, 68(1), 58–66. 10.1007/s11528-023-00911-4

Maurya, S., Verma, R., Khilnani, L., Bhakuni, A. S., Kumar, M., & Rakesh, N. (2024). Effect of AI on the Financial Sector: Risk Control, Investment Decision-making, and Business Outcome. In *2024 11th International Conference on Reliability, Infocom Technologies and Optimization (Trends and Future Directions)(ICRITO)* (pp. 1-7). IEEE.

Maurya, S., Verma, R., Khilnani, L., Bhakuni, A. S., Kumar, M., & Rakesh, N. (2024, March). Effect of AI on the Financial Sector: Risk Control, Investment Decision-making, and Business Outcome. In 2024 11th International Conference on Reliability, Infocom Technologies and Optimization (Trends and Future Directions) (ICRITO) (pp. 1-7). IEEE.

Mbebeb, F. E., & Tanyi, F. B. B. (2019). Alternative Options In Building Workers' incentives: Effects On Job Satisfaction And Perceived Organizational Support In Local Context. *Global Journal of Human Resource Management*, 7(2), 38–53.

McKinsey & Company. (2024, April 2). Retrieved April 25, 2024, from McKinsey & Company: https://www.mckinsey.com/featured-insights/mckinsey-explainers/what-is-generative-ai

Mekala, S., Bhuvana, M., Gupta, D. B., Bhatt, V., Kunekar, P., & Manoharan, G. (2023, September). Natural Language Processing and Deep Learning Techniques to Improve Sentiment Analysis in Social Media Texts. In 2023 6th International Conference on Contemporary Computing and Informatics (IC3I) (Vol. 6, pp. 1751-1755). IEEE. 10.1109/IC3I59117.2023.10397735

Melehy, A. K. (2023). The Impact of AI on the Economy: A Comprehensive Analysis. Available online: https://www.researchgate. net/publication/370400293_The_Impact_of_AI_on_the_Economy_A_Comprehensive_Analysis

Meske, C., & Bunde, E. (2020). Transparency and trust in human-AI-interaction: The role of model-agnostic explanations in computer vision-based decision support. In Artificial Intelligence in HCI: First International Conference, AI-HCI 2020, Held as Part of the 22nd HCI International Conference, HCII 2020, Copenhagen, Denmark, July 19–24, 2020, Proceedings 22(pp. 54-69). Springer International Publishing. 10.1007/978-3-030-50334-5_4

Mhlanga, D. (2023). The Value of Open AI and Chat GPT for the Current Learning Environments and The Potential Future Uses. SSRN *Electron. J.* 10.2139/ssrn.4439267

Mhlanga, D. (2020). Industry 4.0 in finance: The impact of artificial intelligence (ai) on digital financial inclusion. *International Journal of Financial Studies*, 8(3), 45. 10.3390/ijfs8030045

Michael Chui, R. R. (2023, June 14). Retrieved July 7, 2024, from Mckinsey & Company: https://www.mckinsey.com/capabilities/mckinsey-digital/our-insights/the-economic-potential-of-generative-ai-the-next-productivity-frontier#business-value

Miler, R. K., & Bujak, A. (2013). *exactEarthSatellite – AIS as One of the Most Advanced Shipping Monitoring Systems* (pp. 330–337). 10.1007/978-3-642-41647-7_40

Millefiori, L. M., Braca, P., Zissis, D., Spiliopoulos, G., Marano, S., Willett, P. K., & Carniel, S. (2021). COVID-19 impact on global maritime mobility. *Scientific Reports*, 11(1), 18039. 10.1038/s41598-021-97461-734508144

Miola, A., Marra, M., & Ciuffo, B. (2011). Designing a climate change policy for the international maritime transport sector: Market-based measures and technological options for global and regional policy actions. *Energy Policy*, 39(9), 5490–5498. 10.1016/j.enpol.2011.05.013

Mithas, S., Murugesan, S., & Seetharaman, P. (2020). What is your artificial intelligence strategy? *IT Professional*, 22(2), 4–9. 10.1109/MITP.2019.2957620

Miziołek, T. (2021). Employing artificial intelligence in investment management. In *The Digitalization of Financial Markets* (pp. 161–174). Routledge. 10.4324/9781003095354-9

Mogaji, E., Soetan, T. O., & Kieu, T. A. (2020): The implications of artificial intelligence on the digital marketing of financial services to vulnerable customers. Australasian Marketing Journal. 10.1016/j.ausmj.2020.05.003

Mogaji, E., Balakrishnan, J., Nwoba, A. C., & Nguyen, N. P. (2021). Emerging-market consumers' interactions with banking chatbots. *Telematics and Informatics*, 65, 101711. 10.1016/j.tele.2021.101711

Mohajan, H. K. (2019). The first industrial revolution: Creation of a new global human era. *Journal of Social Sciences and Humanities*, 5(4), 377–387.

Mohamed, E. A., & Elnoury, A. (2023). Technological Innovations in the Maritime Sector: A Comprehensive Analysis of Intelligence Knowledge and Industry Dynamics for Graduates Adaptation. *AIN Journal*, 2(46). Advance online publication. 10.59660/467315

Mohanty, B., & Mishra, S. (2023). Role of Artificial Intelligence in Financial Fraud Detection. *Academy of Marketing Studies Journal*, 27(S4).

Morandini, S., Fraboni, F., De Angelis, M., Puzzo, G., Giusino, D., & Pietrantoni, L. (2023). The Impact of Artificial Intelligence on Workers' Skills: Upskilling and Reskilling in Organisations. *Informing Science: The International Journal of an Emerging Transdiscipline, 26*, 039–068. 10.28945/5078

Mujtaba, D. F., & Mahapatra, N. R. (2019, November). Ethical considerations in AI-based recruitment. In *2019 IEEE International Symposium on Technology and Society (ISTAS)* (pp. 1-7). IEEE.

Munim, Z. H., Dushenko, M., Jimenez, V. J., Shakil, M. H., & Imset, M. (2020). Big data and artificial intelligence in the maritime industry: A bibliometric review and future research directions. *Maritime Policy & Management*, 47(5), 577–597. 10.1080/03088839.2020.1788731

Murphy, J., Hofacker, C., & Gretzel, U. (2017). Dawning of the age of robots in hospitality and tourism: Challenges for teaching and research. *European Journal of Tourism Research*, 15, 104–111. 10.54055/ejtr.v15i.265

Murray, B., & Perera, L. P. (2020). A dual linear autoencoder approach for vessel trajectory prediction using historical AIS data. *Ocean Engineering*, 209, 107478. 10.1016/j.oceaneng.2020.107478

Nagaraj Samala, B. S. (2020, April 24). Impact of AI and robotics in the tourism sector: A critical insight. *Journal of Tourism Futures*, 8(1), 73–87. 10.1108/JTF-07-2019-0065

Nah, F., Zheng, R., Cai, J., Siau, K., & Chen, L. (2023). Generative AI and ChatGPT: Applications, challenges, and AI-human collaboration. J. Inf. Technol. Case Appl. Res., 25, 277–304.

Naik, I., Naik, D., & Naik, N. (2023). Chat Generative Pre-Trained Transformer (ChatGPT): Comprehending its Operational Structure, AI Techniques, Working, Features and Limitations. 3rd IEEE International Conference on ICT in Business Industry and Government, ICTBIG 2023. 10.1109/ICTBIG59752.2023.10456201

Naim, A. (2022). Role of artificial intelligence in business risk management. American Journal of Business Management. *Economics and Banking*, 1, 55–66.

Najdawi, A. (2020). Assessing AI readiness across organizations: the case of UAE. In 2020 11th International Conference on Computing, Communication and Networking Technologies (ICCCNT) (pp. 1-5). IEEE. DOI: 10.1109/ICCCNT49239.2020.9225386

Naser, M. Z. (2021). An engineer's guide to eXplainable Artificial Intelligence and Interpretable Machine Learning: Navigating causality, forced goodness, and the false perception of inference. *Automation in Construction*, 129, 103821.

Nechaeva, A. (2023, August 17). Retrieved April 3, 2024, from solimarInternational: https://www.solimarinternational.com/the-impact-of-ai-on-the-travel-industry/

Neelam, K., Rahul, P. S., & Brijesh, S. a. (2023). Artificial intelligence and HRM: identifying future research Agenda using systematic literature review and bibliometric analysis. *Management Review Quarterly*, 455-493.

Negro, A. R., & Mesia, R. (2019). Organization and Society: Understanding Corporate Social Responsibility and The Inclusive Business in The Peruvian Business Environment. *Journal of Applied Business & Economics*, 21(5). Advance online publication. 10.33423/jabe.v21i5.2275

Neubig, S., Baecker, J., Gehring, N., Hein, A., Weking, J., &Krcmar, H. (2022). Data-driven Initiatives of Destinations Supporting Sustainable Tourism.

Neudert, L. M., Knuutila, A., & Howard, P. N. (2020). *Global attitudes towards AI, machine learning & automated decision making*. Working paper 2020.10, Oxford Commission on AI & Good Governance.

Ng, B. (2018, April 12). Retrieved April 10, 2024, from rezdy: https://rezdy.com/blog/pros-cons-artificial-intelligence-travel-industry/

Nguyen, M. Q., Nguyen, T. K. C., & Pham, H. G. (2022). Sustainable Development under the Impacts of the Fourth Industrial Revolution and the Role of Corporate Culture Renovation. *VNU Journal of Science: Policy and Management Studies*, 38(3). Advance online publication. 10.25073/2588-1116/vnupam.4412

Nica, I., Delcea, C., & Chiri ă, N. (2024). Mathematical Patterns in Fuzzy Logic and Artificial Intelligence for Financial Analysis: A Bibliometric Study. *Mathematics*, 12(5), 782. 10.3390/math12050782

Nicastro, D. (2020). 7 Ways Artificial Intelligence Is Reinventing Human Resources. Retrieved from https://www.cmswire.com/digital-workplace/7-ways-artificial-intelligence-is-reinventing-human-resources/

Nieto-Rodriguez, A., & Vargas, R. V. (2023). How AI Will Transform Project Management. Retrieved from Harvard Business Review: https://hbr.org/2023/02/how-ai-will-transform-project-management

Nir Kshetri, Y. K. (2023, October 18). Generative artificial intelligence in marketing: Applications, opportunities, challenges, and research agenda. *International Journal of Information Management*, 75(6), 71–75.

Nistler, J., & Tomas, P. (2023). Graphical use of AI. Retrieved from https://www.vtei.cz/2023/04/

Novianti, W., & Qadri, F. (2020). Design of Information System Human Resource Management. *IOP Conference Series. Materials Science and Engineering*, 879(1), 012126. Advance online publication. 10.1088/1757-899X/879/1/012126

Ochuba, N. A., Adewunmi, A., & Olutimehin, D. O. (2024). The role of AI in financial market development: Enhancing efficiency and accessibility in emerging economies. *Finance and Accounting Research Journal*, 6(3), 421–436. 10.51594/farj.v6i3.969

Odeyemi, O., Okoye, C. C., Ofodile, O. C., Adeoye, O. B., Addy, W. A., & Ajayi-Nifise, A. O. (2024). Integrating AI with blockchain for enhanced financial services security. *Finance & Accounting Research Journal*, 6(3), 271–287. 10.51594/farj.v6i3.855

Okolo, C. T. (2023). The Promise and Perils of Generative AI: Case Studies in an African Context. *ACM International Conference Proceeding Series*, 266–270. Retrieved from 10.1145/3628096.3629066

Oliinyk, I. M. (2023). Prospects for implementing generative artificial intelligence in marketing and trade, Naukovij vìsnik L′otnoï akademìï, vol., p. 110-115.

Olson, G. (2023, March 13). Retrieved April 10, 2024, from Thrifty Traveler: https://thriftytraveler.com/guides/travel/tripit-review/

Omoge, A. P., Gala, P., & Horky, A. (2022). Disruptive technology and AI in the banking industry of an emerging market. *International Journal of Bank Marketing*, 40(6), 1217–1247. 10.1108/IJBM-09-2021-0403

Ooi, K. B., Tan, G. W. H., Al-Emran, M., Al-Sharafi, M. A., Capatina, A., Chakraborty, A., Dwivedi, Y. K., Huang, T. L., Kar, A. K., Lee, V. H., Loh, X. M., Micu, A., Mikalef, P., Mogaji, E., Pandey, N., Raman, R., Rana, N. P., Sarker, P., Sharma, A., & Wong, L. W. (2023). The Potential of Generative Artificial Intelligence Across Disciplines: Perspectives and Future Directions. *Journal of Computer Information Systems*, 1–32. Advance online publication. 10.1080/08874417.2023.2261010

Overgoor, G., Chica, M., Rand, W., & Weishampel, A. (2019). Letting the computers take over: Using AI to solve marketing problems. *California Management Review*, 61(4), 156–185. 10.1177/0008125619859318

Owoc, M. L., Sawicka, A., & Weichbroth, P. (2019). Artificial intelligence technologies in education: benefits, challenges and strategies of implementation. In *IFIP International Workshop on Artificial Intelligence for Knowledge Management* (pp. 37-58). Cham: Springer International Publishing. DOI: 1007/978-3-030-85001-2_4

Oyeniyi, L. D., Ugochukwu, C. E., & Mhlongo, N. Z. (2024). Transforming financial planning with AI-driven analysis: A review and application insights. *Finance & Accounting Research Journal*, 6(4), 626–647. 10.51594/farj.v6i4.1037

Panch, T., Szolovits, P., & Atun, R. (2018). Artificial intelligence, machine learning and health systems. *Journal of Global Health*, 8(2).

Pan, N., Ding, Y., Fu, J., Wang, J., & Zheng, H. (2021). Research on Ship Arrival Law Based on Route Matching and Deep Learning. *Journal of Physics: Conference Series*, 1952(2), 022023. 10.1088/1742-6596/1952/2/022023

Papadimitriou, L., Mpartzeliotis, K., Nikas, S., & Vessala, M. (2017). A Comparative Analysis of Knowledge-Based Firms in High-Tech Sectors and Knowledge Intensive Business Services. In Strategic Innovative Marketing: 4th IC-SIM, Mykonos, Greece 2015(pp. 419-424). Springer International Publishing. DOI: 10.1007/978-3-319-33865-1_52

Parikh, N. A. (2023). Empowering business transformation: The positive impact and ethical considerations of generative AI in software product management – a systematic literature review, Transformational Interventions for Business. *Technology and Health Care*, 269–293.

Park, S. H. (2023). Use of Generative Artificial Intelligence, Including Large Language Models Such as ChatGPT, in Scientific Publications: Policies of *KJR* and Prominent Authorities. *Korean Journal of Radiology*, 24(8), 715. 10.3348/kjr.2023.064337500572

Paschen, J., Wilson, M., & Ferreira, J. J. (2020). Collaborative intelligence: How human and artificial intelligence create value along the B2B sales funnel. *Business Horizons*, 63(3), 403–414. 10.1016/j.bushor.2020.01.003

Pataranutaporn, P., Danry, V., Leong, J., Punpongsanon, P., Novy, D., Maes, P., & Sra, M. (2021). AI-generated characters for supporting personalized learning and well-being. *Nature Machine Intelligence*, 3(12), 1013–1022. 10.1038/s42256-021-00417-9

Paul, R. K., & Sarkar, B. (2023). Generative AI and ethical considerations for trustworthy AI implementation. *Journal ID, 2157*, 0178.

Paulauskaite-Taraseviciene, A., Lagzdinyte-Budnike, I., Gaiziuniene, L., Sukacke, V., & Daniuseviciute-Brazaite, L. (2022). Assessing education for sustainable development in engineering study programs: A case of AI ecosystem creation. *Sustainability (Basel)*, 14(3), 1702. 10.3390/su14031702

Pauline A. Milwood, S. H.-C. (2023, January 15). A Scoping Study of Ethics in Artificial Intelligence Research in Tourism and Hospitality. *Information and Communication Technologies in Tourism*, 2023, 243–254.

Pelot, R., Eng, P., Lin, D., Wu, C., & Hilliard, D. (2009). Spatial Analysis of Maritime Traffic for Maritime Security.

Peng, L., & Zhao, B. (2024). Navigating the Ethical Landscape Behind ChatGPT. *Big Data & Society*, 1-5(1). Advance online publication. 10.1177/20539517241237488

Peponi, A., Morgado, P., & Kumble, P. (2022). Life cycle thinking and machine learning for urban metabolism assessment and prediction. *Sustainable Cities and Society*, 80, 103754.

Peranzo, P. (2019). *AI assistant: the future of travel industry with the increase of artificial intelligence*. Imaginovation. Imagination Turns to Innovation.

Pérez-Campuzano, D., Ortega, P. M., Andrada, L. R., & López-Lázaro, A. (2021). Artificial Intelligence potential within airlines: A review on how AI can enhance strategic decision-making in times of COVID-19. *Journal of Airline and Airport Management*, 11(2), 53–72. 10.3926/jairm.189

Perucica, N., & Andjelkovic, K. (2022). Is the future of AI sustainable? A case study of the European Union. Transforming Government: People. *Process and Policy*, 16(3), 347–358. 1108/tg-06-2021-0106

Phoon, K. F., & Koh, C. C. F. (2018). Robo-advisors and wealth management. *Journal of Alternative Investments*, 20(3), 79–94. 10.3905/jai.2018.20.3.079

Prange, C. I. (2020). Strategic agility–decision-making beyond speed. In Academy of Management Proceedings (Vol. 2020, No. 1, p. 12499). Academy of Management. 10.5465/AMBPP.2020.12499abstract

Prasad, A., & Seetharaman, A. (2021). Importance of machine learning in making investment decisions in the stock market. *Vikalpa*, 46(4), 209–222. 10.1177/02560909211059992

Prashant Balodi, A. T. (2022, December). Role of artificial intelligence in the travel and hospitality industry. *International Journal of Food and Nutritional Sciences*, 11(3), 3138–3149.

Prentice, C., Weaven, S., & Wong, I. A. (2020). Linking AI quality performance and customer engagement: The moderating effect of AI preference. *International Journal of Hospitality Management*, 90, 102629. 10.1016/j.ijhm.2020.102629

Publications, M. (2024). *Generative AI & ChatGPT for Beginners Made Easy 2-Books-in-1: Master Artificial Intelligence Fundamentals, Elevate Your Skills, and Unlock Money-Making Strategies with Conversational AI.* ModernMind Publications.

Qamar, Y., Agrawal, R., Samad, T., & Jabbour, C. (2021). When technology meets people: The interplay of artificial intelligence and human resource management. *Journal of Enterprise Information Management*, 34(5), 1339–1370. Advance online publication. 10.1108/JEIM-11-2020-0436

R, P. (2024, March 4). Retrieved April 25, 2024, from intuz: https://www.intuz.com/blog/generative-ai-in-travel-tourism

Rajagopal, N. K., Qureshi, N. I., Durga, S., Ramirez Asis, E. H., Huerta Soto, R. M., Gupta, S. K., & Deepak, S. (2022). Future of business culture: An artificial intelligence-driven digital framework for organization decision-making process. *Complexity*, 2022(1), 1–14. 10.1155/2022/7796507

Raja, S., Jebadurai, D. J., Ivan, L., Mykola, R. V., Ruslan, K., & Nadiia, P. R. (2024). Impact of Artificial Intelligence in Students' Learning Life. In *AI in Business: Opportunities and Limitations* (Vol. 2, pp. 3–17). Springer Nature Switzerland. 10.1007/978-3-031-49544-1_1

Rajchandar, K., Kothandaraman, D., Manoharan, G., & Kabanda, G. (n.d.). Robotics and its Navigation Techniques: The Present and Future Revelations. Handbook of Artificial Intelligence and Wearables, 189-204.

Rajchandar, K., Manoharan, G., & Ashtikar, S. P. (2024, February). Robustness in Natural Language Processing: Addressing Challenges in Text-based AI Systems. In 2024 11th International Conference on Computing for Sustainable Global Development (INDIACom) (pp. 1435-1439). IEEE.

Raji, B. S. (n.d.). Exploring How Artificial Intelligence (AI) Can Support Start-Ups to Manage Crisis Situations for Future Sustainable Business in the Agri-Food Industry. DOI: 4018/978-1-7998-9815-3.ch014

Raji, B. S. (2022). Exploring how artificial intelligence (AI) can support start-ups to manage crisis situations for future sustainable business in the agri-food industry. In *Future Role of Sustainable Innovative Technologies in Crisis Management* (pp. 192–213). IGI Global. 10.4018/978-1-7998-9815-3.ch014

Ramachandran, K. K., Mary, A. A. S., Hawladar, S., Asokk, D., Bhaskar, B., & Pitroda, J. R. (2022). Machine learning and role of artificial intelligence in optimizing work perceived organizational support and employee behavior. *Materials Today: Proceedings*, 51, 2327–2331.

Rana, T. (2018). The Future of HR in the Presence of AI: A Conceptual Study. SSRN *Electronic Journal*. 10.2139/ssrn.3335670

Randle, O. A., Coleman, A., & Kekwaletswe, R. (2017). *Towards a Motivational based Model for Effective Use of Human Resource Information System in South African Universities*. IEEE. 10.23919/i-Society.2017.8354672

Rane, N. (2023). Role and Challenges of ChatGPT and Similar Generative Artificial Intelligence in Human Resource Management. SSRN *Electronic Journal*. 10.2139/ssrn.4603230

Rane, N., Choudhary, S., & Rane, J. (2023). Sustainable tourism development using leading-edge Artificial Intelligence (AI), Blockchain, Internet of Things (IoT), Augmented Reality (AR) and Virtual Reality (VR) technologies. *Blockchain, Internet of Things (IoT), Augmented Reality (AR) and Virtual Reality (VR) technologies*.

Rane, N., Choudhary, S., & Rane, J. (2024). Artificial Intelligence-driven corporate finance: enhancing efficiency and decision-making through machine learning, natural language processing, and robotic process automation in corporate governance and sustainability. Natural Language Processing, and Robotic Process Automation in Corporate Governance and Sustainability (February 8, 2024).

Rani, S., Babbar, H., Kaur, P., Alshehri, M. D., & Shah, S. H. A. (2022). An Optimized Approach of Dynamic Target Nodes in Wireless Sensor Network Using Bio Inspired Algorithms for Maritime Rescue. *IEEE Transactions on Intelligent Transportation Systems*, 1–8. 10.1109/TITS.2021.3129914

Rani, Y. A., Balaram, A., Sirisha, M. R., Nabi, S. A., Renuka, P., & Kiran, A. (2024, April). AI Enhanced Customer Service Chatbot. In *2024 International Conference on Science Technology Engineering and Management (ICSTEM)* (pp. 1-5). IEEE.

Rasheed, R., & Ishaq, M.N. & ur Rehman, H. (2021). Artificial Intelligence in Corporate Business and Financial Management: A Performance Analysis from Pakistan. Review of Education. *Administration & Law*, 4(4), 847–860.

Rathnayake, C., & Gunawardana, A. (2023). *The Role of Generative AI in Enhancing Human Resource Management Recruitment*. Training, and Performance Evaluation Perspectives. In International Journal of Social Analytics.

Rathore, S. (2023). The Impact of AI on Recruitment and Selection Processes: Analysing the role of AI in automating and enhancing. *International Journal for Global Academic & Scientific Research*, 78-93.

Razak, A., Nayak, M. P., Manoharan, G., Durai, S., Rajesh, G. A., Rao, C. B., & Ashtikar, S. P. (2023). Reigniting the power of artificial intelligence in education sector for the educators and students competence. In *Artificial Intelligence and Machine Learning in Smart City Planning* (pp. 103–116). Elsevier. 10.1016/B978-0-323-99503-0.00009-0

Reddy, R. (2006). Robotics and intelligent systems in support of society. *IEEE Intelligent Systems*, 21(3), 24–31. 10.1109/MIS.2006.57

Rehman, M., Dhiman, D. B., & Cheema, G. S. (2024). Minds and Machines: Impact of Emotional Intelligence on Investment Decisions with Mediating the Role of Artificial Intelligence. International Journal of Engineering, Business and Management, *8*(1), 1-10.

Ren, J. (2021). Research on financial investment decisions based on artificial intelligence algorithms. *IEEE Sensors Journal*, 21(22), 25190–25197. 10.1109/JSEN.2021.3104038

Restoy, F. (2019). Regulating fintech: what is going on, and where are the challenges. *Bank for International Settlements*, 1-7.

Robards, M., Silber, G., Adams, J., Arroyo, J., Lorenzini, D., Schwehr, K., & Amos, J. (2016). Conservation science and policy applications of the marine vessel Automatic Identification System (AIS)—A review. *Bulletin of Marine Science*, 92(1), 75–103. 10.5343/bms.2015.1034

Rodrigue, J.-P. (2020). *The geography of transport systems*. Routledge. 10.4324/9780429346323

Roh, T., Park, B. I., & Xiao, S. S. (2023). Adoption of AI-enabled Robo-advisors in Fintech: Simultaneous Employment of UTAUT and the Theory of Reasoned Action. *Journal of Electronic Commerce Research*, 24(1), 29–47.

Rolnick, D., Donti, P. L., Kaack, L. H., Kochanski, K., Lacoste, A., Sankaran, K., Ross, A. S., Milojevic-Dupont, N., Jaques, N., Waldman-Brown, A., Luccioni, A., Maharaj, T., Sherwin, E. D., Mukkavilli, S. K., Kording, K. P., Gomes, C., Ng, A. Y., Hassabis, D., Platt, J. C., ... Bengio, Y. (2019). *Tackling Climate Change with Machine Learning*. Academic Press.

Roseneil S. (2011). Criticality, not paranoia: A generative register for feminist social research. NORA-Nordic Journal of Feminist and Gender Research, 19(2), 124-31.

Rožman, M., Oreški, D., & Tominc, P. (2023). Artificial-intelligence-supported reduction of employees' workload to increase the company's performance in today's VUCA Environment. *Sustainability (Basel)*, 15(6), 5019. 10.3390/su15065019

Rudra Kumar, M., & Gunjan, V. K. (2022, May). Machine Learning Based Solutions for Human Resource Systems Management. In *ICCCE 2021: Proceedings of the 4th International Conference on Communications and Cyber Physical Engineering* (pp. 1239-1249). Singapore: Springer Nature Singapore.

Ruokonen, M., & Ritala, P. (2023). How to succeed with an AI-first strategy? *The Journal ofBusiness Strategy*. Advance online publication. 10.1108/JBS-08-2023-0178

Russo, D. (2024). Navigating the complexity of generative ai adoption in software engineering. *ACM Transactions on Software Engineering and Methodology*, 33(5), 1–50. 10.1145/3652154

Rust, R. (2020). The future of marketing. *International Journal of Research in Marketing*, 37(1), 15–26. 10.1016/j.ijresmar.2019.08.002

Rutskiy, V., Aljarbouh, A., Thommandru, A., Elkin, S., Amrani, Y. E., Semina, E., & Tsarev, R. (2022). Prospects for the Use of Artificial Intelligence to Combat Fraud in Bank Payments. In *Proceedings of the Computational Methods in Systems and Software* (pp. 959-971). Cham: Springer International Publishing.

Sabir, A. A., Ahmad, I., Ahmad, H., Rafiq, M., Khan, M. A., & Noreen, N. (2023). Consumer acceptance and adoption of AI robo-advisors in fintech industry. *Mathematics*, 11(6), 1311. 10.3390/math11061311

Sakthi, S., Nathan, K., & Karthi, D. R. (2023). Future of Electronic Human Resource Management in the IT Sector. Retrieved from http://eelet.org.uk

Samala, N., Katkam, B. S., Bellamkonda, R. S., & Rodriguez, R. V. (2020). Impact of AI and robotics in the tourism sector: a critical insight. *Journal of Tourism Futures, 8*(1), 73-87.

Samarasinghe, K., & Medis, A. (2020, March 26). Artificial Intelligence Based Strategic Human Resource Management (AISHRM) For Industry 4.0. *Global Journal of Management and Business Research*, 7–13. Advance online publication. 10.34257/GJMBRGVOl20IS2PG7

Sankar, J. G. (2024a). AI-Driven Marketing Success Stories: A Case Note of Industry Pioneers. In *AI-Driven Marketing Research and Data Analytics* (pp. 48-66). IGI Global. 10.4018/979-8-3693-2165-2.ch003

Sankar, J. G. (2024b). Travel Redefined: Future Trends in AI-Enhanced Tourism Experiences. In *AI Innovations for Travel and Tourism* (pp. 135-162). IGI Global.

Sankar, J. G. (2024c). Travel Redefined: Future Trends in AI-Enhanced Tourism Experiences. In *AI Innovations for Travel and Tourism* (pp. 135-162). IGI Global.

Sankar, J. G., & David, A. (2023). Measuring the Service Quality of Artificial Intelligence in the Tourism and Hospitality Industry. In *Handbook of Research on Innovation, Differentiation, and New Technologies in Tourism, Hotels, and Food Service* (pp. 133-155). IGI Global. 10.4018/978-1-6684-6985-9.ch007

Sankar, J. G., & David, A. (2024a). A Comprehensive Examination of Mobile Augmented Reality in Tourism (MART) Adoption: Using the UTAUT2 Framework. In *Contemporary Trends in Innovative Marketing Strategies* (pp. 241-262). IGI Global.

Sankar, J. G., & David, A. (2024b). Transforming the Travel Landscape: Smart Contracts in Tourism Management. In *Decentralizing the Online Experience With Web3 Technologies* (pp. 246-266). IGI Global.

Sankar, J. G., David, A., & Ramasamy, R. (2023). Assessing Water and Sanitation Service Quality at Pilgrimage Sites After COVID-19: An Empirical Investigation. In *Prospects and Challenges of Global Pilgrimage Tourism and Hospitality* (pp. 160-179). IGI Global.

Sankar, J. G., David, A., & Shrutimeena, G. (2024). From Hesitation to Integration: Understanding Digital Healthcare Adoption. In *Multi-Sector Analysis of the Digital Healthcare Industry* (pp. 1-32). IGI Global.

Sankar, G., & Naveenkumar, K. (2018). *Material Handling Management in Third Party Logistics Warehouse. International Journal for Research in Engineering Application & Management.*

Sankar, J. G. (2020a). Customer perception about innovative safety food delivery during lockdown. *Journal of Contemporary Issues in Business and Government*, 26(2).

Sankar, J. G. (2020b). Innovative celebrity endorsement and consumer purchase. *Journal of Contemporary Issues in Business and Government*, 26(2).

Sankar, J. G. (2020c). Innovative consumer behaviour towards sportswear. *Journal of Contemporary Issues in Business and Government*, 26(2).

Sankar, J. G. (2020d). Service Factors Influence on Customer Satisfaction in Innovative Ecommerce. *SANKAR, D.(2020). Service factors influence on customer satisfaction in innovative e-commerce.Journal of Contemporary Issues in Business and Government*, 26(2), 651–656.

Sankar, J. G. (2020e). Service quality of e-Commerce logistics services. *Journal of Contemporary Issues in Business and Government*, 26(2).

Sankar, J. G., & Kumar, G. (2020). Customer perception towards electric two-wheeler innovation. *Journal of Contemporary Issues in Business and Government*, 26(2).

Sankar, J. G., David, A., & Ganesh Kumar, C. (2022). Adaptation of Blockchain Technology In HRM. *Available atSSRN* 4515408.

Sankar, J. G., David, A., & Valan, P. (2023). Examining User Understanding and Perceptions of E-Commerce Data Privacy, Security, and Protection. In *Confronting Security and Privacy Challenges in Digital Marketing* (pp. 159–185). IGI Global. 10.4018/978-1-6684-8958-1.ch008

Sankar, J. G., & Devanand, K. (2020). Social media innovation on consumer buying behaviour. *SANKAR, JG (2020). Social media innovation on consumer buying behaviour.Journal of Contemporary Issues in Business and Government*, 26(2).

Sankar, J. G., & Kiruba Sagar, M, V. (2020). Examining the Risk Factor Associated with UTAUT Model. *Solid State Technology*, 63(2), 1196–1198.

Sankar, J. G., Rajeswari, M., & Dwarak, M. V. S. (2020). To Measure the Service Quality of Film and Television Technology. *Solid State Technology*, 63(2), 1192–1195.

Sankar, J. G., & Srinivasulu, Y. (2014a). A Study of Tourism Industry Impact on Macroeconomic Indicators. *GE-International Journal of Management Research*, 2(11), 2321–1709.

Sankar, J. G., & Srinivasulu, Y. (2014b). Contemporary Sustainable Development Practices in Indian Hospitality Sector: Triple Bottom Line Approach. *SSRN*, 2. 10.2139/ssrn.4204732

Sankar, J. G., Valan, P., & Siranjeevi, M. S. (2020). Various Models to Evaluate Quality in the Service Industry. In *Digital Transformation and Innovative Services for Business and Learning* (pp. 181–194). IGI Global.

Santos, C. (n.d.). Retrieved April 12, 2024, from Stippl.: https://stippl.io/blog/ai-travel-what-are-the-pros-and-cons-for-travelers

Sasikala, J., & Jeganathan, G. S. (2017). A Study on Employee Engagement in Information Technology (IT) Industry. *SSRN*, 1(1), 233–239. 10.2139/ssrn.3536354

Saulat, A. (2018). Four ways AI is re-imagining the future of travel. Mindtree. com.

Schuett, J. (2023). Risk management in the Artificial Intelligence Act. *European Journal of Risk Regulation*, 1–19. 10.1017/err.2023.1

Secure Privacy. (2023, October 4). Retrieved April 11, 2024, from Secure Privacy: https://secureprivacy.ai/blog/ai-personal-data-protection-gdpr-ccpa-compliance

Seeck, H., & Diehl, M. R. (2017). A literature review on HRM and innovation–taking stock and future directions. *International Journal of Human Resource Management*, 28(6), 913–944.

Shah, C. (2023). Generative AI and the Future of Information Access. *Proceedings of the 32nd ACM International Conference on Information and Knowledge Management*, 3–3. 10.1145/3583780.3615317

Shaheen, M., Arshad, M., & Iqbal, O. (2020). Role and Key Applications of Artificial Intelligence & Machine Learning in Transportation. *European Journal of Technology*, 4(1), 47–59. 10.47672/ejt.632

Shambira, L. (2020). Exploring the adoption of artificial intelligence in the Zimbabwe banking sector. *European Journal of Social Sciences Studies*, 5(6), 110–124. 10.46827/ejsss.v5i6.942

Shameem, A., Ramachandran, K. K., Sharma, A., Singh, R., Selvaraj, F. J., & Manoharan, G. (2023, May). The rising importance of AI in boosting the efficiency of online advertising in developing countries. In 2023 3rd International Conference on Advance Computing and Innovative Technologies in Engineering (ICACITE) (pp. 1762-1766). IEEE. 10.1109/ICACITE57410.2023.10182754

Shanmuganathan, M. (2020). Behavioural finance in an era of artificial intelligence: Longitudinal case study of robo-advisors in investment decisions. *Journal of Behavioral and Experimental Finance*, 27, 100297. 10.1016/j.jbef.2020.100297

Sharma, S., Rawal, Y. S., Soni, H., & Batabyal, D. (2023, February). Technological Impacts of AI on Hospitality and Tourism Industry. In *Proceedings of International Conference on Data Science and Applications: ICDSA 2022,* Volume 1 (pp. 71-78). Singapore: Springer Nature Singapore. 10.1007/978-981-19-6631-6_6

Sharma, A. (2022). HRIS-Challenges, Obstacles and Implementation. *Parichay Maharaja Surajmal Institute Journal of Applied Research*, 5(1), 49–53.

Shaw, J. D. (2021). The resource-based view and its use in strategic human resource management research: The elegant and inglorious. *Journal of Management*, 47(7), 1787–1795.

Sheth, J. N., Jain, V., Roy, G., & Chakraborty, A. (2022). AI-driven banking services: The next frontier for a personalised experience in the emerging market. *International Journal of Bank Marketing*, 40(6), 1248–1271. 10.1108/IJBM-09-2021-0449

Shin, D., Koerber, A., & Lim, J. S. (2024). Impact of misinformation from generative AI on user information processing: How people understand misinformation from generative AI. *New Media & Society*, 1–31. 10.1177/14614448241234040

Shoetan, P. O., & Familoni, B. T. (2024). Transforming fintech fraud detection with advanced artificial intelligence algorithms. *Finance and Accounting Research Journal*, 6(4), 602–625. 10.51594/farj.v6i4.1036

Simitha, S., Mugila, P., & Sankar, J. G. (2020). A Study on Customer Relationship Management in Siemens Healthineers. *Solid State Technology*, 63(2), 1199–1203.

Simões, R. V., Parreiras, M. V. C., Da Silva, A. C. C., Barbosa, C. E., de Lima, Y. O., & de Souza, J. M. (2022). Artificial intelligence and digital transformation: analyzing future trends. In *2022 IEEE International Conference on Systems, Man, and Cybernetics (SMC)*(pp. 1462-1467). IEEE. 10.1109/SMC53654.2022.9945429

Singh, C. R., & Manoharan, G. (2024). Strengthening Resilience: AI and Machine Learning in Emergency Decision-Making for Natural Disasters. In Internet of Things and AI for Natural Disaster Management and Prediction (pp. 249-278). IGI Global.

Singh, L. (2023, November 18). Retrieved April 3, 2024, from yellow.ai: https://yellow.ai/blog/chatbot-for-travel/

Singh, A., & Sahoo, D. (2023). Revolutionizing Recruitment: Harnessing the Power of Technology. *IRE Journals*, 6(12), 1343–1355.

Singh, N., & Adhikari, D. (2023). Challenges and Solutions in Integrating AI with Legacy Inventory Systems. *International Journal for Research in Applied Science and Engineering Technology*, 11(12), 609–613. 10.22214/ijraset.2023.57376

Singh, S. K., Rathore, S., & Park, J. H. (2020). Blockiotintelligence: A blockchain-enabled intelligent IoT architecture with artificial intelligence. *Future Generation Computer Systems*, 110, 721–743. 10.1016/j.future.2019.09.002

Siregar, E., & Dachyar, M. (2018). Determining Criteria of Human Resource Information System that Affect Human Resource Performance in Companies Using DEMATEL-Based ANP Method. https://doi.org/10.1051/matecconf/2018248030

Sirimanne, S. N., Hoffman, J., Juan, W., Asariotis, R., Assaf, M., Ayala, G., Ayoub, A., Benamara, H., Chantrel, D., & Hoffmann, J. (2020). Review of maritime transport 2020. *United Nations Conference on Trade and Development.*

Smolarek, B. B., & Scrivener, L. (2021). Examining business-driven education reform by new policy actors: A discursive analysis of UpSkill Houston. *Journal of Education Policy*, 36(3), 349–366. 10.1080/02680939.2019.1686539

Solberg, E., Kaarstad, M., Eitrheim, M. H. R., Bisio, R., Reegård, K., & Bloch, M. (2022). A conceptual model of trust, perceived risk, and reliance on AI decision aids. *Group & Organization Management*, 47(2), 187–222. 10.1177/10596011221081238

Soori, M., Arezoo, B., & Dastres, R. (2023). Artificial intelligence, machine learning and deep learning in advanced robotics, a review. *Cognitive Robotics*, 3, 54–70. 10.1016/j.cogr.2023.04.001

Srivastava, K., & Dhamija, S. (2022, May). FinTech: Application of Artificial Intelligence in Indian Banking. In *Proceedings of International Conference on Communication and Artificial Intelligence: ICCAI 2021* (pp. 601-613). Singapore: Springer Nature Singapore. 10.1007/978-981-19-0976-4_50

Statista. (n.d.). Retrieved July 7, 2024, from statista: https://www.statista.com/topics/10887/artificial-intelligence-ai-use-in-travel-and-tourism/

Stergiou, D. P. (2022). *Social Exchange Theory. Encyclopedia of Tourism Management and Marketing*. Edward Elgar Publishing.

Stipić, V. V. (2021). Interaction of strategic management processes and achieved corporate profitability: Evidence from Croatia. In BH Ekonomski forum(No. 13, pp. 133-149). Ekonomski fakultet-Univerzitet u Zenici.

Stojanović, D., Slović, D., Tomašević, I., & Simeunović, B. (2016). Model for selection of business process improvement methodologies. In *19th International Toulon-Verona Conference on Excellence in Services* (Vol. 5, pp. 453-467). Huelva.

Stopford, M. (2009). *Maritime Economics. Routledge.*

Suffian, A., & Zahari, M. (2017). User Satisfaction on Human Resource Management Information System (HRMIS): A Case Study at Terengganu Police Contingent, Malaysia. Journal of Biological and Environmental Sciences. Retrieved from https://www.researchgate.net/publication/322758387

Sun, J. (2023, December 19). Retrieved April 26, 2024, from World Economic Forum: https://www.weforum.org/agenda/2023/12/how-is-ai-reshaping-the-travel-tourism/

Susann Almasi, A. C. (2023, September 27). Retrieved July 7, 2024, from Mckinsey and Company: https://www.mckinsey.com/industries/travel-logistics-and-infrastructure/our-insights/the-promise-of-travel-in-the-age-of-ai

Svistunov, V. M., Kuzina, G. P., & Lobachev, V. V. (2021). Inevitability of company's corporate culture transformation under conditions of new management technologies. In Engineering Economics: Decisions and Solutions from Eurasian Perspective (pp. 613-623). Springer International Publishing. 10.1007/978-3-030-53277-2_73

Swathi, G., & Pahuja, A. (2024). FinTech Frontiers: Cloud Computing and Artificial Intelligence Applications for Intelligent Finance Investment and Blockchain in the Financial Sector. *International Journal of Intelligent Systems and Applications in Engineering*, 12(4s), 654–659.

Swetaseal. (2023, January 15). Retrieved April 20, 2024, from Medium: https://medium.com/@swetaseal/machine-learning-use-cases-in-tourism-f580d2f14c5b

Synovec, J. R. (2018). Making artificial intelligence real: How brands can use AI to supercharge their marketing stack.

Tabesh, P. (2022). Who's making the decisions? How managers can harness artificial intelligence and remain in charge. Journal of Business Strategy, 43(6), pp.373-380. *The Journal of Business Strategy*, 2021. Advance online publication. 10.1108/JBS-05-2021-0090

Tacheva, Z., & Ramasubramanian, S. (2023). *Challenging AI Empire: Toward a Decolonial and Queer Framework of Data Resurgence*. Advance. 10.31124/advance.22012724.v1

Takyar, A. (n.d.). Retrieved April 9, 2024, from LeewayHertz: https://www.leewayhertz.com/generative-ai-in-travel/

Tambe, P., Cappelli, P., & Yakubovich, V. (2019). Artificial intelligence in human resources management: Challenges and a path forward. *California Management Review*, 61(4), 15–42. 10.1177/0008125619867910

Tan, G. K. S. (2021). Democratizing finance with Robinhood: Financial infrastructure, interface design and platform capitalism. *Environment and Planning A. Economy and Space*, 53(8), 1862–1878.

Tarik Dogru-Dr. True, T. N. (2023, July). Generative Artificial Intelligence in the Hospitality and Tourism Industry: Developing a Framework for Future Research. *Journal of Hospitality & Tourism Research (Washington, D.C.)*.

Tariq, M. U., Poulin, M., & Abonamah, A. A. (2021). Achieving operational excellence through artificial intelligence: Driving forces and barriers. *Frontiers in Psychology*, 12, 686624. 10.3389/fpsyg.2021.68662434305744

Taulli, T. (2023). Generative AI: How ChatGPT and other AI tools will revolutionize business, Berkeley, CA: Apress.

Tavakoli, M., Faraji, A., Vrolijk, J., Molavi, M., Mol, S. T., & Kismihók, G. (2022). An AI-based open recommender system for personalized labor market driven education. *Advanced Engineering Informatics*, 52, 101508. 10.1016/j.aei.2021.101508

Team, 1. (2023, September 20). Retrieved May 2, 2024, from 10xDS: https://10xds.com/blog/transforming-the-travel-and-tourism-industry-with-generative-ai-and-llm/

Tejeda, H., Kumar, A., Smyth, P., & Steyvers, M. (2022). AI-assisted decision-making: A cognitive modeling approach to infer latent reliance strategies. *Computational Brain & Behavior*, 5(4), 491–508. 10.1007/s42113-022-00157-y

Thilagavathy, R., Veeramani, T., & Ramakrishna, B. (2019, March). Role of Augmented Reality and Virtual Reality in Digital World. In *2019 Fifth International Conference on Science Technology Engineering and Mathematics (ICONSTEM)* (Vol. 1, pp. 179-186). IEEE. 10.1109/ICONSTEM.2019.8918727

Tian, X., He, J. S., & Han, M. (2021). Data-driven approaches in FinTech: A survey. *Information Discovery and Delivery*, 49(2), 123–135. 10.1108/IDD-06-2020-0062

Tian, Z., Liu, F., Li, Z., Malekian, R., & Xie, Y. (2017). The Development of Key Technologies in Applications of Vessels Connected to the Internet. *Symmetry*, 9(10), 211. 10.3390/sym9100211

Tiernan, K. (2023, August 28). Retrieved April 1, 2024, from BDO Digital: https://www.bdodigital.com/insights/analytics/airbnb-artificial-intelligence-transform-business

Tijan, E., Jović, M., Aksentijević, S., & Pucihar, A. (2021). Digital transformation in the maritime transport sector. *Technological Forecasting and Social Change*, 170, 120879. 10.1016/j.techfore.2021.120879

Today, A. I., & Tomorrow, A. I. (Rep.). (2017, July). Retrieved January 16, 2018, from ARM with Northstar Research Partners website: http://pages.arm.com/rs/312-SAX-488/images/arm-ai-survey-report.pdf

Torre, G. (2024). Save Time With ChatGPT. *Talent Development*, 78(5), 18–19.

Tripathi, M. A., Tripathi, R., Effendy, F., Manoharan, G., Paul, M. J., & Aarif, M. (2023, January). An In-Depth Analysis of the Role That ML and Big Data Play in Driving Digital Marketing's Paradigm Shift. In *2023 International Conference on Computer Communication and Informatics (ICCCI)* (pp. 1-6). IEEE. 10.1109/ICCCI56745.2023.10128357

Truby, J., Brown, R., & Dahdal, A. (2020). Banking on AI: Mandating a proactive approach to AI regulation in the financial sector. *Law and Financial Markets Review*, 14(2), 110–120. 10.1080/17521440.2020.1760454

Tsolakis, N., Schumacher, R., Dora, M., & Kumar, M. (2023). Artificial intelligence and blockchain implementation in supply chains: A pathway to sustainability and data monetisation? *Annals of Operations Research*, 327(1), 157–210. 10.1007/s10479-022-04785-235755830

Tufa, G., Kant, S., & Dinber, G. N. (2023). Meta- Analysis: Qualitative Review of Human Resource Management Studies. *Advanced Qualitative Research*, 1(1), 42–62.

Tuomi, A. (2023, January 15). AI-Generated Content, Creative Freelance Work and Hospitality and Tourism Marketing. *Information and Communication Technologies in Tourism*, 2023, 323–328. 10.1007/978-3-031-25752-0_35

Turlakova S.S. (2022). Conceptual provisions for managing the behavior of economic agents in the digital space using artificial intelligence tools. Economics and entrepreneurship, 49, 40-54.

Turlakova, S., & Bohdan, B. (2023). Artificial Intelligence Tools for Managing the Behavior of Economic Agents at Micro Level. *Neuro-Fuzzy Modeling Techniques in Economics*, 12(12), 3–30. 10.33111/nfmte.2023.003

Turner, J. (2018). Robot rules: Regulating artificial intelligence. Springer. Journal of Business Research.

Udo, W. S., Ochuba, N. A., Akinrinola, O., & Ololade, Y. J. (2024). Theoretical approaches to data analytics and decision-making in finance: Insights from Africa and the United States. *GSC Advanced Research and Reviews*, 18(3), 343–349. 10.30574/gscarr.2024.18.3.0114

Umamaheswari, S., & Valarmathi, A. (2023). Role of artificial intelligence in the banking sector. *Journal of Survey in Fisheries Sciences*, 10(4S), 2841–2849.

Utpal Chakraborty, S. R. (2023). *Rise of Generative AI and ChatGPT Understand how Generative AI and ChatGPT are transforming and reshaping the business world*. BPB Online.

Vagin, S. G., Klimenko, V. A., Telegina, Z. A., & Aleksashina, T. V. (2022). Improving environmental decision-making in environmental business-management using big data and AI. *Frontiers in Environmental Science*, 10, 951306. 10.3389/fenvs.2022.951306

Van, N. T. T., Vrana, V., Duy, N. T., Minh, D. X. H., Dzung, P. T., Mondal, S. R., & Das, S. (2020). The role of human–machine interactive devices for post-COVID-19 innovative sustainable tourism in Ho Chi Minh City, Vietnam. *Sustainability (Basel)*, 12(22), 9523. 10.3390/su12229523

Velmurugan, T. A., & Sankar, J. G. (2017). A comparative study on motivation theory with Maslow's hierarchy theory and two factor theory in organization. *Indo-Iranian Journal of Scientific Research*, 1(1), 204–208.

Vergara Villegas, O. O., Nandayapa, M., Sossa Azuela, J. H., Cossio Franco, E. G., & Rubin Linares, G. T. (2021). Introduction to the Thematic Issue on Artificial Intelligence for Industry 4.0. *Computación y Sistemas*, 25(4), 681–682. 10.13053/cys-25-4-4057

Verma, A., Lamsal, K., & Verma, P. (2022). An investigation of skill requirements in artificial intelligence and machine learning job advertisements. *Industry and Higher Education*, 36(1), 63–73.

Viglia, G., Furlan, R., & Ladron-de-Guevara, A. (2014). Please, talk about it! When hotel popularity boosts preferences. *International Journal of Hospitality Management*, 42, 155–164. 10.1016/j.ijhm.2014.07.001

VigneshSaravanan, K., JothiThilaga, P., Kavipriya, S., &Vijayalakshmi, K. (2023). Data Protection and Security Enhancement in Cyber-Physical Systems Using AI and Blockchain. In *AI Models for Blockchain-Based Intelligent Networks in IoT Systems: Concepts, Methodologies, Tools, and Applications* (pp. 285-325). Cham: Springer International Publishing.

Vishwakarma, L. P., & Singh, R. K. (2023). An analysis of the challenges to human resource in implementing artificial intelligence. In *The Adoption and Effect of Artificial Intelligence on Human Resources Management, Part B* (pp. 81–109). Emerald Publishing Limited. 10.1108/978-1-80455-662-720230006

Wakjira, G. G., & Kant, S. (2022). Significance of Market Orientation on Business Perceived organizational support With Mediating Role of Employee And Customer Satisfaction In Ethiopia Banks. *Partners Universal International Research Journal*, 1(4), 118–125.

Wamba-Taguimdje, S., Fosso Wamba, S., Jean Robert, K. K., & Tchatchouang, C. E. (2020). Influence of Artificial Intelligence (AI) on Firm Performance: The Business Value of AI-based Transformation Projects. *Business Process Management Journal*, 26(7), 26. 10.1108/BPMJ-10-2019-0411

Wang, L. Z. (2020, June). VacAItionary: AI Travel Itinerary Planning Based on Ant Colony Optimization.

Wang, C., Shen, J., Vijayakumar, P., & Gupta, B. B. (2021). Attribute-Based Secure Data Aggregation for Isolated IoT-Enabled Maritime Transportation Systems. *IEEE Transactions on Intelligent Transportation Systems*, 1–10. 10.1109/TITS.2021.3127436

Ward, B. M. (2019). *Artificial Intelligence in Practice: How 50 Successful Companies Used AI and Machine Learning to Solve Problems*. Wiley.

Webster, S. I. (2022). *Robots, Artificial Intelligence and Service Automation in Travel, Tourism and Hospitality*. Emerald Publishing Limited.

Weeramanthrie, T. T., Thilakumara, C. N., Wijesiri, K. N. A. C., Fernando, N. I., Thelijjagoda, S., & Gamage, A. (2017). ARROW: A Web-Based Employee Turnover Analysis Tool for Effective Human Resource Management in Large-Scale Organizations.

Wei, J., & Wang, R. (2022, December). Application of Artificial Intelligence in the Development of Media Integration under the Background of Smart Media. In *2022 International Symposium on Advances in Informatics, Electronics and Education (ISAIEE)* (pp. 360-364). IEEE. 10.1109/ISAIEE57420.2022.00081

Wichert, A. (2020). Principles of quantum artificial intelligence: quantum problem solving and machine learning.

Widarko, A., & Anwarodin, M. K. (2022). Work Motivation and Organizational Culture on Work Perceived organizational support: Organizational Citizenship Behavior (OCB) as Mediating Variable. *Golden Ratio of Human Resource Management*, 2(2), 123–138.

Wirth, N. (2018). Hello marketing, what can artificial intelligence help you with? *International Journal of Market Research*, 60(5), 435–438. 10.1177/1470785318776841

Wong, E. L. (2021). Analysis of Wealthfront Generation Case Study.

Xia, H., Wang, Y., Jasimuddin, S., Zhang, J. Z., & Thomas, A. (2022). A big-data-driven matching model based on deep Generative re-enforcement learning (GRL) for cotton blending. *International Journal of Production Research*, 1–19.

Xia, H., Wang, Y., Jasimuddin, S., Zhang, J. Z., & Thomas, A. (2022). A big-data-driven matching model based on deep reinforcement learning for cotton blending. *International Journal of Production Research*, 1–19.

Xiao, T. (2021, December). Research on Overcoming about Language Barriers of AI Machine Translation replacing Interpreting under Information Technology. In *2021 International Conference on Aviation Safety and Information Technology* (pp. 12-20). 10.1145/3510858.3510865

Xiao, Y., Li, X., Yao, W., Chen, J., & Hu, Y. (2022). Bidirectional Data-Driven Trajectory Prediction for Intelligent Maritime Traffic. *IEEE Transactions on Intelligent Transportation Systems*, 1–13. 10.1109/TITS.2022.3219998

Yahia, N. B., Jihen, H., & Colomo-Palacios, R. (2021). From Big Data to Deep Data to Support People Analytics for Employee Attrition Prediction. *IEEE Access : Practical Innovations, Open Solutions*, 99, 1. 10.1109/ACCESS.2021.3074559

Yalamati, S. (2023). Revolutionizing Digital Banking: Unleashing the Power of Artificial Intelligence for Enhanced Customer Acquisition, Retention, and Engagement. *International Journal of Management Education for Sustainable Development*, 6(6), 1–20.

Yang, L., Henthorne, T. L., & George, B. (2020). Artificial intelligence and robotics technology in the hospitality industry: Current applications and future trends. *Digital transformation in business and society: Theory and cases*, 211-228.

Yang, X., Wang, Q., & Lyu, J. (2023). Assessing ChatGPT's Educational Capabilities and Application Potential. *ECNU Review of Education*, 1-15.

Yapo, A., & Weiss, J. (2018). *Ethical Implications of Bias in Machine Learning*. 10.24251/HICSS.2018.668

Yeğin. (2020). The place and future of artificial intelligence in marketing strategies. 81st ed. 24 volumes: Ekev Akademi Dergisi. Available online at https://www.ekevakademi.org/makaleler/1000387091_25%20tugba%20yegın.pdf

yellow.ai. (n.d.). Retrieved April 8, 2024, from yellow.ai: https://yellow.ai/case-study/pelago-reimagines-customer-experience-with-gen-ai-powered-conversational-ai-agents/#solution

Yin, J., & Fernandez, V. (2020). A systematic review on business analytics. *Journal of Industrial Engineering and Management*, 13(2), 283–295. 10.3926/jiem.3030

Yunqiang Chen, Q. W. (2019, June 1). An overview of augmented reality technology. *Journal of Physics: Conference Series*, 1237(2), 022082. 10.1088/1742-6596/1237/2/022082

Yusof, S. A. B. M., & Roslan, F. A. B. M. (2023). The Impact of Generative AI in Enhancing Credit Risk Modeling and Decision-Making in Banking Institutions. *Emerging Trends in Machine Intelligence and Big Data*, 15(10), 40–49.

Zahari, A. S. M., Harun, M. A., Hamzah, S. F. M., & Salleh, S. M. (2018). The influence of Human Resource Management Information System (HRMIS) Application towards Employees Efficiency and Satisfaction. *Journal of Physics: Conference Series*, 1019(1), 012077. Advance online publication. 10.1088/1742-6596/1019/1/012077

Zhang, B. Z., Ashta, A., & Barton, M. E. (2021). Do FinTech and financial incumbents have different experiences and perspectives on the adoption of artificial intelligence? *Strategic Change*, 30(3), 223–234. 10.1002/jsc.2405

Zhang, P., & Kamel Boulos, M. (2023). Generative AI in Medicine and Healthcare: Promises, Opportunities and Challenges. Future Internet, 15, 286.

Zhang, Y., & Qi, S. (2019). User experience study: the service expectation of hotel guests to the utilization of ai-based service robot in full-service hotels. *HCI in Business, Government and Organizations. eCommerce and Consumer Behavior: 6th International Conference, HCIBGO 2019, Held as Part of the 21st HCI International Conference, HCII 2019, Orlando, FL, USA, July 26-31, 2019Proceedings*, 21(Part I), 350–366.

Zhang, Y., Xu, S., Zhang, L., & Yang, M. (2021). Big data and human resource management research: An integrative review and new directions for future research. *Journal of Business Research*, 133, 34–50. 10.1016/j.jbusres.2021.04.019

Zhao, Z., Chen, Y., Bangash, A. A., Adams, B., & Hassan, A. E. (2024). An Empirical Study of Challenges in Machine Learning Asset Management. arXiv preprint arXiv:2402.15990.

Zhao, J. (2022). Artificial intelligence and corporate decisions: Fantasy, reality or destiny. *Cath. UL Rev.*, 71, 663.

Zhao, L., Zuo, Y., Li, T., & Chen, C. L. P. (2023). Application of an Encoder–Decoder Model with Attention Mechanism for Trajectory Prediction Based on AIS Data: Case Studies from the Yangtze River of China and the Eastern Coast of the U.S. *Journal of Marine Science and Engineering*, 11(8), 1530. 10.3390/jmse11081530

Zhou, K.-Q., & Nabus, H. (2023). The Ethical Implications of DALL-E: Opportunities and Challenges. *Mesopotamian Journal of Computer Science*, 17–23.

About the Contributors

Jeganathan Gomathi Sankar is a distinguished educator specializing in marketing, currently serving as a faculty member at the BSSS Institute of Advanced Studies. He holds a Master of Business Administration and a Bachelor of Engineering from Anna University and earned his Ph.D. from Pondicherry University. He focuses on information diffusion, ICT, marketing technology, and data science. Sankar has also completed a Postgraduate Diploma in Statistics and Research Methods and Industrial Psychology. His impactful research contributions have been published in reputable journals indexed in Scopus and ABDC. He has actively participated in numerous national and international conferences, earning best paper awards from prestigious institutions such as IIM and NIT. Sankar's teaching philosophy integrates theoretical insights with practical applications, providing students with a comprehensive understanding of contemporary marketing trends. His proficiency in analytical tools such as SPSS, AMOS, STATA, PowerBI, and Python enhances the sophistication of his research endeavors. Known for his engaging teaching style and commitment to academic excellence, he fosters an environment that encourages critical thinking among students. Sankar continues to shape future marketing professionals at the BSSS Institute of Advanced Studies, exemplifying his dedication to advancing knowledge in marketing and technology.

Arokiaraj David is dedicated to fostering academic excellence and leveraging skills to contribute to the development of research-informed teaching activities, an accomplished professional is being sought for a role as an Associate Professor. A wealth of knowledge and expertise is brought to the academic arena through the attainment of a Ph.D. in International Business (Management) from Pondicherry Central University, earned through full-time dedication from 2011 to 2016. The academic journey includes a Master of Business Administration with a specialization in Marketing Management & Human Resources Management from Pondicherry Central University (2008-2010) and a Bachelor of Business Administration in Tourism and Travel Management (2005-2008), both pursued on a full-time basis. Additionally, a Master of Commerce in Finance & Control was pursued at Alagappa University from 2011 to 2013 through part-time engagement, showcasing a commitment to continuous learning. In addition to these educational achievements, a Post Diploma in Computer Application was completed in 2007-08 on a full-time basis, enhancing proficiency in modern technological tools. With a comprehensive academic background, the role of Associate Professor was served at Al Tareeqah Management Studies, Swiss Business School, Ras Al Khaimah, United Arab Emirates. As an aspiring post holder, eagerness to manage and expand income-generating activities, provide academic area leadership, and oversee the design and development of curricula is demonstrated. The goal is to make a significant contribution to the leadership, management, and development of teaching and learning strategies, aligning with academic standards and leading-edge practices. Leveraging experience and knowledge, a commitment to enhancing the quality of education and learning experiences for students while upholding the highest academic standards is maintained.

* * *

Metasebia Adula received the PhD in Business administration degree with Bule Hora University, Ethiopia and currently working as assistant professor at Bule Hora University, Ethiopia. She has over 15 years of governments organization works experience in the different field in women leadership development in Ethiopia. She has published 24 research papers in different international journals.

Kwame Okwabi Asante-Offei is a database professional with over 10 years of industrial experience. Kwame Okwabi holds a Master's degree in Management Information Systems from Ghana Institute of Management and Public Administration (GIMPA) and a Bachelor of Science (Computer Science) degree from Kwame Nkrumah University of Science and Technology (KNUST). He is currently a Database Administrator at Accra Technical University (ATU). Kwame is also a hybrid researcher with an interest in Enterprise Information Systems, Information Systems Security, FinTech Services, Data Science, and e-Learning.

Sunitha Ashtikar is a research associate at SR University.

Ranjit Barua is a Senior Researcher at Centre for Healthcare Science and Technology, IIEST-SHIBPUR. Core research area Bio-Mechanical System, 3D Bioprinting, Tissue Engineering.

Joel Jebadurai Devapitchai is working as an Assistant Professor in Department of MBA, St. Joseph's College of Engineering, OMR, Chennai India. He has published more than 50 research articles in various peer reviewed journals.

Mufaro Dzingirai (Ph.D) is a full-time lecturer in the Department of Business Management at Midlands State University. He is also currently a Senior Fellow at the Nexus Think Tank (Zarawi Trust). Notably, he is a Monitoring and Evaluation Specialist (Internship) at Midlands AIDS Services Organization. Interestingly, he received the Best Paper Presentation Award from the University of Johannesburg (UJ) in 2022. In 2013, he received the MSU Book Prize as the best-graduating student. His research interests include Higher Education, Strategy, Management, Finance, Entrepreneurship, and Development. He publishes in high-impact journals accredited by Scopus and also reviewed many scientific papers in databases like Emerald Insight. More interestingly, he has been hired as a research consultant by both private and public organizations. Lastly, he supervises postgraduate students and has linkages with various universities (national and international) as an external examiner or moderator.

Shashi Kant (PhD) currently is working with the Department of Management, Bule Hora University, Ethiopia. He has published several research papers in Scopus, Springer, WOS, and PubMed reviewed international journals. He already published books on Strategic Management and Entrepreneurship and Perspectives of Marketing. Recently his authored book Computer Applications in Engineering and Management published under CRC Press, Taylor, and Francis. He is certified entrepreneurship trainer of Ministry of Skill Development, India.

Shashi Kant is an Assistant Professor, College of Business and Economics, Department of Management, Bule Hora University, Ethiopia.

Peace Kumah holds a doctorate degree in Business Administration and MBA (Human Resource Management) degree from Wisconsin International University College, Accra, Ghana. She has several years of teaching experience and occupies leadership positions in various educational institutions. Her research interest includes organizational leadership and motivation, change management, and employment relations.

Geetha Manoharan is currently working in Telangana as an assistant professor at SR University. She is the university-level PhD programme coordinator and has also been given the additional responsibility of In Charge Director of Publications and Patents under the Research Division at SR University. Under her tutelage, students are inspired to reach their full potential in all areas of their education and beyond through experiential learning. It creates an atmosphere conducive to the growth of pupils into independent thinkers and avid readers. She has more than ten years of experience across the board in the business world, academia, and the academy. She has a keen interest in the study of organisational behaviour and management. More than forty articles and books have been published in scholarly venues such as UGC-refereed, SCOPUS, Web of Science, and Springer. Over the past six-plus years, she has participated in varied research and student exchange programmes at both the national and international levels. A total of five of her collaborative innovations in this area have already been published and patented. Emotional intelligence, self-efficacy, and work-life balance are among her specialties. She organises programmes for academic organizations. She belongs to several professional organizations, including the CMA and the CPC. The TIPSGLOBAL Institute of Coimbatore has recognised her twice (in 2017 and 2018) for her outstanding academic performance.

William Robert P. is working as an Associate Professor in Saveetha School of Management, Saveetha Institute of Medical and Technical Sciences, Saveetha University, Chennai. He has more than 20 research articles in National and International Journal.His area of Interest is Services Marketing and Financial Services Management.

Saranya S. is working as an Assistant Professor in the Department of Management Studies, NPR College of Engineering and Technology, Natham, Dindigul, India. She has published more than 20 research articles for her credit.

Karuppiah S. P. is working as an Associate Professor in the Department of MBA, St. Joseph's College of Engineering, Chennai. He received his Phd in computer Science And Engineering in Jawaharlal Nehru Technological University, Hyderabad and also finished ME(CSE) in R.M.K Engineering College Affiliated to Anna University, Chennai, He published various Journals in Image Processing and Writing Book for Data Structures and Principles of management. His research interests include Digital Image Processing.

Krishnapriya S. V. is associated with St. Joseph College of engineering OMR, Chennai. She has expertise in finance.

Index

D

E

G

H

I

L

M

N

O

P

S

T

V

W

www.ingramcontent.com/pod-product-compliance
Lightning Source LLC
LaVergne TN
LVHW080629011026
849160LV00014B/1164